Changing Lanes

Urban and Industrial Environments

Series editor: Robert Gottlieb, Henry R. Luce Professor of Urban and Environmental Policy, Occidental College

For a complete list of books published in this series, please see the back of the book.

Changing Lanes
Visions and Histories of Urban Freeways

Joseph F. C. DiMento and Cliff Ellis

The MIT Press
Cambridge, Massachusetts
London, England

MIT Press books may be purchased at special quantity discounts for business or sales pro-
motional use. For information, please email special_sales@mitpress.mit.edu or write to Special Sales Department, The MIT Press, 55 Hayward Street, Cambridge, MA 02142.

This book was set in Sabon by the MIT Press. Printed on recycled paper and bound in the
United States of America.

Library of Congress Cataloging-in-Publication Data

DiMento, Joseph F.
Changing lanes : visions and histories of urban freeways / Joseph F. C. DiMento and Cliff
Ellis.
    p.   cm. — (Urban and industrial environments)
Includes bibliographical references and index.
ISBN 978-0-262-01858-6 (hardcover : alk. paper)
1. Express highways—United States—History. 2. Express highways—Government poli-
cy—United States—History. I. Ellis, Cliff, 1951– II. Title.
HE355.3.E94D56 2013
388.1'220973091732—dc23
2012022866

10 9 8 7 6 5 4 3 2 1

Contents

Preface

When we began writing this book, we found it motivating to discuss our concepts with a widely varied spectrum of potential readers. Somewhat surprisingly, we found nearly everyone with whom we spoke expressed more than a passing interest in the subject matter and seemed to find the topic of urban highway development in the United States intriguing and engaging. At least one reason for their interest became readily apparent: Almost without exception, each person had a tale to tell about how a particular urban highway had affected his or her life or the lives of people they knew or cared for.

Some people had praise for the highways they frequented. They enjoyed the ability to travel from one place to another rapidly and efficiently (except, they would usually add, during rush hour). Their lives had, they believed, not been negatively affected in any way. The majority, however, had a different story to tell, one that often involved some degree of frustration, anger, and loss or, at minimum, curiosity about the choices made by highway developers who had put "that highway/on or off ramp/overpass/bridge right near/over/around/through my city/town/community."

Many with whom we spoke had questions that, to their knowledge, had never even been addressed, let alone satisfactorily answered: Why did they put the road through my parents' house . . . my cousin's store . . . my sister's kids' playground . . . the middle of our city? Why was it built through the poor part of town . . . or the place in our town where those great old houses were? Why did they choose those specific locations? Why are the roads so gigantic? Why didn't they put the highway somewhere else? How did they arrive at those decisions? For that matter, who are "they"?

This volume does not purport to provide specific answers to the questions posed by those people. It does, however, aim to present a comprehensive analysis of the varying contexts in which urban highway decisions were made over the years, the shifting understandings, perspectives, and methodologies that underpinned those decisions, and the changing social, economic, and legal structures that informed, abetted, or constrained the decision-making process. In so doing, we aspire to enable our readers to develop a broad-based, generalized understanding of a complex topic—one that has had a tremendously important role to play in shaping communities, and lives, across our nation.

Acknowledgments

This work would not have come together without the contributions of many generous colleagues. Indispensable were the research, editing, and organizing skills of Dr. Suzanne Levesque, whose professionalism in each area is distinguished.

For research assistance and contributions, we wish to thank the Onondaga Historical Association and research librarians on the main campus and at the Law School of UCI, with special mention of Jeremy Hufton. Jennifer Folz of Clemson University performed admirably as a research assistant during the final phases of the project.

Gregg Tripoli and Dennis Connors at OHA were immensely generous with valuable historical insights and encouragement, as were Ms. Karen Cooney and former OHA Archivist Mike Flanagan.

Portions of this study were produced as part of a doctoral dissertation, completed in 1990, in the Department of City and Regional Planning at the University of California at Berkeley. The support and critical commentary of Roger Montgomery, Judith Innes, Paul Groth, and Christine Rosen were crucial for the completion of this research. Judith Innes deserves special thanks for her many years of encouragement and wise counsel.

Access to the exceptional resources contained in the Institute of Transportation Studies Library at UC-Berkeley was also crucial. Invaluable assistance was provided by Elizabeth Byrne and the staff of Berkeley's Environmental Design Library. The section on Norman Bel Geddes was based on research conducted at the Harry Ransom Center at the University of Texas at Austin. Kathy Edwards and Gypsey Teague of the Gunnin Architecture Library at Clemson University also provided valuable assistance in locating important books and articles.

Over the years Dr. Drusilla van Hengel and Mr. Dean Hestermann did critical primary research work that is background to the I-105 case study.

Ms. Heather Seagle assisted with archival research on the three case studies, and Ms. Megan Lewis provided valuable research assistance for the Syracuse case study.

The University of California Transportation Center, the UCI School of Law, the UCI School of Social Ecology, Clemson University, and Caltrans supplied financial assistance. The original contact with Caltrans was made through Professor Pete Fielding of UCI; this launched interest in the urban freeway as a subject of research in law and urban studies.

When they do their work conscientiously, anonymous reviewers greatly improve most scholarly contributions; in our case the reviewers were analytical, detailed, and helpful, and they offered extremely useful suggestions. We also thank the *Journal of Planning History* for comments on sections of the Syracuse case study work published in other forms therein. Professor Scott Bollens of the Department of Planning, Policy and Design at UCI supplied well informed and useful comments on materials for the Syracuse case. Professors Carol Carozzi and Silvia Saccomani of Politecnico di Torino offered encouragement for continuing this work during a Fulbright funded visit to Turin.

We thank Syracuse University for work done there and especially for making available to us the oral archives of the 15th ward.

Ms. Angie Middleton, Ms. Char Anderson, and Ms. Lynh Tran did important editorial work at UCI.

A book like ours is enhanced by the quality of its visuals. We thank the following organizations and individuals for assisting us in our ability to use photographs and graphics: the American Highway Users Alliance (Daisy Singh); the American Planning Association (Lois Tucker); the American Public Transportation Association (James LaRusch); the Automobile Club of Southern California (Morgan Yates); the City of Milwaukee (Lori Lutzka); GRAEF (Jennifer Kraft); the New Urban News (Robert Steuteville); the UCLA Department of Geography (Kasi McMurray and Matt Zebrowski); and Woodall Rodgers Park Foundation (Annie Black).

We thank Clay Morgan and others at MIT Press for their confidence in our work and for the application of the highest standards in academic publishing.

Finally, books are rarely completed without support from family members, and this is no exception. Cathy Thorne and Deborah Newquist deserve a commendation for putting up with piles of books and articles over many years as this project moved toward completion.

Introduction

Visions of Urban Freeways: Magic Motorways or Daggers in the Heart of Town?

Few decisions have affected American cities as much as those involving urban freeways. These massive infrastructure projects have reconfigured urban form, relocated tens of thousands of people, cost billions of dollars of transportation funds, and supplanted neighborhoods. This is a story of those freeways. We recount the original love affair with the newly invented mode of vehicle movement—the freeway, including freeways through cities. That love affair was influenced by actors ranging from the visionary to the very pragmatic. The professionals involved included highway engineers, urban planners, landscape architects, and architects, with the highway engineers taking the lead role. Both cooperation and conflict emerged as these (mostly) men struggled across half a century to shape urban freeway policy and construction. We review the evolution of their design ideas through time as they tried to respond to rapidly changing demographic patterns with a dramatically evolving concept of how to tackle inner city traffic congestion, ever-growing movement to the suburbs, interstate commerce, and national defense.

We then describe challenges to urban freeway construction as the costs and perceived costs to their completion became increasingly recognized. We chronicle the history of controversies that occurred nationwide, but not in all locales.

Changing Lanes sets the analysis within two contexts. We first address the competing visions of city form and development held by various urban professionals and decision makers. These images varied greatly. Some saw the urban highway as a symbol of modernism and efficiency that, using professional methods, could be integrated into the urban center to improve many elements of the quality of urban life. Others predicted that, without attention to aesthetics and multiple transportation needs, the inner city multiple-lane, limited-access road would counter good city planning. Whatever the vision, in the early decades of high-speed urban corridors the influence of the promise of a new machine age—a romantic one to be sure—was great. Professionals of all kinds believed that municipal problems in American cities would be solved using methods at their disposal.

Our analysis then moves to a second context. We lay out the immensely influential major shifts in the regulatory environment of freeway construction (and the construction of other major public works) in the United States. The several-decades-long (from the 1920s on) infatuation with cars and an unquestioned reliance on urban roads as urban problem solvers changed dramatically in the years of the late 1960s through the 1970s. Congress and state legislatures passed important new laws that guided where freeways can be built, with which funds, after which types of consultation and analysis, and with what impact. Lawmakers and courts required that projects be planned and completed with maximum sensitivity to the environment, with concern for relocation of the displaced, and with active citizen participation, not solely that of technocrats, select business interests, and administrative officials. They required that policy makers consider alternatives other than what, in the 1950s, had become the traditional urban choice.

The story of change is told first in an overall review of urban freeway controversies that arose across the United States. We then focus on three different cases: Syracuse, New York, a Snow or Rust Belt city that early on embraced freeways through its center; Southern California, which rejected some routes and then changed its plans and built what was then the most expensive urban road; and Memphis, Tennessee, which closed its core to Interstate 40.

We aim to describe the history of urban freeways through both a broad overview of competing influences and a narrow focus on the details of cases where the competition played out very differently. As Oscar Handlin argued regarding how urban affairs needed to be described: "how these developments unfolded, what was the causal nexus among them, we shall only learn when we make out the interplay among them by focusing upon a city specifically in all its uniqueness."[1]

Why Syracuse, Los Angeles, and Memphis?

Why examine urban freeways in these three places? For those who know, or knew, these areas the local interest is clear. For readers who do not know these places, the events in the case studies are part of a history that is not only national but also worldwide: the impact of the automobile on the way we live—from East St. Louis to post–World War II Germany. Furthermore, the stories illustrate three different outcomes—a result, we argue, of the changing context in which they played out.

Syracuse illustrates well the decision to go forward with urban freeways early in freeway history and with development planned heavily by nonlocal sources at a time when the uncritical image of the new urban infrastructure was dominant. The urban impact in this mid-size city was significant. Los Angeles took a different path a bit later in freeway history. Many of its planned freeways were, of course, built. However, the one on which we focus, I-105, was a product of many forces that changed freeway development in the post-1960 period. It is the so-called "intelligent" outcome: a product of new law and policy, of the ascendance of new actors, and of more mature design visions. In Memphis, further construction of I-40 was blocked, despite many powerful efforts and many competing design images; its story became an icon in environmental and transportation policy, history, and law.

For each urban freeway decision, we address the role played by professionals with competing visions of the good city—engineers; planners; architects; landscape architects; federal, state, and local officials—and the major influence of larger forces of national and state transportation, environmental, and planning law.

1
Urban Freeways and America's Changing Cities

Origins of Urban Freeway Development

Decisions to develop a system of interstate highways and to make central cities potential sites for them followed inexorably after the assessment that automobiles could move quickly with cross traffic separated and with limited access and high-speed limits; that those roads could link markets, perhaps almost as swiftly as railroads; and that those roads could open up land being used for agriculture or wetlands or parks or recreation.

In the 1920s, New York City conceived a system of controlled-access urban parkways featuring separation of cross traffic, the divided highway, and limitation of access to specific locations. In just a decade, the Los Angeles area became the first major proponent of the new system. In 1934, the cities of Pasadena and South Pasadena approved the Los Angeles County Regional Planning Commission's plans for Arroyo Seco (now the Pasadena Freeway). In 1939, The City of Los Angeles Transportation Engineering Board proposed more than 600 miles of freeways for the region.[1] Later, the California Freeway and Expressway System, which had been created by the state legislature, authorized a grid-like network overlaying the entire Los Angeles basin. The goal was that no Angelino should ever be more than a few miles away from a freeway ramp. Detroit, Chicago, Boston, Washington, D.C., Kansas City, and other American cities also proposed major freeways in the pre–World War II period.

Positive evaluations of the freeway innovation and knowledge of how to build freeways outpaced knowledge of where to put them and what their effects could be.

Unlike Lewis Mumford, most observers did not see the earliest controlled-access roads as threats to community and the urban environment. Mumford wrote in 1958:

Perhaps our age will be known to the future historian as the age of the bulldozer and the exterminator; and in many parts of the country the building of a highway has about the same result upon vegetation and human structures as the passage of a tornado or the blast of an atom bomb. Nowhere is this bulldozing habit of mind so disastrous as in the approach to the city. Since the engineer regards his own work as more important than the other human functions it serves, he does not hesitate to lay waste to woods, streams, parks, and human neighborhoods in order to carry his roads straight to their supposed destination. As a consequence the "cloverleaf" has become our national flower and "wall-to-wall" concrete the ridiculous symbol of national affluence and technological status.[2]

Although not a unique voice, Mumford did not have many early allies. San Francisco landscape architect Lawrence Halprin, whom we discuss in greater depth in chapter 5, listed freeways among the most beautiful structures of our time, commenting that "…because of elevated freeways, vast panoramic views are disclosed which were never seen before....We are in a brilliant kaleidoscope of motion which has enriched our lives and opened up whole new vistas of experience."[3]

Freeways were commonly viewed as signs of social progress. This far more widespread perspective is reflected in the words of the California Division of Highways:

In short, the freeway system is geared to the progress of a civilization as a whole and to some extent will both influence, and be influenced by, the changing character of the area it serves.[4]

Many proponents saw the urban freeway as a major catalyst of urban development, redevelopment, and revitalization. In Kansas City, new urban highways "were supposed to check decentralization, reduce congestion on street cars, separate homes from factories and shops, and prove delightful places along which to shop. Kansas Citians . . . ultimately would enjoy improved health and sound relationships with one another."[5] In Chicago, the head of the city Regional Planning Association said that superhighways "offer the opportunity to protect the regional value of the central business areas . . . to enhance the values of . . . decadent areas and help restore them to tax paying condition."[6]

Automotive Industries, a trade magazine, predicted in 1936 that:

Transportation no longer will be a problem. Most people will be able to walk to work. Pedestrian and vehicle traffic ways will be separated, perhaps on different levels, and walking will once more be safe and pleasant. . . . The city would become a pleasant place to work in and to live in; instead of asphalt jungles, the verdant city without suburbs; instead of obsolete street patterns, an efficient, well integrated network of expressways and arterials.[7]

During the 1930s and 1940s, most engineers and many planners viewed freeways as the indispensable framework for a bold new city of high mobility and economic efficiency. The old neighborhoods near the central business district seemed chaotic and obsolete—obstacles to be cleared away and replaced by new superblocks and wide thoroughfares. As businesses and middle-class residents fled the city for the suburbs, planners and politicians searched for ways to modernize old cities, contain the spread of "blight," and bolster the sagging land values of the central business district. Building a new network of high-speed roads atop the old city grid seemed a critical part of this metamorphosis.

Crucial freeway planning doctrines were forged during the 1930s and 1940s and garnered widespread support during the 1950s as cities were aggressively rebuilt to accommodate the automobile. However, these seminal freeway planning ideas—strongly influenced by rural and suburban precedents—eventually broke down in the inner city, where strikingly different architectural and social conditions prevailed. Conflicts among engineers, planners, architects and landscape architects, and, later, activist citizens and their lawyers emerged as each profession and group struggled for a role in urban freeway planning, newly reconceived to incorporate neglected environmental, aesthetic, and social impacts. Although an imaginative array of ideas for central city freeways emerged from the ferment of the 1960s, the surge of interdisciplinary interest came too late to alter profoundly some actual urban freeway construction (figure 1.1). For other cities, the ferment translated into radical changes in urban freeway plans.

Opportunities for the integration of transportation planning, land-use planning, environmental planning, and urban design were missed, as were chances for fruitful interdisciplinary cooperation. The isolation of freeway planning as a technical exercise in traffic movement led to unnecessarily damaging interventions in the fragile social ecology and physical structure of central cities (figure 1.2).

Urban freeways were built by human actors, not abstract economic and technological forces. Professionals trained in engineering, urban planning, landscape architecture, and other disciplines had to conceive and construct these complicated objects. The worldviews and professional cultures of these groups shaped what transpired on the ground. These worldviews were often tacit and hidden, exerting their influence beneath the more obvious activities of data gathering, technical analysis, and engineering design. But they were also persistent, hard to dislodge, and closely connected with struggles over professional jurisdiction.

Figure 1.1
The Walter P. Chrysler Expressway, seen prior to opening, was the first eight-lane
freeway in Detroit's downtown freeway system. *Source:* American Highway Users
Alliance, *Urban Freeway Development in Twenty Major Cities*, Washington, D.C.,
American Highway Users Alliance, August 1964, p. 27.

Professional Worldviews and the City Building Process

Which theories and images guided highway engineers and city officials
and planners as they selected corridors and designed roadways? How did
they envision the "new city" laced with freeways, modern downtowns,
and rebuilt inner rings? How was the "old city" portrayed? How did
these ideas change in response to transformations in the urban economy,
social system, and cultural environment?

Professionals learn specialized ways of interpreting cities during years
of professional socialization, involving both formal training and practice
in the field. If you ask an engineer, a planner, an architect, and a landscape
architect to identify a problem, gather relevant facts, generate alternatives, and select a course of action, you will probably receive four very
dissimilar documents.[8] Different professions typically produce different

Figure 1.2
Freeways near downtown Cleveland. The Inner Belt (right to left) interchanges with the Willow Freeway. *Source:* American Highway Users Alliance, *Urban Freeway Development in Twenty Major Cities*, Washington, D.C., American Highway Users Alliance, August 1964, p. 21.

critiques of the existing city, images of a desirable future, and prescriptions for planned urban change.

During the parkway building era of the 1920s and 1930s, engineers, landscape architects, and architects collaborated to design some of the country's most beautiful limited-access roads. However, lovely parkways would not be the model for the urban freeways of the post–World War II period. When state highway engineers took over the dominant role in urban freeway building during the 1940s and 1950s, the more modest and context-sensitive parkway and expressway plans of local transportation planners were left behind to be replaced by urban freeways scaled for massive vehicle movements.

The most powerful actors in the story of American freeway building were the highway engineers. They were supported by traffic engineers, transportation planners, and various researchers in the transportation field. Highway engineers were usually educated as civil engineers, and they identified with professional associations or institutions such as the American Society of Civil Engineers, the American Association of State Highway Officials, and the Bureau of Public Roads.[9] Traffic engineers focused more exclusively on the traffic problems of urbanized areas, forming their own association, the Institute of Traffic Engineers, in 1930. The category "transportation planner" is vague but refers to individuals in either public agencies or private consulting firms who engage primarily in the preparation of plans for transit, highway, and street improvements for cities or regions (figure 1.3).

As the lead actors in the domain of urban freeways, highway engineers displayed great confidence in their ability to assess traffic demand, analyze alternatives, and construct elaborate infrastructure, but they hewed to a narrow highway building task that matched their training and legislative mandate. Engineers relied on simplified images of the city and its problems, shied away from the aesthetic and social complexities of urban design, and focused on getting things done. Buoyed by strong public support for more freeways and backed by powerful constituencies, engineers wanted to proceed firmly with the modernization of the city for expanded mobility and economic efficiency.

City planners were not directly in charge of urban freeway building but provided for limited-access arterials in their plans, contributed to transportation policy debates, often supported urban freeway projects, yet also became critics of the urban interstates during the 1960s. In this work we speak of planners and city planners, but the difficulties of defining and bounding the city planning profession are notorious. Debates over the question "Is planning a profession?" appeared in the early planning journals and continue to this day.[10] The early city planners came from backgrounds in architecture, landscape architecture, engineering, law, journalism, and social reform. They retained connections and allegiances to the professions in which they were trained while working to forge a distinct place for city planning in American society. During the 1930s and 1940s, public officials and administrators began to join the planning fraternity. The 1950s and 1960s brought an influx of economists, sociologists, and other social scientists. At no time have clear lines been drawn around the planning field.

City planners laid claim to the comprehensive, long-term guidance of urban physical change but played a subordinate role in the freeway planning process. The planning profession was also fragmented by internal

Figure 1.3
Atlanta, Georgia, as the Downtown Connector was being constructed. *Source:* American Highway Users Alliance, *Urban Freeway Development in Twenty Major Cities*, Washington, D.C., American Highway Users Alliance, August 1964, p. 60.

disputes and could not agree on a consistent policy on urban freeways. Through the 1950s, most planners favored extensive urban freeway networks, although there were some notable dissenters. Many planners changed their minds after actual construction during the 1960s exposed the potential of the new highways to damage city centers, historic neighborhoods, and vulnerable minority populations. Planners advanced worthy arguments for mass transit, coordination of land use and transportation planning, and sensitivity to social and aesthetic factors in freeway design. Unfortunately, planners generally went along with the reductive ideas of Modernist urbanism, with its emphasis on the "motorization of American cities," and missed many opportunities to argue more forcefully for multimodal alternatives.[11]

Architects inhabited the periphery of urban freeway building, although they advanced many proposals for the modernization of the twentieth-century American city and its transportation infrastructure. As a well established profession, architecture presents fewer dilemmas of definition.[12] Even those architects who spent considerable time producing city plans usually identified professionally with the architectural fraternity and obtained the professional credentials required to practice architecture.

However, among urban designers, there is considerable fence straddling. Although trained as architects, many urban designers gravitated toward the larger, urbanistic concerns of the planning profession and made their home there. In such cases, although the term "planner" may be applied, the architectural background of the individual remains an important element of professional identity.

Architects suffered even greater exclusion from freeway policy making than planners, as most people interpreted freeways as works of engineering rather than urban architecture. Architects generated many imaginative proposals for the integration of urban centers and transportation facilities but were brought in to modify freeway designs only after the freeway revolts of the 1960s. Architectural projects for the central city varied widely in their sensitivity to historic urban form. Many Modernist architects envisioned the wholesale clearance of old structures and total re-planning along Modernist principles, including lavish provision of new freeways. Other architects, including members of the urban design concept teams of the late 1960s, advocated design strategies to reduce the impact of freeways on old neighborhoods near the core.

Landscape architecture has clearer professional boundaries than planning, but those boundaries are still permeable. Landscape architects had played important roles in parkway design since the latter half of the nineteenth century, when Frederick Law Olmsted designed his seminal park systems. They pioneered in parkway design during the 1920s and 1930s, emphasizing the integration of roads into the natural landscape, but their talents were neglected in the design of urban freeways after World War II. Like the architects, they gained a stronger voice only after the freeway revolts discredited conventional freeway planning doctrines.

All of these professional groups worked within a highly charged political environment that was dominated by urban growth coalitions and the powerful highway lobby, who were challenged after the 1950s by a formidable array of anti-freeway dissidents. Dissent was strengthened by new environmental, transportation, and housing laws and by public interest law groups that were learning how to work effectively with these new tools.

Before we look to the new legal and regulatory environment that slowed and nearly stopped the momentum for urban freeways, we elaborate the views of several major groups, professions, and disciplines involved in conceptualizing the urban freeway. These views both illuminate the different perspectives of the professions and demonstrate the importance of the influences of dedicated and strong individuals in American urban history.

Professional groups and political actors viewed urban freeways from different angles and tried to shift policy to match their priorities. From various perspectives, urban freeways were perceived as:

1. *Traffic conduits*, designed to expedite the efficient flow of motor vehicles to desired destinations.

2. *Tools of land-use planning and urban redevelopment* oriented toward the comprehensive modernization of the central city.

3. *Large-scale objects of architecture, landscape architecture, and urban design*, with powerful impacts on the physical image of the city.

4. *Economic catalysts* creating access and improving the city's efficiency as a site for the production of goods and services.

5. *Tools of social policy* strongly influencing the spatial distribution of urban residents by race and class.

6. *Components of national defense* providing transportation routes for the movement of men and supplies and evacuation routes for civilians.

Each of these images suggests a particular way of restructuring the city. As guides to policy, they lead to different urban patterns. These images were often seen in hybrid form, blended together to suit shifting economic, political, and professional currents.[13]

As an example, we may contrast the "parkway ideal" of the 1930s with the huge, ten-lane interstates of the 1960s. Parkways were deliberately designed to provide an aesthetic experience for the driver, who could glide through a carefully crafted, sylvan environment free of commercial traffic. When the movement of large volumes of traffic within metropolitan areas assumed priority, the parkway ideal was eclipsed by geometric design for safety and high-volume traffic movement.

Visions of urban freeways were typically embedded within more global interpretations of the existing city and proposals for cities of the future. Highway engineering documents spoke not only of freeways but also of modern, rationally designed cities of expanded mobility and economic prosperity. Planning documents often referenced the concentric ring theory of urban growth and suggested the use of freeways to remove slums and reverse the spread of blight. Lewis Mumford and his colleagues at the Regional Planning Association of America saw freeways as a means to expedite planned decentralization of the urban population into garden cities on the urban periphery. In each case, we can discern a cluster of descriptive analyses, graphic images, and ideas forming an intellectual whole, a way of seeing the city and arguing for change within the arenas of urban policy.[14]

Furthermore, visions of urban freeways were influenced by organizational environments.[15] The highway bureaucracies, both state and federal, were classic examples of large-scale, single-purpose government agencies. Planning bureaucracies had a more limited role as advisors and providers of information, chiefly at the local scale. They were not operating agencies with the power to build. Architects and landscape architects did not have public bureaucracies of their own; they were independent professionals, employees within private architectural firms or employees within bureaucracies controlled by other professional groups. These distinctions in organizational position led to different approaches to the management of urban change, as each group tried to frame problems so that its characteristic methods and solutions would assume greater importance.

City, state, and federal decision makers respond to their understandings of the relationships to each other and to those (the electorate, higher levels of authority) whom they believe keep them in office. In both our general analysis and in the case studies presented herein, we shall see the strong tensions that developed—and led to different outcomes—within this complex decision-making environment.

Varying Visions: Introduction

In the tradition of American city planning, roads were usually considered in tandem with the surrounding urban architecture, not merely as traffic conduits, as is the case in the engineering tradition. Design professionals at the turn of the century were familiar with the importance of arranging streets in a logical and aesthetically pleasing manner, although the old grids of the central cities provided few opportunities for alterations. Outlying areas offered a more empty canvas for the designers' art. Landscape architects and early city planners developed an aesthetic for suburban land development that included broad thoroughfares connecting parks and civic spaces, giving structure to the city and enhancing land values. Frederick Law Olmsted included landscaped boulevards in his plans for parks and suburban developments (e.g., Boston's "Emerald Necklace" of parks linked by landscaped boulevards). George Kessler designed a comprehensive system of boulevards for Kansas City.[16] These boulevards had fewer access points than traditional urban streets and were intended for noncommercial traffic, but they were not true limited-access parkways because they were interrupted at intervals by cross streets (figure 1.4).

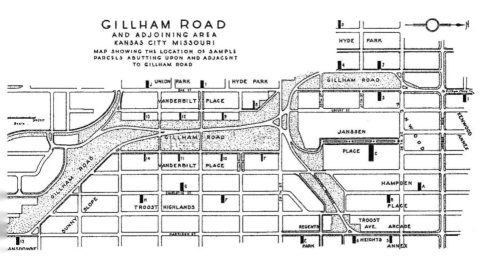

Figure 1.4
Traditional urban "parkway" in Kansas City, with access from cross streets.
Source: John Nolen and Henry V. Hubbard, *Parkways and Land Values*, Harvard
City Planning Studies, Vol. 11. Cambridge, Mass., Harvard University Press, 1937.

The City Beautiful movement placed great emphasis on the proper arrangement and design of streets. Daniel Burnham's 1909 Plan of Chicago
and other plans of this era devote large sections to circulation, typically
using Haussmann-like "regularizations" and radial-concentric street patterns.[17] City Beautiful planners showed only partial awareness of the
coming automobile revolution—the emergence of a city in which the vast
majority of families would own at least one private motor vehicle. City
Beautiful plans still accepted corridor streets lined with buildings, except
for the parkways. The parkways in City Beautiful plans should be distinguished from the later, freeway-like parkways of the 1920s and 1930s.
These earlier parkways were essentially wide streets with landscaped
medians and border plantings. They did intersect with cross streets and
thus were not true limited-access arterials. They were intended for use by
recreational and residential traffic, not commercial vehicles. In the city
center, clearance of slums and their replacement with urban boulevards
and parkways seemed a positive good, worth the costs in disruption and
displacement of residents.[18]

The inherent "logic" of the radial concentric pattern as a system of conduits for traffic was well-known to American city planners long before the
highway research of the 1930s and 1940s.[19] The radials provide access to
the dominant center from all sides; the circumferentials allow movement

from one radial to another and permit through traffic to bypass the congested center. For example, Burnham's *Report on a Plan for San Francisco* (1905) presented a "theoretical diagram" for an urban circulation system using a classic radial-concentric arterial plan (figure 1.5).[20]

While the City Beautiful planners focused on improving the orderliness and aesthetic quality of the city, a different cadre of urban reformers worked for improved low-cost housing, better public health, and the relief of overcrowding. The housing reformers set up their own organization, the National Housing Association, in 1909. They pursued a more specific agenda focused on housing regulations and eventually public housing, maintaining a fitful and not always congenial relationship with city planners.[21] Thus, even before World War I, the planning movement was showing internal fissures that would endure through the freeway building era.

By the 1920s, differences had arisen even among the "physical planning" fraternity over the proper agenda for city planning, and road building in particular. The City Beautiful planners advocated systems of well-landscaped boulevards and parkways, usually in radial configurations, focusing on civic monuments. Streets were to serve a traffic function, to be sure, but they also formed the skeleton of a vast urban design composition, creating public spaces and vistas that would instill the urban populace with awe and reverence. "City Efficient" planners downplayed these aesthetic and moral concerns, focusing instead on the scientific analysis of street patterns in order to move traffic with the least friction. To accomplish this, a hierarchical grid often seemed more practical and efficient and was easier to superimpose on existing American street layouts.

The rise of the City Efficient planners marked a shift within the planning movement from "civic design" to functional planning, viewing the city primarily as an efficient site for production and consumption.[22] Harland Bartholomew and other leading planners of the 1920s hoped to transform city planning into a scientific enterprise by means of land use, economic, and transportation surveys linked to proven principles of rational urban structure.[23] City planning was conceived as the orderly accommodation of urban growth, guided by a master plan and enforced by zoning ordinances and subdivision regulations. Marc Weiss has argued that this type of planning was both invented and propagated by planners, working in conjunction with large-scale developers who strongly supported public measures to preserve land values in middle- and upper-class residential areas and in the central business districts.[24]

Mainstream American city planners were concerned about the decline of American central cities because those central areas represented a huge

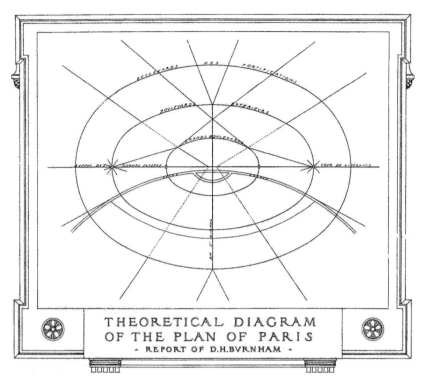

Figure 1.5
Theoretical diagram for a rational circulation system, based on Paris. *Source:* Daniel H. Burnham and Edward H. Bennett, *Report on a Plan for San Francisco*, San Francisco, Sunset Books, 1905.

accumulation of fixed capital. Central city interests feared a precipitous devaluation of these assets as the result of blight and excessive decentralization of economic activity to the suburbs. Harland Bartholomew played a leading role in defining the problem of urban blight and advancing proposals for clearance or rehabilitation of the core frame around the central business district. The construction of wide new arterials was consistent with City Efficient planning, which prescribed land-use sorting, modernized circulation systems, and the replacement of obsolete urban areas.

Unlike highway engineers, city planners did not build strong connections with the federal government during this period. American city planners were based mainly in local government, and even there they had a tenuous foothold in lay planning commissions, supplemented by small staffs or hired consultants. There were no strong regional planning

organizations.[25] Planning did receive federal sanction through the prom-
ulgation of the Standard Zoning Enabling Act (1924), the Standard City
Planning Enabling Act (1928), and the U.S. Supreme Court decision in
Euclid v. Ambler (1926).[26] But planning lacked the type of institution-
building strength that the highway builders mastered early on.[27]

Rural Origins of the Highway Builders

Highway engineering in the United States emerged from rural experience,
a key fact in understanding the history of urban freeway planning. The
Bureau of Public Roads was founded in 1895 as the Office of Road Inquiry within the Department of Agriculture. The bureau's original mandate was to improve rural roads. City streets were left entirely to the municipalities, and the bureau's original orientation and program of research
concentrated on non-urban highways. Like city planning, the bureau
emerged during the Progressive Era, as middle- and upper-class reformers
pushed for more efficient and honest forms of public administration.[28]
Ostensibly, the new bureaucracies would "depoliticize" city management
and apply the criteria of business efficiency to the public domain.
    The first state highway departments were formed during the 1890s.
The American Association of State Highway Officials was founded in
1914 and, working in conjunction with the Bureau of Public Roads,
gradually became a powerful political lobby for highways as well as a
conduit for the dissemination of highway policy and technical expertise
throughout the nation.[29] Federal aid for the construction of roads was
inaugurated with the Highway Act of 1916.[30] The institutional structure
established at this time, using federal supervision and state implementation, proved extraordinarily durable. Even when the bureau and the states
moved into urban areas, the cities would be "outsiders" to this venerable
federal–state relationship. The Bureau of Public Roads and the American
Association of State Highway Officials became authoritative voices in the
making of highway policy.
    Road builders had another advantage. Highway engineers built a
product that almost everyone seemed to want—more roads. This was a
commodity with virtually unlimited demand. Highway engineers did not
experience recurring doubts about the worth of their activities, although
there were battles over which bureaucracies would control the highway
planning function in government.[31] The engineers had a clear image of
their designated mission. They were concerned about their status in society, political clout, educational credentials, and employment prospects,

but did not doubt the importance of their central task—to build modern highways. As a profession organized around a single, unambiguous function, highway engineers found the tasks of institutional consolidation, establishment of technical credibility, and definition of professional turf simpler than for city planners. In another sharp contrast with planners, highway engineers received strong support from a powerful cluster of private economic groups: the automobile, oil, rubber, glass, heavy equipment, and construction material industries, along with elements of labor dependent upon automobile manufacture and road construction for jobs. Planners had no such focused constituency.

Highway engineers also moved quickly to establish a strong, wellfunded highway research organization. The Highway Research Board was founded in 1921 as a prestigious institution for sponsoring, coordinating, and disseminating technical highway research. This played no small part in establishing the credibility and expertise of the highway builders, who developed a public image as masters of "facts" determined by objective, disciplined inquiry. Their form concepts radiated the aura of scientific research, whereas those of planners and designers often seemed to emerge from trial and error or artistic intuition.[32]

Louis Ward Kemp has summarized the highway engineers' ideology at this time: build enough highways to accommodate traffic; develop scientific methods of location, design, and construction; and create a "highway policy subsystem," an interlocking directorate of private lobbying groups, congressional supporters, federal agencies, centralized research forums, and professional associations to push for more highways.[33] However, this emerging community of highway builders had not yet developed an array of form concepts for urban arterial construction. Their chief concern was the construction of a unified highway system between farms and cities and connections between cities. The internal circulation systems of urban areas fell outside their mandate and remained an underdeveloped area of concern.

The Automobile Takes Center Stage

The rapid growth in automobile ownership during the 1920s elevated traffic congestion to a new plane.[34] In addition, technical developments in the automobile were forcing changes in road design. As David Jones, Jr., has pointed out, during the 1920s, the auto, which had been "a canvastop sporting vehicle," was transformed into "a hard-top, enclosed, allweather utility vehicle" suitable for commuting, shopping, and all other trips.[35] Larger and more powerful cars also required better roads for safe, efficient handling.

At first, city planners and traffic engineers attacked the traffic problem with rationalized thoroughfare plans, traffic control devices, and proposals to expand existing streets.[36] Street widening provided a measure of relief but had inherent limits. Extra lanes could be added with relative ease to streets with wide sidewalks or median strips, but once that space was converted to new lanes, expansion required eating away at adjacent buildings, a very expensive proposition. In heavily built-up areas with multistory buildings fronting directly on modest sidewalks, large-scale widening was prohibitively expensive.[37]

Between 1920 and 1930, many cities expedited traffic by building viaducts spanning railroad yards, industrial zones, rivers, and other obstacles to smooth vehicle flow. These viaducts were not full-scale elevated highways because they only spanned limited areas and connected directly with the surface street system at their termini.[38] Bridge approaches also provided experience with the construction of freeway-like segments within urban areas.[39]

Another city planning and traffic engineering strategy was the creation of new road hierarchies instead of the uniform grid. The grid made all streets equally available for through traffic. A hierarchy separated traffic into through and local streams, keeping the through traffic out of quiet residential areas. Existing grids could be reworked by designating selected streets as collectors and widening them or making them one-way. Other strategies included better signalization, signal timing, and elaborate parking restrictions.[40]

These incremental measures could only accommodate a limited amount of new traffic. During the 1920s, for more and more experts on urban transportation, it seemed that a qualitative "leap" toward a new scale of speed and capacity was needed, rather than expensive modifications of street patterns laid down many decades before. Large volumes of automobiles could only be handled in specialized channels devoted exclusively to the movement of motor traffic, free from at-grade intersections and accessible only at widely spaced intervals by specially designed entrance and exit ramps.[41]

Piecemeal traffic accommodation measures such as street widening did have impacts on the form and function of the central city, although nothing as dramatic as the later freeway building operations. Adapting urban form to the automobile almost always entailed significant costs. Street widening chiseled away at spacious sidewalks and planted median strips:

"parkways" became traffic conduits. One-way traffic schemes tended to convert quiet residential streets into busy arterials. Thus, as freeway proponents would repeatedly argue, the non-freeway alternatives for expediting traffic were not benign and exacted their own toll on the quality of city life.

Visionary Plans of the 1920s and Early 1930s

During the 1920s architects, engineers, and planners generated an array of inventive proposals to build whole new cities around automobile infrastructure, rather than chip small incremental improvements into the recalcitrant material of existing urban landscapes.[42] Although few of these proposals were ever implemented, they seeded the intellectual landscape with concepts and images of cities thoroughly adapted to the motor age.

Le Corbusier unveiled his famous urban proposals in the 1920s and early 1930s: "A Contemporary City for Three Million People" in 1922, the Plan Voisin for Paris in 1925, and the Radiant City during the early 1930s.[43] In Le Corbusier's Modernist city plans, broad highways and transit lines penetrate to the city center, but all transportation modes are segregated on separate levels. Traditional corridor streets have been abolished. Land uses are rigidly separated (figure 1.6).

In the 1920s, the American architects Raymond Hood, Harvey Wiley Corbett, and Hugh Ferriss, who were aware of Le Corbusier's startling ideas for urban reconstruction, produced their own impressive array of futuristic renderings, which percolated into popular magazines and movies.[44] In their skillful renderings, broad highways penetrate the central city, slicing through phalanxes of skyscrapers, but on separate levels from pedestrians and parking facilities. These architectural visions introduced the profession and segments of the wider public to an impressive catalog of technological "solutions" to the conflict between the automobile and the city. These proposals involved massive new construction, not the piecemeal alterations pursued by municipal traffic engineers and city planners. They purported to be final and comprehensive, not incremental and subject to frequent revision.

But there is a great gap between the drafting board and the inner councils of urban transportation policy. Prominent architects often produced what might be called a "divided portfolio." To earn a living, they designed individual buildings for private clients, geared to the economic and political realities of the urban real estate market. On the side, they produced urban design and city planning projects with no identifiable client or plan

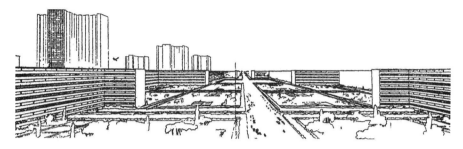

Figure 1.6
Le Corbusier's Contemporary City (1922) as reproduced in *Architectural Record* 73 (January 1933): 15.

of implementation.[45] Architects were not in charge of public works or city planning, and their influence could only be gradual and indirect, a slow permeation of the public mind with new possibilities. Certainly, as visual presentations, the future cities of Le Corbusier, Corbett, Hood, Ferriss, and others were entrancing in their modernity and contrast with the past. They made the public conscious of alternatives, moving the idea of urban freeways steadily toward acceptability.

The work of Fritz Malcher during the late 1920s and early 1930s straddled the fence between visionary urban design and pragmatic traffic improvement. Malcher worked out a complicated array of street designs for ensuring the uninterrupted flow of traffic, christened "The Steadyflow Traffic System."[46] In a 1931 article in *American City*, Malcher presented a plan for a whole city organized around his methods for efficient traffic flow.[47] In Malcher's drawings, we can see an urban form built completely around the elaborate road hierarchies and turning lanes required to accommodate the uninterrupted movement of the motorized vehicle.

Early Freeway Plans

Some cities began designing freeway networks during the 1920s. The Detroit Rapid Transit Commission published a plan for superhighways integrated with rail rapid transit in 1924, and a freeway plan for Chicago was unveiled in 1928.[48] The renderings of the Detroit "Super-Highway" show a broad thoroughfare with rapid transit tracks in the median, separated from the auto lanes by stately rows of trees (figure 1.7). There is a Fifth Avenue–style tower for traffic signals operated by a traffic policeman at the intersection. The "parkway" ambience is reinforced by groups of pedestrians ambling along only a few feet from the freeway, as though it were a Parisian boulevard. Such idealized images were common in the early freeway literature. Planners had not yet grasped the dimensions of the new "machine space" created by motor highways; using images left over from a slower, quieter age, they gave it human-scale attributes that could not be maintained in reality.[49]

Some planners joined pro-highway urban "growth coalitions," hoping to coordinate new expressways with other physical planning improvements. Planners saw *their* profession as the indispensable guardian of the city's physical form and assumed that they would play a leading role in

Figure 1.7
Detroit Superhighway Plan of 1924. *Source:* Detroit Rapid Transit Commission, *Proposed Super-Highway Plan for Greater Detroit*, 1924.

determining the location and design of new urban highways. Here, planners misjudged their future involvement in freeway planning, failing to see that they would be overshadowed by single-purpose highway agencies.

In the United States, the most prescient thoroughfare plan of the 1920s was the *Regional Plan of New York and Its Environs* (RPNYE), which portrayed a complete transportation network for the New York region. This network closely resembles the freeway system eventually built by Robert Moses.[50] The RPNYE was the most technically sophisticated plan of its time, drawing upon reams of detailed urban research and a stellar array of leading professionals from planning, architecture, transportation, and urban economics. The highway component of the RPNYE was not a pure radial-concentric pattern, but a hybrid between the grid and a radial-concentric plan.[51]

The RPNYE transportation proposals are also significant for the urban design detail provided. In a seeming holdover from the City Beautiful, the RPNYE's architects produced skilled renderings of proposed improvements. Unlike later freeway plans that contained mainly tables, graphs, maps, and bird's-eye views, the Committee on the Regional Plan of New York and Its Environs devoted substantial effort to exploring the architectural components of its proposed urban thoroughfares.[52]

Conclusion

In this chapter, we began our description of the conceptual evolution of the modern urban freeway. We laid out the understandings of urban challenges that led professionals of many kinds to address the role of roads, in their existing forms and in their future and futuristic forms, in solving problems variously understood as economically based or as based on infrastructure or transportation movement needs.

We saw that the perceived advantages of a new form of urban transportation, with separated grades, limited accessibility, and high speeds, were being identified. These alleged benefits included urban development, redevelopment and revitalization, and decreased vehicular congestion. Understanding of these "goods" came in great part from generalizing from the success of building roads in rural areas, from admiration of the few already built limited-access roads, and from lovely plans for others yet to be built. Some critics of the evolving notions and of the early freeway attempts could be found, but many of the disadvantages and costs of channeling traffic through central cities were not understood.

We described very different views of the function of urban transportation systems on the parts of highway engineers, planners, landscape architects, and architects, although we also identified times where their visions, not fully developed, converged. We anticipated the important role played by the engineering profession, a role that we make more specific in the following chapters. And we noted that while these visions were developing (and to some extent competing), the automobile was taking an ever more central role in American life. It was being popularized, idealized—even romanticized—in popular culture as a vehicle to a richer and freer future.

In the next chapter, we note the range of interests and constituencies that supported and bought to dominance the varying visions of the professions that would conceptualize, design, build, and eventually critique high-speed highways through urban cores.

In chapter 2, we pay greater attention to the decade of the 1930s; we describe the slowing of momentum for urban freeways during the Great Depression, but we also recognize the opportunities for building laid out in the New Deal. In addition, we encounter early successful examples of urban parkways and turnpikes and great ideas for more of these sylvan structures in major American cities. We also see that, despite the Depression, the automobile continued to create great demands and challenges for urban traffic movement.

2

The 1930s: Forays into the Urban Realm

Initial Opportunities for Urban Freeway Construction

With the onset of the Depression in 1929 and its deepening during the following years, American cities experienced severe fiscal stress and retrenchment. Funds for highway improvements dwindled. The ambitious urban plans of the 1920s now seemed completely unrealistic, as cities tried to cope with more pressing issues of unemployment and the maintenance of basic services. Ultimately, however, in conjunction with the pump-priming initiatives of the New Deal, the 1930s would offer the first opportunities for significant urban freeway construction. President Franklin D. Roosevelt's programs of federally funded public works enabled Robert Moses, the country's premier public entrepreneur, to take his urban projects off the drawing board and into the city. As World War II approached, some of the most famous exemplars of urban freeways were constructed, such as the Henry Hudson Parkway and Gowanus Parkway in New York City and the Arroyo Seco Parkway in Los Angeles. The Pennsylvania Turnpike opened in 1940. These exemplars, in turn, influenced the codification of urban freeway policy during the war years.

The Depression slowed the rate of automobile expansion, but pressures on traditional street networks continued to build. Car registrations in 1930 totaled almost 23,000,000; by 1940, they had reached almost 27,400,000.[1] This was stagnation compared with the 1920s but did not end the search for solutions to urban traffic congestion. The limited-access highway within the built-up area of the city remained on the agenda.

In 1930, urban freeway planning was still a poorly charted landscape. Rural and suburban parkways served as models of new free-flowing thoroughfares for the auto age but only on the urban fringe. Boulevard and parkway elements of City Beautiful plans had been completed in Chicago, Philadelphia, and other cities, but these were not true limited-access thoroughfares and often involved only the widening and embellishment of existing surface streets.[2] Approaches to large bridges had required clearance of congested areas but only for a limited distance on each side of the spans. The "superhighway" plans for Detroit and Chicago portrayed extensive networks of limited-access highways, but the cities lacked the funds to build the segments that traversed expensive central city land (figure 2.1).[3]

The 1930–1938 period saw the construction of numerous influential exemplars. Robert Moses' urban parkways and bridges showed public officials, engineers, planners, and designers that limited-access roads could be pushed into urban centers, often with considerable attention to aesthetics and associated amenities. Thus, when urban freeway planning doctrine was made more explicit during the war years, the authors of national policy could gaze upon actual achievements rather than paper plans.

Urban Freeway Planning: First Forays of the Highway Engineers

During the 1930s, the highway engineering profession, led by the Bureau of Public Roads at the federal level, began to make its first forays into the realm of urban freeway planning. This was not entirely a matter of choice: the bureau's turf was being invaded by other political actors. After Roosevelt's election in 1932, New Deal economists wanted to use highways as employment generators. Superhighway advocates called for a national system of divided, high-speed roads, and toll-road builders wanted to construct new toll highways outside the federal-aid system. The bureau faced the specter that its hegemony in road-building affairs would be gradually chiseled away.[4] As Bruce Seely has pointed out, the bureau was aware of the need for federal aid for urban highways, endorsing "legislation to include urban portions of state highway systems in the federal-aid network in 1930 and 1932," proposals that were finally enacted in the Hayden–Cartwright legislation of 1934.[5] But as urban freeways rose higher on the national public works agenda, the bureau sought to ensure that new urban highways would not fall under the jurisdiction of other divisions of government.[6]

Thus far, the highway engineer's mission had been to improve farm-to-market roads and construct a rationally connected system of national highways, the federal primary system. Neither the Bureau of Public Roads nor the state highway departments had a tradition of cooperation with municipal officials on urban highway design. The formidable research

Figure 2.1
Growing traffic congestion created pressure to construct new roads and bridges.
Source: Norman Bel Geddes, *Magic Motorways*, New York, Random House, 1940.

capabilities of the bureau and the Highway Research Board had not been directed at the problem of integrating highways into existing cities.

The highway engineers' inherited experience with rural freeway building influenced both their theory and practice as they gradually crossed inside city limits after the early 1930s. Rural highway deficiencies differed from the problems that engineers would later face in the cities. In rural areas the roads often meandered, following section lines and avoiding topographical obstacles; there were many dangerous turns and curves. Rural roads often failed to form an interconnected system for long trips. Poorly designed vertical alignments created dangerous blind spots and roller-coaster effects where highways passed through hilly terrain. The obstacles to rural highways were chiefly natural features—rivers, streams, hills, valleys—rather than man-made structures.[7]

During the 1920s, highway engineers also learned how quickly highway improvements could become obsolete. Widened roads quickly filled with traffic, necessitating further rounds of improvements. Larger and faster vehicles required stronger pavements and wider turning radii. Highway engineers saw that the solution to these rural problems was a coordinated freeway network that linked points of traffic generation by the shortest possible distance, removing physical obstacles where necessary, and sized to handle traffic loads well into the future.[8]

Highway engineers had acquired valuable experience in the technical aspects of highway design: alignments, pavement and subgrade materials, bridge construction, and roadside landscaping. But rural highway building provided few insights into the formidable problem of tampering with the social ecology, economic life, and architectural heritage of existing cities. Thus, the highway engineering profession entered the 1930s with neither an explicit body of knowledge about the insertion of freeways into built-up districts nor accumulated experience at that task. Cost consciousness, traffic service, and safety requirements dominated the highway planning process.

City Planners and the New Thoroughfares

The city planning profession entered the 1930s on the defensive; municipal planning budgets were slashed as cities reacted to the precipitous decline in tax revenues. Only employment with New Deal agencies kept many planners solvent during the Depression. The profession had few resources to deploy in new domains such as urban highways.[9]

During the 1920s, city planners presented themselves, in large part, as technical problem solvers with practical solutions to traffic congestion and land-use conflicts. Remaking the city for the automobile formed a critical part of the "scientific" land-use planning that dominated American city planning practice. Automobile accommodation seemed popular with business and the general public, future-minded, democratic, and conducive to improved urban economic performance. The automobile industry anchored the emerging mass production economy and was not a force to be quixotically opposed. As a struggling profession heavily reliant on either consulting contracts or municipal employment, city planning's market niche provided for only limited independence from the views of local political elites and business interests. In such a climate, planners embraced technical tasks that steered clear of social conflict or utopian challenges to the status quo.[10]

Variations of the radial-concentric or "spider web" pattern of arterials dominated the planning discourse of the day. Karl B. Lohmann's *Principles of City Planning* (1930), an important instructional and reference text, endorsed this pattern.[11] The book reproduced the highway scheme from the *Regional Plan of New York and Its Environs*, remarking that "The theoretical figure of a spider's web cannot perhaps be duplicated in every plan, but at least it can be approximated."[12] Lohmann mentioned the "superhighways" of Detroit in a brief paragraph and deemed the new highways on the horizon "spectacular expressions of the present-day needs of metropolitan traffic" but did not explore their implications for urban form.

Planners were still struggling to determine what kind of city they should be striving to build at a time when the motor vehicle and electrification were breaking down old pressures for compactness. Champions of the garden city ideal saw the urban fringe as a new frontier where proper planning could finally occur; incremental changes to old patterns would not work. Clarence Stein wrote in 1939 that:

Within the next half century the larger cities of America will be rebuilt or replaced. . . . They must go. . . . It is impossible now to develop a new plan in the old framework. . . . Replacing building by building or even block by block will not suffice.[13]

Stein's colleague in the Regional Planning Association of America, Benton MacKaye, had developed his "Townless Highway" concept during the late 1920s. MacKaye advocated the construction of new communities placed off to the side of new regional highways, thus avoiding the creation of "motor slums" and "ribbon development."

Instead of a single roadtown slum, congealing between our big cities, the townless highway would encourage the building of real communities, at definite and favorable points off the road.[14]

New towns would decant population from the urban core, lessening the need for elaborate freeway networks through the central city. Thus, the garden city ideal could be reconciled with a large radial-concentric regional freeways system, linking a smaller, restructured central city with both suburbs and satellite communities.[15]

For many city planners, America's central cities seemed hopelessly resistant to the current array of planning remedies, and it seemed wiser to concentrate on planning new communities properly on the urban fringe.[16] In 1930, John Ihlder pointed out that "City planning heretofore has given most attention to the development of new areas. This was logical not only because the new areas presented easier technical problems and a freer field for the new art or science, but because in the new areas support was more readily secured, opposition more readily overcome."[17]

In 1932, Harland Bartholomew declared that "The average American city is about the most wasteful of all the creations of man. . . . Our cities are faced with wholesale economic disintegration."[18] In his Presidential Address to the National Conference on City Planning in June 1931, Bartholomew lamented planning's ineffectiveness:

While any generalization is but a hazardous guess, it is doubtful whether city planning is much more than 5 per cent effective in the largest cities nor more than 25 per cent effective, on the whole, in the smaller cities. While city planning under present practices is more or less hopeless in the largest cities, it can be made 75 per cent to 90 per cent effective in the smaller cities, to their economic benefit as well as to their social and esthetic advantage.[19]

But Bartholomew, unlike many of his colleagues, insisted that planners must attack the problem of central city decay rather than retreating to the suburbs. In the same address, he argued that "the greatest deficiency of current city plans" was the "lack of attention to the preservation of values or the rehabilitation or re-planning of those vast areas of old residential property that are found in every city between the downtown business districts and the suburbs." Despite his pessimism about the current efficacy of planning, Bartholomew insisted that "we could and should plan to rebuild these blighted districts," providing them with the amenities of the decentralized city: "good houses, less congestion, more open space and attractiveness." In addition, "through use of the neighborhood unit," planners could encourage "personal interest in the community in place of the individual indifference of today."[20]

Bartholomew's call to stem further decay of neglected gray areas was timely, but planners' prescriptions often reflected their dislike of old urban districts and penchant for clean-sweep remedies. For example, in 1933 the Detroit City Planning Commission proposed the clearance of a large slum area and its replacement with uniform, geometrically arranged apartment blocks. The proposal included a new grade-separated highway at the northern end of the cleared site. The old street grid was eliminated, replaced with superblocks containing apartments arranged on culs-de-sac. The plan would have provided open space and freedom from cross traffic, but only by abolishing the traditional corridor street, a form concept increasingly associated with obsolete industrial cities and urban decay.[21]

Some planners and urban officials saw transportation improvements as an opportunity to clear out dilapidated urban districts, particularly those forming a "ring of blight" around high-value properties of the central business district. Harold S. Buttenheim, editor of the journal *American City*, observed in 1931:

Another trend of thought—though marked as yet by little accomplishment except as incidental to other projects—is the rehabilitation of the blighted areas of American cities. One of the most practicable legal means of action in the United States is through such major projects of boulevard building as were carried out in Paris through the efforts of our fellow member Baron Haussmann.[22]

Thus, the clash between highway projects and traditional, fine-grained urban form could be framed as a beneficial one, with the new arteries clearing and replacing undesirable urban tissue. Planners lacked a complex canon of central city urban design that would have provided a sound basis for integrating new arterials into the historic city. In any case, most urban observers did not view proposed urban freeways as matters of architecture or civic design that required as much careful treatment as a cluster of buildings or a subdivision. Freeways were seen as engineered structures, built for economy and convenience, providing the mobility essential for modern commerce.[23]

New Arterials and Urban Design

During the 1930s, planners, engineers, and public officials still believed that new urban parkways or freeways could be made compatible with the existing city. Parkways enhanced the rural landscape; why couldn't they do the same in the city? And perhaps utilitarian highways might be threaded into built-up areas with some sensitivity, if designers would marshal their talents to confront the problem. Thus, in the absence of clear precedents, planners began to search for answers to the emerging conflict between the freeway and the city (figure 2.2).

The 1930 *Report on a Thoroughfare Plan for Boston*, prepared by the Boston City Planning Board and planning consultant Robert Whitten, illustrates the insights and foibles of early urban highway planning.[24] As we will discuss in greater detail when Boston appears as a "cameo city" in chapter 6, the plan portrayed a system of "express roads" roughly radial concentric in form. Outside the central business district (CBD), new radial express roads would be carved through existing residential districts where necessary. In the core, the plan recommended construction of a "Central Artery" cutting through the heart of historic Boston, presaging the Central Artery that was actually built in the 1950s, and which has now been demolished and replaced with an underground freeway.

To his credit, Robert Whitten did discuss the relation between the new urban highways and the three-dimensional urban environment. He was aware that elevated structures could cause problems with noise, vibration,

Figure 2.2
Two proposed configurations for threading elevated highways through the central city. *Source:* Boston, City Planning Board, *Report on a Thoroughfare Plan for Boston*, Robert Whitten, Consultant, 1930.

and blockage of views and sunlight. Still, he decided that elevated highways were the only workable means of traversing densely built-up downtown areas in the absence of preexisting linear corridors such as rivers or vacant waterfront lands.

As a matter of first impression the erection of additional elevated structures in Downtown Boston is very objectionable. The comparison of course is with the present noisy and ugly elevated railway structures. It must be remembered, however, that the proposed upper level roadway will occupy the central portion only of a broad avenue; that it will be but two-thirds the height of the elevated structure in Atlantic Avenue; that great care will be taken in its design to make it attractive and to reduce noise and vibration; that it will be used by motor vehicles and not by railroad trains; that it is probable that hard tire vehicles would be excluded; that a vehicular subway would interfere with sewers and with present and future rapid transit subways; and that it is not physically and economically possible to take care of the large volume of traffic on the street surface.[25]

Clearly, Whitten was worried that his elevated highway proposal would draw criticism. His mitigation measures, though, were not very convincing. Ultimately, he fell back upon the last line of defense: given existing engineering and financial constraints, only elevated highways could move large streams of traffic through Boston's central business district.[26]

Whitten's renderings of his elevated highways showed startling juxtapositions of the new arterials with adjacent buildings, similar to the elevated railways found in a number of large American cities, including Boston. The abutting eight- to ten-story buildings formed a canyon, with the highway at the bottom, and the proposal clearly presented problems with noise reverberating off the building façades and the accumulation of fumes and dust at street level. But this scheme did have the advantage of not requiring extensive demolition of existing structures in the urban core: the highway was inserted *into* the corridor street, albeit threateningly, rather than demanding its complete removal. Even entrance and egress were handled by ramps in the center of the highway connecting with the street below, reducing the need for land clearance to create room for large interchanges.

Whitten acknowledged that elevated transit structures were undesirable, but he believed *that automobile thoroughfares would be different.* They could be designed attractively, and cars generated less noise than trains. Like so many other planners, Whitten saw urban highways as a new technical invention that could be mastered and guided by technical experts. Although somewhat uncouth, highways could be aesthetically treated and rendered suitable for urban life.

Whitten's plan fused both forward-looking and traditional road forms. His elevated structures and surface radials marched across the urban landscape like the roads of the future, but he placed two large traffic circles near the CBD to handle traffic distribution and intersection with a major cross street—a primitive solution by later standards. Perhaps this seemed a logical space-saving choice for the congested center. Throughout the 1920s and early 1930s, planners continued to use design fragments deriving from park and City Beautiful plans of the early 1900s. They were still willing to strike compromises with the old urban fabric, rather than give engineering design criteria complete priority.

During the 1930s, a number of large American cities either initiated or continued to elaborate ambitious plans for limited-access urban thoroughfares. Chicago's plan for a "Comprehensive System of Elevated Super-Highways" was discussed in *City Planning* for April 1931:

[T]he scheme for a comprehensive system of elevated superhighways radiating out fanshape from a rectangular by-pass route around the four sides of our central business district, commonly called the "Loop," and extending outward from the Loop to the borders of the city north, northwest, southwest, and south.[27]

Also, Chicago's Outer Drive along the lakefront was cited frequently in the planning and engineering literature as a model of elegant urban parkway design.[28] Planning for a comprehensive urban expressway system for Chicago continued throughout the 1930s (figure 2.3).[29]

Los Angeles lagged behind New York City in parkway and freeway construction during the 1930s, but both public and private groups began to position the city for freeway dominance in the coming decades. In 1937, the Automobile Club of Southern California produced a *Traffic Survey*, which proposed a regional expressway grid.[30]

Two plates in the report show that the authors had considered the urban design aspects of freeway construction. The plate "Motorway Through a Residential District" showed enormous grassy buffer zones between the freeway and adjacent housing. In spread-out Los Angeles, planners could envision an extravagant use of land to shield residents from noise and fumes. The plate "Motorway Through a Business District," however, adopted a completely different strategy. Instead of separating the freeway from its CBD environment, the freeway was constructed through a sequence of large office buildings in a "joint-use" scheme similar to the visionary architectural plans of the 1920s. The *Traffic Survey* vigorously embraced an extensive expressway system for the Los Angeles region, but this 1937 plan portrayed the new motorways as either *spacious parkways*

Figure 2.3
Chicago superhighway proposal of 1939. *Source:* Chicago, Department of Super-highways, *A Comprehensive Superhighway Plan for the City of Chicago*, prepared by Charles E. De Leuw, William R. Matthews, and A. J. Schafmayer, 1939.

or *elements of urban architecture.* In 1939, the Los Angeles municipal engineers followed suit with their own comprehensive parkway plan for the Los Angeles basin.[31] As the renderings and text clearly show, however, this was still an urban parkway plan, not a plan for ten-lane freeways.[32] These urban design features were later diluted or abandoned when interstate design standards eclipsed the more modest expressway standards of municipal planners and engineers (figure 2.4, figure 2.5, and figure 2.6).

Symptoms foreshadowing later conflicts over professional dominance in the highway planning field were already visible in the 1930s. In a 1930 article in *American City*, Richard Schermerhorn, Jr., a planner and landscape architect in New York City, worried that aesthetic measures were being applied to highways as cosmetics, after all of the major decisions had already been made by engineers. This was like "starting the job in the middle" and relegated the role of the landscape architect to the "incidental planting of shrubs and vines." Schermerhorn argued that "Highway structures such as bridges, culverts, underpasses, etc, should be designed by architects or landscape architects instead of engineers."[33]

Some prominent architects influenced public debates over transportation planning through their utopian "cities of the future." The Corbusian metropolis of skyscrapers, apartment blocks, lavish open space, and rapid transportation systems received its latest incarnation in *The Radiant City*, worked out between 1929 and 1935.[34] Le Corbusier offered little help

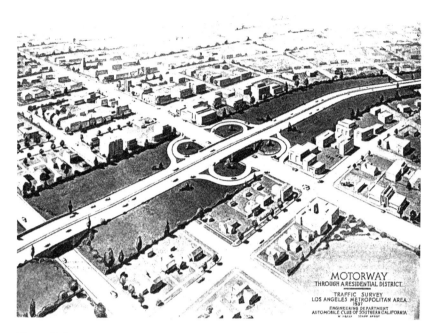

Figure 2.4
Buffering an urban motorway with wide swaths of landscaping. *Source:* Automobile Club of Southern California Archives, *Traffic Survey: Los Angeles Metropolitan Area Nineteen Hundred Thirty-seven*, 1937.

to the planner looking for ways to build freeways in dense city centers with minimal disruption. He envisioned the abolition of large expanses of existing urban centers and the erection of new megastructures above or through them. This type of urban design required the clean slate that practicing city planners would encounter only in new town projects or the large-scale urban renewal projects of the 1960s.[35]

Similarly, Frank Lloyd Wright's "Broadacre City" of 1935 proposed abandonment of the overcrowded metropolis and its wholesale replacement with an open landscape of single-family houses dispersed throughout a rural freeway grid.[36] Wright offered nothing for the planner or architect trying to locate a new thoroughfare through a jumble of nineteenth-century row houses, warehouses, or office buildings.

Despite occasional forays into urban design, however, most architects concentrated on individual buildings for private clients and left highway design to the engineers and landscape architects. As Eliel Saarinen had observed in 1925, "It is true that during later years something of the art

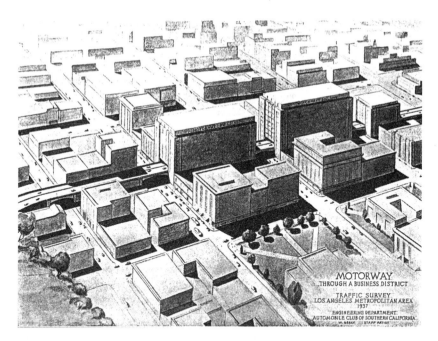

Figure 2.5
Building a motorway into the architecture of the central city. *Source:* Automobile Club of Southern California Archives, *Traffic Survey: Los Angeles Metropolitan Area Nineteen Hundred Thirty-seven*, 1937.

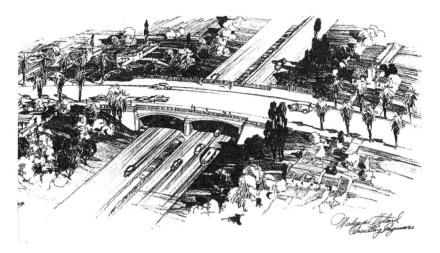

Figure 2.6
Proposed parkway for Los Angeles. *Source:* Los Angeles, Transportation Engineering Board, *A Transit Program for the Los Angeles Metropolitan Area*, 1939.

of City Building—City Planning—had been taught in the schools, but as yet this art is more or less foreign to the usual system of architectural education. It is not yet acknowledged as a necessary foundation to the education of the architect."[37]

The Urban Parkways of Robert Moses

While architects and planners searched for form concepts on the drafting board, Robert Moses was preparing to use New York City as his palette. Moses had already envisioned an array of arterial improvements for New York City by the 1920s, based largely on a long heritage of arterial plans for the New York region. He saw that if automobile owners were to use his beaches and recreation areas, they would need spacious access routes out of the central city to the points where his parkways began.[38] The corrupt Tammany administration had made little progress on these improvements. Construction had begun on the Triborough Bridge in 1929, but the project ground to a halt between 1930 and 1932. The West Side Highway along the Hudson River had been launched in 1927 but advanced sluggishly and stopped completely in 1931.[39] With plans to spare but no efficient administrator to marshal resources and push construction, New York City appeared unable to complete any major transportation projects to meet the needs of its burgeoning population.

Throughout the 1920s, Moses surveyed the landscape of New York City, imagining radical transformations of its physical form. By 1930 he was ready to unveil his plans to the public. On February 25, 1930, before an audience attending the New York Park Association's annual dinner, Moses mapped out an elaborate system of parkways, boulevards, and bridges covering the New York region.[40] Closely resembling the highway plans in the *Regional Plan of New York and Its Environs* (RPNYE), Moses' proposals described a roughly radial-concentric pattern focusing on Manhattan.[41] Moses portrayed these arterials not as harsh bands of concrete, but as parkways bordered with grass, trees, and recreation areas. The entire project appeared to be an extension of his rural parkway-building activities, a means of penetrating the dreary grayness of the city with sylvan ribbons and recreational facilities for public use. This image of continuity with the beautiful parkways of Long Island and Westchester County quelled opposition that might have arisen on aesthetic grounds.

Moses used form concepts already elaborated in the RPNYE, a modified radial-concentric configuration. This was a radical plan to rebuild New York for the automobile. However, the growth-generating capacity

Figure 2.7
The West Side Highway in New York City, one of the first elevated urban expressways. *Source:* Norman Bel Geddes, *Magic Motorways*, New York, Random House, 1940.

of metropolitan freeway systems was only dimly perceived at this time. As Robert Caro points out, the meaning of the automobile—and of parkways—was quite different during the 1920s and 1930s from its later connotations. Although the auto was rapidly becoming the chief means for the journey to work, it retained the aura of a recreational vehicle. Planners could still imagine building enough new roads to satisfy demand and making those roadway miles beautiful works of landscape architecture. The Westchester and Long Island parkway models promised a high standard of aesthetic achievement in highway design. Free at this time of significant challenge, Moses sold his public works package to a receptive public eager for more roads—and construction jobs during hard economic times.

Even Lewis Mumford, in *The Culture of Cities*, viewed the automobile as a beneficent liberator of urban dwellers from the cramped confines of the industrial city. Rationally planned regional highway networks could help to "break up the functionless, overgrown urban masses of the past," replacing the "mono-nucleated city" with the "poly-nucleated city."[42] For Mumford, new highways would offer *escape from* the congested center. Moses, however, had no intention of abandoning the great metropolis. In his vision, new freeways would offer increased *access into* the heart of the city. Penetration, not bypasses, marked his plans.

The most publicized freeway exemplar by Moses during the 1930s was the Henry Hudson Parkway, the northern section of the "West Side Improvement" connecting the Battery with Moses' Henry Hudson Bridge, which linked the northern tip of Manhattan with the Bronx. This impressive work of urban engineering received universal praise, appearing, for example, on the cover of *American City* in November 1937.[43] The project appeared to live up to its parkway designation magnificently. Throughout part of its length, the new arterial boasted tennis courts, playgrounds, promenades, and an elaborate boat basin.[44] In addition, automobile drivers were treated to an unfolding panorama of New York City as they entered the city from the north; the "view from the road" was a thrilling one.

But as Robert Caro explains in detail, a knowledgeable person, aware of the preexisting landscape and the social geography of the city—a person actually walking along the parkway through its whole length rather than viewing it abstractly from above or driving along it in an automobile—might have seen a more qualified triumph of urban engineering. As the parkway passed through Harlem, it became a stripped-down highway devoid of the landscaping treatment dispensed so freely in other areas of the city.[45] The parkway damaged Inwood Hill Park in the northwestern corner of Manhattan, eliminated the last freshwater marsh left in New York City, and cut through the quiet community of Riverdale across the bridge from Manhattan.[46] Virtually the entire Manhattan waterfront along the Hudson River was now occupied by an automobile thoroughfare, soon to be carrying record numbers of automobiles with all of their noise and fumes. There would be no peaceful expanse of waterfront along the Hudson, untainted by the background roar of speeding machines (figure 2.8).[47]

Uncritical admiration was bestowed upon another important Moses freeway conceived during the 1930s and opened in 1941: the Gowanus Parkway along the southern waterfront of Brooklyn. An *Architectural Forum* article on the Gowanus Parkway intoned:

Like a Roman road the highway cuts through dreary city . . . and sweeps across its incongruous confusion and decay. There is a new scale to this structure that is truly contemporary, and next to it the incongruous disorder of our environment is shown up as hopelessly indefensible. Sweeping through the old city and over it—it is the first real taste of the coming urbanism.[48]

In this picture, the old city *lacks order*. Land uses are mixed together, stores below apartments, light industry amid stores, schools and churches scattered throughout. Against this "disorder," the article posits a new type of order—"the coming urbanism"—in which each land use is in its proper place, sorted into separate districts, with each district linked by spacious automobile thoroughfares.

The neighborhoods near the Gowanus are deemed lacking in health and vitality. The metaphor of "decay" implies the need for strong solutions, such as surgical removal of the diseased tissues. The new freeway stands out sharply against the dingy background of the old city; it soars *above*, marking a clean, unobstructed path for modern traffic.

Urban professionals of the late 1930s and early 1940s portrayed a rational, modernized city as the inevitable wave of the future. Their imagined modern city radiated only positive symbolism: elevation, clarity, hygiene, speed, rational order, and the beneficent use of state power. In contrast, the old city was cloaked in negative images of disorder and decay.

Planning professionals of this era did not see the social and spatial order that was embodied in old urban neighborhoods. The neighborhoods near the Gowanus Parkway were not slums. As Caro relates in *The Power Broker*, the mixed-use ethnic neighborhood of Sunset Park provided a decent, functional environment for its inhabitants. Scruffy on the outside, its urban densities, mixed uses, and public spaces supported a traditional,

Figure 2.8
The Henry Hudson Parkway in 1937. *Source:* The Benjamin and Gladys Thomas
Air Photo Archives, Fairchild Collection, UCLA Department of Geography.

non-suburban type of city life. The Gowanus Parkway disrupted that order by enshrouding Sunset Park's main commercial street in shadows,
noise, and fumes, driving out businesses and encouraging encroachment
by disruptive activities from adjacent warehouse and vice districts.[49]

Professional images of the industrial city—images that exaggerated
the dysfunctional characteristics of high densities, mixed uses, and old
buildings—are traceable to a cluster of causes, in addition to the real
health and social problems associated with urban poverty. For strong
reasons, planners and engineers of the 1930s viewed the clearance of
gray areas and their replacement with roads as unambiguous benefits.
New highways would generate jobs, and during the Great Depression
this was a first priority. Virtually everyone endorsed the rapid construction of large public works projects providing work for the masses of
unemployed. Robert Moses knew how to design, finance, and construct
such works.

Moses did not possess comprehensive transportation plans that were based on a thorough analysis of highway impacts on future urban land use, travel patterns, social geography, and urban design. He did not try to produce such plans. But he did have detailed, buildable plans for urban public works. High-quality planning studies require time, and time was scarce. Public officials saw few convincing reasons to block freeway projects worth hundreds of millions of dollars in order to quell the lingering doubts of a few critics. During the 1930s technology carried a strong positive sign, unchallenged by anxieties about environmental impacts. To most observers, Moses produced highly visible "solutions" to complex urban problems at a time when no one else seemed to have any alternatives. Urban highway projects promised to rejuvenate the central city economy and provide new jobs during a time of economic crisis.

Throughout this saga, Moses presented himself and his works as the product of apolitical expertise in service to the public interest. He was a master at marshalling data, constructing arguments, and presenting plans that made his alternatives appear to be the only rational ones. He successfully framed the problems facing the city in terms that pointed toward his solutions. He would close off debate, sometimes by simply bullying opponents but also by deploying barrages of information and seductive renderings prepared by his select corps of professional landscape architects, architects, and engineers.[50]

Finally, the research methods used by planners, designers, and engineers were not geared to the discovery of the internal social ecology or architectural value of older urban neighborhoods. Planners counted what was easily countable and pertinent to accepted indices of social or economic well-being: population density, crime rates, income, physical defects in housing, tax rates, and land values. These data, along with a superficial scan of building façades, could reveal a "slum" where there was actually a reasonably stable low-income community. Thus the scientific "objectivity" of planning studies was compromised by biases built into the methods of analysis.

As the first builder of urban highways on a large scale, within the most prominent city in the nation, at a time when other cities were groping for tangible solutions to traffic congestion and mass unemployment, Moses became the model of how to get things done and a node of innovation diffusion for urban freeway form concepts. For Moses, the negative regulations and laborious studies of planners had little attraction. Planners produced no structures on the ground, no monuments, no soaring towers of concrete and steel.

Outlines of Urban Freeway Doctrine

During the 1930s, city planners and transportation experts developed ambitious plans for major thoroughfare systems. Some used traditional boulevard or parkway designs, but many included the limited-access features that increasingly seemed essential for smooth traffic flow. Parkways were deemed the most desirable form, but where land was unavailable for wide rights-of-way, planners did not hesitate to prescribe elevated structures winding through the man-made canyons of the central city. On the metropolitan scale, radial-concentric or modified grid freeway systems emerged as the preferred patterns.

Still, all of these proposed highways were of modest scale in comparison with the later swaths of the interstate system, which were designed to the high geometric standards of the 1950s and 1960s. In the 1930s, city planners and engineers hoped that the freeway would be a *manageable insertion into the urban fabric*. As Robert Whitten wrote in 1932:

Unless the completed expressway has elements of charm and beauty, it will probably prove somewhat crude and deficient from the standpoint both of traffic efficiency and of preventing the blighting of adjacent areas. It must not be cramped but must have natural flowing lines. It must be spacious, with room for shrub and tree and for the dispersion of the traffic sound waves. It should have a pleasant, park-like appearance that will add some elements of interest and distinction to the neighborhood through which it passes.[51]

This remained the ideal, but even Whitten himself allowed these principles to be compromised in his plan for Boston's Central Artery. In other cities, too, highway plans displayed a restraint in size and design that rendered them more compatible with the existing city than urban freeways of the post–World War II period. Planners moved haltingly toward an urban freeway aesthetic during the 1930s, but they focused on the most obvious visual and acoustic problems, largely neglecting more elusive social and economic impacts on adjacent populations.

Planners and engineers of the 1930s were confident that urban freeways could open up a new world of efficient personal transportation while simultaneously improving the environmental quality of the city. They had no vivid awareness that there might be painful trade-offs between accessibility and other dimensions of urban life.

As one planning board member expounded:

Now that science has shown the possibilities through modern street designing, a new era has dawned. Through the facilities of two-level streets, of properly designed traffic arteries, of underpasses, arcades, and of the other contributions to scientific street design, there now is the assurance that access can be provided to any part of the city where it is worthwhile. Leading business men already have grasped this idea; within five to ten years from now it will be common property.[52]

The planning and engineering professions concentrated on improving traffic flow to the central business district and on the careful planning of new suburban communities. Although stemming blight also emerged as a challenge, most planners believed that large areas of the core frame would have to be cleared if land values in the center were to be ensured. New highways converging on the CBD seemed essential.

Within the urban political economy of the 1930s, planners and engineers had few incentives to search for what Jane Jacobs would later call the "ordered complexity" of the central city or to devise an urban form to sustain that complexity. The urban ethnographies of the Chicago School of sociology provided some insights into the social ecology of the central city, but these were tinted with the Chicago sociologists' own unexamined preconceptions about urban life and form.[53] The planning profession made use of the ecological theory of urban land-use succession (e.g., the concentric ring theory), in combination with neoclassical theories of land economics, but showed little inclination to explore inner-city neighborhoods sympathetically from a cultural geographic perspective. Certainly, that would have done little for their legitimation as a "science" of urban change. More commonly, the professional imperative was to transform these areas to fit middle-class norms of order and social propriety.

In addition to their tenuous hold on a professional market niche, city planners' diffuse goals and methods put their profession at a disadvantage in competition with single-purpose highway bureaucracies and skillful public entrepreneurs for control over the city-shaping initiatives of the public sector. As the planning profession delved into whole new domains during the New Deal—regional resource planning, social policy, economic development, municipal finance and administration—transportation planning competed with a growing list of other concerns for the planner's time and attention. Planners had no research apparatus to document the complex relationships between highways and urban form. They could not become respected experts on highways with the same authority as the engineers of the Bureau of Public Roads, state highway departments, public authorities, and leading consulting firms.[54]

Conclusion

The years of the New Deal continued the pump priming for the coming of the urban freeway. Despite the lack of funds on the part of governments, including the cities themselves, for construction of the newly conceptualized transportation systems, there were some exemplars of what the innovation could be. On-the-ground examples were the parkways of Westchester County and Long Island that were, or seemed to be, compatible with green space, pedestrian and recreational activities, and residential and commercial life. The parkway was appreciated as an entity of charm and beauty. A few inner-city highways were built—those of Robert Moses in New York—and plans proliferated for major urban roads in Boston, Chicago, Los Angeles, and New York.

We saw in this chapter the continuing influences of the rural road experience and of major concerns for better traffic movement and for removal of urban blight. Engineers continued to play strong roles amid a much lesser influence of planners and even some laments of landscape planners about the momentum of this great city intruder. Notions of the urban freeway were influenced by towering figures with major plans—plans not concerned with preserving old neighborhoods and their values. The visions were those of Le Corbusier, Wright, and Moses, not those of Jane Jacobs. Throughout the decade, the automobile remained a beneficial liberator in the minds of many Americans.

3

Urban Freeways and National Policy, 1939–1945

Urban Freeway Policy Transformed

Between 1939 and 1945, the nation moved from Depression to war. As production shifted to war goods, non-defense highway construction was curtailed, but the lull was used to forge the freeway plans that would shape the postwar urban world. Diverse strands of urban freeway thought were woven together into coherent doctrine in two key federal documents: *Toll Roads and Free Roads* (1939) and *Interregional Highways* (1944).[1] Here, the radial-concentric pattern—penetrating the urban core—was endorsed by prestigious highway engineers and city planners. Inner beltways were envisioned around renewed central business districts. New urban freeways would be used to clear out slums and blighted areas.

As David Jones, Jr., and Brian Taylor have persuasively argued, this was the period when more modest plans for urban parkways and expressways were replaced with plans for ambitious high-speed urban freeways; planning for transit was pushed aside; and the potential for a closer connection between highway planning and land-use planning receded.[2] As Jones has noted:

Tasking highway departments to play a principal role in the metropolitan arena—the principal role, as it turned out—was a conclusive event. . . . Freeways displaced parkways as the focal technology of urban road programs; transit development was displaced from the metropolitan agenda; and planning for transportation was severed from planning for adjacent land use. This was the significance of the battery of highway legislation adopted in 1941, 1943, 1945, and 1947.[3]

During the 1930s, urban freeways had risen on the national agenda, especially in New York City, where Robert Moses pushed through an unprecedented sequence of large-scale public works. Los Angeles was not far behind, building the first segment of its ambitious parkway plan, the Arroyo Seco Parkway. Engineers and planners debated the pros and cons of transcontinental highways and their urban extensions, but New Deal funds flowed mainly toward ad hoc projects chosen to provide employment. Between 1936 and 1938, the Bureau of Public Roads deflected several proposals in Congress to build a national system of toll highways, but the need for some kind of interregional system, including major urban components, seemed evident to most engineers and planners.[4] The German autobahns—which avoided cities—had captured the fancy of many American highway engineers, and Robert Moses had shown that limited-access highways could be threaded into congested urban cores. Throughout the Depression, Americans retained their technological optimism, their faith that the nation could recover from hard times and get back on the road to material progress. The public admired great works of engineering, and the provision of new freeways for the private automobile promised to combine individual choice and state power in a beneficent combination.[5]

Many streams of freeway planning, research, and visionary design crystallized in the United States around 1939. In the realm of public policy, the Bureau of Public Roads issued *Toll Roads and Free Roads* in April of that year, a document that marked a decisive turn toward planning for urban freeways. In the realm of visionary design, the New York World's Fair of 1939 showcased Norman Bel Geddes Futurama exhibit, located fittingly in the General Motors pavilion. Futurama showed millions of Americans a compelling image of a sleek, orderly, conflict-free city designed to carry large volumes of automobiles safely and smoothly. *Toll Roads and Free Roads* and Futurama helped to steer both expert and public opinion toward the freeway "solution" to the country's urban transportation problems. Then, in 1944, the publication of *Interregional Highways* and the passage of the Federal-Aid Highway Act of 1944 solidified the intellectual and legal foundations for the urban interstates of the postwar era.

Norman Bel Geddes: Futurama and *Magic Motorways*

As the Depression wore on, Americans continued to seek escape routes from a dreary, oppressive present. The New York World's Fair of 1939 satisfied that need with dozens of vivid images of a better future made possible by machine-age technology.[6] The hit of the fair was Norman Bel Geddes' Futurama exhibit, which portrayed an imaginary "City of 1960" in which all the nagging problems of the troubled industrial cities of the 1930s had been solved (figure 3.1). In Bel Geddes' own words:

Futurama is a large-scale model representing almost every type of terrain in America and illustrating how a motorway system may be laid down over the entire country—across mountains, over rivers and lakes, through cities and past towns—never deviating from a direct course and always adhering to the four basic principles of highway design: safety, comfort, speed and economy.[7]

Bel Geddes fleshed out his concepts in his *Magic Motorways* book of 1940, which provided "a dramatic and graphic solution" to the problem of "the complex tangle of American roadways."[8] *Magic Motorways* devoted little space to the problem of integrating new freeways into *existing*

Figure 3.1
View of the "City of the Future" diorama in the Futurama exhibit at the New York World's Fair of 1939. *Source:* Norman Bel Geddes, *Magic Motorways* (New York, Random House, 1940).

cities. Bel Geddes envisioned a clean slate where the designer could deploy his concepts at will. He saw old cities as traffic disasters, and his book contained an extensive catalog of contemporary safety hazards and obstructions to smooth traffic flow (figure 3.2). The old city, whether defined by an "organic" street pattern or a rigid grid, was in hopeless conflict with efficient motor travel. In Bel Geddes' pithy phrase, "There is not much chance left for tinkering."[9]

Bel Geddes did not believe that *interregional* highways should penetrate to the centers of cities.[10] He argued that direct penetration would only cause "congestion and confusion." He also rejected building circumferential beltways as part of an interregional system because they would force drivers to navigate in arcs *around* cities, thereby losing "a quality that is essential to a highway, namely that of being the shortest distance between two points."[11] Bel Geddes' solution was to locate the transcontinental freeways off to one side of major cities, with connections to the urban center and environs via feeder highways.

Figure 3.2
Example of traffic congestion in American cities. *Source:* Norman Bel Geddes, *Magic Motorways* (New York, Random House, 1940).

A great motorway has no business cutting a wide swath right through a town or city and destroying the values there; its place is in the country, where there is ample room for it and where its landscaping is designed to harmonize with the land around it.[12]

But this statement is misleading, because Bel Geddes' "feeder roads" and inner-city "express boulevards" are actually large freeways in themselves (figure 3.3). True, they are not the main trunk highways of the interregional system, but they are still huge thoroughfares, as a glance at the Futurama model reveals.

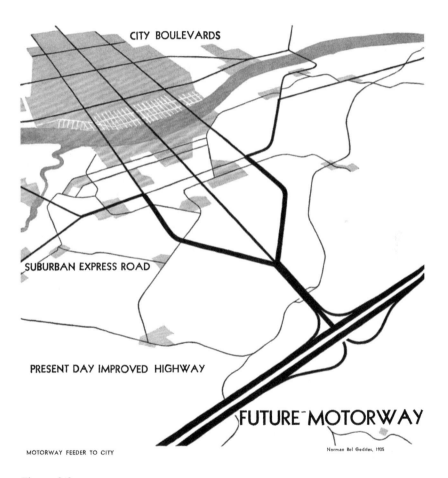

Figure 3.3
Interregional motorway bypassing the central city, with urban feeder highways branching off and connecting with "express boulevards." *Source:* Norman Bel Geddes, *Magic Motorways* (New York, Random House, 1940).

In Bel Geddes' scheme, the high-speed urban feeders "sweep off from the [interregional] motorway in great wide curves that permit traffic to head for the city at an unreduced 50-mile-an-hour-speed." They then "fan out and form a tributary system that connects with the express boulevards within the city."[13] Notably, Bel Geddes proposed that at this interface between suburban feeder roads and urban express boulevards, travelers would be required to transfer to public transit or smaller, city-size cars and buses. The careful hierarchical separation of channels would be paralleled by distinctions between vehicle types, with large, high-powered vehicles reserved for long-distance intercity trips (figure 3.4).[14]

Figure 3.4
"Express boulevards" and skyscrapers in the center of the "City of Tomorrow."
Source: Norman Bel Geddes, *Magic Motorways* (New York, Random House, 1940).

In his chapter "Accelerating City Traffic One Hundred Per Cent," Bel Geddes explained the proper design of traffic facilities in the city center. The solution derived directly from the many multilevel traffic separation plans proposed since the 1920s.[15] Complete separation of high-speed through traffic and slow local traffic is achieved. There is a local street grid and an expressway grid. "The streets themselves are all one way and of only two widths—100 feet and 80 feet." In addition, "Their regulation speed is 30 miles an hour." Upon this "city grid" is superimposed an expressway grid at ten-block intervals, with complete grade separation from the city grid in a "basket-weave pattern," allowing for speeds of 50 mph.[16] Pedestrians in the city center find a safe haven in a separate level above the automobile zone, with easy access to floors in each building explicitly designed for pedestrian access. All parking occurs within the buildings; the streets are completely clear of parked vehicles (figure 3.5).

The building and open space patterns of Futurama strongly resemble Le Corbusier's urban plans of the 1920s and early 1930s. Futurama is configured by a large grid composed of 500-by-200 foot superblocks. Most of the superblocks are covered with low five-story structures, but approximately every tenth block is punctuated with a huge skyscraper, "a steel and glass shaft reaching high into the air, set back with gardened

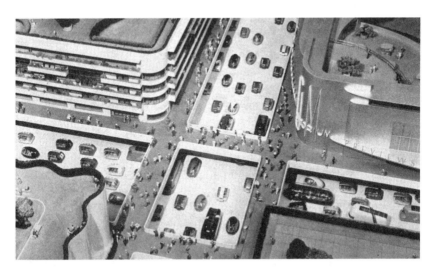

Figure 3.5
In the city center, sidewalks are elevated to the second-story level. *Source:* Norman Bel Geddes, *Magic Motorways* (New York, Random House, 1940).

terraces and separated from the next great tower by at least two blocks of large green park."[17]

In a somewhat anomalous aside, Bel Geddes wondered whether "Perhaps there is no need for private cars to come within certain congested areas of a city" and suggested that modern, efficient subway systems could drastically reduce the need for people to drive themselves.[18] But Bel Geddes did not pursue this intriguing thought. *Magic Motorways* was a book about modern roads, with no room for lengthy digressions on alternative modes of urban transportation. Bel Geddes' faith in the automobile as the savior of the American city was unwavering.

Almost ten million people experienced Futurama, legitimizing urban freeways for a substantial public. Highway engineer Frank T. Sheets wrote that

There may arise certain practical questions when this exhibit is viewed. But I venture this opinion, that of every 100 people who are fed through the ramps into that awesome chamber of highway prophecy, 100 emerge from the exit with a very positive conviction that some heroic measures are needed, both in engineering, planning, and financing, if tomorrow's needs are to be met.[19]

But the direct effect of Futurama on actual freeway planning remains unknown, despite its evidently strong effect on the public imagination. Bona fide power brokers like Robert Moses considered the exhibit a mere "work of the imagination." Moses told Bel Geddes that "you are simply taking a look into the future; that you don't want your recommendations to be taken too seriously by practical work-a-day people who must live in their own time."[20]

Bel Geddes' Futurama exhibit portrayed a city without slums, a city delivered from all the social ills of industrial capitalism through the application of expert design. As a social vision, Futurama reinforced the illusion that Americans all belonged to one big middle class, with technology carrying the entire population forward into a new world of affluence and freedom. Like the talented stage designer that he was, Bel Geddes rearranged the scene before him without confronting issues of power, economic inequality, or social conflict.

Bel Geddes called for thorough planning, and his urban scenarios could never have been implemented without the visible hand of a centralized state, but he said little about the political obstacles to his daring plans. He was at home in the manageable world of stage and industrial design, not in the frustrating world of politics. Bel Geddes could imagine, draw, and build detailed models of "universal solutions" for urban disorder, but his implementation strategies were abstract. He recommended the creation of a "National Motorway Planning Authority" staffed by experts and "independent of factional politics."[21] But in a domain so entangled with the national economy, real estate development, and urban social conflicts, the wish for apolitical solutions was utopian and ideological, screening the struggle for power, wealth, and status played out on the urban scene.

As with so many other architectural utopias of the 1920s and 1930s, the physical elements of Futurama could be detached from their rhetoric of apolitical, technocratic harmony and adapted to the purely commercial purposes of corporate capital.[22] The cities portrayed in Futurama would, indeed, be utopias for Shell Oil and General Motors, the sponsors of Bel Geddes' urbanistic explorations. With everyone on wheels, and the entire national landscape built around the automobile, mass markets for gasoline, oil, and hundreds of other auto-related products would be built into American urban form for the next century.[23]

Although one cannot demonstrate direct connections between Futurama and subsequent state policies, it clearly projected vivid images of an appealing automotive future to a large popular audience. Bel Geddes' urban visions and industrial designs were dramatic, compelling, and immediately understandable by the untrained observer, quite unlike the boring, statistic-packed reports of the highway and planning bureaucracies. Futurama stocked the social consciousness with images of an auto-dominated future, precisely at the time when politicians, highway engineers, and planners were forging the diverse strands of urban freeway planning thought into funded public policy (figure 3.6).

Toll Roads and Free Roads

President Franklin D. Roosevelt had maintained a strong interest in highway planning developments since the 1920s, when he served on the Taconic State Park Commission in New York.[24] He followed the debates over transcontinental highways during the mid-1930s and, in 1937, requested that the Bureau of Public Roads (BPR) produce a report on the feasibility of a national system of three east–west and three north–south toll highways. The Federal-Aid Highway Act of 1938 authorized and funded the study.[25] The resulting research effort, supervised by bureau chief Thomas H. MacDonald, yielded findings and proposals that bore the imprimatur of the nation's most prestigious highway research agency and strongly influenced subsequent national policy. The bureau's report, *Toll Roads and Free Roads*, published in 1939, rejected the toll road idea, suggested an alternative system of free highways extending into and through cities,

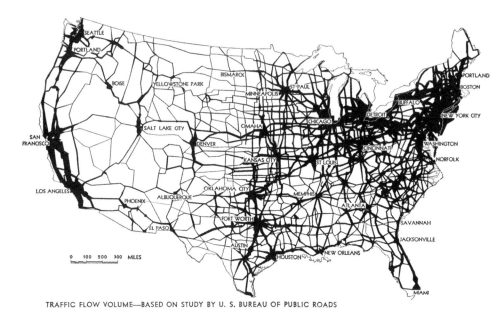

TRAFFIC FLOW VOLUME—BASED ON STUDY BY U. S. BUREAU OF PUBLIC ROADS

Figure 3.6
Graphic from *Magic Motorways* showing traffic flow volumes in the United States, based on Bureau of Public Roads data. *Source:* Norman Bel Geddes, *Magic Motorways* (New York, Random House, 1940).

and offered specific suggestions for inserting such highways into built-up urban areas.

Toll roads were rejected because the study indicated that only a small portion of the mileage would pay its own way.[26] The report then outlined an alternative "free" system of 26,700 miles. With war imminent in Europe, the bureau also emphasized the military importance of highway improvements in order to augment industrial capacity and carry military traffic if necessary. At this time, the bureau wanted to argue vigorously for the urban segments of an interregional system, because the nation's worst traffic problems were now in urban, not rural, areas. However, FDR viewed the proposed highways mainly as connectors between cities, so the bureau's urban emphasis was toned down.[27]

The section on "A Master Plan for Freeway Development" focused on the condition of existing cities and sketched a rough theory of urban freeway design. Here we find the first lengthy analysis at the federal level of the urban freeway challenge. As such, it deserves a close reading, not merely for its technical recommendations but for the assumptions about urban society and built form woven into the text.

The BPR engineers who authored *Toll Roads and Free Roads* did not question the strategy of automobile accommodation in central cities. They declared that "the only course that promises a really satisfactory solution is the provision of adequate facilities for conduct of the heavier entering traffic streams through the city at or near its center, and on to appropriate exit points." This meant that *radial freeways* penetrating *into and through* the city center had to be built: only these new arterials would provide traffic service where it was most urgently needed. Also, in conjunction with economic relief efforts, such freeways would generate jobs where most of the unemployed were located, in the central cities.[28]

The report rejected the idea that bypass routes could solve the urban congestion problem. The swelling of traffic volumes on urban highways was caused by "a multiplicity of short movements into and out of the city," not through traffic headed for destinations beyond.[29] Bypass routes would siphon off a relatively small portion of traffic, because "As all traffic maps show, the greater part of the heavy traffic at a city entrance is an in-and-out movement of local generation."[30] This finding marked a clear shift from preoccupation with rural highways to the realization that a system of *urban* freeways would have to be built if growing volumes of automobiles were to be accommodated.

Toll Roads and Free Roads explicitly addressed commuter traffic, "a heavy movement of purely city traffic that mounts to high peaks in the morning and evening rush hours."[31] This traffic moved primarily from "peripheral city areas and suburbs" to the city center and did not have business in the "intermediate city sections," that is, the older neighborhoods encircling the central business district, the streets of which formed a persistent obstacle to smooth through movement to the CBD.

Confronting the Existing City

The authors of *Toll Roads and Free Roads* saw that the construction of express highways in urban areas would present serious right-of-way difficulties. Examples of successful urban freeways therefore loomed large as the highway planners searched for models showing how obstacles could be overcome. Judged "outstanding . . . both for their completeness and the vigor of their execution" were two Robert Moses creations, the West Side Highway and Henry Hudson Parkway, along with the Westchester County parkway system and the Merritt Parkway in Connecticut. Also mentioned were a freeway segment in St. Louis and Roosevelt Boulevard in Philadelphia.

The BPR engineers focused on two types of obstacles to urban freeway building: the need to acquire and clear expensive urban land, and the engineering difficulties of constructing elevated or depressed highways through congested areas criss-crossed with existing utilities and infrastructure. The paramount concern was the "damage to, or obliteration of, private property" due to its impact on total freeway costs. Engineering and economic criteria dominated the analysis. This was not a comprehensive view, addressing the impacts on existing social networks, architectural resources, and cheap rental housing stock for the urban poor. For the authors of *Toll Roads and Free Roads*, the central question was as follows: How can we get these inevitable facilities built at reasonable cost?

The urban freeway proposals in *Toll Roads and Free Roads* were embedded in a theory of urban spatial change derived from the Chicago School of urban sociology and mainstream urban land economics.[32] The Chicago sociologists maintained that competing social groups struggle over the use of urban land, producing a "natural" process of invasion and succession that translates spatially into concentric rings around the city center, each with a distinct social and economic character.[33] More affluent groups gradually move outward from the core into more spacious and salubrious residential areas. Low-income groups inherit the aging structures vacated by the outward migration. As in a biological ecosystem, each social group struggles with the physical environment and other social groups to carve out a niche supporting its distinctive "form of life."

This sociological approach was reinforced by the theories of land economics, which argued that urban spatial structure is determined by competitive bidding for urban land. This competition for advantageous locations yielded a high-rent central business district, a ring of transitional uses, and an outer ring of desirable suburbs.[34] The report's planning prescriptions mirror the weaknesses of these theories. Spatial outcomes produced by urban actors are construed as "natural" processes; new technologies "cause" changes in urban form; and urban environments "determine" the behavior of their residents. We shall examine each of these in turn.

Toll Roads and Free Roads, like many other documents addressing the issue of urban blight during the 1930s, explained blight as the product of a natural process of urban expansion. According to this model, as the CBD grows outward, nearby residential neighborhoods are gradually infiltrated by commercial uses. Landlords convert single-family homes to apartments for lower-income groups. Speculators holding properties on the edge of the CBD defer maintenance and milk tenants while waiting to sell out at CBD land prices. Clearance of these areas for new freeways could be construed as a beneficial, indeed natural, step in the evolution of the city toward a more efficient form.[35]

Toll Roads and Free Roads manifested technological determinism in its attribution of city-shaping powers to the automobile. But automobiles are inert objects. Only people using automobiles in particular ways shape cities. During the 1930s and 1940s, specific social actors were attempting to restructure the American city to increase automobile use and limit alternative forms of transportation.[36] The auto certainly made it possible for the middle classes to flee from the central city to the suburbs, but the extent of this transformation was influenced by other social forces.[37] Treating the automobile as an inexorable cause of a new urban structure obscured the transportation and urban form alternatives that still remained open in 1939. *Toll Roads and Free Roads* advanced a plan for an automotive "City Inevitable."[38]

Toll Roads and Free Roads also used a version of environmental determinism common in planning and architectural thought of the 1930s. Planners equated the removal of blighted buildings with the removal of social problems attributed to the buildings' users.[39] New urban freeways could thus be construed as both enhancers of mobility and cures for inner-city social disorder and physical decay. But the theory fails to distinguish between physical structures and their current use (e.g., single-family homes divided into small apartments) and to distinguish physical structures from the social groups occupying them at a particular historical moment (e.g., apartment buildings or hotels, originally of decent quality, neglected by slum landlords and rented out to struggling low-income groups). There were, to be sure, sizable inner-city areas that were beyond repair, where clearance and rehousing of residents was the only option. But in many cases the buildings and streets of the old city had been livable urban environments during the streetcar era and were not, in themselves, causes of social pathology. Environmental theories of the 1930s discredited these dense, mixed-use, pedestrian-scale environments, making clearance for freeways seem an unambiguous social benefit.

For modernizing planners and engineers of the 1930s, the old industrial city formed an intractable obstacle to new, more salubrious patterns of urban life. Urban freeways could help to reverse the course of urban decay and create new urban forms for the motor age.

It is apparent that the whole interior of the city is ripe for the major change that it must undergo to afford the necessary relief to pressures generated by the effort to force the stream of twentieth-century traffic through arteries of the early nineteenth century.[40]

Although written in dry, bureaucratic language, *Toll Roads and Free Roads* embraced images of modernity as eagerly as the more impassioned prose of Norman Bel Geddes and the architectural utopians of the 1920s. Traffic improvements were given an almost magical power to improve the urban environment.

A Pattern for New Urban Freeways

Toll Roads and Free Roads bestowed the sanction of the Bureau of Public Roads on a particular pattern of urban freeways: the hub-and-wheel pattern.[41] For efficient traffic service, radial freeways should penetrate to the city center from all feasible directions. Landlocked cities would have radials along all four compass points, whereas a city situated along a body of water might receive arterials from only two or three directions. Connection between the radials would be provided by "a circumferential or belt-line route forming an approximate circle around the city at its outer fringe."[42] Larger cities might also require an inner beltway.

In some cases it may be feasible to construct the distributing belt line within the city—generally somewhere within the ring of decadent property surrounding the central business area. Such a belt line, connecting at appropriate points with radial arteries extending out of the city, may avoid the cutting of a new route directly through the business sections, and may either serve as a substitute or supplement for the outer belt line.[43]

Thus, some cities might require two beltways, one through the "core frame" surrounding the central business district and one on the periphery. Those cities requiring only one beltway faced a choice of locating it either through the core frame or somewhere near the periphery of built-up land. The Baltimore example used in the report displays one version of this pattern, with six radials penetrating to the urban core. Here, however, the belt line is approximately 5 miles from the center and thus is not an example of a true inner-city belt line cutting through the core frame of the CBD. In the absence of an inner belt, the Baltimore radials terminate confusingly in small traffic loops, an obsolete solution even by the standards of the accompanying *Toll Roads and Free Roads* text (figure 3.7).[44]

The authors of *Toll Roads and Free Roads* saw little worth saving in the ring of aging property surrounding the central business district. The old urban areas dating from before 1900 contained "countless impediments that embarrass the movement of twentieth-century traffic."

An old city, growing by the coalescence of numerous ancestor villages, the irregular and discontinuous street plan of [the old city] is the despair of the stranger and the daily inconvenience of its own citizens.[45]

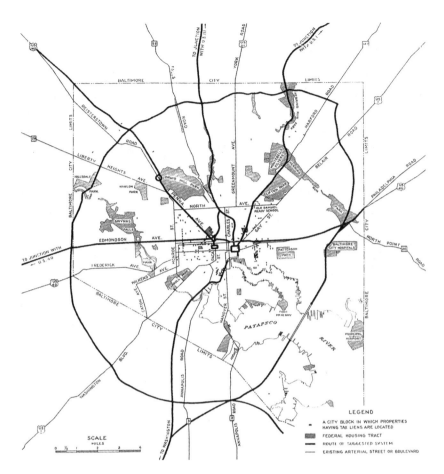

Figure 3.7
Tentative plan for Baltimore express highways. *Source:* Bureau of Public Roads,
Toll Roads and Free Roads, 1939.

Old streets were viewed only as obstacles to the movement of motorized traffic (figure 3.8).

The *Interregional Highways* Report of 1944

The *Interregional Highways* report, written between 1941 and 1944, reinforced the analyses in *Toll Roads and Free Roads* and codified many
of the basic planning doctrines for America's postwar urban freeways.
By 1941, American involvement in the war seemed closer than ever, and
defense needs rose to the top of the national agenda. In April, President

Figure 3.8
Photograph of a "decadent area" on the fringe of a central business district. Areas like this were targeted for removal through freeway construction. *Source:* Bureau of Public Roads, *Toll Roads and Free Roads*, 1939.

Roosevelt appointed a committee of experts, the National Interregional Highway Committee (NIHC), to study the need for a national system of interregional highways, the form such a system should take, and the potential of such a large construction project to utilize industrial capacity and manpower at the end of hostilities. The president believed that a substantial agenda of domestic public works projects might provide the economic stimulus to avert a depression. The NIHC's report, *Interregional Highways*, was finally published in January 1944.[46]

The committee was chaired by Thomas H. MacDonald, Commissioner of Public Roads of the Bureau of Public Roads, then part of the Federal Works Agency. Other members from the highway engineering profession included G. Donald Kennedy, highway commissioner for the state of Michigan, and Charles H. Purcell, state highway engineer for California. The committee boasted several representatives from the realm of urban and regional planning. Frederic A. Delano, chairman of the National Resources Planning Board, had been involved in numerous planning activities since the turn of the century. Harland Bartholomew was the preeminent planning consultant of the day, operating from his consulting firm headquartered in St. Louis. Rexford Guy Tugwell had been an economics

professor at Columbia, a member of Roosevelt's "Brain Trust," chairman
of the Resettlement Administration, and in 1941 was chairman of the
newly founded New York City Planning Commission. The final member
of the committee was Bibb Graves, former governor of Alabama, who
died shortly after the committee was formed.[47]

The committee investigated five possible freeway systems and determined that one of 33,920 miles—third largest of the five—would best
serve traffic needs.[48] The report estimated that more than 4,400 miles of
this system would lie within city boundaries.[49] As a "supplement" to this
basic system, the authors recommended up to 5,000 additional miles of
circumferential and distributing routes required to serve traffic adequately in the larger cities.[50]

The committee discussed the relationship between the proposed freeways and urban form in the chapter "Locating the Interregional Routes
in Urban Areas." As in *Toll Roads and Free Roads,* the concentric ring
theory of urban spatial structure was set forth.[51] The committee noted
the migration of offices, industries, and retail establishments to suburban
areas but did not predict the exact spatial pattern that new automotive
suburbs would take.

The committee perceived a relationship between rapid decentralization
and the decline of the old neighborhoods surrounding the central city.
Decentralization, although a beneficial trend overall, was seen as harmful
when "excessive" and ungoverned by a rational plan for orderly growth.
City planners were "really just now coming to grips with . . . decentralization or dissipation of the urban area to an extent not economically
justified."[52] Clearly, the new interregional highways would exert a strong
influence on future land use.

Unwise location of the interregional routes might not be sufficiently powerful
to prevent a logical future city development, but would be powerful enough to
retard or unreasonably distort such development.[53]

In a promising recommendation, the committee emphasized that urban
route selection should be the cooperative result of local and state officials
and even endorsed the creation of *metropolitan authorities* to design a
rational pattern of arterials in complex urban areas composed of many
municipalities.[54]

Interregional Highways devoted an entire section to "Principles of
Route Selection in Cities." The critical question was whether the new interregional highways should penetrate to the city center. The committee
decided that the new freeways "should penetrate within close proximity

to the central business area," as so many important traffic destinations were downtown, including rail and water terminals.[55] But, "how near they should come to the center of the area, how they should pass it or pass through it, and by what courses they should approach it, are matters for particular planning consideration in each city." The committee then offered an array of suggestions for corridor location. These suggestions provide a kind of guidebook for subsequent freeway planning, and most of today's freeways occupy corridors determined by these principles codified in 1944 (figure 3.9 and figure 3.10).

Because the existing urban pattern often had a star shape, with the points composed of mass transit or highway corridors, there were "wedges of undeveloped land" between these built-up areas. These areas had remained undeveloped because of poor transportation service, difficult topography, or reservation for public use. The committee recommended using these corridors for radial freeways penetrating to the city center. Provision of highways in these wedges would open this land for development, a deliberate strategy designed to achieve a more compact urban

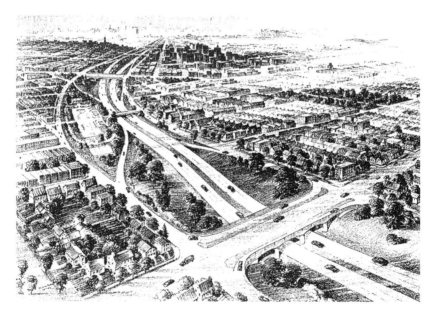

Figure 3.9
Rendering showing an interregional highway passing through a residential area within a city, with a block-wide right-of-way, depressed sections passing under important cross streets, and border areas designated for "neighborhood recreational purposes." *Source:* National Interregional Highway Committee, *Interregional Highways*, 1944.

Figure 3.10

Elevated interregional highway through the city center. *Source:* National Interregional Highway Committee, *Interregional Highways*, 1944.

pattern. Fearing "excessive decentralization," the committee preferred development on this land closer to the central city, rather than scattering new development on the urban periphery.[56]

On the issues of circumferential and distribution routes, *Interregional Highways* offered advice similar to that in *Toll Roads and Free Roads:*

In the larger cities more than one circumferential route may be needed. A series of them may be provided to form inner and outer belts, some possibly within the city itself, others without. In the largest cities one such route may be required as a distributor of traffic about the business center.[57]

The report also recommended the integration of the new urban freeways with major traffic generators such as railway terminals, wharves, airports, wholesale markets, sports arenas, and new industrial areas.

The section on "Minimization of Street Intersections" contained several crucial suggestions for threading freeways through the urban fabric without blocking off existing streets or building numerous grade overpasses and underpasses:

• The new freeways should run *parallel to the normal rectangular street plan*, rather than cutting across the existing street grid along a diagonal or curve, which would generate numerous complicated intersections.

• Location *near or above railroad rights-of-way* presented problems of smoke, noise, and unsightliness, but these could be mitigated by the use of electric or diesel locomotives and the provision of "appropriate screening and landscaping." Railroad rights-of-way offered the great advantage of reducing intersections with cross streets, as they usually already served as linear barriers interrupting the street grid.

• *Riverbanks and the valleys of small streams* often provide linear corridors into the heart of the city. The report notes that these stream valleys have historically given rise to "a very low order of development—neighborhoods of cheap, run-down houses and shacks, abject poverty, squalor, and filth." If cleared and used for freeways, these corridors would offer routes only rarely interrupted by transverse streets, often penetrating directly into the central business district.[58]

• Finally, the committee noted that expensive intersections could be reduced by locating the new freeways *along the boundaries of parks and other large tracts of city or institutional property* that interrupt the regular rectangular street plan.[59]

Schematic diagrams illustrated the recommended urban freeway locations.[60] In "large cities," interregional highways should run directly into the city center, along the edges of the central business district. In the example provided, "three interregional routes intersect at the city and all must pass within convenient reach of the large central business section." One of the freeways runs along a riverbank throughout its entire length, cutting through the old waterfront area along the river's edge near the CBD. A second enters the city through a wedge of undeveloped land, passes by the business district, crosses the river, and exits the city on the other side. A third freeway crosses the city from east to west, "skirting the business district." These three centrally focused radial routes are supplemented by interregional circumferentials positioned further out from the city center (figure 3.11).[61]

The CBD parking problem could be solved by extensive construction of underground or multistory parking garages.[62] These garages should be located near the inner beltway encircling the downtown:

A wholly satisfactory termination of express highways in large cities will probably not be found short of the provision of a limited-access distribution route located circumferentially about the central business section.[63]

This inner belt would, in theory, (1) expedite the transfer of vehicles between the freeways and downtown streets, (2) distribute cars more evenly throughout the central area, and (3) enable cars to drive on freeways

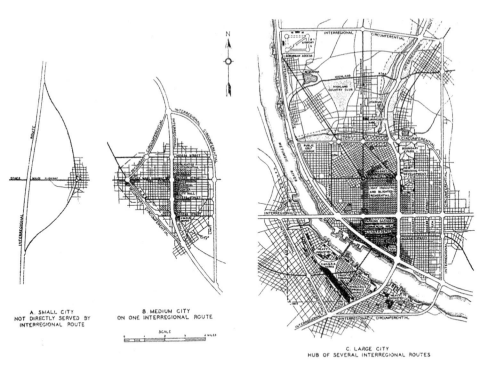

Figure 3.11
Recommended locations of interregional routes through small, medium, and large cities. Note the complete encirclement of the central business district of the large city. *Source:* National Interregional Highway Committee, *Interregional Highways*, 1944.

virtually all the way to their downtown destinations, exiting the freeway at or near conveniently located parking structures.

Like *Toll Roads and Free Roads, Interregional Highways* portrayed extensive freeway networks as the only solution to urban congestion. Waterfronts, parks, and other public lands would have to be used as freeway corridors, because of their low dollar cost and provision of linear paths through the existing street system. In central business districts, the proposed routes would create a kind of moat around the downtown, separating the office and retail uses of the CBD from the blighted areas of the core frame.

Interregional Highways did emphasize that the new highways should be part of "a rational plan of future land use that will assign more or less specific areas to each of the principal classes of use—residential, cultural, business, industrial, etc."[64] The planners on the committee did make sure that the integration of land use and transportation was mentioned. The committee also showed considerable foresight in recommending that urban highway planning be guided by a metropolitan authority. However, the authors did not propose that the urban freeway program be subject to complete reexamination or drastic alteration based on city planning principles. As Bruce Seely has written:

Perhaps the most significant feature of the report, however, was the acceptance of the BPR's narrow engineering approach to highway construction by the two regional planners (Tugwell and Bartholomew) and the politician (Graves). . . . At various points in the committee deliberations, the planners raised the possibility that highways could revitalize urban business districts, control decentralization, and guide urban land use and growth. The report did mention these points, recognizing that highways had a permanent impact on urban development. But traffic service always ranked first among the purposes of highways. . . . Indicative of this narrow viewpoint was the report's failure to examine the relationship of roads to alternative forms of transportation.[65]

Federal Legislation of the Early 1940s

Congress finally acted upon the recommendations of the Bureau of Public Roads by passing the Federal-Aid Highway Act of 1944, which designated a National System of Interstate Highways "not exceeding forty thousand miles in total extent so located as to connect by routes, as direct as practicable, the principal metropolitan areas, cities, and industrial centers, and to serve the national defense."[66] When the Bureau of Public Roads and the state highway departments reached agreement on the interstate locations in 1947, 2,900 miles were in urban areas, with location decisions on 2,300 more urban miles (for circumferential and distributing routes) deferred until better traffic studies could be performed. Thus, of the 40,000-mile interstate system conceived in 1944, approximately 5,200 miles were to be located in urban areas.[67]

The 1944 legislation finally brought state and federal highway engineers officially onto the urban stage, a stage already occupied by city planners, architects, municipal engineers, and local officials. However, despite the strong recommendations in *Interregional Highways* that highway planning and city planning be carefully coordinated, the 1944 legislation did not require that state engineers clear their plans with city planners or local officials. Route designation was to be by "joint agreement" of the state highway departments and the Bureau of Public Roads. The legislation did not require a comprehensive transportation planning process for metropolitan areas.[68] Understandably, some planners feared that unprepared cities would "find themselves in the position of having to accept highway routings selected by agencies which are not familiar with and have no real understanding of local conditions."[69]

Freeway Planning Thought on the Threshold of the Postwar World

By 1945, a substantial body of urban freeway building theory had been codified and disseminated. Both *Toll Roads and Free Roads* and *Interregional Highways* bore the imprimatur of the federal government, and the latter had been signed by two of the most famous planners of the 1930s, Harland Bartholomew and Rexford Tugwell. The works of Robert Moses had been deemed models worthy of imitation by planners and engineers across the nation. The Federal-Aid Highway Act of 1944 placed the federal government and the state highway departments in leading positions to shape urban freeway patterns for the postwar world (figure 3.12).

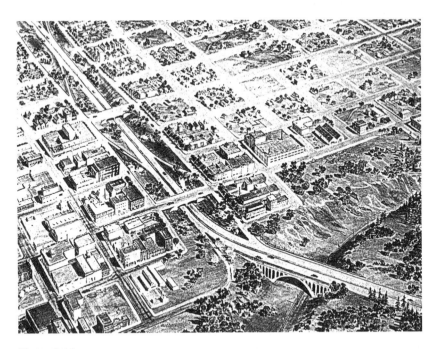

Figure 3.12
Proposed depressed "thruway" for Portland, Oregon. *Source:* Robert Moses et al., *Portland Improvement* (New York: William E. Rudge's Sons, 1943).

Although the parkway model of urban highway design was praised and invoked as an example of successful limited access construction, a shift was already under way toward larger, more utilitarian arterials. This coincided with what David Jones has called "the passing of the baton" in urban freeway planning from local officials to the state highway depart-ments.[70] The highest priority of the states was the efficient movement of high volumes of traffic through the cities, with other city planning con-cerns such as land use and coordination with mass transit pushed into the background.

Replication of the parkway ideal in dense urban areas seemed increas-ingly impractical due to high land costs and the difficulty of disrupting existing activities. Not surprisingly, the elevated freeway seemed more and more tempting, as it could cut through old neighborhoods on a minimal right-of-way, did not require costly excavation like depressed highways, and would still allow cross traffic to pass underneath.[71] Engineers envi-sioned "By-Passing Cities in the Vertical Plane." On maps these freeways would penetrate through the heart of the city, but on the ground they would soar above the congested grid of existing streets (figure 3.13).[72]

Urban freeways raised many troubling questions about future urban patterns, and rifts between highway builders and city planners could be seen. At one extreme, Robert Moses expressed disdain for comprehensive planning when he declared that "We do not believe in revolution. The city is not going to be torn up and rebuilt on a decentralized satellite or other academic theory. Therefore, we do not have to wait for the painting of the new, big, over-all picture constantly referred to by revolutionary planners."[73] Even those highway officials sympathetic to city planning of-ten viewed the new highways as "the framework of the city and regional plan," with the remainder of the city plan derivative from the critical highway element.[74]

Some planners and urban commentators, such as the members of the Regional Planning Association of America, did propose radical rearrange-ments of the urban pattern, but for practicing professionals these ideas seemed quite out of reach. As Paul Oppermann, assistant director of the American Society of Planning Officials, wrote in 1939, "It would be pos-sible of course to reconstruct our towns and cities in such a way that they would be more efficient, more convenient, and better to look at. Instead we are following the 'practical' course and solving the immediate prob-lems as well as we can."[75]

Most urban experts did agree, however, that the old urban fabric of mixed-use corridor streets was obsolete and that the transition zone

Figure 3.13
An elevated "thruway" portrayed as a compatible addition to an urban neighborhood. *Source:* Robert Moses et al., *Portland Improvement* (New York: William E. Rudge's Sons, 1943)

around the CBD was an inviting location for new freeways to serve the CBD.[76] As Magali Larson has observed, the engineers, planners, and Modernist architects of the 1930s and 1940s consciously sought to erase historic urban forms and replace them with new patterns from their drafting boards. The city was seen as a tool or complex machine, and "Inefficient and worn-out tools are replaced."[77] The new arterials seemed an essential part of the emerging modern city of straight lines, rapid movement, and segregated functional zones.[78]

The American public shared the fascination of the engineers and planners with technical solutions to urban problems. During the 1930s and 1940s, visions of a new society propelled by the machine to new heights of prosperity tempted a population just recovering from the worst economic crisis of the century. Urban freeways, it seemed, could provide public infrastructure for the unlimited movement of private vehicles for the masses.

Architects and planners of the 1930s and 1940s viewed large swaths of the old industrial and commercial cities of the eighteenth and nineteenth century as expendable. Those places were old enough to seem "obsolete" without being old enough to seem "historic."

During the 1930s, cities devoted few resources to assisting the central city poor, especially if they belonged to racial minorities, and these groups remained essentially voiceless in the formation of urban policy.[79] The idea of blocking major public works because of their impact on poor neighborhoods had little support. In addition, freeway boosters argued that freeway-induced economic growth would benefit all members of the urban polity.

As America entered the postwar world, highway engineers and city planners were poised to map urban freeway routes with only limited awareness of their long-term impacts. The process would be top-down, controlled by experts. A host of variables remained outside mainstream freeway planning methodology. For the moment, inadequate funding and rural opposition to expensive urban projects kept urban freeway construction on hold. But the freeway planning theories of the 1940s had already set engineers and planners on a collision course with inner-city neighborhoods, defenders of urban parks and waterfronts, historic preservationists, and sundry other opponents of the unrestrained motorization of the American city.

Conclusion

In the period addressed in this chapter, new freeways became the subject of national policy. Two federal documents, *Toll Roads and Free Roads* and *Interregional Highways*, crystalized the visions of the superhighway for America and for its cities.

Side by side with these federal contributions were the visionary notions of stage designer Norman Bel Geddes, who, in his book *Magic Motorways* (1940) and in his Futurama exhibit in the General Motors pavilion of the New York World's Fair of 1939, showcased for millions of Americans "architectural utopias"; these had dominant roles for urban roads in a city sleek, orderly, and designed to move automobiles safely and smoothly.

The first of the federal reports, *Toll Roads and Free Roads*, was funded under the Federal-Aid Highway Act of 1938 and written by Bureau of Public Roads engineers. It laid out a system of thousands of miles of roads for America. The report saw Moses' projects as outstanding contributions to the urban environment and followed the Chicago School of sociology's understanding of urban form and development. Roads were both enhancers of mobility and cures for inner-city social disorder.

At the end of the period addressed in this chapter, the *Interregional Highways* report of 1944 appeared, reinforcing the analysis of *Toll Roads and Free Roads*. Among its topics was whether roads should penetrate city centers; it offered ideas on how to thread freeways through those centers, and it presented ideas for controlling costs of this major infrastructure initiative by locating roads along parks and other public lands. The two reports saw extensive freeway networks as the solution to urban congestion.

In 1944, the Federal-Aid Highway Act designated a national system of interstate highways, and, by 1947, almost 3,000 miles in this system were planned to be located in urban areas. The law further solidified the important role of engineers in the work of urban development and provided for a top-down, expert-dominated approach for decision making for city freeways.

By the mid-1940s, the sylvan parkway concept was seen as unrealistic for the nation's needs. However, until the period addressed in the next chapter, the construction of urban roads remained on hold.

4

Postwar Urban Freeways: Scaling Up for a City on Wheels, 1946–1956

From Concepts to Construction

Between 1946 and 1956, the freeway planning concepts worked out during the late 1930s and the war years were elaborated, expanded, and applied to particular cities. As state highway engineers, aided by the Bureau of Public Roads, assumed control of freeway planning and construction in urban areas, design for traffic service and high-speed safety overshadowed earlier proposals to weave expressways into the fabric of the existing city and combine the new highways with mass transit. Parkway ideals receded as engineers sized new urban freeways for growing volumes of motor vehicles.[1] City planners expressed some misgivings about wholesale commitment to large urban freeway systems and devised some imaginative proposals for mixtures of freeways and transit, but most accepted the new freeways as beneficial improvements. Architects wove freeways into their schemes for rebuilt central cities, often using multilevel strategies to mitigate impacts and preserve pedestrian space, but they stood outside the freeway planning system and had little effect.

Although the freeway plans prepared by city planners during the late 1940s were intrusive enough, these plans did preserve some elements of the parkway tradition of the 1930s, such as limited widths, heavy landscaping, transit medians, and design speeds below 50 mph. There was some attempt to coordinate arterials with land-use patterns, redevelopment activities, and transit planning. However, this more moderate thread of freeway planning doctrine eventually faded under the pressure of mounting traffic volumes and the institutional might of the highway community.

Preparing a New Generation of Freeway Plans for American Cities, 1946–1950

Between 1945 and 1947, the Bureau of Public Roads and the state highway departments worked out tentative routes for the interstate system. In 1947, they agreed upon 37,700 miles of the 40,000-mile system specified in the legislation, and an official map was published.[2] Approximately 2,900 miles ran through urban areas. Routes for the remaining 2,300 miles of the system were not specified at this time; these miles would be devoted to urban circumferential and distributing routes, to be designated at a later date after more detailed urban transportation studies.[3]

The urban freeway corridors roughed out during the mid-1940s were not based on sophisticated city planning studies. Alan Altshuler has described the highway planning process as it occurred in Minneapolis–St. Paul in his classic text, *The City Planning Process.*[4]

The Highway Department's engineers had relied on their knowledge of existing desire lines. To estimate future traffic, they had simply projected vehicle registration trends. . . . To the extent that these data were insufficient, they had relied on their engineering experience and common sense.[5]

But these early corridor decisions displayed remarkable durability, in spite of their weak analytical base. Their authors acquired a vested interest in their correctness and deflected demands for reappraisal and change. Placed on planning and engineering maps, they began to influence subsequent decisions about urban development.

The engineers' hurriedly prepared freeway plans of 1945–1947 proved somewhat premature because money for construction was not forthcoming. Powerful political and bureaucratic obstacles prevented the shift from rural to urban freeway building that the 1944 legislation had seemed to promise. Although "cities" were supposed to receive 25 percent of the funds, "most rural-dominated state highway departments funneled the funds to fringe locations and small towns."[6]

This delay gave the state highway departments time to conduct more thorough analyses of traffic patterns. Minneapolis–St. Paul conducted a full-scale origin–destination study in 1949. But as Altshuler relates, the engineers "were unworried about the possibility that they might have located the freeway routes erroneously in 1945-46. They expected, indeed, that the 1949 survey would provide irrefutable proof that their route choices had been the best possible."[7] Highway engineers wanted accurate land-use forecasts to predict future vehicle trips, but not even major cities like Minneapolis and St. Paul had such information. The engineers made do with rough estimates provided by the region's municipalities.[8] Although opposed by St. Paul's chief planning engineer, the state highway department's proposed route locations were approved by the city in 1947. Similar events occurred in other large American cities.[9]

The role of freeways in shaping future urban development went largely unexamined, obscured by a narrow focus on traffic service. Highway planners forged ahead and made decisions, acting on limited information. By initiating a new pattern of accessibility, they froze into place key components of the urban pattern. Later land-use and traffic studies were often used only to adjust the number of lanes or interchange spacing, rather than to reevaluate locations.

Doctrines of the Highway Engineers

Highway engineers did not consider their planning activities to be "urban design"—it would not have occurred to them to frame the task that way—but their decisions still created the transportation skeleton for postwar urban form. The manuals codifying standards for highway location and design institutionalized an array of form concepts, which strongly influenced subsequent urban patterns.[10]

The American Association of State Highway Officials (AASHO) submitted interstate design standards to the Bureau of Public Roads in 1945. These standards specified what an interstate highway had to be: minimum widths, geometric design, freeway types, spacing of interchanges, and so on. Thus, interstate freeways could be modified only in limited ways as engineers mapped them onto existing urban landscapes.[11]

During the late 1940s, the Bureau of Public Roads argued that urban freeways were the only solution to the congestion problem and that they could be effectively linked with plans for slum clearance and redevelopment.[12] However, the state highway departments had little interest in linking the two programs. The whole idea of close integration at the federal level faded when the Housing Act of 1949 set up a separate bureaucracy for urban redevelopment.[13]

BPR chief Thomas H. MacDonald made "The Case for Urban Expressways" in a 1947 article by that title.[14] He argued that "long-range planning of adequate highway facilities will save many cities from stagnation and decay." Opposition to urban expressways was inevitable, but cities that refused to face the facts and accommodate automobile growth would lose business and suffer depreciation of property values in the central business district.

MacDonald attempted to refute three common arguments against urban expressways. First, critics argued that new freeways would destroy housing during an acute housing shortage. MacDonald rejoined that, indeed, many dwellings would have to be removed, but central city freeways would usually "pass through 'blighted' sections where property values are low, and most of the buildings are of the type that should be torn down in any case, to rid the city of its slums."[15] Even in the slums, though, MacDonald asserted that "*no matter how urgently a highway improvement be needed, the homes of people who have nowhere to go should not be destroyed. Before dwellings are razed, new housing facilities should be provided for the dispossessed occupants.*" However, the article did not indicate how this could be accomplished.

Second, MacDonald denied that the new urban freeways would be "big ditches" acting as barriers between neighborhoods. Overpasses at selected street intersections would preserve links between neighborhoods and even increase accessibility for drivers by improving traffic flow on local streets. Finally, MacDonald denied that it would be cheaper to widen existing streets in central areas than to build new freeways. Because many of the more feasible street widenings had already been performed by 1947, any future strategies of this sort would reap limited gains in traffic flow at great cost in destroyed property. If unlimited traffic accommodation were the goal, a freeway system was the only logical choice.

MacDonald argued that urban freeways would save the central cities by smoothing the path of central business district (CBD)-bound cars to the center, while non-CBD traffic could bypass the congested core without using surface streets at all. Urban freeways would free the city center of traffic congestion and restore its competitive advantage: "the question for our large cities is not can they afford express highways, but how can they possibly afford to be without them."[16] In addition, as a redevelopment tool, freeways would

help to check the accelerated growth of blighted areas, which are the product of traffic congestion, lack of planned land use, and the failure to create attractive opportunities for the investment of private capital.[17]

Joseph Barnett, chief of the Urban Road Division of the Bureau of Public Roads, articulated similar ideas in "Express Highway Planning in Metropolitan Areas" (1946–1947).[18] He maintained that only the "generous provision for free-flowing facilities" could solve the urban congestion problem and that origin–destination data were the single most important type of information in determining preliminary expressway locations.

Following *Toll Roads and Free Roads* and *Interregional Highways,* Barnett recommended that central city routes be placed in the deteriorated fringe areas around the central business district. These areas had deteriorated "because no agency existed to control city development." They were unstable zones, areas in transition, older residential districts in which the property owners were waiting for conversion to commercial uses.

Barnett also rejected the option, advanced by some planners, of building freeways only outside the central city. He endorsed depressed freeways as the most desirable design alternative in urban areas. Admitting that an elevated structure "blocks off light, creates a potential nuisance below, and seriously damages property on both sides," Barnett thought that these effects could be mitigated by the provision of frontage roads and the use of areas under the freeway structures for business purposes.[19] On the other hand, elevated structures allowed almost all surface streets to pass under the freeway.

Barnett listed fifteen principles for the design of freeways. It is instructive to analyze the hierarchy of these 1947 guidelines.[20] The first five all dealt with traffic-carrying efficiency. The sixth mentioned that "the facility should be integrated with the city plan." The ninth directed that "important structures such as major bridges and buildings should be left intact." Finally, the fifteenth and last principle was that "the facility should be pleasing in appearance."

Barnett clearly stated that "the highway engineer must appreciate that, in the location and design of urban arterial facilities, he is participating in city planning" and that the engineers must "cooperate intimately with all other agencies interested in the planning, development, operation, control, and general welfare of the city." But he assumed that sensible city planning analysis would support both freeways and slum clearance. Like many engineers, Barnett divided the city planning profession into two groups: pragmatic, down-to-earth realists and impractical dreamers.

We have heard a great deal about ivory tower planning and long haired planning. It is unfortunate that a few wild-eyed broad plans which might ignore the realities can bring discredit on broad planning generally. . . . The plans which appear to give the best results are not those which start as broad over-all plans but those which are built up piece by piece from the compelling and overwhelming desires of individuals in great numbers.[21]

Barnett rejected the hopes of "visionary enthusiasts" that freeways could rehabilitate cities by themselves but argued that freeways could perform the "triple function" of acting as (1) dividers or boundaries between residential neighborhoods or between areas of different land use, (2) as conduits to the central business district, and (3) as routes for through highway traffic.[22] Mass transportation and pedestrian circulation were mentioned as topics that should be covered in the preliminary engineering report, but these topics were not pursued.

The comments on Barnett's paper, which were published in subsequent *American Society of Civil Engineers Proceedings*, gave evidence of some disagreement among engineers about proper freeway design. Harry Lochner, a consulting engineer, argued that the new freeways should be designed from the beginning to carry mass transportation vehicles, recreational facilities should be provided on residual pieces of land taken for freeway construction, and freeway planners should be aware that they will be *causing* development and not just *serving* it.[23]

Merrill D. Knight, Jr., an engineer with the Bureau of Public Roads, reiterated the importance of integrating freeways with a sound land-use plan and noted that origin–destination data only reflect existing conditions and must be correlated with accurate projections of future land use. Knight also proposed "setting values on classified land uses as potential traffic generators." As Knight phrased it, "The determination of the pattern for future urban growth constitutes the most complex phase of selecting locations for proposed expressways."[24]

A number of engineers challenged Barnett's unfavorable evaluation of elevated freeways. Others agreed that they should only be used as a last resort, and preferably only in industrial areas. The tendency of freeways to *generate* traffic as well as service existing traffic was noted by R. H. Baldock.[25] One commentator did notice that "in all this express highway planning, including New York and New Jersey state highways, nowhere has the writer seen any provision for the pedestrian—he is the forgotten man."[26]

The strongest dissent came from George H. Herrold, the planning engineer for St. Paul, Minnesota.[27] Herrold argued that a freeway does not "solve" the downtown congestion problem: "it increases speed and removes some frictions; and it moves people faster to the areas of congestion," but in downtown areas large numbers of cars still converge on a land area that could not accommodate those quantities of bulky vehicles. Herrold also challenged Barnett's contention that city planning studies have often resulted in "a jam that prevented progress."

Possibly someone was stubborn or had a limited technique. However, cities are full of things called "progress" that were put there before all the facts were known. There are many activities in a city other than moving around in an automobile.[28]

Herrold bluntly asserted that "except where strategically located," an urban freeway is a wide swath of inhospitable land use that "introduces a disrupting force to all the factors of good living." He proposed an auto-free central business district:

No passenger cars should be allowed inside the circumferential route. People would transfer from automobiles to shuttle buses and taxi cabs, or they would walk to their destination. From an economic standpoint, it would be far better to improve mass transportation to the highest standards possible, and then later to follow up with motor express routes. Building express routes first will increase congestion to a self-limiting status. Building up mass transportation will move the people where they need to go and may stop the disintegration of central districts.[29]

Herrold's notion of the pedestrianized downtown received little support from highway engineers, mainstream planners, and urban politicians at this time, although it would resurface in later decades.

Although highway engineers routinely endorsed integration of highways with city plans, the engineering literature contained a persistent undercurrent of mistrust. Engineers questioned the practicality of planners' schemes for urban regeneration and noted the frequency of plan-making without implementation. Charles M. Noble, the New Jersey state highway engineer, asked "What do we mean by planning? Is it merely an artistically prepared drawing, about which there is a great deal of high-minded discussion, put on public display for a short time and then relegated to the files of yesteryear to gather dust?"[30] Here, the highway engineers were echoing planners' own self-doubts about their ability to define "good city form" and devise policies to achieve it.[31]

Highway engineers were sensitive about opposition to urban freeways long before the highly publicized freeway revolts of the 1960s. In his 1948 article, Noble attributed opposition to the relatively small number of people who would be directly affected by the new freeways through loss of homes and businesses. In his view, these people were loud and organized, whereas the vast majority who would benefit from the new freeways were diffuse and hard to mobilize. In addition, Noble argued, "the public is confused by charges and counter charges and does not know where its interest lies."[32]

Elmer Timby, president of the Engineering Division of the American Roadbuilders Association, clarified the engineering perspective on highway development in the city core during U.S. Senate hearings on the planning, location, and design of the urban highway system:

It is, for some, easy to become so engrossed in considering the many ways that highway planning can be used as a tool for positive urban development that one loses sight of the fact that roads and streets serve the essential purpose of a circulatory system, thus allowing the urban complex to function as a unit. . . . Today, except in unavoidable occasional spots, the land taken is generally the least usable or the most rundown in the area . . . the radial highway generally increases the value of adjacent property, often spectacularly, thus increasing the real estate tax base of the metropolitan area. The process of design and location of metropolitan expressways frequently involves the highway program in such major social problems as urban renewal and relocation. Typically, the central business district is surrounded, or nearly surrounded by a belt of land which has been stricken by urban blight. These neighborhoods, in many cases, were good residential neighborhoods at one time, but unfortunately have deteriorated into slum areas. The highway can be an extremely valuable tool in bringing about a rehabilitation of urban slums not only as a means of clearing away unsafe and unsanitary buildings, but also by making the adjacent land more eligible for higher use.[33]

Safety and efficiency were the guiding principles for the highway engineers, says Frank Griggs, a transportation engineer who worked on the New York State Thruway. "The engineers were trained in getting people from point A to point B in the cheapest, fastest, and safest manner." Cheap often meant through wetlands, only later recognized as valuable, or through slums, bulldozed before residents could organize. "We didn't realize that poor people might not want to move—even if we thought it was for their own good," Griggs says.[34]

City Planners Prepare for the New Freeways

For city planners, serving traffic was only one problem on their agenda. They had to consider other modes of transportation, impacts on future land use, and how to fit new freeways into the existing urban pattern.[35] Understandably, they developed a more varied array of alternatives.

In particular, planners pressed for the integration of freeways with mass transit. *Urban Freeways* (1947), jointly produced by the American Institute of Planners and the American Transit Association, put forth numerous proposals for combining rail and bus transit with the urban freeway system.[36] A number of leading planners believed that scatteration could be reduced by creating new nuclei of residence, commerce, and industry around bus or rail transit stations built at intervals along the freeway.[37] In theory, these stations would counteract the tendency of freeways to generate formless sprawl. They would complement the linear nature of the freeways, as suburban railroad stations had created nodal settlement patterns along railroad routes between 1840 and 1900. Freeways would become part of the public transit system, rather than a ruthless competitor. The elegant renderings included in *Urban Freeways* suggested that mass transit, as well as the private automobile, might be streamlined and modernized (figures 4.1, 4.2, and 4.3). Stations could be attractively designed, transit vehicles upgraded, and trains run speedily along freeway medians. Automobile commuters might be persuaded to leave their cars in the suburbs rather than drive them into congested central business districts.

Although highways for private vehicles remained their first priority, during this period some highway engineers also endorsed the integration of rail transit with highways. The BPR's Thomas H. MacDonald stated that "The interest of public transportation and of over-all street and highway transportation can never be divergent. They must be parallel. Indeed in many cases they are coincident."[38] Municipal engineer Lloyd Aldrich of Los Angeles also endorsed the idea of using freeway rights-of-way for transit.[39]

However, with only a few exceptions, these early proposals came to nothing. Most mass transit systems were still privately owned at this time, and transit planning was not seen as a public responsibility or "public work" deserving of federal funding. Joint-use schemes presented problems of coordination between private transit companies and highway officials across numerous local jurisdictions. The transit proposals would also have significantly increased the right-of-way and construction costs of the new freeways, and highway engineers wanted highway funds to flow exclusively to highway construction, not to ancillary transit, landscaping, or urban design projects (figure 4.4).[40]

A few prominent city planners were skeptical about proposals for overreliance on massive freeway construction in central cities. In 1950,

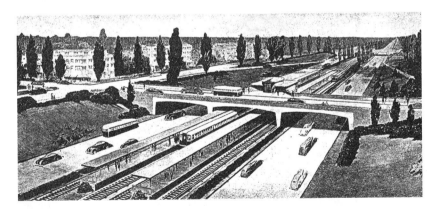

Figure 4.1
Proposal for a freeway with transit right-of-way in median. *Source:* American Institute of Planners, Committee on Urban Transportation, *Urban Freeways,* 1947.

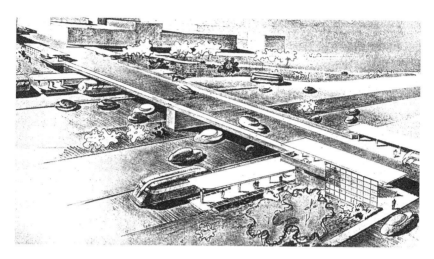

Figure 4.2
Proposed freeway with bus terminals. *Source:* American Institute of Planners, Committee on Urban Transportation, *Urban Freeways*, 1947.

Figure 4.3
Proposal for freeway with transit right-of-way in median and cluster of high-density residential units nearby. *Source:* American Institute of Planners, Committee on Urban Transportation, *Urban Freeways*, 1947.

Figure 4.4
Chicago's Eisenhower Expressway (formerly the Congress Street Expressway), one of the few examples of a rail transit line in a freeway median strip. *Source:* American Highway Users Alliance, *Urban Freeway Development in Twenty Major Cities*, Washington, D.C., American Highway Users Alliance, August 1964, p. 22.

Walter Blucher of the American Society of Planning Officials argued that no amount of freeway building would ever solve the traffic problem.

I helped spend a great many millions of dollars for street widenings in the city of Detroit. I helped invent the super-highway . . . but I cannot say that there is less congestion upon the public streets, less turmoil at terminals or fewer accidents than when we started this tremendous program of acquiring additional right-of-way for the movement of automobiles.[41]

Henry Churchill also warned against excessive highway building. Congestion "is an insoluble problem as long as our cities continue their present street patterns, and make them worse—not better—by building highways that act as feeders to the centers. It is an insoluble problem as long as we control neither the intensity to which land can be used, nor the use to which the private automobile can be put."[42]

At the other extreme, some local planning officials were quite willing to abandon the old city. In a 1945 article titled "The City Means Nothing to Traffic," Peter P. Hale, an engineer and associate of the New Haven City Plan Commission, declared that "traffic has given cities their form, and that therefore, traffic will change cities' form, or take it away altogether." Hale claimed that few people like the environment of the existing city and that only the large amounts of money sunk in existing buildings and infrastructure prevent "the full, immediate disintegration of the city into a series of scattered urban centers." The planner's task was to grasp the emerging opportunities "to create a perfect civic expression of the motor age even at the expense of allowing the city proper to languish until this first job is done." Hale warned that cities that failed to adapt to traffic would be left behind economically as businesses moved to new urban centers more amply provided with traffic-handling facilities.[43]

Mainstream city planning texts continued to endorse extensive urban freeway networks, as long as they were integrated with general plans and did not cut through stable neighborhoods. The second edition of the classic planning reference *Local Planning Administration* (1948) repeated the information from the 1941 edition and said nothing new about urban freeway systems. Remarkably, the text did not indicate that freeways posed a critical new challenge to the planning profession's ability to guide urban development. There was no premonition of unpredictable impacts or citizen protest.[44]

Another important city planning text, Harold M. Lewis's *Planning the Modern City* (1949), discussed limited-access roads in considerable detail. Lewis was the son of Harold P. Lewis, famous for his work on the *Regional Plan of New York and Its Environs*, and he continued to promote the highway planning principles of the Regional Plan Association. The parkway tradition of Frederick Law Olmsted, Gilmore Clarke, and the young Robert Moses still lived on in the New York region, although it was being eroded by constant pressures to upgrade old facilities and build new ones to higher geometric standards. Lewis addressed the role of autobahn-style express highways in urban areas. He endorsed the construction of the New York Thruway as an intercity connector but denied that whole networks of these autobahnen were necessary in urban areas.

Although it has been suggested that a network of limited-access thoroughfares might provide the skeleton of the street pattern of an entire city, it is doubtful whether such expensive construction would be justified on this scale. Few cities would ever need more than two or three of these routes and then only for streets carrying a large proportion of through traffic. These expressways are comparable to railways in cost and carrying capacity and should be treated very much the same in the city plan; in other words, they are not a part of the regular street pattern, although they should be tied in with it.[45]

Lewis endorsed a mix of highway types for the New York region, with both parkways for noncommercial vehicles and freeways open to truck traffic. Lewis's proposals were tame in comparison with those of S. E. Sanders and A. J. Rabuck, who in *New City Patterns* presented scenarios for a radical reconstruction of the city along the lines of Le Corbusier.[46] The authors rejected traditional city form in favor of "cells," each devoted to a particular land use.[47] Within the cells, the superblock idea is imposed relentlessly. The central business district module (adequate for a city of 200,000, modules to be added for each increase in 200,000 population) are divided into an office zone and several commercial zones, with the offices housed in twenty- and thirty-story slab skyscrapers, the department stores in twelve-story buildings, and other functions in two-story buildings. Pedestrian pathways are separated entirely from vehicular roads. The various residential modules are similarly structured according to rigid geometric principles, with every building type and land use in its place.

New City Patterns was a recycled Corbusian fantasy, a city entirely purged of traditional city form. A creation of the drafting board, it had little chance of being implemented in the near future. But along with dozens of other schemes promulgated by architects and planners, *New City Patterns* prepared the soil for subsequent assaults on the remnants of the nineteenth century city. These texts cataloged the deficiencies of the old city and magnified the benefits of the new. They helped to legitimize form concepts in which extensive freeway networks were essential elements.

Bits and pieces resembling these Modernist diagrams were eventually built across the nation, along with the adjacent freeways, although not in the profusion called for in the initial plans. In keeping with the limits of city planning in the United States, overall city form could not be planned; but in large projects under private control—subdivisions or redevelopment projects—fragments of visionary planning and architectural doctrine could be realized (figure 4.5).[48]

In the creation of powerful images of great cities rebuilt for the automobile, no one surpassed Robert Moses and his talented group of engineers and designers. In *Selected Measures for the Partial Relief of Traffic Congestion in New York City*, submitted to the New York City Planning Commission in 1946, Moses demonstrated his mastery of the freeway planning document.[49] In the aerial views, the freeways appeared

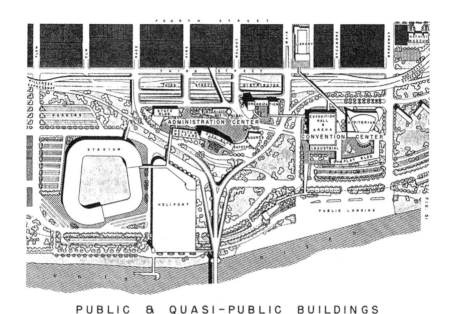

PUBLIC & QUASI-PUBLIC BUILDINGS
IN THE
RIVERFRONT REDEVELOPMENT PLAN

SCALE IN FEET
NORTH   400   0   400   1200

CITY PLANNING COMMISSION
CINCINNATI OHIO   METROPOLITAN MASTER PLAN

Figure 4.5
Plan for the redevelopment of the Cincinnati waterfront, including a major expressway and array of public facilities. *Source:* Cincinnati Planning Commission, *The Cincinnati Metropolitan Master Plan and the Official City Plan of the City of Cincinnati*, General Consultants, Ladislas Segoe and Tracy B. Augur, 1948.

as impressive additions to the city's infrastructure, cutting bold pathways through the high-rise landscape of Manhattan. Street-level views, on the other hand, made the freeways seem far less intrusive than they would have been in reality. One rendering showed an elevated expressway hugging the ground as it passed before a cathedral. The freeway occupies a small corner of the drawing, implying that it would scarcely alter the surrounding city (figure 4.6).

Through such clever packaging techniques, elevated freeways were portrayed as good neighbors, or even architectural assets, rather than as invasive structures adding pollution and noise to surrounding neighborhoods. Numerous other plans used aerial views and renderings to present proposed freeways in a favorable light.[50] Needless to say, the perspective

Figure 4.6
Proposed freeway across Manhattan. *Source:* New York, City Planning Commission, *Selected Measures for the Partial Relief of Traffic Congestion in New York City*, prepared by Gano Dunn, W. Earle Andrews, and Gilmore D. Clarke, 1946.

from high above the city, as though one were hovering in a helicopter, provided almost no useful information about the actual impact of freeways at ground level (figures 4.7, 4.8, 4.9, and 4.10).

Another critical issue was where to put the thousands of cars that would flood into downtown after the construction of urban freeways. According to many highway engineers, large parking garages near the freeways would solve the problem.

The Neglected Vision of the Urban Designers

As both urban redevelopment and central city freeways loomed on the horizon, planners had reason to ponder the adequacy of their physical planning heritage. Had the profession drifted into the unimaginative repetition of conventional, two-dimensional land-use plans? Could these plans respond to the complexities of central city reconstruction?

Christopher Tunnard, director of the Graduate Program in City Planning at Yale, had serious doubts. In 1951, he appealed for a resurgence of urban design within city planning and specifically mentioned urban freeways as examples of the eclipse of aesthetic sensibility in urban public works construction.[51] He lamented the marginalization of urban design, indeed its demotion to a cosmetic or embellishment.

This I think, has been our mistake—considering Civic Design as something which comes after "planning" . . . I am therefore appealing for a greater role to be given the creative professions in city planning, to lift city planning out of the plane of workability and expediency on which it now rests, to change something of the surgical approach of the city planner to that of the artist.[52]

Tunnard asked why "Civic Design has been neglected, even forgotten, for so many years?" and targeted the dominance of four subgroups within the design professions. The first and most populous group consisted of "utilitarian planners who deal largely in two-dimensional land use allocation." Although land-use planning was an essential and legitimate activity, it tended to become a form of sterile land-use sorting.

Beware of the planner who calls himself a practical man. It may mean that he has no imagination, or it may mean that he will always substitute expediency for long range planning. . . . Planners who look on the city as "a market, a place to work, an arena for the ambitious, a passage-way' (as Haussmann said) have made the city increasingly impossible as a place in which to live.[53]

Tunnard's second nemesis consisted of technocratic planners and architects who exalted technique "with lavish compliments being paid to the engineer as the true architect of our time. . . . This kind of romanticizing

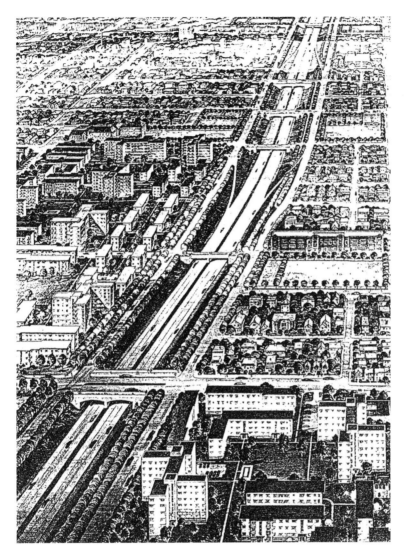

Figure 4.7
Proposed expressway for Detroit with adjacent land redeveloped for high-rise housing. *Source:* Detroit Transportation Board, *Detroit Expressway and Transit System*, prepared by W. Earle Andrews, Ladislas Segoe, and DeLeuw Cather and Company, 1945.

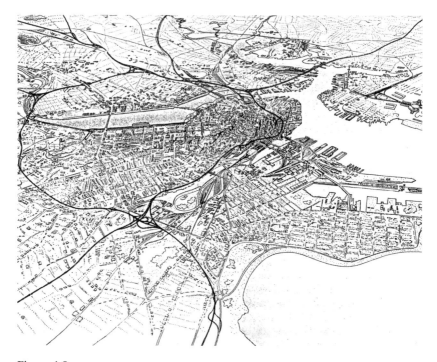

Figure 4.8
Aerial view of proposed Boston highway system. *Source:* Charles A. Maguire and Associates, *Master Highway Plan for the Boston Metropolitan Area*, 1948.

shows a confusion of judgment and a loss of the measure by which we judge our surroundings." Third, Tunnard critiqued "neoromantics" who tried "vainly to recreate the past in our modern world" through pictur-esque design or who accepted modern building styles but surrounded all their structures in a sea of greenery.

It is hard to go along with the notions of those who wish to place the city on a lawn because of an overly-romantic wish to make the town and country one. The town has its own character and, although sadly lacking green space at the present time, would lose its identity altogether if the neoromantics had their way. Take a walk through any new suburban area and see what has happened to the street; it has lost all character because of the mistaken notion that part of a metropolitan area can be made to look like a New England village.[54]

Finally, Tunnard criticized designers who pursued "originality for its own sake, the cult of the new." In their search for startling architectural ef-fects, these designers abandoned "the tradition of quiet anonymous build-ing" and robbed the city of "the pleasures of a quiet street architecture."

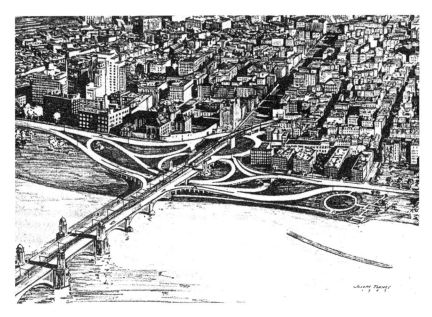

Figure 4.9
Proposal for Longfellow Bridge Interchange, Boston. *Source:* Charles A. Maguire and Associates, *Master Highway Plan for the Boston Metropolitan Area*, 1948.

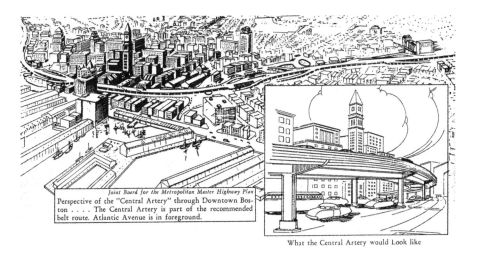

Joint Board for the Metropolitan Master Highway Plan
Perspective of the "Central Artery" through Downtown Boston . . . . The Central Artery is part of the recommended belt route. Atlantic Avenue is in foreground.

What the Central Artery would Look like

Figure 4.10
Rendering of proposed Central Artery through Boston. *Source:* Theodore McCroskey, Charles A. Blessing, and J. Ross McKeever, *Surging Cities*, Boston, Greater Boston Development Committee, 1948.

Tunnard had in mind those imitators of Wright and Le Corbusier who were happy only with unusual building sites and bizarre building forms. Tunnard constructed a powerful indictment of the orthodoxies of *three* professions: city planning, highway engineering, and architecture. All of them, he argued, were failing to produce a livable city. He detected a damaging one-sidedness in American physical planning practice, a failure to devise physical planning patterns to match the diversity and unpredictability of urban life.

We have passed the stage of the two-dimensional land-use diagram; . . . How much longer can we coast along on the modest reputation for good-looking civic design achieved by Radburn, Greenbelt and Baldwin Hills Village?[55]

Tunnard felt that planners had no convincing aesthetic for the central city. Suburban design principles were inapplicable there, and attempts to build inner-city versions of Radburn only destroyed the special qualities of the large metropolis. For Tunnard, this was also a mistaken strategy for professional advancement. In their search for professional legitimacy based on "science," planners had neglected aesthetics, potentially "their strongest weapon" for winning the public over to their cause. As Tunnard concluded, "In city planning, sociology, engineering and pressure salesmanship are rated higher than esthetics. While this remains true, can you blame people for not being interested or informed?"[56]

Highway Engineering Methodology and Urban Form, 1946–1956

During the first postwar decade, highway engineers continued to expand their methods for both traffic forecasting and technical freeway design. Riveted to the more narrow task of highway planning for traffic-carrying efficiency—free of the urban design conundrums troubling city planners—they could pursue the "normal science" of steady, incremental research-based advancement.[57]

Traffic Analysis

For highway engineers of the 1940s and early 1950s, "planning" meant the assessment of travel demands, not comprehensive transportation planning. Highways were built to accommodate traffic, not reshape the urban pattern; hence, the focus on improving traffic surveys. Early surveys simply counted the number of cars and trucks passing checkpoints on various thoroughfares. During the 1920s and 1930s, origin–destination studies based on interviews with drivers were introduced.[58] They provided more detailed information about driver behavior, which could be expressed graphically in the form of "desire lines" showing where drivers wanted to go. The city could be viewed as an immense map of "driver desires," and freeways could then be designed with the proper locations, number of lanes, interchanges, and other design features to handle the expected traffic.[59]

Unfortunately, origin–destination surveys merely showed the existing demand for trips, which could be projected into the future only by dubious techniques.[60] Freeways themselves created corridors of development and generated new traffic.[61] Highway engineers actually needed a vision of *future land uses* to be served by the new freeways. There was no way to avoid an intersection with city planning, and that convergence would come to pass during the 1950s.[62]

Cost–Benefit Analysis

Highway cost–benefit calculations might have prompted a more thorough analysis of freeways and urban form, but the opportunity was missed. The official formulas emphasized benefits to drivers such as saving of travel time, gasoline, and vehicle wear and tear.[63] Costs were usually limited to right-of-way acquisition and the actual design and construction of the highway. This methodology almost always made a new freeway in an urban area look economically sound, as long as it did not parallel another freeway too closely. Because there was no existing method for assessing complex, diffuse impacts on the surrounding city, land values were often used as a proxy variable. The method often overlooked the long-term influence of freeways on the urban environment, as only short-term land price changes were captured in the analysis. And finally, the method did not compare the freeway against other possible configurations of transportation and land use attainable with public funds; it only compared particular areas before and after the construction of freeways (figure 4.11).[64]

Variables that could not be easily quantified with the measuring methods available at the time—such as aesthetics, social cohesion, energy efficiency, and many elusive "quality of life" factors—were either excluded from the freeway planning process or given minor weight.[65] This strategy preserved the scientific aura of engineering methodology but only by postponing an accurate assessment of the impact of the highway on the city.[66] Analysis of the intricacies of city form appeared to be a methodological swamp, but all of the "soft" variables excluded by highway planning methods of the late 1940s and early 1950s would come back to haunt the highway community in the 1960s (figure 4.12).

Figure 4.11
Boston's Central Artery, showing the stubs that were supposed to connect with the Inner Beltway. *Source: Urban Freeway Development in Twenty Major Cities,* American Highway Users Alliance, Washington, D.C., August 1964, p. 34.

Planners and highway engineers increasingly sparred over the very meaning of "planning." The engineers' urban freeway proposals were structuring a transportation system, land-use pattern, and ultimately a "form of urban life"—all without systematic evaluation of alternative urban patterns. Forecasting of traffic was not the same as planning of cities. But forecasting meshed easily with free market doctrine, which claimed that sovereign consumers could select the best urban pattern by "voting" with their housing and transportation dollars from the alternatives presented to them by producers. City planning in its "strong" meaning—the conscious, deliberate shaping of urban form through some degree of centralized control—still suffered from negative connotations of government regimentation, economic inefficiency, and the loss of hallowed freedoms.

Figure 4.12
A large swath of dense urban fabric in Boston was razed to build the Central Artery, as shown in this aerial photograph from 1952. *Source:* The Benjamin and Gladys Thomas Air Photo Archives, Fairchild Collection, UCLA Department of Geography.

New Developments in Freeway Planning and Design

During the 1950s, changes in motor vehicle design, combined with increased traffic volumes, placed pressure on engineers to design freeways wholly devoted to traffic-carrying efficiency and safety requirements. More modest parkway and expressway concepts were gradually crowded out. Larger and more powerful autos and trucks required wider lanes, more gradual curves, and stronger pavements. Visibility standards were also increased.[67]

Highway engineers continued systematically to analyze the way that drivers responded to changes in highway design. This "operational research" involved viewing the freeway as a complex system subject to scientific or engineering analysis to improve capacity and safety performance. Researchers "suggested similarities between traffic engineering and the principles of fluid mechanics."[68] The freeway was viewed as a conduit carrying thousands of metal capsules piloted by organisms with specific behavioral limitations (vision, reaction times, orientation skills, capacity to follow driving rules). Thus, scientific principles could be formulated to determine features such as divided lanes, access controls, urban grade separations, acceleration and deceleration lanes, interchange spacing, signs, roadside distractions, and driver orientation.[69] Freeways governed by these new principles would have to be even wider and more gently curved to handle future vehicles. Improvements in safety and capacity thus brought new limitations on the ability of designers to thread freeways through congested urban areas. The imperatives of freeway design conflicted more and more harshly with the old scale of the central city, with its fine-meshed grids and complex land-use mixtures.

Highways and Landscape Architecture

The concept of "the complete highway" was launched in 1943 by the joint Highway Research Board–American Association of State Highway Officials Committee on Roadside Development, with the goal of fitting highways more carefully into the surrounding environment.[70] The committee enunciated four requirements for the complete highway: utility, safety, beauty, and economy.[71] The requirement of beauty involved designing alignments so as to avoid scarring the landscape, to preserve scenic values, to keep the roadside free of clutter, and to provide attractive landscaping. Some highway engineers and administrators chafed against the new demands, fearing that they would drain resources from the primary task of laying pavement.[72]

In spite of initial skepticism, landscape design did gradually become institutionalized within the highway planning process, but in a marginal position that never proved satisfying to the landscape architecture profession. State highway departments hired "landscape engineers," usually to deal with the planting of vegetation along rights-of-way. Typically, landscape architects wanted highways to be more like landscaped parkways and for landscape design principles to be incorporated into all phases of the design process, not pasted on at the end as a cosmetic. Landscaping involved added costs, and poorly placed trees could create safety hazards, but roadside elements could also increase safety by improving driver orientation and preventing boredom. In addition, careful choice of alignments using landscape design principles could eliminate the need for extensive cut-and-fill operations.[73]

Overall, however, the potential contribution of landscape architecture to urban freeway design was not exploited during the postwar decade. It was their skill at urban design and land planning that might have shifted the course of urban freeway planning, but landscape architects were restricted to a more limited role as designers of roadside landscaping. The considerable achievements of landscape architects in the design of rural and suburban highways were not paralleled in the urban domain.[74]

Exploring the Land Use–Transportation Connection

During the early 1950s, research on the relationship between land use and transportation flowered. Both highway engineers and city planners had gradually come to realize that knowledge about future land uses and their traffic-generating potential was necessary for freeway planning. Freeways did not just service urban development; they also initiated land-use conversion by increasing accessibility. It made no sense to plan highways without considering future land uses.

In *Urban Traffic: A Function of Land Use*, Robert B. Mitchell and Chester Rapkin outlined a framework for researching the traffic-generating properties of different urban activities.[75] Mitchell and Rapkin argued that traffic problems could only be solved through "the planning, guidance, and control of change in the pattern of land uses in the interests of efficiency."[76] Planners needed to know both the traffic consequences of the allocations of land portrayed in their land-use plans and the likely impacts of new transportation facilities on land use. Mitchell and Rapkin did not provide answers to these riddles; rather, they laid the foundations for a research program. The challenge was quickly taken up by the directors of the first metropolitan traffic studies.

The first systematic modeling of the relation between land use and transportation was the Detroit Metropolitan Traffic Study, under the direction of J. Douglas Carroll, which was completed in 1956. Carroll and his associates attempted to develop mathematical models correlating different land uses with trips. A gravity model was used to determine the number of trips from one portion of an urban zone to another. Once the relationships were determined, planners could plug in the land-use allocations from Detroit's master plan and predict future traffic loads.

These pioneering developments drew more planners into the highway planning process, but as forecasters and data providers rather than as shapers of the metropolitan spatial pattern. The planners' role was the more modest one of improving the existing freeway planning process by providing cheaper, more accurate projections of future traffic demands, assuming a conventional pattern of urban growth along lines determined by the existing real estate market.

Ideas of Architects and Urban Designers

Architects stood outside the highway policy-making process but continued to produce schemes for incorporating new freeways into rebuilt city cores. Architectural texts of the early postwar period repeated the theme that the freeway and the city could be integrated through innovative design. Theoretically, by segregating land uses and separating pedestrian spaces and streets, city dwellers could have both pleasant central city environments and the mobility provided by the auto.

The Heart of the City, published under the auspices of the Congrès Internationaux d'Architecture Moderne (CIAM) in 1952, offered a collection of essays by architects on the future of the urban core. Jose Sert argued that motorized vehicles should not be allowed in city centers; they "must reach different points of the perimeter of these areas and find the necessary parking facilities right there, but the land inside these perimeters should be only for pedestrian use, and screened from the noise and fumes of the motors."[77] The conflict between the freeway and the core would be solved by a radical separation of functions. Other contributors offered variations on the theme of radical re-planning of city centers to eliminate traditional corridor streets.

But not every author in *The Heart of the City* endorsed Le Corbusier's surgical approach to the renewal of historic cities. British architect W. J. Holford ventured that "Operations like those performed by Haussmann on the body of Paris, or by Robert Moses on the much younger New York, renew vitality for a time, but lead to further thrombosis and congestion before long."[78] Urban designer Robert C. Weinberg, reviewing the book in the *Journal of the American Institute of Planners*, applauded CIAM's advocacy of pedestrian plazas downtown, but expressed serious reservations about the rigidity of the designs:

A curious geometric sameness runs through many of the patterns, leading one to wonder whether these "cores," if they were conceived in any relationship to the spirit of the locality for which each is intended, may not imply that, in the opinion of CIAM, our future urban communities, from one end of the world to the other, will display a deadly sameness, with only the minimum concession to differences of climate and topography.[79]

Also at this time, architect Victor Gruen devised his famous plan for Fort Worth that involved enclosing a pedestrianized downtown within a freeway loop and phalanx of parking garages.[80] Like so many other plans, however, the Gruen plan ran aground on the inertia of existing political and property arrangements. Private garage and parking lot operators opposed the plan. Gruen himself, looking back in 1973, judged that the plan was not implemented because "The city and state authorities resented that fact that the plan was developed by private enterprise, that the project was far ahead of its time, and that federal assistance for urban redevelopment was not at that time available."[81] In any case, the Gruen plan served as an influential example of blending CBD pedestrianization with a vast freeway network—clearly an application of the shopping mall concept, which Gruen had pioneered, to the downtowns of large American cities.

Leading architects and experts on the city center conducted a round-table discussion on "How to Rebuild Cities Downtown" in the *Architectural Forum* of June 1955.[82] The article warned that "the life-blood of the older center appears to be drained out along every superhighway" but argued that it was completely unrealistic to propose the abandonment of the downtowns of large cities. Through intelligent design the downtown could be saved. In the article's summary of "18 ways to solve" the problem, the participants came up with familiar recipes for solving the central city traffic problem.

An improved highway pattern is the first essential for handling people coming downtown by automobile. This must include peripheral expressways, along with peripheral parking terminals, so a change-over can be made to mass transportation. It must include through expressways not going through the downtown core to keep traffic off the streets that will do no business downtown; it must include ring expressways placed well within the city but directly outside the downtown core. . . . It must include other expressways that do spill directly into the core.[83]

The concept of a freeway loop around the central business district—an idea articulated in both *Toll Roads and Free Roads* and *Interregional Highways*—continued to fascinate planners and architects looking for relief from congestion in the city center.[84] But notes of skepticism were sounded. Planner Walter Blucher and others questioned whether such huge investments of public funds should be devoted to the automobile and whether downtowns could accommodate any more vehicles.[85] But the dominant view was that of transportation consultant Wilbur Smith, who argued that the tide of automobiles could not be stopped; it could only be channeled.

In the final analysis, physical planners and urban designers could agree on little except the obsolescence of traditional central city patterns. There was some consensus that the downtown expressway loop was a useful idea, although the long-term social and economic impacts of that strategy remained vague. Planners had no "science" of good city form, only a disparate array of form concepts, each serving a particular conception of proper urban life.[86] An urban future with some type of large-scale freeway network seemed inevitable; the radial-concentric pattern, with an inner belt around the CBD, had emerged as the most plausible form concept; but beyond that dozens of questions remained unanswered about the effects of such a massive new arterial system on the visual form, economic vitality, and social structure of the urban core.

Conclusion: On the Eve of the Interstates

Between 1946 and 1956, the seminal ideas codified in *Toll Roads and Free Roads* and *Interregional Highways* were refined, elaborated, and expanded. Initial planning was begun on the interstate system, with state highway departments taking the lead and emphasizing traffic-carrying efficiency. The planning and design professions stood outside the highway planning community, speculating somewhat apprehensively about the long-term effects of urban freeways, but still hopeful that city planning goals would be integrated into any program of construction (figure 4.13).

The pre-World War II parkway model of urban highway design faded from view and was replaced by ambitious plans for utilitarian arterials devoted to traffic-moving efficiency. State highway departments consolidated their hold on the urban freeway planning process, eclipsing local planning and public works officials.[87] The highest priority of the states was the efficient movement of high volumes of traffic through the cities, with other city planning concerns such as land use, provision of housing, and coordination with mass transit pushed into the background. The idea of integration at the federal level ended with the creation of a separate bureaucracy for urban redevelopment.

During this waiting period—while the interstate system remained underfunded—engineers, planners, and designers engaged in inconclusive debates about the best form for the new urban freeways. Most of the important issues were raised—whether penetration of the core was necessary, elevated versus depressed designs, the relation of freeways to land use, division of neighborhoods, displacement of the poor, and the aesthetic impact of freeways on central city form—but these were only simmerings, not yet full-blown conflicts demanding major changes in the canon of urban freeway design. Urban freeways were not quite "real" yet: most were lines on maps, awaiting adequate funding.

Figure 4.13
The Whitehurst Freeway along the Georgetown waterfront, the first freeway in Washington, D.C.; it opened to traffic in 1949. *Source: Urban Freeway Development in Twenty Major Cities*, American Highway Users Alliance, Washington, D.C., August 1964, p. 38.

In 1955, the state highway departments and the Bureau of Public Roads defined the remainder of the interstate routes—the urban mileage that had been designated in 1947 but not mapped. These routes were published in *General Location of National System of Interstate Highways*, known as the "Yellow Book."[88] The Yellow Book's maps for most large American cities show the hub-and-wheel pattern from *Toll Roads and Free Roads* and *Interregional Highways* modified to accommodate the topographical and land-use characteristics of each metropolis. Los Angeles was something of an exception, deploying a system closer to a grid, albeit with a noticeable bending of routes toward the downtown.[89]

The freeway funding dilemma was finally solved with the passage of the Interstate and Defense Highway Act of 1956, which provided for 90 percent federal funding of the interstate system, the remainder to be provided by the states.[90] The fiscal obstacles to metropolitan freeways fell away. The urban freeway program would now be fueled with billions of dollars, an irresistible force pushing old doubts and questions aside.

As David Jones has noted, the 1946–1956 period marked the ascendancy of California as the leader in urban freeway planning, gradually edging out New York. New York's postwar "Thruway" pioneered in intercity freeway design, but Los Angeles became the city that committed itself unreservedly to the freeway and the private automobile.[91] Engineers and public officials increasingly looked to Southern California for models of the emerging freeway landscape.

Highway engineers possessed the plans, the self-confidence, and the legislative mandate to build urban interstates and other elements of the federal system. They had agreed-upon models for freeway location and design. By framing the task as one of traffic service through extensive freeway construction and by paring away intractable city planning concerns, they could act decisively, unencumbered with the burdens of comprehensive city planning. Their view of urban modernization was not complicated by the tangles of aesthetic, social, economic, and environmental variables that produced indecision among planners and architects. They had simple models and data for those models. Their approaches were vindicated in what were seen as the successes of practical men such as Robert Moses. Those planners who were considered relevant bought into the solutions with technocratic contributions, and what little role remained for urban designers came at the end: marginal cosmetic additions.

The planning profession was unprepared for the freeway building era that would be unleashed by the 1956 act. In 1956, veteran planner Tracy B. Augur, writing in the *Highway Research Board Bulletin*, asked: What kind of urban pattern is best suited to the conditions and requirements of our time? But Augur confessed:

Unfortunately, as vital as these questions are, we know very little about the answers. That is one of the most important fields in which research is needed and one of the most neglected. . . . As badly as this country needs action to develop better urban patterns, it needs, even more, the fundamental research on which sound patterns can be based.[92]

But only limited time was left for research. The mass production of urban interstates would soon be under way.[93] As we see in the next chapter, between 1956 and 1970, urban freeway form concepts developed during the previous three decades became blueprints for actual construction. State highway engineers led the way. However, opposition to the urban freeway, fostered in part by those with other visions of the form, function, and value of inner-city neighborhoods, also began to grow and to have on-the-ground effects.

5

Changing Visions and Regulations for Highway Planning

The Federal and State Roles and Urban Routes

In a 1970 essay reviewing the Eisenhower presidency and its accomplishments, Daniel Moynihan decisively and dramatically declared:

> [T]here was one program of truly transcendent, continental consequence. This was a program which the twenty-first century will almost certainly judge to have had more influence on the shape and development of American cities, the distribution of population within metropolitan area and across the nation as a whole, the location of industry and various kinds of employment opportunities (and, through all these, immense influence on race relations and the welfare of black Americans) than any initiative of the middle third of the twentieth century. This was, of course, the Interstate and Defense Highway System. It has been, it is, the largest public works program in history. Activities such as urban renewal, public housing, community development, and the like are reduced to mere digressions when compared to the extraordinary impact of the highway program.[1]

A federal "interstate highway program" has, in effect, been in existence since 1916, only 3 years after Henry Ford began mass production of the Model T. In that year, Congress approved the first in a series of programs of continuing federal aid for highways, apportioning funds among the states amounting to half of the construction costs of "rural post roads," the roadways over which mail was transported.[2]

The Federal Highway Act of 1921, which superseded the Federal Aid Road Act of 1916 , stated that federal officials should "give preference to such projects as will expedite the completion of an adequate and connected systems of highways, interstate in character." In addition, it called upon each of the states to designate a formal system of "primary or interstate highways" and "secondary or intercounty highways" for federal aid purposes. The primary highways were not to exceed three-sevenths of the total mileage designated for federal aid, and the secondary highways were to make up the balance of the total mileage. However, the three-sevenths limitation was ignored by federal and state officials, who considered all roads within the federal aid system to be "primary" roads.[3]

The contemporary Dwight D. Eisenhower National System of Interstate and Defense Highways, commonly known as the interstate system, traces its origins to a series of studies that began in the late 1930s. These studies were authorized under the Federal-Aid Highway Act of 1938, which required the Bureau of Public Roads, the forerunner of the Federal Highway Administration, to study the feasibility of constructing a system of three north–south and three east–west transcontinental highways. These superhighways were initially proposed as a network of toll roads. The bureau's report, *Toll Roads and Free Roads*, showed that such a toll network would not be self-supporting; instead, the report advocated a toll-free interregional network of highways.[4]

In 1941, President Franklin D. Roosevelt appointed a committee, headed by Commissioner of Public Roads Thomas H. MacDonald, of the Bureau of Public Roads, to assess the need for a national system of expressways.[5] The National Interregional Highway Committee produced its report, *Interregional Highways*, in 1944. The report advocated the construction of a system of 33,900 miles of rural roadways, in addition to 5,000 miles of auxiliary urban roadways.[6]

In response to this and other initiatives, Congress passed the Federal-Aid Highway Act of 1944 and began the creation of the National System of Interstate Highways. The act declared that up to 40,000 miles of roadway would be located to "connect by routes, direct as practical, the principal metropolitan areas, cities, and industrial centers, to serve the national defense, and to connect at suitable border points, routes of continental importance in the Dominion of Canada and the Republic of Mexico."[7]

The act provided a federal share of 50 percent for construction costs for primary, secondary, and urban highways. In creating what was called the ABC program, the aim of Congress was to meet the needs of individual states for development of an interstate network of main highways and farm-to-market and feeder roads. For the first time, federal funding for urban extensions was provided.[8] The act directed the designation of the interstate system but did not specify that the system was to be financed differently from the primary program (50 percent). Subsequent to this act, state highway agencies prepared, often for the first time, comprehensive highway plans for urban areas, indicating the preliminary locations of the proposed interstates.[9] But no funds were actually set aside for construction. Instead, state highway engineers were authorized to "draw" on their state's ABC funds.[10]

Although the system had been named the National System of Interstate Highways, the federal provision followed the traditional federal aid highway practices in place since 1921. There was no comprehensive plan of development. According to practice, state and federal officials would share expenses, leaving day-to-day construction to state agencies and private contractors.[11]

In effect, lack of a comprehensive plan was a foreshadowing of the conflicts that have continued over time. On the one hand, truck operators and state road engineers urged expressways with a view toward maximizing traffic flow. Business and urban leaders argued for the use of expressways as a part of a plan to revitalize downtowns and surrounding neighborhoods.[12]

From the earliest days of federal planning, routes through urban areas were contemplated "to provide direct connection into and through all of [the] cities" of the system.[13] They were not provided for, however, until the 1950s. By September 1955, the "Yellow Book," as it was known in the highway planning profession, contained maps of the urban areas for which the government had approved urban interstate sections: they numbered one hundred.[14]

A freeway is defined by the American Association of State Highway Officials (AASHO) as "an expressway with full control of access . . . distinguished from all other expressways by the degree of separation of crossroads and the manner of providing access. A freeway has no cross traffic at grade."[15] Before 1956, 480 urban freeway miles were under construction or completed in the nation's largest cities. Greater than half of the mileage lay within the boundaries of metropolitan New York, Chicago, and Los Angeles.[16] The urban system was designated to be 8,600 miles in length.

By the mid-1950s, 6,500 of the planned 40,000 interstate miles had been constructed at a cost of $1 billion, and $232 million had been spent throughout the country on 19,900 miles of farm-to-market roads. Rising construction costs, shortages after the war, and more expensive building standards slowed the construction of urban and interurban arteries.[17] However, the states appeared to prefer to build less expensive highway projects that could serve their own citizens with their federal apportionment.[18] In this way, the "national directive" plodded forward.

In 1956, Congress declared it essential to the national interest to provide for the completion of the interstate system throughout the United States. In the Federal-Aid Highway Act of 1956, the federal share for interstate construction was fixed at 90 percent. The act, which fostered the largest public works program ever adopted until that time,[19] also raised federal highway user taxes, including the gas and tire taxes, and placed a levy on heavy vehicles. Perhaps the greatest significance of the act was its creation of the Highway Trust Fund. All of these revenues would be available for expenditures without further congressional authorization.[20]

Until this time, the gas tax, imposed as a temporary Depression measure in 1932, was separate from the highway program. Unmarked funds for highway programs had been drawn from the general revenue. This linkage demonstrated the first comprehensive congressional commitment to the completion of the program. Thus, "in light of financing and other provisions in the 1956 Act, it is entirely appropriate to say that the modern 'Interstate System' originated in 1956."[21]

Shortly after the passage of the act, Lewis Mumford, whom this volume introduced in earlier chapters, expressed a different perspective on the interstate highway system and its impacts on urban and rural areas. Mumford believed that crucial elements of a workable transportation system were being ignored in favor of one based strictly on the automobile. In his book *The Highway and the City*, Mumford wrote:

When the American people, through their Congress, voted a little while ago (1957) for a twenty-six-billion-dollar highway program, the most charitable thing to assume about this action is that they hadn't the faintest notion of what they were doing. Within the next fifteen years they will doubtless find out; but by that time it will be too late to correct all the damage to our cities and our countryside, not least to the efficient organization of industry and transportation, that this ill-conceived and preposterously unbalanced program will have wrought. Yet if someone had foretold these consequences before this vast sum of money was pushed through Congress, under the specious, indeed flagrantly dishonest, guise of a national defense measure, it is doubtful whether our countrymen would have listened long enough to understand; or would even have been able to change their minds if they did understand. For the current American way of life is founded not just on motor transportation but on the religion of the motorcar, and the sacrifices that people are prepared to make for this religion stand outside the realm of rational criticism. Perhaps the only thing that could bring Americans to their senses would be a clear demonstration of the fact that their highway program will, eventually, wipe out the very area of freedom that the private motor car promised to retain for them.

The fatal mistake we have been making is to sacrifice every other form of transportation to the private motorcar and to offer, as the only long-distance alternative, the airplane. But the fact is that each type of transportation has its special use; and a good transportation policy must seek to improve each type and make the most of it. This cannot be achieved by aiming at high speed or continuous flow alone If you wish casual opportunities for meeting your neighbors, and for profiting by chance contacts with acquaintances and colleagues, a stroll at two miles an hour in a concentrated area, free from needless vehicles, will alone meet your need. But if you wish to rush a surgeon to a patient a thousand miles away, the fastest motorway is too slow. And again, if you wish to be sure to keep a lecture engagement in winter, railroad transportation offers surer speed and better insurance against being held up than the airplane. There is no one ideal mode or speed: human purpose should govern the choice of the means of transportation. That is why we need a better transportation system, not just more highways.[22]

The Evolution of Urban Freeway Planning

Between 1956 and 1970, urban freeway form concepts that were developed during the previous three decades became the blueprints for actual construction. State highway engineers, with the support of local growth coalitions, pushed radials and inner beltways through old neighborhoods and industrial districts, linking central business districts with emerging regional highway networks. A learning process was also inaugurated, as deficiencies in freeway planning and design became apparent. Under pressure from coalitions of freeway opponents, engineers and planners gradually developed more sophisticated approaches to inserting freeways into built-up areas. As with so many other city planning issues, public controversy served as a belated, contentious form of technology assessment.[23]

City planners, urban designers, and observers of urban affairs mustered effective criticism of urban freeway building only late in this process, after most of the critical decisions had already been made. As early as 1948, Frank H. Malley proposed that "the highway designer, in the collective interests of the community, can go further than the interests of the highway user, by utilizing those methods and techniques of city planning which will assist the highway engineer in fitting the expressway into a functional and orderly land use pattern for the urban area."[24]

However, despite much conciliatory rhetoric, planners and designers were perceived by many members of the highway community as interlopers, capitalizing on the newfound prominence of highway issues and the availability of money for highway-related research.

The design professions did launch a productive research agenda on freeways and urban form during the late 1950s, but they were able to achieve only modest alterations in freeway design. Where freeways were stopped or modified, it was through grassroots protest, litigation, and federal legislation, rather than technical arguments or academic research. In 1957, the AASHO issued a new codification of standards for interstates and other urban freeways in *A Policy on Arterial Highways in Urban Areas.*[25] This well-known "Red Book" summarized and legitimized the principles of urban freeway planning we have traced back to the 1920s and earlier.

The fundamental logic for roadway construction in urban areas used by the highway engineers is set forth clearly in the manual:

If the urban area is to continue to grow and prosper, the highway network should not only accommodate the existing demand but also be amenable to efficient and orderly enlargement, commensurate with the demands of the predictable future. It is therefore necessary to expand the present travel as determined from the origin-destination data into the future by a logical method. The future travel demand is then compared with the capacity of the existing street and arterial route network. This comparison serves to indicate the general location and type of additional facilities or the expansion of existing facilities, or both, required to accommodate adequately the anticipated demand.[26]

Although the engineering criteria in this manual were not labeled "urban design guidelines," they constituted a *de facto* design canon limiting the options for locating freeways in the central city. The authors acknowledged the importance of land-use considerations in freeway location but in language too vague to provide meaningful guidance (figure 5.1).

The influences of commercial, industrial, residential, and civic uses of land are major controls in urban highway location. . . . Ultimate development combined with existing development gives the structure of the future city to which arterial improvements are fitted.[27]

The manual did offer some specific suggestions for the location of arterial routes:

• through wedges of unused land between ribbons of developed areas;

• through blighted areas, particularly those subject to redevelopment;

• along railroads and the shorelines of bodies of water; and

• adjacent to borders of parks and other sizable tracts of city and institutional property.

These recommendations resembled very closely the urban highway location criteria defined in *Interregional Highways* in 1944. These routes would keep land costs down and minimize disruption of the existing street grid, but at a considerable cost in destruction of other urban values: parks, low-cost housing stock, and access to waterfronts.

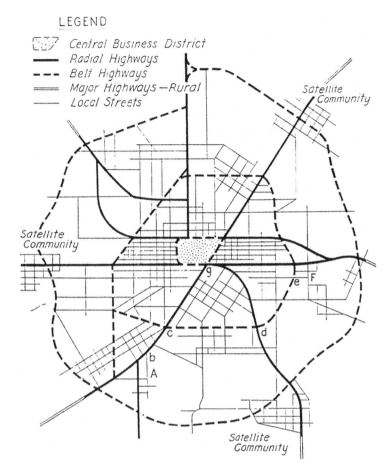

LEGEND

░░░ Central Business District
▬▬ Radial Highways
- - - Belt Highways
═══ Major Highways —Rural
──── Local Streets

Satellite Community

Satellite Community

Satellite Community

Figure 5.1
Basic pattern of urban arterial highways. *Source:* American Association of State Highway Officials, *A Policy on Arterial Highways in Urban Areas*, 1957.

Design speeds limited the engineers' ability to fit the new freeways into crowded urban districts because high speeds ruled out any but the most gradual of curves. The manual specified that design speeds for at-grade expressways could vary from 40 mph in built-up areas to 60 mph in outlying areas, with 50 mph recommended as a more fitting design speed for a modern urban facility.[28] Right-of-way for a six-lane at-grade expressway would ideally consist of at least 275 feet. Freeways of this magnitude created a difficult mismatch with the fine-grained street grids of the central city.

Although *A Policy on Arterial Highways in Urban Areas* did recommend that highways be designed so as to present a pleasing appearance, this theme was placed in the background. The manual admitted that an elevated freeway on a narrow right-of-way "presents a visual barrier, blocks off light, produces objectionable traffic noises, and sometimes creates a nuisance area below."[29] Joint-use opportunities received some attention; there were discussions on placement of freeways over or through buildings and on the use of space under viaducts.[30] The manual also discussed the incorporation of transit facilities in freeways, but with little enthusiasm.[31]

Overall, from an urban design point of view, the 1957 AASHO manual presented a limited array of ideas for integrating freeways into existing cities. Freeway building was defined as an engineering job. Nothing in federal highway legislation placed a premium on city planning, urban design, or social concerns. Not surprisingly, highway engineers subsequently paid little attention to those issues and presented the new thoroughfares as universal benefits for all urban dwellers.

There is some evidence that President Eisenhower did not realize that the interstates would run through, rather than around, cities until almost 3 years after the passage of the 1956 act. The president's concerns about the program led him to request, in July 1959, that his advisor General Bragdon conduct a review of the urban interstates. An interim report was completed in March 1960.[32]

Gary Schwartz has summarized the Bragdon recommendations as follows:

(1) That inner belts be eliminated; (2) that circumferentials be preferred over arterials or spurs; (3) that spurs be substituted for routes going all the way through the city; and (4) that spurs be kept to minimum length.

These changes would have permitted the elimination of 1,700 miles of urban freeways. However, the Bragdon inquiry did not result in any changes to the interstate program. General Bragdon moved on to another position shortly thereafter, and his recommendations quietly died for lack of attention.[33] The inertia of existing highway policy was immense, and it is unlikely that Bragdon or anyone else could have redirected urban freeway policy in such a radical fashion at that late date.

Some responses to existing highway planning policy surfaced at the 1957 Hartford Conference on "The New Highways: Challenge to the Metropolitan Region." Clearly, many urbanists were troubled by the potential impacts of the interstate program on American cities. Planner/

architect Carl Feiss called for a moratorium on new highway construction until cities had prepared plans to accommodate them.[34] Edward T. Chase, one of the organizers of the conference, worried that "The program exists as an unrelated enterprise, isolated from metropolitan planning and indeed even from the transportation system it is supposed to rejuvenate."[35] He noted the "notorious" gulf between planning officials and highway engineers and suggested that the state highway departments were "not famous as reservoirs of first-rate planning talent." Closing on an upbeat note, however, Chase saw a promising sign in the formation of the new Urban Research Committee of the Highway Research Board, which would be devoted to exploring the impacts of highways on cities.

Mortgage banker James W. Rouse hoped that the new freeways could be used creatively to define new neighborhoods and remove traffic streams from existing surface streets.[36] J. Douglas Carroll, Jr., director of the Chicago Area Transportation Study, admitted that controversies over location were "heightened by the fact that the specialists just don't know what is best. . . . The way to optimize location is not clear."[37] Luther Gulick, president of the Institute of Public Administration, declared that it would be "a colossal blunder to think that we should rebuild our old cities and plan our new urban and suburban developments or 'New Towns' primarily 'to take care of the automobile'. . . . We know now that we will get nowhere if we put the automobile first, and forget other needs and values."[38]

In 1957, journalist Grady Clay asked whether the Federal Highway Program would produce "Miracle Miles or a Big Mess?" He suspected that highway routes had been selected with only perfunctory attention to city plans, sometimes on the basis of outdated maps, and with limited input from city planners. He observed that freeway planning maps failed to portray either the social or morphological complexity of the city. Clay ventured that "expressways within the built-up portions of our city, are truly a form of architecture, the most expensive public architecture in our generation." As such, they deserved concerted effort to fit them satisfactorily into the urban landscape.[39]

The 1958 Sagamore Conference
At the 1958 Sagamore Conference (at Syracuse University), the First National Conference on Highways and Urban Development, "55 top highway officials, mayors, public works directors, city planners, traffic

engineers, and business and civic leaders" met to discuss the urban highway program.[40] As with any such convocation of experts, one must be
careful to distinguish pious resolutions from substantive policy making.
Certainly, the Sagamore Conference produced renewed endorsements of
city and regional planning as an important determinant of freeway location and design. As the conference documents affirmed, "Mere token cooperation of highway and city officials will not suffice. A real working relationship right from the initial phases of the highway program is vital."[41]

The conference documents announced that the interests of highway
engineers and city planners were basically the same. Both believed that
downtowns could only remain competitive if they were equipped with a
full array of expressway connections. They disliked the traditional corridor street, which allegedly spawned congestion and blight, but were
receptive to the notion that some downtown streets should be replaced
with pedestrian malls.[42]

In a paper given at the Sagamore Conference, Joseph Barnett testily
defended the highway engineers from criticisms that they were ignoring
city planning principles.

In deference to the most vociferous critical element, let me say right off that one of
the most important items which a highway engineer looks for is a comprehensive
and firm city plan. This assertion has been made for several decades but has not
been accepted in good faith because many cities do not have adequate city plans
so highway engineers have had to proceed without them. Where a city plan has
been available, highway engineers by and large have seriously considered the elements in that plan and, insofar as it was economical and practical to do so, have
located urban arterial highways and determined the appropriate highway types in
conformity therewith.[43]

Within this framework, city planning could assist the highway builders
through provision of land-use information and regulatory power over future land use, offering predictability of traffic generation. But if planners
and architects were to thrust issues of urban aesthetics, social welfare,
race, or economic justice to the forefront, they would be transgressing
their appropriate role in the transportation planning process.

Lawrence Halprin: The Landscape Architect as Freeway Designer
Landscape architect Lawrence Halprin broke new ground in urban freeway planning with his consulting work in San Francisco during the early
1960s. This work culminated in the book *Freeways* (1966).[44] Halprin
walked a line between the highway engineers and their critics, praising
some freeways as "magnificent examples of engineering which have risen

to the status of exciting art" and condemning others as inept intrusions that have "demeaned the cities which they were meant to serve." He argued that freeways must be reconceptualized as "a new form of urban sculpture in motion."

Halprin acknowledged the technical engineering standards involved in freeway construction but argued that these had to be fused with the skills of the designer. Freeway design would thus become "an intuitive act of the most demanding and imprecise kind." Engineering principles could be specified precisely, but evaluations of aesthetic, sociological, and physical impacts on the urban environment depended "on value judgments of the most intuitive kind."[45] Halprin skillfully played upon the tension between the freeway as liberator and destroyer, utilitarian concrete mass and sculptural object. He warmly embraced that distinctively modern experience, rapid motion in a powerful road machine, "Planing over the land at tree-top level—the roofs of houses below you—almost like flying."[46]

These vast and beautiful works of engineering speak to us in the language of a new scale, a new attitude in which high-speed motion and qualities of change are not mere abstract conceptions but a vital part of our everyday experiences.[47]

Freeways could create magnificent panoramic views of the city in a "brilliant kaleidoscope of motion which has enriched our lives and opened up whole new vistas of experience." But they could also destroy precious urban values.

Freeways have done terrible things to cities in the past decade, and in many instances have almost irrevocably destroyed large sections of the cities which they were meant to serve.[48]

Depressed freeways often formed "great ditches" between neighborhoods. Elevated freeways blocked out light and air, generated noise, and the areas beneath them often became blighted zones of rubbish-strewn asphalt. Halprin also criticized inner freeway loops, which "have served, in fact, to strangulate the downtown core in a noose, isolating it visually and socially from the rest of the city."[49]

Regardless of the degree to which Halprin's ideas could be co-opted by highway builders, *Freeways* was a markedly different treatment of the whole issue of freeway design, illustrating the different professional "worlds" inhabited by the physical designer and the highway engineer. Halprin's book was packed with drawings and pictures of freeways taken from all angles. The style was literary, and at times rhapsodic, rather than dry and technical. Analysis of urban form occupied center stage, rather than calculations of efficiency.

Mainstream City Planning and the New Freeways

Especially after the Housing Act of 1954 injected new vigor into programs for urban renewal, city planners believed that the central city could be saved through planning initiatives. Urban renewal promised the clearance of decayed slum districts in the core frame and their replacement with a new-built environment for the expanding service economy (office towers, luxury housing, convention facilities, cultural centers). Select inner-city neighborhoods could be renovated for middle-class people returning to the central city. Planners and other growth coalition members saw transportation improvements as a critical element of central city renascence. New highways would allow middle- and upper-class white collar workers and shoppers to speed in and out of the central business district (CBD) without congestion and without encountering the inhabitants of the troubled "gray areas." The urban poor would be just a blur on the streets below the freeway viaducts.[50]

At the same time, the flight of industrial jobs to the suburbs would remove the economic rationale for having large working populations in the city at all, and old industrial land could be recycled for new economic activities. Although low-income groups could not actually be expelled from the city, as there was no place for them to go, they could be spatially contained by a combination of market forces and public housing policies.[51]

Despite the strengthening of the prestige, funding, and technical apparatus of the planning profession after World War II, planners still struggled to achieve a stronger influence on urban policy. Other professions such as engineering, architecture, landscape architecture, and public administration also claimed elements of the city as their proper domain.

A sympathetic public official, addressing planners in a 1957 article in the *Journal of the American Institute of Planners*, wrote the following:

> But you have not yet been in operation long enough to convince the doubters and the potential rivals; you have not translated your pretensions and your aspirations into understandable, convincing and dependable examples of what you and your planning techniques can do in the competition of the marketplace.[52]

This same official cautioned that new freeways, if improperly planned, would only help traffic "to move more swiftly through the surrounding blight" and warned planners that if they did not assert themselves, they would be bypassed during the coming decades of rapid urban change.

More than a few city planners believed that, despite the profession's increasing numbers and institutional solidarity, planning was somehow failing to shape a better urban world. Catherine Bauer captured this mood in her 1957 article "Do Americans Hate Cities?" published in the *Journal of the American Institute of Planners*.[53] Discussing the reactions of some foreign visitors to American cities, she remarked that "The Ferry Building Freeway row [in San Francisco] amazes them." In a great European city, to deface such a building "with an elevated highway would be as unthinkable as to transform the Tuileries or the Tivoli Gardens into parking areas."[54]

Searching for the reasons why Americans rejected stronger urban planning and compact urban form, Bauer placed the blame largely on governmental chaos: "The metropolitan community is incapable of making any decisions about its structure, or the disposition of future development, because it does not exist as a governmental entity."[55] Bauer also diagnosed an almost neurotic desire to escape from urban problems by fleeing to outlying areas, rather than by confronting troubling issues of race, class, economic decline, and inadequate services. "Whole communities become tagged, and a kind of class warfare ensues between different segments of the metropolitan area that militates against any chance of united action, however strong the need for it." Although Bauer discerned some pro-city counterforces on the horizon, she left it an open question whether escapism or urbanity would ultimately triumph.

Urban Design and the Problems of Urban Freeways

During the late 1950s and early 1960s, architects, landscape architects, and the urban design wing of the planning profession gradually augmented their critique of conventional urban freeway building. Their concern was expressed in articles such as "Expressway Blight" (1959), which attacked the design blunders of Boston's Central Artery.[56] The author complained of "muffed opportunities for redevelopment and renewal," faulted designers for their timidity in that face of "the occult mysteries of traffic surveys and right-of-way engineering," and wondered how "this most expensive of urban expressways could have possibly been made so ugly."[57]

Moreover, by the early 1960s, it was clear that the urban freeway form concepts of the 1940s and 1950s were producing unexpected impacts on central cities. Freeway planning—far from being a technical exercise—turned out to be politically explosive, value-laden, and fraught with aesthetic dimensions. The design and engineering professions continued to spar over issues of highway location and design while projecting an image of consensus during periodic conferences on freeways in the urban setting.

Urban Design Concept Teams

Belatedly, in a few cities urban designers achieved a more prominent role in urban freeway design. The Baltimore urban design concept team of the late 1960s included engineers, architects, planners, transportation consultants, sociologists, and various other professionals and was chaired by Nathaniel Owings of the prestigious Skidmore, Owings & Merrill architecture firm. The team tackled the intractable problem of Baltimore's inner-city expressways and devised a less intrusive network than the massive tangle of roads, bridges, and interchanges proposed by the state highway department for the city's downtown and Inner Harbor.[58] The designers proposed the deletion of a large bridge across the Inner Harbor and the conversion of several through-routes to boulevard-scale spurs leading into the downtown (figure 5.2).

In Chicago, another multidisciplinary design team, also including architects from Skidmore, Owings & Merrill, produced an imaginative plan for the proposed Chicago Crosstown Expressway.[59] The original freeway plan called for an eight-lane elevated structure. In the concept team design, the eight-lane freeway was divided into two depressed, four-lane channels, approximately three blocks apart. This defined an expressway corridor, with land in the middle slated for parks, playgrounds, light industry, retail centers, and mass transit facilities. The project was never built, however, and this segment was deleted from the freeway system in 1979.

In 1968, the *Highway Research Record* published an issue devoted to "Team Concepts for Urban Highways and Urban Design."[60] Remarks made by the new Federal Highway Administrator, Lowell K. Bridwell, illustrated the shift in attitude at the federal level induced by the freeway revolts.

Highway planning, notwithstanding all of its highly diverse and complicated engineering detail, is not and cannot be a completely quantifiable process. . . . the highway facility is only one element or thread in the fabric that represents the city, neighborhood, or area concerned. I am not aware that God granted all wisdom to any particular discipline. What I am aware of is that no single professional discipline represents all of the talent and training and experience necessary for the task we now face.[61]

Bridwell tried to hew a path carefully between highway proponents and critics. Other authors were more blunt. Andrew F. Euston, director of Urban Programs for the American Institute of Architects, asserted that "Failure in basic decision-making lies at the beginning of nearly all the highway controversies."[62]

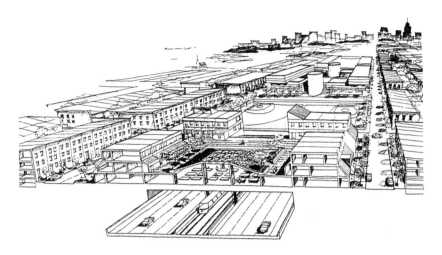

Figure 5.2
Joint-use proposal for Baltimore. *Source:* Urban Design Concept Associates, *Project Description* (Baltimore), 1969.

As a rule, in America our large-scale public construction projects have . . . been designed unresponsively. Until recently, human needs rarely have been considered. Thus, in the design of urban highways, "user needs" was merely one of those euphemistic semantic tools that clouded an issue. "Auto needs" were what was meant.[63]

Euston referred to highway and street planning as "design failure at [a] colossal scale" but offered a thread of hope by claiming that "responsive urban design methodology can be applied today." Unfortunately, "this methodology is late in coming, and it could have been encouraged considerably more than it was."

Milton Pikarsky, Commissioner of Public Works for Chicago, defended highway planners by pointing out that "in hundreds of urban areas, urban highway projects have been satisfactorily completed and are serving the public" and "when you consider the accomplishments and the magnitude of the work, you must agree that the criticisms and mistakes are almost minor in comparison."[64]

Finally, architect Archibald Rogers summed up the strategy of the urban design concept team. Rogers rejected the old style of narrow highway planning directed only at highway users, with a skewed accounting of costs and benefits. He argued that an effective urban highway planning process would have to deal with redevelopment of the entire highway corridor, involve "the broadest kind of multidisciplinary team," be conducted in a "fishbowl" of public scrutiny, and work toward a conception of the highway as "potentially a great work of civic architecture."[65]

After a long hiatus, and decades after the inception of urban freeway construction, landscape architects and architects had been called in to produce freeway designs more sensitive to their urban context. In collaboration with engineers, they produced a more elaborate catalog of design alternatives for freeways in central cities. However, these ideas arrived after the polarization of the political landscape and had only a limited impact on actual freeway construction during the 1960s. The strongest challenge to urban freeway building came through grassroots protest, which was translated into legislative restrictions and, in some cases, deletion of controversial segments.

From Panacea to Pariah?

By the late 1960s, citizen protest and political stalemate over controversial freeway segments, in conjunction with the widespread political and social upheaval of the times, forced public officials to reassess the complex social, economic, and aesthetic impacts of large-scale infrastructure projects. The eager, uncritical acceptance of urban freeways as emblems of growth, prosperity, and rising standards of living gradually began to wane. Freeway protests grew louder, and pressures for reform led to a spate of legislation curbing the freedom of highway engineers to locate and build new arterials. As a result, the regulatory environment in which the construction of urban highways began was soon to be radically transformed.

The Evolution of the Regulatory Environment

The evolution in urban highway planning concepts was both reflected in and fostered by changes in the regulatory framework within which planning decisions were made.

The Highway Act of 1962

As pressure mounted to modify the highway planning process, Congress finally passed legislation requiring the integration of highway planning with metropolitan planning. The Highway Act of 1962 required that, starting in July 1965, urban freeways be based on a comprehensive transportation planning process.[66] The final sentence in the section requiring such a planning process stated:

After July 1, 1965, the Secretary shall not approve under section 105 of this title any programs for projects in any urban area of more than fifty thousand population unless he finds that such projects are based on a continuing, comprehensive transportation planning process carried out cooperatively by states and local communities in conformance with the objectives stated in this section.[67]

The language of the act was vague, however, and its requirements could be satisfied without radically altering the existing pro-highway thrust of transportation planning. In their analysis of this period, Levin and Abend conclude that the highway community interpreted the planning requirements of 1962 act narrowly to mean status-quo-reinforcing land use/transportation modeling, rather than vigorous exploration of alternatives to extensive urban highway networks.[68]

During the 1960s, the Bureau of Public Roads (BPR) conducted an extensive program of research and technical training and assistance to expedite the new methodologies and the highway planning process. Gradually, the manner in which urban transportation planning had historically been conducted was altered. By the legislative deadline of July 1, 1965, all of the 224 then-existing urbanized areas included under the Federal-Aid Highway Act of 1962 had initiated an urban transportation planning process.[69]

During the mid-1960s, however, the critical thrust directed at urban highways continued, as freeway and urban renewal conflicts prompted planners and architects to question the state of urban design in the United States. Central city rebuilders, once clad in great expectations, now seemed to be faltering due to flawed designs and unanticipated social consequences. Catherine Bauer Wurster captured the mood of many planners and architects:

[T]here is a spreading sense of uneasiness and uncertainty. The opportunity is here, but do we really know how to build great cities? . . . Architecture as the art of giving significant three-dimensional form to cities, never more important than today, has never been given less attention.[70]

Formation of the Department of Transportation, 1966

By the mid-1960s, the impacts of a lack of coordination among the disparate entities involved in the development of the interstate system had become obvious. In 1966, Senator Warren Magnuson, at the behest of the Johnson administration, proposed the creation of a twelfth Cabinet department, to be known as the Department of Transportation (DOT). The DOT was established on October 15, 1966. Its purpose was "to bring together transportation functions and activities now carried on by some

35 existing departments and agencies." The department was to have a budget of $6.2 billion and a staff of almost 95,000 people. The intent was expressed in S. 3010, the bill endorsing its creation:

The Congress hereby declares that the general welfare, the economic growth and stability of the Nation and its security require the development and implementation of national transportation policies and programs conducive to the provision of fast, safe, efficient, and convenient transportation at the lowest cost consistent therewith and with other national objectives, including the efficient utilization and conservation of the Nation's resources. The Congress therefore finds that the establishment of a Department of Transportation is necessary in the public interest and to assure the coordinated, effective administration of the transportation programs of the Federal Government; to facilitate the development and improvement of coordinated transportation service, to be provided by private enterprise to the maximum extent feasible; to encourage co-operation of Federal, State, and local governments, carriers, labor, and other interested parties toward the achievement of national transportation objectives; to stimulate technological advances in transportation; to provide general leadership in the identification and solution of transportation problems; and to develop and recommend national transportation policies and programs to accomplish these objectives with full and appropriate consideration of the needs of the public, users, carriers, industry, labor, and the national defense.[71]

Public reaction to the proposal was widely disparate. In a statement made during the Congressional hearings, Walter G. Baskerville, Sr., president of the Upper Mississippi Towing Corp. of Minneapolis, Minnesota, expressed the following concerns:

Many factors have no doubt contributed to the development of the outstanding transportation system which our country now enjoys. It would seem to us that in the governmental sphere two of the key factors in the success formula are (1) the fact that Congress itself has carefully reviewed the economic justification of all public funding and (2) independent agencies have been permitted to function within the areas properly prescribed for the particular agency by Congress. . . . In view of its long and able performance on transportation matters, Congress should not be asked to disqualify itself in favor of a new Secretary. No evidence justifying the granting of such carte blanche authority on transportation policy has been offered. . . . We strongly urge that Congress retain its proper function of the formulation and economic evaluation of proposals for investment of public funds in the transportation field.[72]

Engineers and architects made their views heard. Charles E. Shumate, president of the American Association of State Highway Officials and chief engineer of the Colorado Department of Highways, made clear that highway development had historically been, and should continue to be, guided by highway engineers[73]:

Because of the cooperative and engineering nature of the Federal-aid highway program, the State highway departments feel strongly that the Federal Highway Administrator must always be an experienced, outstanding, recognized highway administrator-engineer, who knows the program well and who is well known to, and respected by, the State highway departments. Much of the past and present success of the program is definitely attributable to the fact that such persons have always been named to the top Bureau of Public Roads position. . . . We prefer not to leave such matters entirely to experts in other transportation forms and to academic transportation economists. Highway transportation daily affects the travel and way of life of practically every person in this country, and will continue to do so, so long as the freedom of choice is not infringed and highway transportation is not subordinated by some revolutionary effort to artificially fertilize some other transportation mode.

Morris Ketchum, Jr. FAIA, President of the American Association of Architects, was concerned that the proposed Department of Transportation would usurp the responsibilities of the Department of Housing and Urban Development in designing and creating urban highways:

We view an efficient and economical transportation system as an asset to national growth. We are familiar with the formidable problems which occur in our metropolitan areas because of poorly planned transportation programs when formulating a master plan for a metropolitan area. . . . We believe urban transportation decisions fall within the purview of the Department of Housing and Urban Development since, in President Johnson's words, it "bears the principal responsibility for a unified Federal approach to urban problems." We recognize, however, that the proposed Department of Transportation will have concomitant responsibilities for coordinating transportation programs and policies. . . . It would be unfortunate to curtail the Department of Housing and Urban Development in this one area of urban planning before it has had an opportunity to demonstrate its utility.[74]

The potential for strife between the two departments had been anticipated by President Johnson. In his transportation message, the president declared that the future of urban transportation depended upon wide-scale, rational planning requiring the cooperative efforts of the secretary of Housing and Urban Development and the secretary of the new Department of Transportation. President Johnson stated: "I shall ask the two Secretaries to recommend to me, within a year after the creation of the new Department, the means and procedures by which this cooperation can best be achieved—not only in principle but in practical effect."[75]

Section 4(f) of the Department of Transportation Act of 1966 declared a national policy that special effort should be made to preserve the environment. Section 4(f) covered land consisting, in part, of publicly owned parks, recreational areas, wildlife and waterfowl refuges, and all historic sites:

It is hereby declared to be the national policy that special effort should be made to preserve the natural beauty of the countryside and public parks and recreation lands, wildlife and waterfowl refuges, and historic sites. The Secretary of Transportation shall cooperate and consult with the Secretaries of the Interior, Housing and Urban Development, and Agriculture, and with the states in developing transportation plans and programs that include measures to maintain or enhance the natural beauty of the lands traversed. After August 23, 1968, the Secretary shall not approve any program or project which requires the use of any publicly owned land from a public park, recreation area, or wildlife and waterfowl refuge of national, state or local significance as so determined by such official unless (1) there is no feasible and prudent alternative to the use of such land, and (2) such program includes all possible planning to minimize harm to such park, recreational area, wildlife and waterfowl refuge, or historic site resulting from such use.

The 1967 U.S. Senate Hearings on Urban Freeways

In 1967, the U.S. Senate conducted hearings on urban highways, and these sessions provide a useful perspective on freeway debates during this transitional period of the great freeway building era. Representatives from each of the professions involved in urban freeway planning stepped forth to duel over the proper strategy for freeway location and design.

The 1967 hearings solicited information from five groups of people: (1) general urban experts; (2) professionals and specialists in particular aspects of urban life; (3) political leaders at the local level; (4) state, regional, county, and city level officials responsible for planning and building urban highways; and (5) federal officials responsible for urban affairs.[76]

William Slayton, the executive vice president of Urban America, opened the hearings with a critique of existing highway planning practice.[77]

The cost accounting applied to urban highways until now has been deficient in that the ledger shows the costs of the program only in terms of land acquisition, design, and construction. It does not show such real and tangible costs as the additional street and storage capacity required at the point of egress; the taking of land from the tax rolls; the dislocation of the people in the highway's path; the reduction in value of adjacent property; the division and disruption of neighborhoods stemming from insensitive location; and the visual blight resulting from insensitive design.[78]

Slayton pinpointed the unfortunate consequence of this skewed cost accounting. Whenever more expensive, environmentally sensitive freeway proposals were put on the table, the costs were seen as "a painful extra" rather than as an integral, justifiable expense of building freeways in urban areas. Hence, much of the excellent work done by engineers, planners, and urban designers to make freeways more compatible with cities often went unused due to lack of funds. Slayton also noted that it was "rather late in the game" for multidisciplinary concept teams to be assembled. He found it "incredible that the Baltimore effort is regarded as bold and experimental."[79] Slayton carefully qualified his critique by saying that he was not accusing highway planners of insensitivity or of being unaware of externalities. He acknowledged a "steady broadening of outlook, particularly in the leadership of the Bureau of Public Roads."[80] However, Slayton clearly arrayed before the senators a disturbing list of flaws in the highway planning process.

Robert Durham, the president of the American Institute of Architects, expanded the critique. Durham lamented the lack of solid knowledge about urban problems: "Our social and physical environment is poorly understood compared to other fields of inquiry. Unfortunately, we seem to know more about the moon than we do some of the things affecting the city."[81] In the absence of a clear urban policy, single-purpose planning projects continued to shape the city in thoughtless ways. "In city after city, a review of the corridor and the route selection design procedures reveals a somewhat threadworn catalog of statutory criteria."[82] Durham noted the absence of architects and landscape architects in the early location and design phases of highway planning:

I have actually seen a State highway department call in an architect as an architectural consultant one day a month and the architect is sent down to the State capital and is faced by 300 engineers and the architect goes from table to table making little blue marks on final drawings. . . . Under such circumstances, he is not really a consultant. He is adding little bits of cosmetics to a system which is so massive and so detailed and so technical that he is not really being given the place he should on a team.[83]

John Fisher-Smith, chairman-elect of the Committee on Urban Design of the American Institute of Architects, reinforced Durham's accusation that the designers had been shunted to the periphery of the highway planning process.

There is a tendency to fluff over the architect, the planner, as being aesthetes, whereas once you as a decisionmaker have made the decisions about the location, the use, the budget, and all these other public program decisions, you have really finished the major design elements of the project.[84]

Thus, in 1967, professional conflict between architects and engineers had not abated. More than a few architects resented their marginalization as decorators or salvage crews for freeways designed earlier without their participation.

Architect Norman Klein of Skidmore, Owings & Merrill, a participant in the Baltimore urban design concept team, presented an outline
of that project to the committee. Senator Len Jordan asked Klein why it
had taken 10 years to recognize the need for such teams to design urban
highways. Klein responded by citing a "cultural lag" or "sluggishness"
within government in responding to new circumstances. Only within the
past few years had engineers, city planners, and architects developed the
ability to talk constructively with one another about freeway issues. Also,
"the government is beginning to become more responsive to the outcry"
from cities affected by freeways.[85]

The most biting criticism of highway planning came from Ian McHarg,
then chairman of the Department of Landscape Architecture and Regional Planning at the University of Pennsylvania and partner in the consulting firm of Wallace, McHarg, Roberts & Todd. McHarg submitted a copy
of "A Comprehensive Highway Route Selection Method Applied to I-95
between the Delaware and Raritan Rivers, New Jersey," illustrating his
overlay method and ecological criteria for highway location. McHarg declared that "when one thinks about social costs it is clear that, by and
large, highways have been among the most blatant destroyers of the
American environment, both natural and social values." He then attacked
the intellectual narrowness of engineers:

I think plumbers are marvelous men, and our society could not endure without them, and highway engineers are very decent people too, just so long as it
is understood that highway engineers can only treat a highway as it deals with
inanimate things, with projectiles, and we limit their competence to pavements,
bridges, and geometrical alinement, [sic] but add a leavening of those people who
understand something about the nature of man and something about the nature
of biophysical processes. . . . Sir, I think plumbers are absolutely admirable, but we
don't ask them to design cities. I think the problem about highways is we permit
engineers to have a profound effect upon cities and, in effect, to design them.[86]

Carl Feiss—who had argued for a moratorium on urban freeway
building 10 years earlier so that adequate city plans could be prepared—
suggested that many freeway conflicts could have been averted through
careful multidisciplinary planning, although it was probably too late for
consensus solutions where freeway controversies had become too vitriol-
ic.[87] Feiss viewed the conventional public hearing process as inadequate;
it was often a mere "gesture" rather than a serious probing of impacts and
public attitudes. He also questioned how much real choice cities had in
dealing with proposed highways, when the "fragrant carrot" of 90 percent federal funding made highway construction fiscally irresistible.[88]

Edward J. Donnelly, representing the engineering profession, heartily endorsed the idea of multidisciplinary design teams and emphasized that lack of funding, not professional narrowness, was the real culprit with urban freeway difficulties.

Urban highway planning and design obviously are primarily engineering functions; but, just as obviously, the day is past when urban highways can be planned within narrow bounds. Highway planning for our cities of today and tomorrow, to be effective, must consider a wide range of urban problems and must take into account a wide range of factors related to the urban environment. . . . The engineering profession is firmly committed to the principle of the "interdisciplinary team" approach to the solution of urban problems. We believe that the complexity and magnitude of the problems of our cities make it essential that the various professions and disciplines collaborate to the fullest extent possible in seeking solutions to those problems. . . . To this end, four of the national engineering societies represented here today, the National Society of Professional Engineers the American Institute of Consulting Engineers, the American Society of Civil Engineers and the Consulting Engineers Council, together with the American Institute of Architects, the American Institute of Planners, and the American Society of Landscape Architects recently have developed and adopted a 'Guide to Professional Collaboration in Environmental Design' for use by the members of the participating professional societies. The guide emphasizes the desirability and need for collaboration among all environmental design professionals, and sets forth guidelines and tenets aimed at promoting and facilitating cooperation and teamwork among professionals who deal with research, planning, design, and construction of man's living environment. . . . In the overwhelming number of cases, a miles-per-dollar yardstick has been imposed on highway planning and design, and money simply has not been provided to meet advancing environmental standards and requirements.[89]

Rex M. Whitton endorsed design concept teams but argued that highway engineers had a successful track record and should remain the lead actors. In his view, the mistakes made by the highway community were "minor" in comparison with the magnitude of their achievement.[90]

The representatives from AASHO, John O. Morton, J. Burch McMorran, and A. E. Johnson, defended the highway builders' record, insisting that "the State highway departments had been doing much cooperative planning before it was an official requirement. This planning had been in the form of contacts with all affected public officials, planners, professional staff, and combined with the public hearing process."[91] Although outwardly welcoming the interdisciplinary design approach, Morton questioned both the motives and the competence of non-engineers who had criticized the highway planning process.

Very early in the program we realized that there would be problems arising from our mistakes, but it also became very apparent that we now had many people wanting to get into the act now that the program was so big, so important, and glamorous, and involved so much money. It was definitely attracting disciplines and professions that had taken little or no interest in highways previously. We began to hear immediately from many instant and self-proclaimed experts, where they had not been in evidence before. There were a few people in each of these groups who did have some background and experience, and contributed constructively, but they were extremely limited in numbers.[92]

Morton claimed that the vast majority of people were satisfied with the existing highway planning system; it was only when you tried to placate the last 2 percent of the population—"the so-called artistic and creative people"—that controversies got out of control.[93] He also painted an unflattering portrait of city planning as a profession with no agreed-upon standards, subject to personal "opinion or preference" rather than factual analysis. He requested the senators to refrain from modifying the highway program just because there had been trouble in a few controversial locations that were "special cases."[94]

Anthony Downs of the Real Estate Research Corporation offered some important testimony on the social and economic impacts of the new freeway systems. In his opinion, radial freeways bestowed the greatest benefits on the suburbs and the CBD, "thereby causing a relative decline in the desirability of older in-city neighborhoods which lie between downtown and the suburbs."[95] Downs also argued that "the construction of radial expressways linking downtown with suburban areas has tended to increase the degree of racial segregation in our larger metropolitan areas," although he attributed no racist motives to the highway planning authorities. There were three dimensions to the race issue: (1) highways made suburbanization possible, and the new suburbs were usually segregated by race; (2) highway construction displaced disproportionate numbers of blacks in the central city; and (3) a disproportionate share of nonconstruction costs of highways (blighting effects, noise, pollution, visual intrusion, community disruption) had been imposed on low-income blacks in the central city.[96] Downs believed that "both Congress and the agencies concerned have . . . been relatively insensitive to some of the socially disruptive or undesirable effects of these roads upon the lower income groups in our metropolitan areas, particularly in the central cities."[97]

Using the 1967 Urban Highway Hearings as a barometer of professional attitudes, it is clear that deep rifts still separated designers, planners, and urbanists from the highway planning community. These divisions, rooted in conflicting professional agendas and views of the city, persisted because they emerged not from isolated skirmishes over particular projects but from deep-seated conflicts over resources, status, and power to shape the built environment.[98]

Catalysts of Change, and Legal Legs on Which to Stand

It was not only among the professionals and public policy officials that an evolving understanding of the limits of the model approach to thinking about urban highways was appreciated. The general public, in small sectors and numbers, was beginning to see freeways in urban areas in ways much different from the Futurama vision.

By 1967, the *New York Times* could summarize (in an article "White Roads Through Black Bedrooms"), "No longer is it sufficient for a highway to carry vehicles efficiently and speedily from Point A to Point B. Now, it is felt, a highway should melt esthetically into a neighborhood. It should contribute to development of the neighborhood's economic and social life. It should disrupt and uproot minimally. . . . Plans that do not include sociological, economic and esthetic considerations simply will not be approved by Washington."[99]

The National Historic Preservation Act
The bill that would eventually be passed as the National Historic Preservation Act was introduced in two versions—as S. 3035 and S. 3039. At a 1966 hearing on the relative merits of each bill Senator Edmund Muskie stated:

My concern today is that the program for national preservation be strengthened and accelerated as rapidly as possible. Time is against us. In too many cases we will be too late. Nearly half the 12,000 structures listed in the Historic American Buildings survey already have been destroyed. . . . Historic preservation can be achieved without blunting progress. In truth, historic preservation will enrich our progress. . . . In a changing, growing society, our landmarks take on increasing importance. They add stability to our lives. They are a point of orientation. They establish values of time and place and belonging. They are a humanizing influence.[100]

At the hearing, written comments were received from Morris Ketchum, Jr., president of the American Institute of Architects (AIA). Mr. Ketchum commented that the AIA's involvement in the efforts to preserve historically significant buildings began at the 1890 AIA convention, whereupon the institute called for the formation of a Committee on Historic Buildings to preserve historic structures—particularly architecturally significant structures—across the nation. He added that the institute, working with the Library of Congress and the National Park Service, organized the Historic American Building Survey in 1933 and formed the National Trust for Historic Buildings in 1949 to assist in the preservation of sites, buildings, and objects of historical or cultural significance.[101]

However, Mr. Ketchum added, "the current preservation effort is not sufficient to stop the tide of destruction. Senator Muskie noted as he introduced S. 3098 that so many historically significant structures had already been destroyed that in another five years there might be no need for this legislation. We support S. 3098 in every respect. . . . S. 3098 is exceedingly timely legislation. It establishes a program this country has needed for years."[102]

Another respondent, George B. Hartzog, Jr., director of the National Park Service, commented:

Historic Preservation is the goal of citizen groups in every part of the country. . . . This Historic Sites Act of August 21, 1935 enacted a national policy to preserve historic sites, buildings, and objects of national significance for the inspiration and benefit of the people of the United States. Much has been accomplished under this Act. Sites and objects have been preserved in Federal and non-Federal ownership. The National Survey of Historic Sites and Buildings has been undertaken, as has the Historic American Buildings Survey. . . . Much remains to be done in order to safeguard our country's heritage. . . . The time has come to renew and strengthen our efforts for historic preservation by involving more creatively all levels of government with the efforts of private organizations and individuals.[103]

With the passage of the National Historic Preservation Act of 1966, the National Register of Historic Places (NRHP) was created. Under the act, strict regulations were placed on construction projects that had the potential to impact historical, cultural, or archeological resources. Although the act did not forbid construction on these sites entirely, it did, at times, provide an additional means by which those who opposed a particular highway project could protest its construction. In chapter 6, we will see that roadway projects in the cities of Baltimore and New Orleans were, in fact, stopped by protestors using, among other tools, this legislative safeguard.

The Federal-Aid Highway Act of 1968

In 1968, 2 years after the passage of the Department of Transportation Act of 1966, the Federal-Aid Highway Act of 1968 declared anew a national policy of preservation of natural beauty of the countryside and public park and recreation lands, wildlife and waterfowl refuges, and historic sites. The statute, which increased the mileage of the interstate system from 41,000 to 42,500 miles and extended the completion date to 1974, established a highway relocation assistance program. This was to provide payments to property owners forced to move because of highway building.

Fostering Early Citizen Involvement

By 1969, it had become clear that citizen participation in the highway planning process was ineffective because any significant citizen involvement occurred too late in the process, at a point in time when the proposed highway had already been designed. In early 1969, the Federal Highway Administration revised its policies and procedures to establish a two-hearing process for highway projects, thereby replacing the single hearing. The first hearing was mandated to be held prior to any decision on route placement, in order to allow citizens the opportunity to question or comment on the need for, and location of, the proposed project. The second public hearing focused on the specific design features and location of the proposed roadway. When, in late 1969, it was determined that even a two-hearing process was insufficient, the planning process was further amended to require citizen participation in all phases. As a consequence, highway planning agencies became responsible for obtaining public comments and perspectives.[104]

The 1970 National Environmental Policy Act and Its State Versions

The National Environmental Policy Act (NEPA; 42 USC 1970) was passed in 1969 and became law in 1970. NEPA set a national policy of protection of environmental resources. Not fully understood at the time of its enactment, it was to cause an unparalleled change in decision making in the federal government. It required that agencies use a systematic interdisciplinary approach to environmental planning and evaluation in decision making that might have an impact on the environment. For major federal actions significantly affecting the quality of the human environment, an Environmental Impact Statement (EIS) was mandated.

State versions of NEPA followed, including two statutes that played important roles in two of the three case studies presented in this volume. California's Environmental Quality Act (CEQA) became law in 1970, and the New York State Environmental Conservation Law (SEQRA) was passed in 1975. Although the state of Tennessee did not enact a "wide-ranging" environmental statute similar to NEPA, the state did enact the Tennessee Water Quality Control Act in 1971. This statute, along with its 1977 amendments, has acted to regulate rural and urban highway planning in Tennessee since its enactment.[105] Both sets of laws, federal and state, covered highway agencies.

The Federal-Aid Highway Acts of 1970 and 1973, and the Uniform Relocation and Real Property Aquisition Policies Act

In 1970, when Massachusetts announced a halt on construction of principal unbuilt expressways, Governor Sargent of Massachusetts said: "I have decided to reverse the transportation policy of the Commonwealth of Massachusetts. The decision has immediate effect on the metropolitan Boston area, long-range effect on the state as a whole, and, it is my hope, major effect on the entire nation."[106] He went on to offer a plan of an appeal to Congress and a proposal for a state amendment to allow broader use of highway funds according to the Federal-Aid Highway Act of 1970.

The Federal-Aid Highway Act of 1970 authorized states to use urban area highway funds for traffic-reduction projects and addressed the need to promote air quality. In 1970, the Uniform Relocation and Real Property Acquisition Policies Act (23 USC 1970) was passed. It required the states to ensure "fair and reasonable" relocation payments, to operate a relocation assistance program, and to ensure that adequate relocation housing is available. Many other laws and regulations in the 1970s were addressed to transportation planning and highway agencies.

The Federal-Aid Highway Act of 1973 renewed the 1970 act, authorized more than $18 billion, and allowed for the substitution of transit projects for withdrawn interstate portions such as Boston's Southwest Expressway.

The Clean Air Act

The Clean Air Act was amended in 1970, at which time it became a truly regulatory statute as contrasted with its earlier functions of study and planning. It required each Air Quality Management District to develop plans (State Implementation Plans) to meet national standards (National Ambient Air Quality Standards) for criterion pollutants. These pollutants could be implicated in highway construction and use, but the Clean Air Act did not directly regulate highway construction. It did, however, provide for citizen suits that could be targeted toward highway construction and siting.

The Balance of Power Shifts

Environmental legislation in the late 1960s and early 1970s armed citizens and local governments with legal tools to challenge unpopular freeway segments.[107] Freeways that were captured in this newly constructed regulatory net underwent much more scrutiny than earlier freeways. The environmental legislation of the late 1960s and early 1970s did have teeth, and by providing a basis for litigation by freeway opponents, it changed the balance of power in urban freeway controversies.[108]

Thus, by the mid-1970s, construction of urban freeways faced a very different legal context than it had a couple of decades earlier. Public outrage and legally fostered public participation had rendered the freeway construction arena far more sophisticated and contentious.

The hearings held to ensure funding for the completion of the interstate highway system through Washington, D.C., serve to illustrate this point.[109]

Approximately eighty witnesses were scheduled to be heard during 3 days of congressional hearings on H.R. 16000, which authorized completion of the interstate system within the District of Columbia. Mr. Charles Cassel, an architect and a member of the Black United Front, spoke on behalf of a committee formed "to coordinate the actions of member associations which oppose any further planning or construction of freeways in the Metropolitan Washington area." Mr. Cassel stated that citizens in the district were "completely aware that no solution to this crisis is valid which accepts the premise that the automobile is a fixed factor around which all plans must center," and that "all serious and objective studies have proven what every other major city in the world discovered scores of years ago . . . that it is sensible and sane to move large numbers of employees from radially located points of residence to a limited size central employment area through rapid, mass rail transit, located essentially beneath the busy and already congested service area where people live, work, shop, and recreate." Mr. Cassel went on to describe the "vested interests" behind freeway construction as "the road gang . . . who insist on creating more massive concrete canyons containing accelerated treadmills for rapidly dumping pollution-generating vehicles into a downtown area, which is already hopelessly congested during rush hours and whose vehicle handling capacity cannot be improved."[110]

Reginald Booker, chairman of the Emergency Committee on the Transportation Crisis, made his organization's position very clear: "We say no more white man's roads through black bedrooms. This is the resounding battle cry of those people who I should say are poor black people and white people, black mostly who are fighting against the freeway bulldozer." Mr. Booker called the entire freeway construction program "a case of racism, whether this is by accident or by design." Mr. Booker stated that Department of Transportation Secretary Alan Boyd had referred to the freeway in Washington, D.C., as "a classic example of racism." Mr. Booker continued: "Surely those vested interests, those groups in Washington, D.C., as they are effectively called the road gang, the cement manufacturers, the tire manufacturers, surely those people who advocate freeways and people who sit in Congress who advocate freeways are sowing the seeds of racial disorder in a garden of racism and they are surely to reap a harvest of rebellion here in Washington, D.C."[111]

Highway construction now faced a more sophisticated legal context than it had a couple of decades earlier. Citizens could more easily get to court for review of decisions of highway agencies; environmental impact assessment was standard; relocation assistance was required; and decision making on roads and highways and freeways was no longer exclusively the province of highway agencies. There had been a sea change in public policy since the birth of the freeway.

Conclusion: Changing . . .

In this chapter, we have described critically influential changes in the environment for freeway planning and implementation that occurred in the postwar period.

The nation's thoughts about ambitious freeway programs began in the early 1900s (table 5.1), but it was not until the actions of the Franklin D. Roosevelt administration that the notion of building a major infrastructure system of roads moved toward reality. The Federal-Aid Highway Act of 1944 established the national system of interstate highways and highlighted its function in serving the nation's defense. At that time funding was to be provided; however, it would be more than a decade before federal monies would actually arrive. In the meantime, support for construction of urban freeways had to come from local interests.

By the mid-1950s, some criticism of urban freeway building was identifiable, but concerns were expressed late in actual cases and usually could not decrease the momentum of engineers and highways officials—envisioned in and programmed by their Red and Yellow Books on implementing a national freeway system. What's more, there continued to be a limited inventory of ideas regarding what to do about freeways in cities. For the most part, the task of moving cars through the urban core was seen as an engineering job. The gulf between engineers and other urban professionals remained fairly wide, despite a number of meetings where professionals came together to address the larger questions of the function of roads in cities.

Table 5.1
Timeline of Major Urban Freeway Decision-Making Events

1916
• Congress approves the first in a series of programs of continuing federal aid for highway construction.

1921
• The Federal Highway Act of 1921 is passed. Preference is to be given to construction of a connected, interstate highway system. States are called upon to designate primary and secondary highways for federal aid purposes.

1929
• Despite the growing number of automobiles and increasing traffic congestion, the Great Depression curtails funding for previously planned highway improvements throughout the nation.

1930s
• Robert Moses maps out an elaborate system of parkways, boulevards, and bridges for the New York region.
• Moses' Henry Hudson Parkway is completed.
• Roosevelt's federally funded public works program, the New Deal, offers the first opportunities for significant urban freeway construction.
• Highway engineers make initial forays into the realm of urban freeway planning.
• Karl Lohmann's *Principles of City Planning* endorses a "spider web" pattern of arterials, which dominates the era's planning discourse.
• Planners begin to search for answers to emerging conflicts between freeway and city.
• *Report on a Thoroughfare Plan for Boston* portrays a system of roughly radial express roads with a "Central Artery" cutting through the city's historic heart.

1934
• The Hayden–Cartwright legislation includes urban portions of state highway systems in the federal-aid network.

1935
• Le Corbusier's *The Radiant City* envisions abolition of large expanses of existing urban centers and erection of new megastructures above or through them.
• Frank Lloyd Wright's *Broadacre City* proposes replacement of overcrowded cities with an open landscape of homes dispersed throughout a rural freeway grid.

1937
• The Automobile Club of Southern California publishes its *Traffic Survey*, proposing a regional grid of expressways and a joint-use scheme in which motorways in the city are seen as elements of urban architecture.

1938
• The Federal-Aid Highway Act of 1938 authorizes the Bureau of Public Roads (BPR) to conduct feasibility studies for construction of a system of six transcontinental highways.

Table 5.1 (continued)

1939

• BPR's report, *Toll Roads and Free Roads*, is published, advocating a system of toll-free highways. This marks a decisive turn toward planning for urban freeways.

• The 1939 New York World's Fair is held. Norman Bel Geddes' influential Futurama exhibit, viewed by 10 million people, promotes freeways as the solution to urban transportation woes.

• California legislation gives cities the right to veto freeway extensions.[112]

• Urban professionals of the late 1930s and early 1940s portray a rational, modernized city as inevitable and portray old city sections as disordered and decayed.

1940s–1950s

• Freeway planning concepts of the 1930s and early 1940s are elaborated, expanded, and applied to certain cities. State highway engineers and the BPR assume control of freeway planning and construction in urban areas.

• Bel Geddes' book *Magic Motorways* is published. It portrays old cities as being in hopeless conflict with motor travel and advocates construction of transcontinental freeways off to the sides of existing major cities, with feeder highways as connecting elements.

1941

• FDR appoints a National Interregional Highway Committee (NIHC) to assess the need for a national system of expressways.

• Moses' Gowanus Parkway along the southern waterfront of Brooklyn is completed.

1943

• The joint HRB–AASHO Committee on Roadside Development introduces the concept of the "complete highway," which they define as combining utility, safety, beauty, and economy. Highway engineers fear a drain of resources from their primary task of laying pavement; however, landscape design does eventually become institutionalized in the highway planning process.

1944

• The NIHC's report, *Interregional Highways*, is published. It advocates construction of 33,900 miles of rural roadways and 5,000 miles of auxiliary urban roadways and codifies basic planning doctrines for postwar urban freeways.

• With passage of the Federal-Aid Highway Act of 1944, Congress creates the National System of Interstate Highways and solidifies intellectual and legal foundations for postwar urban interstates. Its ABC program provides 50 percent of construction costs for primary, secondary, and urban highways.

1944–1945

• State highway agencies work to prepare comprehensive highway plans for urban areas showing locations of proposed interstates.

• New York's Urban Arterial Laws of 1944 and 1945 authorize the state to prepare an urban highway program with the state responsible for creation of a master highway plan for each city in New York with a population of more than five thousand.[113]

Table 5.1 (continued)

- The AASHO submits interstate design standards to the BPR.

1946–1956
- Seminal ideas codified in *Toll Roads and Free Roads* and in *Interregional Highways* are elaborated, refined, and expanded. Initial planning on the interstate system begins, with state highway departments taking the lead, marginalizing local planners and public works officials, and emphasizing traffic-carrying efficiency. Planners and design professionals, as outsiders, speculate about long-term effects of urban freeways on city planning goals.
- California takes the lead in urban freeway planning. Engineers and public officials increasingly look to Southern California for freeway models.

1946
- The Vieux Carré (New Orleans) elevated riverfront expressway concept is prepared.
- Robert Moses submits *Selected Measures for the Partial Relief of Traffic Congestion in New York City* to the New York City Planning Commission. His work portrays elevated freeways as architectural assets as opposed to negative structures for the surrounding neighborhoods.

1947
- The BPR and state highway departments determine tentative routes for the interstate system and publish an official map of the system: 37,000 miles of the planned 40,000 were agreed upon; approximately 2,900 miles are located in urban areas.
- Syracuse city arterials, including a central loop around the downtown business district, are envisioned and a funding source identified.
- In "The Case for Urban Expressways," BPR Commissioner Thomas H. MacDonald refutes common arguments against urban expressways and advocates for replacement housing prior to razing of existing housing.
- The American Institute of Planners and the American Transit Association jointly produce *Urban Freeways*, which sets forth proposals for combining rail and bus transit with the urban freeway system.
- Joseph Barnett, chief of the Urban Road Division of the BPR, writes "Express Highway Planning in Metropolitan Areas" (1946–1947); he maintains that only "generous provision of free-flowing facilities" could solve urban congestion problems.
- George H. Herrold, planning engineer for the city of St. Paul, argues that, "except where strategically located," urban freeways negatively impact urban living. He argues for pedestrianized downtowns, but his arguments receive little support from engineers, planners, or politicians at the time.

1948
- The second edition of *Local Planning Administration* is published. This edition adds nothing new to the discussion of urban freeway systems that was presented in the 1941 edition.

Table 5.1 (continued)

1949

• The Housing Act of 1949 sets up a separate bureaucracy for urban development, precluding close integration of highway development and urban redevelopment at the federal level.

• S. E. Sanders and A. J. Rabuck publish *New City Patterns*, advocating radical reconstruction of the city along the lines of Le Corbusier and rejecting traditional city form in favor of "cells," each devoted to a particular land use.

Early 1950s

• Research on the relationship between land use and transportation begins to flourish with the realization among engineers and planners that knowledge about the traffic-generating potential of future land uses is essential for freeway planning.

• Architect Victor Gruen devises a plan for Fort Worth that includes a pedestrianized downtown within a freeway loop accompanied by parking garages. Although not implemented, his plan serves as an influential example of blending core pedestrianization with an extensive freeway network.

1951

• Christopher Tunnard, director of the Graduate Program in City Planning at Yale, appeals for a resurgence of urban design within city planning. He specifically denotes urban freeways as exhibiting a dearth of aesthetic sensibility in urban public works construction.

1952

• *The Heart of the City*, a collection of essays by architects on the future of the urban core, is published. Many authors suggest that only a radical separation of city functions would resolve conflict between core cities and freeways. Other authors suggest elimination of traditional corridor streets to create pedestrianized cores.

1954

• The Housing Act of 1954 passes, catalyzing programs for urban renewal that feature replacement of decayed slum areas with new-built environments for an expanding service economy and for middle-class citizens returning to cities. Transportation improvements are seen as a critical element of central city renaissance.

1955

• State highway departments and the Bureau of Public Roads define the remainder of the interstate routes (urban mileage designated but not mapped in 1947) in *General Location of National System of Interstate Highways*, known as the "Yellow Book."

• June issue of *Architectural Forum* publishes a roundtable discussion among leading architects and city experts on "How to Rebuild Cities Downtown," which suggests that intelligent design could save downtowns and offers eighteen principles to be implemented.

Table 5.1 (continued)

• Residents in the path of the Western Freeway in San Francisco organize to fight the proposed route.

Mid-1950s
• 6,500 miles of 40,000 planned interstate miles completed at a cost of $1 billion.

1956–1970
• Urban freeway form concepts developed during the previous three decades become blueprints for construction. State engineers and local growth coalitions push radials and beltways through old neighborhoods and industrial districts.

• Under pressure from opponents, engineers and planners develop more sophisticated approaches to construction of freeways in built-up areas. As deficiencies in planning and design become apparent, a learning process is initiated.

• Various universities (the University of Illinois and the Massachusetts Institute of Technology) initiate research efforts into ways to improve aesthetic/perceptual experiences through highway design.

1956
• The Interstate and Defense Highway Act of 1956 passes, creating the Highway Trust Fund and providing 90 percent federal funding for the interstate system. With concerns about expense minimized, design for high volumes and high speeds replaces the aesthetic concerns of the earlier parkway tradition.

• The *Detroit Metropolitan Area Traffic Study*, the first systematic modeling of the relationship between land use and transportation, is completed.

• BPR approves I-40 alignment through Overton Park in Memphis.

Late 1950s to Early 1960s
• Architects, landscape architects, and urban design planners augment critiques of conventional urban freeway building.

1957
• AASHO issues a new codification of standards for interstates and other urban freeways in *A Policy on Arterial Highways in Urban Areas*, known as the "Red Book." The Red Book defined freeway building as an engineering job, legitimized principles of urban freeway planning from the 1920s and earlier, limited options for locating freeways in central cities, and placed no emphasis on city planning, urban design, or social concerns.

• Federal legislation allows circumferential routes to be included as mileage of urban interstates.

• The Hartford Conference on "The New Highways: Challenge to the Metropolitan Regions" is held and reveals widespread concerns about potential impacts of the interstate program on cities.

• The Urban Research Committee of the Highway Research Board is formed to explore highway impacts on cities.

• Carl Feiss, architect and urban planner, argues for a moratorium on urban freeway construction until adequate city plans can be prepared.

Table 5.1 (continued)

1958
• The Sagamore Conference, the First National Conference on Highways and Urban Development, is held. Fifty-five top highway officials, mayors, public works directors, city planners, traffic engineers, and business and civic leaders discuss the urban highway program.
• "A Theory of Urban Form," by Kevin Lynch and Lloyd Rodwin, assesses existing urban form theory and proposes a framework for future research into the interrelationships between urban forms and human objectives.
• Lewis Mumford, long-time critic of conventional city planning doctrines and 1950s-era urban freeway programs, denounces the interstate system as an "ill-conceived and preposterously unbalanced program."

1959
• President Eisenhower's concerns about the interstate program lead him to request a review of the urban program by General Bragdon, whose recommendations would have eliminated 1,700 miles of urban freeways. However, they were not implemented and resulted in no changes to the interstate program.
• The San Francisco Board of Supervisors adopts a resolution opposing all freeways proposed in the San Francisco Master Plan.
• The *Chicago Area Transportation Study* augments the methodology pioneered in the earlier *Detroit Metropolitan Area Traffic Study* in which rapidly evolving advancements in computer technology were to enhance transportation data gathering and analysis and enable better demand assessments. However, these advances were not matched by equivalent advancements for assessment of freeway impacts on urban activities and did not challenge underlying assumptions of previously chosen transportation systems.
• Edgar M. Horwood and Ronald R. Boyce publish *Studies of the Central Business District and Urban Freeway Development*. They conclude that freeway impacts on the CBD are too entangled with numerous other variables to allow effective analysis.

Early 1960s
• Freeway protests begin in numerous cities, including Philadelphia, New York, Indianapolis, Cleveland, San Antonio, and Washington, D.C., among others. The revolts spawn a popular literature of protest, which begins to change formerly positive perspectives on highway building.
• Kevin Lynch's *Image of the City* lays the foundations for a more systematic approach to urban design based on cognitive maps of city residents. Although widely accepted among planners and designers, it did not redirect ongoing freeway and urban renewal projects.
• Landscape architect Lawrence Halprin argues that design skills must be incorporated into technical engineering standards for freeway construction and that freeways must be reconceptualized as "a new form of sculpture in motion."

Table 5.1 (continued)

1961

- Jane Jacobs publishes *The Death and Life of Great American Cities*, prompting reconsideration of zoning, land-use planning, and Modernist urbanism by some architects, landscape architects, and city planners. In her work, urban freeways are identified as a key city-wrecking force. However, economic and political forces promoting urban freeways remain strong; most highway builders, traffic engineers, and city planners fail to heed her critique.

- In "Architecture and the Cityscape: Notes on the Primitive State of Urban Design in America," (*AIA Journal* 35, no. 3, March 1961), Catherine Bauer Wurster describes a "spreading sense of uneasiness and uncertainty" related to city building among planners and architects.

- In "The Architect and the Planner" (*AIA Journal* 35, no. 3, March 1961), Charles Blessing blames urban problems on a failure to create an "effective joint working relationship" among professional groups involved in city building.

- Interstate 81 officially opens between Watertown and Syracuse.

1962

- The Highway Act of 1962 passes, requiring integration of highway planning and metropolitan planning. The act's vague language allowed for status-quo-reinforcing land use/transportation modeling for urban highway networks and did not force vigorous exploration of alternatives.

- The Hershey Conference is held. Highway engineers, planners, and designers meet in an attempt to reconcile conflicts, but little or no substantive progress is made.

- Kevin Lynch and Donald Appleyard publish *The View from the Road*, which argues that freeways should create stimulating experiences for drivers. Their work does not address the inherent conflict between enhancement of drivers' experiences and maintenance of livability for residents.

- Christopher Alexander and Marvin Manheim pioneer graphic techniques for mapping and overlaying highway design requirements to create optimum highway locations. Designed for use in rural and suburban areas, their method's impact on urban freeway planning was limited.

- An amendment to the Federal-Aid Highway Act requires the federal government to give "due consideration" to the "probable effect" of highway projects on urban areas.

- Opposition to Baltimore freeways is expressed in a major public hearing.

- Landscape architect Lawrence Halprin is asked by California state officials to produce an array of alternatives for the Panhandle Freeway, indicating a shift toward an urban design perspective.

1965

- At the Williamsburg Conference, engineers, architects, planners, and political officials meet again to discuss the impacts of highways on the urban environment.

Table 5.1 (continued)

"The Williamsburg Resolves," general principles of urban freeway design, result. The participants agree upon a greater emphasis on urban design and upon increased dissemination of information to the public.
• The federal Civil Rights Act passes.

1966
• Formation of the Department of Transportation: Section 4(f) of the Department of Transportation Act of 1966 declares a national policy that special effort should be made to preserve the environment.
• The Freedom of Information Act passes.
• San Francisco's Embarcadero Freeway is abandoned.
• The New Orleans City Planning Commission concludes that the North Claiborne area shows "existence of severe blight"; little damage is foreseen for a decision for a future I-10 to be routed through the district.
• The Model Cities Program is authorized by the Demonstration Cities and Metropolitan Development Act of 1966.
• The National Historic Preservation Act is passed, establishing the Register of Historic Places and placing stringent regulations on construction with the potential to impact historic, cultural, or archeological resources.

1967
• The freeway debates and protests of the late 1960s begin to erode formerly uncritical acceptance of urban freeways.
• U.S. Senate hearings on urban highways are held. Testimony is heard from representatives of five major groups involved in urban freeway planning at the local, county, state, regional, and federal levels.
• Vieux Carré (New Orleans) lawsuit is filed.
• Nashville I–40 legal challenge fails.
• Construction on I-496 in Philadelphia begins.
• The San Francisco City Planning Department declares its opposition to more freeway construction in favor of development of public transit systems.

1968
• The Federal-Aid Highway Act of 1968 declares again a national policy of preservation of natural beauty of the countryside and public park and recreation lands, wildlife and waterfowl refuges, and historic sites. Relocation and replacement housing requirements are now mandated and funded as costs of construction.
• Remarks made by Federal Highway Administrator Lowell K. Bridwell in the *Highway Research Record* demonstrate a shift in attitude at the federal level elicited by the freeway revolts.
• The Fair Housing Act passes.
• *The Freeway in the City* is authored by leaders in the fields of highway engineering, architecture, landscape architecture, and planning. It offers a far richer array of design alternatives than the AASHO's 1957 Red Book but fails to question the basic mission of construction of large-scale urban freeway systems.

Table 5.1 (continued)

- The Department of Transportation allows funds earmarked for San Francisco freeways to be used for the Century Freeway in Los Angeles.
- Miami's downtown expressway is completed.

1969
- Vieux Carré freeway plans are scrapped.
- The National Environmental Policy Act (NEPA) passes.
- The Federal Highway Administration's "two-hearing" regulation is adopted.
- Westway (New York City) lawsuit is filed.

Late 1960s
- Urban designers begin to achieve a new prominence in urban freeway programming in a few cities. The Baltimore urban design concept team of engineers, architects, planners, transportation consultants, sociologists, and other professionals achieves success in devising a less intrusive network of roadways than that proposed by the state highway department.

1970
- The governor of Massachusetts announces a new state transportation policy: (1) opposing freeways designed for meeting peak-hour demand; and (2) promoting mass transit.
- The Federal-Aid Highway Act of 1970 authorizes states to use urban area highway funds for traffic-reduction projects and addresses the need to promote air quality.
- The Uniform Relocation and Real Property Acquisition Policies Act (23 USC 1970) passes; it requires that relocation payments, assistance programs, and housing be made available.
- The Clean Air Act is amended.
- California enacts the California Environmental Quality Act (CEQA).

1971
- Seattle I-90 lawsuit is filed.
- FHWA accepts New York City's Westway into the national interstate system.
- Tennessee enacts the Tennessee Water Quality Control Act.

1972
- A coalition files a lawsuit challenging the route of I-105 (Century Freeway) through Southern California cities.
- The governor of Massachusetts announces a decision to drop the Inner Belt and Route 2 extension.

1973
- The Federal-Aid Highway Act of 1973 passes. It includes provisions allowing "urbanized areas" to exchange federal interstate funds for other transportation projects and results in the de-designation of approximately 190 miles of the interstate system.

Table 5.1 (continued)

1975
• New York enacts the New York State Environmental Conservation Law (SEQRA).

1976
• A mediation process effects an inter-jurisdictional agreement in the Seattle I-90 case.

1977
• A settlement is reached in the I-105 (Century Freeway) controversy.

1978
• The I-40 alignment through Overton Park is defeated.
• President Carter's National Urban Policy is declared.

1985
• The Westway project is halted.

1993
• Century Freeway (I-105) opens.

By the mid-1960s, there was some recognition of the need for what were labeled multidisciplinary teams; these would include design professionals. The impacts and political nature of siting and the characteristics of urban freeways were slowly coming to be understood. An uneasiness and uncertainty replaced the optimism and confidence about what freeways were doing and would do to America's cities.

By the late 1960s, a spate of legislation began to reflect the concerns of the critics. New laws focused on environmental protection and quality, historic preservation, and relocation assistance—fundamental concerns of urban change but which to that point had been considered outside of the analytical purviews of freeway builders.

In the next chapter, we see how controversies over freeways played out across America—often with very different outcomes—sometimes even in the same city. We examine the contexts in which highway planning decisions were made in several cities. We describe how differences among decision makers and professional groups involved in each case manifested themselves and the physical results of ultimate choices.

6

Urban Freeway Tales: Three Cities among Dozens

Urban Freeways: Impacts and Controversies

As we have seen, perhaps no set of decisions has had more of an effect on America's cities than the development of a system of interstate highways using central cities as potential sites for portions of their placement. Massive highway infrastructure projects have reconfigured urban form, moved hundreds of thousands of people, cost billions of dollars of public funds, and supplanted many neighborhoods.

From the earliest days of federal planning, routes through urban areas were contemplated—"to provide direct connection into and through all of [the] cities" of the system.[1] Yet as we have described, they were not sufficiently funded until the 1950s. By September 1955, the "Yellow Book" contained maps of the one hundred areas for which the government had approved urban interstate sections.[2] Syracuse, Memphis, and Los Angeles were included[3] (figures 6.1, 6.2, and 6.3).

Urban highway decisions affected cities throughout the United States in various forms, with variable intensity, and with different impacts. Some critical writings called urban freeways "Daggers in the heart of town."[4] Controversies over their construction arose in Atlanta, Baltimore, Boston, Charleston, Cleveland, Detroit, Honolulu, Indianapolis, Los Angeles, Memphis, Nashville, Newark, New Orleans, New York, Philadelphia, Pittsburgh, Portland, Richmond, San Antonio, San Francisco, Seattle, and Washington, D.C., among other places.[5]

Some controversies revolved around aesthetics; some around strategies preferred by commercial and industrial interests; some around transportation system efficiency; some around a nascent concern for environmental protection and historical and neighborhood preservation; and some around race.[6] By the 1960s, Federal Highway Administrator Francis C. Turner nonetheless could argue that the urban freeway issue was a small

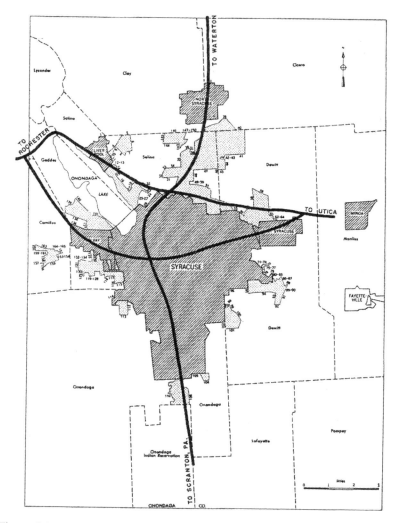

Figure 6.1
Map of Syracuse, New York, illustrating interstate highway segments designated
in the 1955 Yellow Book. *Source:* U.S. Department of Commerce, Bureau of Public
Roads, *General Location of National System of Interstate Highways.*

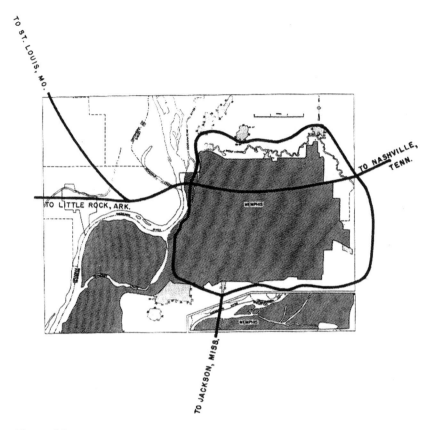

Figure 6.2
Map of Memphis, Tennessee, illustrating interstate highway segments designated
in the 1955 Yellow Book. *Source:* U.S. Department of Commerce, Bureau of Public
Roads, *General Location of National System of Interstate Highways.*

one: "the total mileage involved is only on the order of 150 miles out of
42,500 and 16 cities out of more than 200 that we are working in. . . . A
small percentage in anybody's figures book."[7]

Urban freeway decisions are idiosyncratic, but certain factors stand
out in helping to explain them. Among the most important is timing. For
it was not until the early 1970s that the true effects of the major policy
shift in approaches to highway building were felt. In brief, the visions of
major highways through cities moved from the benign, or more positive,
to the highly contested. The dominance of professions and the impact of
important and charismatic leaders shifted. In the early years of the Merritt (New York) and Pasadena (California) highways, for example, with

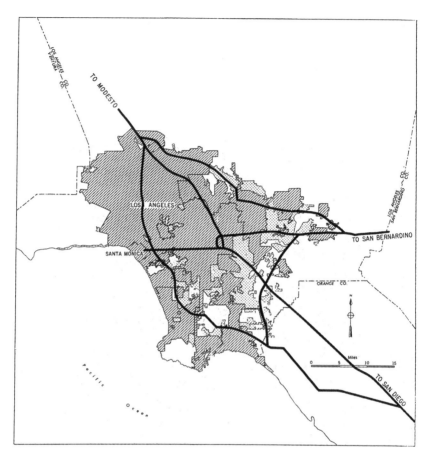

Figure 6.3
Map of Los Angeles, California, illustrating interstate highway segments designated in the 1955 Yellow Book. *Source:* U.S. Department of Commerce, Bureau
of Public Roads, *General Location of National System of Interstate Highways.*

little citizen participation apart from limited public hearings on specific
routes,[8] technical experts laid out plans for major transportation facilities. Those plans, which often included noncontested condemnation of
and considerable alteration of the physical environment, were then implemented through standard routines by agency colleagues.[9] Here is how one
veteran of Caltrans, the former California Highway Department, put it:

When I first became a right of way agent, back in, oh gosh, 1956 I guess it was,
engineers pretty much ran things. And they had a line here and a line here, and it
was a straight line that met those points. And, of course, the highway commission

basically adopted the route by setting the terminal points. And the Department of Public Works, which it was then, would then do the route. And basically the route was pretty much established by the Division of Highways . . . there was probably less of a social awareness in those years than there finally came to be after the federal laws required that there be housing bonuses and relocation costs and things like that."[10]

Snapshots of Urban Freeway Controversies in Several Cities

The following section briefly reviews, in cameo form, the controversies that arose in several of the cities listed at the start of this chapter, along with their eventual conclusions. As we will see, the controversies in these cities frequently shared similar characteristics; however, the outcomes experienced were often very different—sometimes even in the same city.

Subsequently, we will present in-depth analyses of urban highway planning and construction in our three case study cities: Syracuse, New York; Memphis, Tennessee; and Los Angeles, California. We will examine the contexts in which urban highway planning decisions were made in those cities, including a review of the legal, sociopolitical, and economic elements that helped to inform highway planning decisions in the era in which decisions were made in each case. We will look at the decision makers and the professional groups—engineers, architects, landscape architects, urban planners—involved in the decision-making processes in each case. We will examine the nature of the controversies that arose, or did not arise, in Syracuse, Memphis, and Los Angeles as a result of urban highway proposals put forth by highway planners for the three cities. Finally, we will examine the physical outcomes that occurred in the cities and the ramifications of those outcomes for the urban areas and their residents.

Baltimore: Some Roads Scrapped and One Built "to Nowhere"

In Baltimore, the neighborhoods of Harlem Park, Fells Point, and Federal Hill were all listed as "obsolescent" by the Homeowners Loan Corporation in 1937, and all were chosen as potential sites for Baltimore's proposed east–west expressway.

The city had begun planning for the construction of the east–west expressway in 1939 with the employment of three local engineers, known collectively as the Advisory Engineers. The Advisory Engineers recommended that a portion of the expressway be constructed along the Franklin–Mulberry corridor, through the community of Harlem Park. During this era, as already noted, urban highways were perceived by the engineering community and by city planners as a framework for a more efficient and mobile city and as a means of "blight removal." However, the Advisory Engineers' plans were not implemented during this era. Over the subsequent two decades, the city of Baltimore called for more iterations of highway plans.[11]

The subsequent seven expressway proposals differed in their recommendations for specific routes through the city. However, all proposals used the Franklin–Mulberry corridor for a portion of the alignment, thereby institutionalizing Harlem Park as a route for the road. As a result, many Harlem Park residents ceased to invest in their homes, in anticipation of the condemnations that appeared imminent. By the 1960s, Harlem Park was filled with deteriorating properties and abandoned homes.[12]

The April 1959 iteration of the expressway plans, known as the "10-D plan," integrated the previous proposals into a cohesive plan for the development of an east–west expressway through the city. All three neighborhoods, Harlem Park, Federal Hill, and Fells Point, were incorporated into the 10-D east–west expressway plan. The 10-D plan was published in October 1961, at a time when the negative impacts of urban highways were becoming apparent, and when city planners' and the public's perceptions of these roadways as an unambiguous public good had shifted to a far less positive perspective. Upon publication, the 10-D plan immediately ignited controversy and opposition that, during the middle 1960s, was unorganized and erratic.[13]

The Relocation Action Movement (RAM), the first of several groups that would unite to oppose highway construction in the city, was founded in late 1966 by working-class African Americans from the neighborhoods of Harlem Park and Rosemont. RAM's early emergence on the scene, at a time when opposition to the expressway had not coalesced into a strong anti-highway force, had an intense effect on the group's strategy. Rather than protesting the construction of the road, RAM's goal was to ensure just compensation for those being displaced by highway construction.[14]

With the assistance of Stuart Wechsler, a Congress of Racial Equality (CORE) representative, RAM leaders met with Alan Boyd, President Johnson's Secretary of Transportation and head of the U.S. Department of Transportation. The group's leaders also met with Governor Spiro Agnew. With the support of federal and state allies, RAM influenced the enactment of a state law to ensure replacement-cost compensation for displaced individuals, in addition to a subsidy of up to $5,000 to cover moving expenses.[15] However, the city council was able to condemn the Franklin–Mulberry corridor alignment, purchase the homes inside the condemnation lines, and begin bulldozing them by 1969.[16]

This was a far different outcome than that experienced in the neighborhoods of Fells Point or Federal Hill. As Andrew Giguere writes[17]:

In the cases Federal Hill and Fells Point . . . condemnation lines were contested, highway plans were excoriated and sent back to the drawing board, law-suits, injunctions and appeals were filed. At the same time that RAM was voicing its opposition to the highway and mailing position statements to Mayor McKeldin, a little known organization called the Movement Against Destruction was making big statements to the press and to city officials. . . . Citing facts and figures with an obvious comprehension of the complexities of the "traffic evaluation summary," MAD sought to undercut the authority and knowledge of planners. MAD also cited the ballooning costs of road construction and argued that "efficient modes of mass transit" would complement the city far better than a destructive highway network.

Between 1968 and 1975, MAD dramatically altered the dynamics of the Baltimore freeway revolt. By the middle 1970s, a united group of community organizations opposed the road builders. As MAD began to challenge construction across the entire city, its organizational network slowly expanded to encompass the entire city.[18]

MAD members attended policy meetings, challenged council members and the mayor with position statements and letters, and waged an aggressive media campaign. Its participation in the public process allowed MAD to disseminate information about the road to its constituents and member organizations, to local, regional, and national media outlets, to politicians, and to "freeway fighters" in other cities.[19]

After Earth Day 1970, the passage of the Clean Air Act, and the rapidly growing interest in environmentalism in the popular culture, MAD began to focus on environmental issues such as noise and air pollution. The Volunteers Opposed to Leakin Park Expressway (VOLPE), an organization closely aligned with MAD, successfully solicited the support of the Sierra Club in filing a lawsuit against a portion of the roadway planned to run through Leakin Park.[20]

MAD also sought to highlight the historic nature of specific areas of the city; however, it was the Southeast Council Against the Road (SCAR) and the Society for the Preservation of Federal Hill and Fells Point (The Society) that ultimately ensured the survival of these neighborhoods by advocating for their inclusion on the National Register of Historic Places.[21]

As noted in chapter 5, the National Historic Preservation Act (NHPA) was passed in 1966. The act established the National Register of Historic Places (NRHP), the official list of the nation's historic places deemed worthy of preservation. The NRHP serves as a means of assisting and coordinating the identification, evaluation, and protection of America's historic, cultural, and archeological resources. Although sites that qualify for inclusion in the register are not exempted from state or federal modification via highway construction, they are protected by stringent regulations on construction.[22] As was the case with the new laws related to environmental protection, the emergent legal protection given to sites that had never previously been accorded protection under the law reflected a change in legal perspectives and provided a legal basis on which anti-freeway arguments and lawsuits could be constructed.

Many of the homes in Fells Point were built in the late-eighteenth and nineteenth centuries. The Society's first objective, therefore, was to catalog and categorize the hundreds of historic structures in the community. To that end, members of The Society conducted surveys of the historic buildings in Fells Point, which were then compiled into reports by Robert L. Eney, architectural historian and founding member of The Society. As a result of these efforts, the Fells Point Historic District was officially added to the NRHP on March 28, 1969. Over the course of the next 2 years, a similar survey would be conducted in Federal Hill, which would be added to the NRHP in 1970.[23]

By 1985 in both Federal Hill and Fells Point, formerly abandoned, boarded-up structures were being or had been replaced by dozens of renovated and restored homes. According to the Baltimore City Taxpayers Coalition, tax assessments had risen more than 300 percent in both historic districts. Plans for an expressway through Fells Point or Federal Hill were abandoned. Fells Point and Federal Hill are now beloved historic districts that provide residents and visitors to the city with high-end shopping, dining opportunities, and popular night-life venues.[24]

A large part of The Society's success must be attributed to the fact that many of its members came from affluent city neighborhoods or suburban Baltimore County. The Society, therefore, possessed far greater resources than RAM or MAD, which permitted it to host public events that helped to elicit widespread support for its cause, to finance historic and architectural surveys, to purchase and restore buildings, and to create effective advertisements publicizing the historic waterfront that they wished to protect.[25]

Baltimore's story is thus a mixed one. Fells Point and Federal Hill were spared from highway construction. However, less than 3 miles away, a 1.39-mile-long highway, an integral segment of the east–west expressway, forms a 30-foot-deep trench slashing through the neighborhood of Harlem Park.[26] The construction of this road, known as the "Highway to Nowhere," "Interstate Zero," or the "Highway in the Ditch," destroyed 900 homes and displaced fifteen hundred working-class African Americans.[27]

The advent of MAD and other oppositional organizations overshadowed a now largely forgotten and yet quite important highway planning attempt on the part of the city of Baltimore. In October 1966, the prominent architectural firm of Skidmore, Owings & Merrill was commissioned to spearhead a joint planning venture—the urban design concept team (UDCT)—which was envisioned to be a collaborative urban freeway design effort on the part of architects, engineers, economists, planners, and sociologists. The UDCT was charged with developing a high-quality design freeway integrated within the urban fabric to provide maximum social and economic benefits with minimum disruption. The UDCT, the largest experiment in urban design ever attempted, offered the hope that comprehensive planning might be possible throughout the nation. By the time of its institution, however, public confidence in the merits of the highway project had waned, and public opposition to the project was intense. The professional communities involved in the planning effort eventually turned their attention elsewhere, convinced that socially advantageous, comprehensive renovation was impossible. Despite its lack of ultimate success, the UDCT exemplified the differences between highway engineers and architect planners, highlighted ethical issues relating to conflict of interest and the legitimacy of the clients involved in highway development, and illustrated the potential and the limitations of citizen participation in the planning process.[28]

In a paper entitled "Architects and Planners in the Middle of a Road War: The Urban Design Concept Team in Baltimore, 1966-1971," the author addresses the clash of professions in the UDCT case, which was conceptualized during the period before construction of some urban freeways and applied in the Baltimore case. The author asserts that Skidmore, Owings & Merrill attempted, both professionally and through the use of some guerilla and arguably questionable and professionally unethical tactics, to influence the outcome of the 10-D plan. This put the UDCT in direct conflict with the engineering professionals involved in the project, who were considerably angered to have their professional conclusions questioned.

Boston: Cycles of Freeway Defeats

Freeway battles in Boston were frequent and numerous. The 1948 master plan for the Commonwealth of Massachusetts included the construction of several transportation facilities. Among them was the "Inner Belt," a controlled-access, multilane loop route designed to connect downtown Boston with neighboring radial expressways. The proposed Inner Belt

Expressway, a 7.3-mile loop around the northern, southern, and western periphery of downtown Boston, was delineated in the *1948 Master Highway Plan for the Boston Metropolitan Area* during the postwar era when freeway engineers began to dominate the field of highway construction based on "modern" goals of efficiency and mobility in transportation networks. During this era, the "City Efficient" vision eclipsed earlier visions of the "City Beautiful" that had been manifested in parkway development.

The Inner Belt Expressway was to be constructed per the design standards recommended in the *Master Highway Plan*: six 12-foot lanes to be separated by a variable median strip, with 12-foot-wide emergency shoulders and contiguous service roads located within a 300-foot-wide right-of-way. Along the route's depressed sections, in the more heavily urbanized areas, the expressway was to be built within a 170-foot-wide right-of-way.[29]

In 1955, the federal Bureau of Public Roads (BPR) included the Inner Belt in the national network, thereby ensuring that the Massachusetts Department of Public Works would be reimbursed for 90 percent of the Inner Belt's $44 million cost. The larger portion of the Beltway was to be designated as I-695, with a small section between the Southeast Expressway and Southwest Expressway to be designated as I-95.[30]

A portion of the Inner Belt's route had been located on either side of Cambridge. In Cambridge, city councilors, residents along Brookline Street and Elm Street, and state legislators would all speak against the highway; however, no prominent local group had been, up to that time, organized specifically to oppose the highway. By fall 1965, Cambridge was the last obstacle in the way of the completion of the Inner Belt project. Formal plans for the Boston section of the highway would be announced in December.[31]

By early fall 1965, however, a small group of young professionals, whose membership included an assistant professor at Harvard, a planner for the Boston Redevelopment Authority, a young architect, and a real estate broker, joined forces to fight the Inner Belt. This group brought new skills to the battle, along with a new strategy that differed greatly from the prevailing plan of the city council.[32]

Earlier planners believed that the proposed route was a good choice because it went through low-value real estate, thereby representing a means of carving out "deteriorating" areas. The new planners, however, saw the Inner Belt as a destructive force to neighborhood stability, uprooting thousands of families who would be unable to replace the homes they lost.[33] This represented a shift in perspectives in the planning community from that of urban highways as tools of blight removal and city rejuvenation to that of urban highways as destructive to the social fabric of the community.

As demolition along the Inner Belt right-of-way commenced in Roxbury and the South End, the Cambridge group, acting in conjunction with residents and civic leaders, organized a coalition of various community groups along the proposed route to oppose the Inner Belt.[34]

Opponents criticized the studies and analyses done by the Department of Public Works as being faulty and biased.[35]

Fred Salvucci, later transportation secretary under Governor Michael Dukakis in the 1970s and 1980s, was one of the leaders of the Inner Belt protests. Salvucci, who possessed a degree in civil engineering from the Massachusetts Institute of Technology, served as transportation consultant to then Boston Mayor Kevin White. His opinions had significant influence with city and state officials. Eventually, the protests led by Salvucci attracted the attention of Representative Thomas P. ("Tip") O'Neill, who also protested the prospective demolition of neighborhoods along the proposed route. The protests against the Inner Belt quickly extended to Beacon Hill and to Capitol Hill.[36]

By the beginning of the 1970s, the impetus for the construction of the Inner Belt had shifted to opposition toward the roadway. President Nixon's transportation secretary, John A. Volpe, whom we encounter in several of the stories in this chapter, a longtime Massachusetts Department of Public Works commissioner, began campaigning for a more balanced national transportation policy and for the transfer of funds that had been earmarked for urban highway construction to mass transit systems.[37] This crucial modification in the legal underpinnings and visions that had previously informed highway construction provided the incentive needed for a dramatic refocusing of transportation strategies away from urban freeway development and toward alternative forms of public transportation.

As noted in chapter 5, Governor Sargent of Massachusetts halted the construction of principal unbuilt expressways in the state in 1970, thereby reversing the transportation policy of the Commonwealth of Massachusetts. He also appealed to Congress to allow broader use of highway funds under the Federal-Aid Highway Act of 1970. As we have seen, the Federal-Aid Highway Act of 1973 renewed the 1970 act, authorized more than $18 billion in funding, and allowed for the substitution of transit projects for withdrawn interstate portions such as Boston's Southwest Expressway. Furthermore, in response to vocal community opposition,

Boston's Mayor White called for a complete halt on construction within Route 128. As Allan Sloan noted, these policy shifts had a significant impact on urban freeway construction:

In making this move, the governor and his advisors began to look for advice on transportation matters not to the bureaucracies that had formulated the original plans and developed the policies and programs that were being implemented, but to ad hoc non-governmental groups and their spokesmen within the metropolitan community who had been urging a change in basic policy. When this process began, no one expected that the results of citizen participation would be a complete revision of the basic program but this is exactly what happened.[38]

New studies would consider not where to build but whether to build expressways and how to integrate mass transit and other traffic system management techniques. A re-study organization was created and named the Boston Transportation Planning Review (BTPR). Its work, federally funded at 90 percent, began in 1971. In December 1972, on the recommendation of the BTPR, the governor announced his decision to drop the Inner Belt and Route 2 extension.

Boston had made a major policy conclusion: Expressways should not be built on a scale large enough to satisfy the potential peak-hour demand for auto travel to and from downtown Boston because improved public transit, not highways, was the form of transportation that should serve commuters.

The only major new highway facility to be constructed within Route 128 was a two-lane bus tunnel from downtown to the airport.[39] Two other major projects were also allowed. The Central Artery depression was permitted. Major improvements were also acceptable in the southwest corridor, including new arterials to maximize development potential.[40]

On May 23, 1974, the never-built Inner Belt through Boston was among the first of the proposed interstates to be exchanged for mass transit funding under the Federal-Aid Highway Act of 1973.[41]

Miami: Thousands of People Displaced

In Miami, plans for an interstate urban highway began early. A 1955 plan gave way to one developed by the Florida State Highway Road Department in conjunction with county agencies and assisted by Wilbur Smith and Associates.[42,43]

Miami's civic leaders not only saw the federal provision of highway funds as an opportunity to solve local traffic problems and rejuvenate the ailing central business district but also perceived an opportunity to reorganize the city's racial profile. With those objectives in mind, the route of the future Interstate 95 was shifted from its earlier proposed location along an abandoned railway corridor to cut through Overtown, a largely black residential area and business community. Highway planners also planned to site an enormous, four-level, elevated interchange directly in the center of Overtown's black business district. The interchange connected with an East–West Expressway (the future Interstate 395), which slashed through additional areas of Overtown as it wended its way west to suburban areas and the airport and east to Miami Beach.[44]

The plan was endorsed by local politicians, business and civic leaders, developers, newspapers and television stations, and the governing commissions of Miami, Miami Beach, and Dade County. The expressway was touted as being good for business and tourism, in addition to resolving traffic congestion.[45]

Not everyone, however, was in favor of the freeway proposals. Opposition to the plan arose almost immediately and was largely limited to white property owners and white small business owners. More than five hundred people appeared at a state road department public hearing held in February 1957, where at least fifty citizens expressed their concerns regarding losing their properties, the negative impact of the proposed elevated sections of the expressway, and the large number of road closings that would result from construction.[46] In an article appearing in the *Journal of the Historical Association of Southern California*,[47] Raymond Mohl writes: "Expressway supporters from the Miami-Dade Chamber of Commerce, in a statement sent to Governor Collins, quickly denounced the 'small but vocal' group of self-interested opponents, and then fell back on the theme of growth and progress: 'This community can no longer afford to allow timidity and indecision to stand in the way of progress.'"

Initial opposition to the freeway project diminished quickly within the white community and was mostly extinguished within only a few months of the public hearing held in February. Among Miami's black community, there were no demonstrations, protest movements, or public meetings held in an attempt to prevent the completion of the freeway project. The civil rights movement was in its infancy and, according to Mohl, Miami's black citizens had very little political clout during the 1950s and seemed "mostly stunned and immobilized by the anticipated housing losses."[48] The Miami branch of the NAACP had been under attack by a state legislative committee, which alleged that the association had been infiltrated by communists, and the group's attention was diverted from the housing problem. Although an ardent white housing reformer named Elizabeth Verrick instituted a decade-long, one-woman campaign to raise public consciousness about the black citizens who would be displaced by the freeway construction, her fervent efforts could not prevent the freeway plans from being realized.[49]

The downtown expressway was completed in 1968 without any public hearings in the directly affected community. By the time the roadway was completed, thousands of black homes had been lost, and the black business district had been destroyed. The gargantuan downtown interchange, which alone consumed forty blocks, took the housing of about ten thousand people.[50]

New Orleans: Vieux Carré Riverfront Expressway Defeated but I-10 Constructed

Proposed urban freeway sections within blocks of each other in New Orleans experienced very different fates. The Vieux Carré urban freeway case began with a concept of Robert Moses in 1946. The Louisiana Highway Department hired Moses, who, we have seen, was already a major figure in the freeway and infrastructure communities from New York City, to reform the chaotic New Orleans transportation system. Moses prepared a plan that called for an elevated riverfront expressway, justifying it as an aid to the Vieux Carré District by "lifting . . . traffic . . . to the viaduct . . . to create additional space on the surface streets so that docks and warehouses could be serviced more efficiently than at the present time."[51]

In 1957, the New Orleans Chamber of Commerce established the Central Area Committee. The committee supported the Moses plan, and it became the main proponent of the New Orleans expressway.

To that point, there was no central formal and definitive opposition to the expressway concept. In fact, some preservationist organizations concluded that a freeway would relieve congestion in the area. The committee, the Louisiana Highway Commission, and the city planning commission also concluded that an elevated highway would revitalize the business district. Later, however, public hearings were held, and in 1965 the preservationist movement clarified its goal: to seek alternatives for any expressway project in the Vieux Carré District.[52] In the same year, as by then required by federal law, the Louisiana Highway Department held another hearing to address the economic effects of the project. Both opposition and support for the project were manifest. After consideration of a tunnel alternative, the Louisiana Highway Department concluded that the elevated option was the safest, most feasible, and least expensive approach. In 1966, an attempt to require a more comprehensive study and to review alternatives failed.[53]

Preservationists then turned to a national effort. The National Trust for Historic Preservation called upon the U.S. Department of Housing and Urban Development to establish an interagency task force to study the riverfront project. In 1967, preservationists filed suit in federal court relying on a number of state and local laws restricting architectural design and modernization to that which would maintain the quaint and distinctive character of the Vieux Carré District. Plaintiffs later added the argument that final approval of the secretary of the Department of Transportation should be withheld until he could find that the project was based on a "continuing comprehensive planning process," as defined in the amended Federal-Aid Highway Act, and until he found that no "feasible and prudent" alternative to the use of the land existed as required by the act. Other arguments were based on the National Historic Preservation Act of 1966.[54] Despite this opposition, by 1969 it seemed apparent that the Secretary of Transportation would approve the expressway. However, President Richard Nixon assumed power in January 1969, and soon thereafter federal approval of the freeway was withdrawn—apparently because the Advisory Council on Historic Preservation had not commented on the project.[55] Shortly thereafter, in July 1969, the new Secretary of Transportation, John Volpe, canceled the Vieux Carré expressway. He found that the proposed freeway "would have seriously impaired the historic quality of New Orleans' famed French Quarter."[56]

Another neighborhood in New Orleans, however, also facing an interstate freeway decision, experienced a very different outcome. By 1966, the city planning commission had concluded that the North Claiborne area was severely blighted and that developing a highway system through the area would not result in any significant damage.[57] The I-10, which displaced many black businesses and predominantly black residential areas, is sited in part at North Claiborne, about a mile from the Vieux Carré District.

New York: Robert Moses versus Jane Jacobs

At the height of his career, Robert Moses was one of the most powerful political figures in New York. Anthony Flint asserts, "Moses ran his own government, with its own seal, its own police, a fleet of cars, and even a yacht. Moses had written the legislation creating the authority, including his own job description, terms and bylaws, and the power to issue bonds and collect revenue from tolls. He was the most public figure in New York who had never been elected to anything, at one time holding twelve different city and state positions simultaneously—all of them appointments."[58]

Ironically, Robert Moses may himself have sown the seeds of dissent that led not only to his own decline but also to the downfall of proposed urban expressways across the United States. In 1962, secure in his largely unopposed success in constructing urban expressways throughout the East, Moses began to push for the construction of the Mid-Manhattan Expressway and the Lower Manhattan Expressway. Both roadways were planned to run east–west across Manhattan; both had been included in the city planning commission master plan for a new network of arterials in 1941; and both had been approved by the state legislature in 1944. However, funding for the two massive projects was unavailable until the passage of the Federal-Aid Highway Act of 1956. After the act's passage, Moses began his drive to turn conceptual plans into concrete reality.[59]

To Moses' frustration, the concept of the Mid-Manhattan Expressway, an express connection between the Lincoln and Queens-Manhattan tunnels that would have served crosstown traffic from the tunnels, local crosstown traffic, and through traffic between Long Island and New Jersey, was abhorrent to many "largely affluent and politically influential forces" in the prospering district endangered by the proposed expressway. Opposition was vehement from the outset, and the project was soon scrapped.[60]

In spite of this setback, Moses continued to press for the construction of the Lower Manhattan Expressway, an elevated, ten-lane expressway that would have cut a 350-foot-wide corridor through the densely populated neighborhoods of the Lower East Side, the Bowery, Chinatown, Little Italy, and what would later be known as SoHo. Construction of the expressway would have required the destruction of 416 residential buildings, 365 retail stores, and 480 other commercial establishments. It would also have resulted in the eviction and relocation of 2,200 families.[61]

Jane Jacobs's battle against Robert Moses and the proposed expressway raged for almost a decade—from 1962 until 1971, when the project was finally quashed. In the course of the long struggle, Jacobs helped to organize the residents affected by the proposed project and orchestrated well-photographed and publicized demonstrations against it. Jacobs also recruited influential allies to her cause—including Lewis Mumford, the New York Society of Architects, Artists Against the Expressway, and the Lower East Side Businessmen's Association. In direct opposition to Moses' concept of the automobile as the fulcrum around which transit plans should revolve, Jacobs insisted that densely populated urban neighborhoods would function much better through a reliance on mass transit, walking, and bicycling. Jacobs's intense campaign against the expressway began to bear fruit, as the press began to depict the expressway in a powerfully negative fashion. On December 11, 1962, the mayor and the Board of Estimate began to halt the condemnation proceedings along the expressway's planned route. They also began the process by which the expressway would be excised from the city map of planned arterials.[62]

That victory, however, did not end the war. Moses continued to fight for the development of the expressway, eliciting the continued support of powerful interests in favor of the expressway and portraying Jacobs and her followers as obstructionists. Jacobs and her followers, however, had gained a powerful ally. John Lindsay, a Republican congressman who was running for mayor of New York, had become a friend and ally of Jacobs in an earlier battle over urban renewal in Manhattan. Lindsay adopted the campaign against the expressway as a plank in his platform, thereby garnering the support of the very large constituency opposed to the project.[63]

Lindsay used his position in Congress to stall federal funding and the approval process for the expressway in Washington, D.C. Moses' crusade in favor of the expressway continued unabated; however, Lindsay's delaying tactics allowed a powerful new force to join the opposition—the historic preservation movement. Beginning in the early 1960s, a coalition of citizens began to oppose the demolition of historic buildings on the basis that much of the city's cultural and historical heritage was being destroyed. As Flint points out, "In the Lower Manhattan Expressway fight, historic preservation became quite literally a roadblock.[64]

Years of bitter skirmishes and contentious debate followed, years of battles in which the momentum swung first this way and then that—either for the project or against it. Lindsay, who had been elected mayor, vacillated in his stand against the expressway and called for other proposals to modify Moses' plans, none of which were deemed acceptable by all parties involved in the confrontation.[65]

When Jacobs was arrested and charged with disorderly conduct while addressing New York State transportation officials at a public hearing on the expressway on April 10, 1968, her supporters rioted. Her arrest became "the talk of the town."[66] At her subsequent appearance at the courthouse, the disorderly conduct charge against her was dropped and changed to second degree riot, inciting a riot, obstructing public administration, and criminal mischief. Flint states: "All of New York, it seemed, rushed to the defense of the nationally acclaimed author of *The Death and Life of Great American Cities* . . . neighborhood residents put on events in her honor and held fund-raisers for her legal defense."[67]

Mayor Lindsay perceived that Jacobs's arrest had permanently tarnished the image of the Lower Manhattan Expressway and portrayed it as a project "pushed by heartless bureaucrats who would go to any lengths to subdue public opposition." Lindsay returned to his original opposition to the expressway and, on July 16, 1969, declared the project officially dead. Governor Rockefeller concurred, omitting it from the 1971 list of proposed projects eligible for federal funding. Moses' reign as New York's master roadway builder had ended. Jacobs had won, and her victory in Manhattan resounded nationally.

New York: The Westway Urban Freeway Defeated

The original West Side Highway, the world's first elevated highway, extended from the southern tip of Manhattan to Yonkers. The highway was originally designated NY 9A north of the Holland Tunnel and NY 27A south of the Holland Tunnel and was part of the comprehensive, limited-access network of parkways conceptualized for the city of New York by Robert Moses.

The original elevated highway, which stretched from West 72nd Street south to Chambers Street, was built between 1927 and 1931. The highway was then extended south from Chambers Street to the Brooklyn-Battery Tunnel approach between 1945 and 1948. At 72nd Street, the West Side Highway connected to Moses' Henry Hudson Parkway to the north.

As discussed earlier, Moses' urban highway proposals for the city were widely acclaimed during an era where urban highways were seen as essential for city growth and prosperity, when their construction provided desperately needed jobs, when their traffic-generating capacity was not understood, and when the environmental and social costs of their construction were seen as necessary evils or ignored entirely.

In 1971, the Federal Highway Administration (FHWA) accepted the highway into the national interstate system. In 1973, a portion of the West Side Highway collapsed, and in 1974 a replacement for the elevated roadway was formally introduced and referred to as Westway. From the Battery to 42nd Street, a partly depressed expressway would run under a park that, with other land uses, would be built on land reclaimed from the Hudson River.[68] The project was planned to be a six-lane artery.

In 1974, legal action against Westway was commenced under the National Environmental Policy Act (NEPA) and the Clean Air Act. Planning for the highway continued through a decade-long series of this and other legal challenges. Ongoing support for Westway came from the Secretary of Transportation, the New York governor, and, at various times, the New York City mayor. In 1981, President Reagan gave New York Mayor Koch a symbolic check for $85 million to pay for right-of-way acquisition.

However, community opposition continued to grow, and further legal actions were taken. The cases revolved around predicted environmental problems, significantly the impact on fisheries habitat, and on the failure of government fully to disclose these impacts. An increase in traffic generation, with its concomitant noise and pollution, and the economic costs of construction (estimated at more than $2 billion) were also cited by opponents of the highway.

Westway "died in 1985, the victim of community opposition, litigation, and diminishing political support."[69] A permanent injunction was entered prohibiting the grant of a landfill permit for Westway, federal funding of Westway, and construction of Westway by the state.[70]

San Francisco: The General Case—Defeated

Citizen opposition to several freeways in the San Francisco area during the 1950s was "vociferous."[71] Neighborhood groups organized to contest proposed freeways on the grounds that they required too much property, degraded neighborhoods, required unattractive structures, and destroyed neighborhood business centers.

For most of its history, San Francisco served as the hub of the Bay Area, the center of a "Venetian Confederacy" held together by ferry connections to adjacent settlements.[72] During the 1930s, the Golden Gate Bridge and the Bay Bridge finally provided new automobile connections to the north and east.

During the late 1940s and early 1950s, San Francisco's leaders wanted to propel San Francisco into the coming age of postwar economic growth. San Francisco differed from many other cities in its more stalwart commitment to transit but not in its belief that easy auto access to the central city was essential for economic growth and that surrounding neighborhoods would have to suffer freeway impacts for the good of the city as a whole. Urban freeways were not imposed on the City of San Francisco from without. They were welcomed and planned for by the city itself.

During World War II, San Francisco planners foresaw a circumferential expressway along the waterfront, more bridges, and expanded highway connections to the south. Freeway elements also figured prominently in the Master Plan of 1945, prepared under the direction of L. Deming Tilton. The maps for this plan show a proposed freeway along the Embarcadero connecting the Golden Gate Bridge with freeway routes to the south, a freeway through the Panhandle to Golden Gate Park, and a free-way through the Mission District.[73]

In 1948, prestigious national planners were hired to produce a com-prehensive transportation plan, which contained an extensive freeway system—roughly radial-concentric, with adaptations to topography—supplemented by major transit improvements. The San Francisco City Planning Commission used this 1948 "Transportation Plan for San Fran-cisco" as a foundation for its own plan, the Trafficways Plan of 1951.[74]

Inner-city freeway construction began during the 1950s, at first through industrial areas where aesthetic matters seemed secondary and where the lack of residents in the affected areas limited opposition. The San Francisco freeway revolt originated with freeways proposed for the western section of the city, in the Inner Sunset area near Golden Gate Park.[75] When the state Division of Highways initiated preliminary stud-ies and surveys of routes through the city in 1955, neighborhood groups mobilized and stopped several segments.

Parts of the Embarcadero Freeway and the Central Freeway were com-pleted in 1959—both ran largely through industrial, waterfront, or low-income mixed-use areas. They were elevated, boxy, and devoid of design elegance. They quickly set strong negative precedents for urban freeway construction in San Francisco's built-up areas. The Embarcadero Freeway, which ran along the city's northern waterfront, was finished up to Broad-way, but its ungainly double-deck structure provided excellent ammunition for freeway opponents. The Central Freeway was also partially finished, mainly through an industrial area but on its northern end cutting through neighborhoods of Victorian houses and apartment buildings.

Citizen protest forced engineers, planners, designers, and public of-ficials to engage in a belated form of "technology assessment," a search for some freeway pattern that would minimize negative impacts on San Francisco's densely packed neighborhoods and make the proposed routes more palatable to the citizenry. Urban design considerations were finally emphasized. Landscape architect Lawrence Halprin and other designers produced some imaginative design alternatives. But the freeway debate was already polarized; the least obtrusive solutions were prohibitively expensive, and, in the end, the freeway building program was terminated in the political arena.

On January 23, 1959, the San Francisco Board of Supervisors regis-tered the public's antipathy toward the freeways in Resolution Number 45–59. The resolution opposed construction of all freeways proposed in the San Francisco Master Plan and resulted in the termination of several proposed links to the interstate system.[76] The freeways opposed by the supervisors all passed, at least in part, through middle-class residential areas, neighborhoods capable of mounting enduring, politically sophisticated opposition. Freeways routed mainly through industrial and lower-class areas, however, were not deleted.

In presenting a statement from San Francisco Mayor John F. Shelley at the 1967 Federal-Aid Highway Act hearings, Legislative Representative Maurice Shean summarized the seasoned San Francisco position:

> Proponents of freeways may minimize the expected effects of traffic noise, exhaust fumes, general nuisance, and the number or displaced families and businesses upon the community, but the objecting public has been and will be hostile and a force to be reckoned with. Proposed new freeways are regarded by many as rivers of noise, gas, exhaust and constant never-ceasing motion; a "river to be kept away from my door." . . . If, in San Francisco, [a] new start takes time, it is time which can well be spent in giving mass transportation the leg up it requires if we are ever to achieve a "balanced" transportation system. I would suggest that a fresh start will mean a number of things, a few of which follow. A maximum emphasis on urban design considerations that must be part and parcel of any roadway: Here I mean such things as views to be created rather than blocked; major landscaping; a blending of the road with the land and its uses, rather than an imposition upon it; the creation of park systems rather than the desecration of them; and the enhancement of neighborhoods, rather than tearing them apart. A total rethinking of present highway standards in terms of lane widths, speeds, grades, and the like. Who cares if we lose some speed in our dense urban areas if in doing so we can save homes, people, views, land, and esthetic values?[77]

The freeway battles that stopped or restricted freeway construction in Northern California, however, had an additional outcome: The controversies in San Francisco led to the eventual allocation of highway funds from projects there to routes in Southern California. The Century Freeway, one of our case studies, received a portion of these funds.

Seattle: A Road Built—Expensive and Redesigned

Studies on the planned Interstate 90 in Seattle date back to 1944. Engineering and design work began in 1957. In 1963, after a public hearing on three alternatives, the state selected a corridor that soon received Bureau of Public Roads approval. The original plan was for a fourteen-lane highway, but controversy arose over size and location. In 1970, federal officials approved the proposed location and authorized acquisition of property for right-of-way.

In 1971, residents brought a lawsuit against the state and the federal highway administrations to halt further property acquisition until defendants complied with the relocation provisions of the Federal-Aid Highway Act of 1968; the federal agency complied with NEPA; and new public hearings on the proposed route were held. By August 1972, the courts had found the Environmental Impact Statement (EIS) on the project inadequate. The highway department made design changes to address some of the opponents' objections, including dedicating lanes for rapid transit.

In 1976, a mediation process brought about an inter-jurisdictional agreement that included design and access changes incorporated into the final EIS. That document was then determined adequate, and an earlier imposed injunction on property acquisition was dissolved. In 1989, a 7-mile stretch of the interstate opened, at that point "the most expensive segment of freeway ever built."[78] The segment included a floating bridge, a triple-decker tunnel with a level dedicated to pedestrians and bicycles, and a concrete-slab roof over some sections. In 2001, an earthquake damaged the viaduct. How to replace or repair it became a modern urban freeway controversy; positions were articulated that it should be a new elevated highway, a tunnel, or a surface street integrated into the street grid. In a March 2007 referendum, voters rejected both a new elevated highway and a tunnel. As of October 2011, however, two projects are now planned to replace the SR 99 Alaskan Way Viaduct along Seattle's waterfront: the SR 99 Tunnel Project and the SR 99 South Holgate Street to South King Street Project. As a result of the SR99 Tunnel Project, the central waterfront section of the Alaskan Way Viaduct will be replaced with a bored tunnel underlying downtown Seattle. The tunnel is planned to connect to the new SR 99 roadway under development south of downtown Seattle and to Aurora Avenue in the north of the city.[79] The SR 99 South Holgate Street to South King Street Project will replace the southern mile of the Alaskan Way Viaduct, near Seattle's port and stadiums, with a new roadway having wider lanes and meeting current earthquake standards.[80] Street, transit, seawall, and waterfront improvements are also being planned by King County, the City of Seattle, and the Port of Seattle as part of the Alaskan Way Viaduct program.[81]

Washington, D.C.: The Three Sisters Bridge and the Highway System in the District
Formulated in the early 1960s, the proposed highway plan for Washington, D.C., would have created an elaborate 329-mile wheel-and-spokes network of freeways in and around the city. Freeways sections traversing several urban residential neighborhoods and an Inner Loop through the

downtown area were called for, in addition to the construction of a new Potomac bridge at Three Sisters Islands near Spout Run—the proposed Three Sisters Bridge.[82]

U.S. Department of Transportation Secretary Alan S. Boyd was adamant in stating that both the Department of Transportation Act and the Federal-Aid Highway Act of 1962 required him to investigate the potential impacts of the proposed bridge. Boyd's stand held implications for federal policy-making regarding the construction of urban freeways throughout the nation.[83]

In the District of Columbia, the Committee of 100, which was founded in 1923 to "sustain and to safeguard the fundamental values derived from the tradition of the L'Enfant Plan and the McMillan Commission,"[84] assumed a prominent role in challenging freeway plans for the district, including the interstate highway plans that would have created high-speed interstate corridors through city neighborhoods. By fall 1966, the Committee of 100 had formed liaisons with groups protesting freeway decisions in New Orleans, Philadelphia, San Francisco, and other cities.[85]

Frederic Huette, of the Executive Committee of the Catholic Interracial Council of Washington, D.C., spoke to the anger and betrayal felt by some of those who would have been affected by the completion of the proposed highway system in the district:

Is it to be that, on the question of urban freeways, that the will of money interests, and the agencies of power that they control, are to prevail . . . ? . . . We oppose the basic plan of the forces of greed, thirsting for all that highway trust fund money to build unneeded and unwanted freeways, freeways which serve the interests of money only and pollute our air and environment, serve also as "Chinese walls" to divide our community physically, socially, spiritually, into ghettos, black and white, rich and poor.[86]

The "Washington Freeway Battle" began with a proposal by highway planners in the district and in Maryland to construct a freeway extension through Rock Creek Park to downtown Washington. The Committee of 100 joined the National Park Service, the National Capitol Planning Commission, and many national and local organizations to oppose the plan. Highway planners also proposed a freeway extension down Wisconsin Avenue to Tenley Circle, with one fork cutting through Rock Creek Park and Melvin C. Hazen Park, and a second fork running down Glover-Archbold Park to the Potomac. The committee also opposed this plan and united in litigation with the families that had donated most of Glover-Archbold Park to prevent intrusion into the stream valley woodland contained within the park.[87]

The committee garnered support from civic groups throughout the district in its attempt to defeat the freeway plan. Acting in conjunction with the District of Columbia Federation of Civic Associations, the committee sued in the federal courts.[88] On February 9, 1968, the U.S. Court of Appeals ruled in favor of the freeway protestors and enjoined construction on the grounds that the District of Columbia's Department of Highways had neglected to adhere to proper procedure, including convening public hearings.[89]

After the decision, however, President Richard M. Nixon, who was involved in freeway policy making, stepped in to assure District Representative Natcher, who had pressed for the proposed project, that "the District of Columbia is firmly committed to completion of these projects as the Federal Aid Highway Act of 1968 provides." Immediately thereafter, the disputed sections were re-designated as part of the interstate highway system. By September 17, the initial contract for construction of the Three Sisters Bridge had been awarded.[90]

In response, demonstrators occupied the Three Sisters Islands, preventing bulldozers from reaching the construction site. After a short period of time, the demonstrators were arrested, handcuffed, and removed from the site.[91]

The Committee of 100 intensified its opposition. Even Secretary of Transportation Alan Boyd let it be known that he opposed Three Sisters Bridge. However, Natcher threatened to remove monies earmarked for Washington, D. C.'s subway system unless the freeways and the bridge were built. Fearing that the entire Metro system would be jeopardized, the D.C. Council voted to approve the Three Sisters Bridge and several other proposed highways on August 9, 1969. One month later, Volpe ordered work on the Three Sisters Bridge to begin in a week.

However, a temporary restraining order issued in October 1969 stopped construction. In August 1970, John Sirica, chief judge of the U.S. District Court, ordered work on the bridge to cease. In his opinion, Sirica wrote that proper planning procedures had not been followed and that the comments of the local community had not been adequately heard.[92]

The city, fearing the loss of its subway funding, immediately filed an appeal in the U.S. Court of Appeals, but Sirica's decision was upheld by the appeals court in August 1972 and the Supreme Court refused to review the case. Meanwhile, the National Capital Planning Commission and the city government "quietly dropped the freeway proposals from transportation master plans, even though they knew this would irritate Rep. Natcher. Their hope was that a court victory would make freeway plans (and the spending of political capital) unnecessary. They also hoped that the winds had shifted to the point where they could deliver Metro money via some new route."[93]

Finally, in 1976, Secretary of Transportation William T. Coleman announced that his department would guarantee all monies needed for Metro to build its entire 103-mile system if Congress would free up Washington's mothballed share. According to Bob Levey and Jane Freundal Levey (2000), "Then and only then, under intense pressure from Democratic leaders on Capitol Hill, did William Natcher fold his cards" and abandon his plans for Washington D.C.'s highway system.[94] The controversy formed a contextual backdrop for national legislation, the Federal-Aid Highway Act of 1973, which, as noted in chapter 5, allowed Highway Trust Funds to be reallocated and used for the construction of mass-transit systems. At that time, President Nixon joined with urban politicians, environmentalists, and transit advocates to oppose inflexible funding requirements for urban highway construction in favor of reallocating highway funds for the construction of mass transit.[95]

Three Cities among Dozens: Syracuse, Memphis, and Los Angeles

The above cameos introduced the range of actors and influences—professional, political, and citizen based—that led to quite different outcomes throughout the United States. Controversy related to highway development spared few regions and few neighborhoods within cities.[96]

The balance of this chapter provides a more in-depth review of decision making on urban freeways in American metropolitan areas and uses as exemplars the cities of Syracuse, New York; Memphis, Tennessee; and Los Angeles, California.

The analysis is set within the context we have set forth of competing and evolving visions of the design of urban highways and sea changes in the regulatory environment of freeway construction in the United States. As discussed in chapter 5, that environment was set in the 1940s and early 1950s and shifted dramatically in the late 1960s and the 1970s. Congress and state legislatures passed important new laws that guided where freeways can be built, how they may be funded, which types of consultation and analysis must precede their funding and construction, and what kinds of environmental, social, aesthetic, and economic impacts may be permitted as a result of their construction. Lawmakers and courts required that projects be planned and completed with maximum sensitivity to the environment, with concern for relocation of the displaced, and with active citizen participation. They required that policy makers consider alternatives other than the traditional urban choices of the 1950s.

The cases presented herein suggest that the municipalities fall into a class whose fates are dependent to a great extent on major forces linked to the transportation sector, but whose urban infrastructure decisions are not alike. These outcomes are related to a set of interacting phenomena—from timing of transportation decisions within an environment of changing state and federal funding opportunities and environmental law to governmental philosophy about fiscal issues and about how to maintain a vital central city core.[97] The degree of acceptance of various visions of super roads and their benefits—often associated with professional affiliations—also played a central role in the very different city stories we tell.

As this chapter will demonstrate, the case study cities experienced three very different outcomes: Syracuse, a snow and Rust Belt city, embraced freeways through its center early on. Los Angeles built some, rejected others, and then changed its plans for one and built the then most expensive urban road, the Century Freeway. Memphis closed its core to Interstate 40, a transcontinental road.

For each urban freeway decision, we address the role played by national and state transportation and environmental and planning law; by state and local engineers and other professionals; by funding and urban development options (real and perceived); by understandings of desirable urban design choices and their effects; by local activism, both grassroots and institutional; by political orientation of local administrations, including toward fiscal options; and by other urban policy choices faced by the local government.

Syracuse: "Benefits Like Those from the Construction of the Erie Canal"
Syracuse, New York, is a Central New York city with a population of 140,658.[98] It is located at the confluence of the New York State Thruway (incorporated in 1958 as portions of the interstate system), Interstate 690, and Interstate 81. It is very roughly equidistant from Canada and Pennsylvania and from Buffalo and Albany.

The city's population increased rapidly in several historical periods. Similarly, loss of population has occurred in a relatively brief historical period, roughly from 1960 to the present. Growth has been linked at various times to the city's natural resources, including salt (the city got its name because of the similarities between it and Siragusa in Sicily), and its location on important transportation routes. The city was a major point on the Seneca Turnpike and other early New York roads and on the Erie

Canal, which was important in the city's development in the years from 1830 to roughly 1920. It was also located on major train routes for much of the twentieth century.

During the period of decision making on interstates in the Syracuse area, thruways, interstate highways, state highways, and arterial highways were the responsibilities of the New York State Thruway Authority and the State Department of Public Works. The county highway superintendent, who was appointed by the Board of Supervisors and reported to that organization's Highway Committee, was responsible for county roads. In each town, a highway superintendent had charge of all town roads.[99]

By one measure, interstate highway development in Central New York began with the New York State Thruway. In 1942, the state of New York began plans for what would become the Governor Thomas E. Dewey Thruway. As first conceived and funded, the thruway was neither an interstate freeway nor did it go through a major city center in Upstate New York; but in 1958, it became integrated into the interstate system.

However, what would become Interstates 81 and 690, passing through the heart of the city, began as a road concept in the 1940s. In 1944, the Syracuse–Onondaga County Post-War Planning Council (hereafter, the planning council) addressed the area in which the interstates would ultimately be built.[100] In a major report entitled *Postwar Perspective, A Report to the People of the City of Syracuse and the County of Onondaga, 1944*, the planning council said that the state proposed to relocate a section of the road known as Route 11, beginning at a point about 1½ miles south of Lafayette, a village south of Syracuse. The report included details on location and size.[101]

Postwar Perspective contained a vision of modern highway development for the city—a vision that would be central to the aspiration of future highway planners and public officials but with varying degrees of priority. The plan included (1) a "belt line" around the city (providing for a highway without difficult turns or steep grades and allowing traffic to reach the outskirts of the city without having to pass through congested streets), on which through traffic, particularly trucks, could bypass Syracuse if desired;[102] (2) the state thruway, bypassing the city to the north; (3) other east–west thruways in the general direction of Erie Boulevard, a major east–west street formerly the route of the Erie Canal; (4) north–south thruways; (5) a high-speed thruway connecting downtown with the university and medical center; and (6) an alternate plan, a complete loop around the central district[103] (an alternate for future consideration). The system, it was determined, would decrease congestion and traffic accidents and, in doing so, help maintain the economic vitality of Syracuse.[104]

There was little controversy about whether the urban freeway plans should go forward. All Syracuse mayors, planners with few exceptions, and most businesspeople were supportive.[105] Also supportive were the New York State Department of Public Works, the New York Central Railroad, the Medical College, Syracuse University, urban renewal program officials, highway user groups, the trucking industry, both of the major newspapers, and real estate interests. There was a bit more controversy over design, but even that was relatively muted, and some of it came after the fact of construction.

In 1946, the city planning commission revealed the relative importance of local and state influences on the routes through the city. It noted that the district state highway engineer of the state Department of Public Works had undertaken detailed planning of the principal arterial routes through the urban area of Syracuse. The commission said it had been "consulted on a number of occasions by the state engineers." It expected that the state would submit the tentative proposals to the commission for review and comment. The commission reminded that it had jurisdiction over the comprehensive plan of the city, including major thoroughfares.[106]

The state document itself appeared one year later; it described how the state Department of Public Works had prepared plans for "a modern arterial route system." It consisted of three major high-speed connections from the Ontario-Mohawk Thruway, south–north and west–east routes across the city, and a relocation of Route 5 west to the city center. It also described arterials circumferential to the central business district.[107]

The report gave details on lane number for "the expressway type" routes of twin pavements separated by substantial malls. They would be limited access, interchanging with major streets. For two parts of the system, mileage was noted and totaled about 18 miles.

The major role that the state actually played in siting is evidenced in a planning commission document written about a decade later, when the route was partially opened. Speaking of a section under construction, the commission said, "Details of the exact location of the arterial through the city have not yet been made public by the State Department of Public Works." The commission was able only to "presume" where the route would actually run.[108] In addition, "the Mayor expressed disappointment" about where the east–west route through his city would be.[109]

By this time, the economic future of the city had been linked to highway construction, "the greatest single element in the cure of city ills."[110]

Observers had for a time focused on the city's streets as a limiting factor in its future growth. A special study of Syracuse by *Fortune* magazine concluded:

Street layout adequate for carriage and pedestrian was wholly inadequate for automobile and bus. Upon land that once provided plenty of breathing space, plenty of elbowroom for a few tens of thousands, there were now crowded more than 200,000 souls, and still more thousands poured in and out every day. . . . It takes too long to go to work, too long to shop, too long to get to the park, too long to get out of town, too long to get in town, too long to get to school, to the train, to the airport. It costs too much in terms of wasted time, rubber, gasoline, and nerves to transfer goods, to make deliveries, to make business calls.[111]

In 1947, state engineering officials wrote to Mayor Frank Costello to inform him that the state was prepared to advance the construction of arterial highway improvements within the city of Syracuse in conformance with "the comprehensive development plan" (described in an attached report).[112] In 1944, legislation had set forth a new policy with respect to city thoroughfares connecting with state highways. Previously, the engineers noted, state highway funds were used almost exclusively in rural districts; the new policy allowed the state to improve and develop arterial routes within the cities themselves, permitting the state to construct "many desperately needed improvements" that formerly could not be built because cities could not finance them. The state said it was submitting the plan for city consideration because "projects should not be undertaken within a city until it is certain they fit into a master plan of development which it is mutually agreed is financially practical and will redound to the best interests of the city, its urban area and the State."[113]

The state engineers now envisioned the "belt line": the loop would be formed partially by north–south and east–west routes together with improved arteries along identified Syracuse streets. A part of the northern section would be depressed, whereas other parts would be at grade. Existing railroad (D.L.&W) structures on the West Street leg of the loop were incorporated into the plan.[114]

The system would be financed through the Postwar Reconstruction Fund, with surplus revenues collected during the war years, with continued regular federal highway construction aid, and with appropriations from anticipated state revenues.[115] In a section on assessed land values, the report noted that the worth of important sections was dependent upon getting rid of the "evils" of congestion, delays, and accidents.[116]

The belief that the success of Syracuse was heavily based on its central place in an overall transportation network was widespread. When Sergei

Grimm was head of the commission, the planning commission said that the state proposal would be "the greatest physical improvement contemplated in the city of Syracuse since the railroad elevation and its effects on the city may be equal to that of the construction of the Erie Canal."[117] In the report, the engineers wrote that Syracuse was in an exceptionally favorable market location: a 300-mile radius from Syracuse includes the Boston, New York, Philadelphia, Cleveland, and Pittsburgh metropolitan complexes, with a population of more than 42.5 million, in the "richest concentrated market in the world."[118]

An understanding of the relationship between highway construction and removal of substandard uses was offered: acquisition of needed wide rights-of-way in mixed-use border areas "where a blight condition now exists" would eliminate much substandard development. New open space along the proposed routes would encourage the rehabilitation of the remaining properties and enhance values in the entire area. As to the critical issue of cost, it was estimated at about $23.5 million, of which the city's share would be one half of the cost of "right-of-way," about $5,278,000.

At the same time (1947), state engineers also envisioned north–south and east–west routes. The east–west highway (which was to become I-690) also saw considerable planning before the Federal-Aid Highway Act of 1956. The northern section of the north–south route (which would become I-81) saw extensive planning prior to the act's passage.

In 1947, the city council approved the state plan by a close vote. However, the vote at the county legislature was much more decisive: 28–6, split along party lines.[119]

On March 27, 1950, the planning commission gave its general endorsement to the route, concluding that the plan would attempt to minimize damage to participating neighborhoods while providing some traffic relief to the overcrowded streets on Syracuse's north side. The planning commission had said that its earlier approval of the Arterial Route Plan was in principle, and not in reference to the exact locations of the routes. Those locations would not be fixed until an "exhaustive and detailed study" was done both by state engineers and local officials "familiar with local conditions."[120] Nonetheless, through its chairman, Thomas E. Kennedy, the planning commission said the proposed Arterial Route System "was not a matter of choice," and the commission commended the state Department of Public Works "for its splendid report."[121] The commission did point out that the state procedure did not allow for free exchange of information,"[122] but as to general location, the plan corresponded substantially with the city's own postwar planning project plan.[123]

In 1953, progress in implementing parts of this vision was described. One of the main arterials was ready for construction. Preliminary plans for another arterial (a major north–south element, Oswego Boulevard) had been processed. Work on the construction contract drawings was at "such an advanced state" that state Department of Public Works officials hoped that the entire route—from the thruway to the central district— "could be put on the construction program for next year." Also in 1953, citing limitations of the state plan, the city presented its study of two alternatives, one an "overhead structure hugging the NY Central Elevated route," the other "a subsurface route."[124] This report, appending an article on the tunnel and viaduct in Seattle, said both elevated and cut-and-cover construction were common throughout the country.[125]

Arterial Development/Urban "Redevelopment"
Several dynamics of urban development were now influencing each other. Major funding sources for highway construction were becoming available, first through state and then through state and federal sources. Some of those funds were linked to highway plans that were superimposed on the city. At the same time, solutions were being sought for what was perceived to be a blighted urban core. The Syracuse economy was strong, but development was perceived as limited by "non-economic problems"; constraining factors included "water, sewage disposal, educational facilities, roads and governmental administration."[126]

Linking urban redevelopment and highway construction was part of the general thinking of some of the leading builders of the time, including Robert Moses[127] (discussed at greater length in chapters 1 and 5 of this volume). "Urban highways could serve as an important tool. . . . Blighted and slum areas could be redeemed through the proper location of expressways. Such rebuilding could be expedited through excess condemnation techniques which allowed land taken for highway right-of-way to be used for urban renewal purposes."[128] This view was advocated at the federal level as well.[129] Thomas H. MacDonald, commissioner of the federal Bureau of Public Works, attempted to include highway construction as a technique for urban renewal in the Federal Housing Bill of 1949. President Harry S. Truman successfully opposed the addition; he feared that the bill might not pass if it were too broad.[130]

In Syracuse, recognition of the renewal/transportation link continuously evolved. By 1954, a very strong interest in urban redevelopment, or "slum clearance," was evident, especially in regard to the 15th Ward near city hall. The city was looking for funds from the state, and developers were advocating private-sector actions supported by governmental monies to improve this and nearby sections of the city core. State funds were available for clearance, and the city was increasingly focusing on the decay and civil embarrassment of sections of the ward. The mayor and others called for control of migration of farm workers to the area. At one point, the military became involved, and a Marine tank was used to demolish a few "shacks" in the area.[131] Newspaper articles described the makings of "a possible race riot" as a result of "evils nurtured in slums, and the 15th Ward as a "keg of dynamite."[132]

Various ideas were offered for blight removal in the ward. A small group of builders proposed a solution, billed as the answer to "the 15th Ward slums."[133] The four builders offered a strategy in "Housing . . . U.S.A.," which they described as the bible of the National Association of Home Builders, and focused on costs. They concluded that the cost of obtaining "slum land" at its market value, clearing it, and getting it ready for redevelopment made reconstruction economically unfeasible "unless state and city pay a substantial part of the cost of acquiring the land."[134] The builders proposed a master plan for transportation, highways, and freeways, in addition to redevelopment of blighted areas not susceptible to rehabilitation in accordance with the master plan.

By February 1954, the city had applied for federal funds for a project affecting the 15th Ward, which would entail clearance of the buildings near city hall. Then-mayor of Syracuse Donald Mead concluded that explorations in connection with Title 1, which he described as "a combined slum clearance, land re-use federal program," "might be the logical approach" to the situation in the 15th Ward.[135]

Thus, by the mid-1950s, the city was simultaneously seeking funding for slum clearance and for arterial development—this while still dependent on higher levels of government for highway planning. Syracuse in the period also was committed to a fiscal conservatism that required identification of funding sources before projects would be approved. Borrowing was shunned.[136] Furthermore, as in many cities at the time, the mainstay of public finance at the local level was the property tax, which had fallen precipitously nationwide.[137]

When properties that could be put to various uses were being considered for arterials, they could be resold only for limited purposes, in order not to interfere with the reuse of the property for highways. One part of a proposed route would result in elimination of blighted residential structures, while some properties were excluded until a later time or a different place, as they would be needed for links with one or another

of the arterials.[138] By 1954, highway decisions were affecting other decisions in the 15th Ward, including those related to building of playgrounds,[139] football fields, and public housing.[140] Public housing for four
hundred families and people to be displaced from substandard homes by
a proposed highway adjoining a former playfield site was announced.[141]
Another housing area was to be on a site different from one originally designated,[142] because property values in the proposed north–south
state arterial link would increase and make the property too expensive
for public housing and more suitable for business.[143] Washington Street,
which had been "regarded historically as the worst residential street in the
city,"[144] would be obliterated by the Townsend St. Arterial.[145]

The area around the 15th Ward was beginning to be seen as a substantial urban policy challenge. In an article entitled "Trouble Feared," the
Post-Standard reported that "the doubling of the Negro population in 10
years, along with the difficulty of the Negro in moving out of the ghetto
because of racial barriers have created an overcrowded condition that
many experts felt may someday lead to troubles. The 15th Ward contains
some of the country's worst slums."[146]

This perspective on their community was not shared by residents of
the 15th Ward, whose opinions on the highway placement were not solicited by decision makers. Former residents of the 15th Ward did, however,
share their thoughts on their community at the "Que Reunion," which
is held semi-annually in Syracuse. At the reunion, attendees reminisced
about a time when "you didn't have to lock your doors and everybody
knew everybody."[147]

Lorraine Merrick, native Syracusan and former deputy supervisor of
Syracuse City Schools, added: "The 15th Ward was a community. People
who didn't know the 15th Ward have different perceptions about what the
15th Ward was all about. It was a very diverse community. A real community, extended family didn't necessarily have to be an aunt or an uncle. It
could be a next-door neighbor. Families worked together. . . . It's unfortunate that young people can't experience the things we had."[148]

The opinions of the 15th Ward residents, however, were given little,
if any, weight in the highway decision-making process. In fact, the belief
was widespread among the residents that "urban renewal"—as opposed
to highway construction—was the reason behind the demolition of the
15th Ward.

According to Clarence Dunham, a former Onandaga County legislator
who represented the south side of Syracuse, "Urban renewal came along
and destroyed our neighborhood. All the blacks and majority of Jews

lived together [;] there were a mixture of Italians, Irish and other ethnic groups. Back in the 1930s and 40s our neighborhood was very small so everybody knew everybody—every family knew every family."[149]

From the perspective of another former resident: "Homes were not the only thing lost in the demolition of the 15th Ward. Small businesses, churches and schools were also destroyed. Urban renewal destroyed a close-knit community where parents disciplined each other's children."[150]

As Diane Ravitch and Joseph P. Viteritte assert:

Most of that ward was demolished in the 1960s . . . as part of a grand plan of what was then called 'slum clearance,' driven by notions of 'urban cleansing.' It was combined with major interstate highway construction that cut through and destroyed many old city neighborhoods, white as well as black. But only the black Fifteenth Ward was virtually bulldozed out of existence. . . . What the city got [as a result] was wider highways on concrete stilts, more parking lots and garages, and a few new high-rise apartments and commercial buildings.[151]

The perceived future economic benefits attributed to highway construction, in combination with the substantial incentive of federal funding, however, weighed heavily in the city's decision to pursue freeway construction. Funds that would be secured from the highway program were substantial.[152] Syracuse's investment of around $10.2 million in an accelerated arterial program would generate an estimated federal–state commitment of almost $40 million. Even the small-percentage city contribution, however, would be an exception to Syracuse's highly conservative economic policy, a hallmark of city administrations for decades.

In May 1955, the regional director of urban renewal for the Federal Housing and Home Finance Agency assured Mayor Mead, members of the city planning commission, and the common council of federal aid for "slum clearance and urban renewal." In his praise of the Syracuse plan, among the benefits he saw in its realization were "less vulnerability" to suburban competition because of traffic improvements. "The big question is whether you can afford to keep your slums. You're supporting them whether you know it or not."[153]

The annual report of the city planning commission stated that the proposed urban renewal program had opened up new solutions for the city's "knotty problem."[154] Both the city and the state "could effect large savings on arterial-route development costs" if rights-of-way were acquired in connection with "very large" urban renewal projects. Some 350 acres would be involved, including the north–south and other arterials, and coordination of arterial route plans with those for urban renewal was "in prospect."[155]

Up to that point, despite grand plans, the city had authorized only bonding ($3,150,000) for the first arterial project (Oswego Boulevard) where land taking had begun; there had been an "unexpected failure of prospects" for federal and state aid for programming.[156] Sometime around 1956, the city planning commission published a report that addressed the challenge of finding funds for clearing blighted areas, undertaking redevelopment, and engaging in the tasks of urban renewal.[157] The report outlined negotiations with state and federal highway officials and urban renewal agencies to save on the right-of-way cost of arterial routes where they pass through redevelopment areas by "writing down" this cost with clearance grants before proceeding under arterial law.

Still, finding sources for the local share was a problem having "not the slightest prospect" of resolution, a "staggering challenge."[158] "Reduction in cost of development of the arterial routes [is] . . . among the purposes of redevelopment of the area."[159]

The arterial–blight link had been addressed explicitly by Sergei N. Grimm, executive secretary of the city planning commission from 1938 to 1957. His plan would (1) permit the city to acquire arterial rights-of-way and (2) authorize the city to turn the land, or portions of it, over to the state as the municipal share of arterial financing.[160] Grimm noted that in order to take advantage of major savings on the city's share of arterial route costs, the city would need to become involved in land taking on a "gigantic scale."[161] Instead of piecemeal "scattered sites" housing and the splitting of urban renewal activities into smaller clearance projects, the plan would be a comprehensive approach to the city's housing, slum clearance, renewal, and arterial land-acquisition problems.[162] Later, Grimm calculated the savings on arterial right-of-way (based on a possible 50 percent state urban renewal contribution) as $500,000.[163]

By March 1957, the displacement ("moving") of residents in the 15th Ward was proposed. Grimm showed the route of proposed arterial highways through the 15th Ward and described demolitions, renewals, and improvements that would create a cultural center in the middle of the blighted area.[164] Grimm specifically pointed to the north–south arterial highway as "an eventual aid." By May of the same year, the state had outlined a $50 million arterial route plan through the city; it would take a decade to complete.

According to Grimm, arterials were part of a dynamic plan making available new sites for displaced business establishments by undertaking clearance projects.[165] He believed that Syracuse "badly needed a modern highway network. . . . The resulting reduction in downtown congestion and increased accessibility would markedly improve the economic condition of the area." This might encourage suburbanization, but Grimm, trained as a civil and mining engineer, did not consider it a planner's duty to influence where people choose to live.[166]

By late 1956, the route for the North–South Route 11 highway was approved with little participation of the people to be displaced, although several other groups did have input.[167] At a hearing conducted in accordance with the new federal highway act, more than one hundred attendees represented what was described as "practically every segment of community life: the Syracuse Chamber of Commerce, the Manufacturers Association; the Penn-Can Highway Committee; the Syracuse Automobile Club and the Dairymen's League. City Engineer Potter Kelly, voiced strong approval of the expressway."[168]

The National Interstate and Defense Highways Act of 1956 added to the state's ability to go forward with the highway plans for Syracuse. To qualify for 90 percent National Highway Program funding, New York included Syracuse's network in the interstate system and built the roads as interstate highways. In avoiding a large financial burden, the city sacrificed planning and approval power for debt avoidance and had little to say about interstate section siting.

Adding to the acceptability of sacrificing local input to achieve economically desirable projects was the orientation in the administration of New York Governor Nelson Rockefeller toward state-guided massive construction projects to address racial and environmental issues. Rockefeller tripled the annual rate of road construction compared with that of the previous gubernatorial administration. Although some of the state largess came after Syracuse leaders had made urban highway commitments (or acquiescences), the Rockefeller administration reinforced the notion that deference to state funding was responsible.[169]

Not until 1958 did Mayor Anthony Henniger and one common council member oppose parts of the state plan: to build a string of high-speed highway bridges through the city in what local newspapers referred to as "the heart of the community." The mayor said he had not realized that the plans "had gone so far" and he had learned that elevated highways "have ruined other cities."[170]

The many 15th Ward families displaced by the project were given little assistance in finding suitable replacement housing. The only information provided to the residents was in the form of printed handbills listing dates for vacating properties and a demolition timetable. Descriptions of government-planned uses for the parcels to be vacated were distributed.

Financial reimbursements for lost residences were considered equitable and sufficient support for the families who had lost their homes.[171]

Nor was sufficient replacement housing available for all of the families who had been displaced: In a May 5, 1957, *Post-Standard* article entitled "Only 718 Units In Housing For Uprooted," the newspaper reported:

A total of 3,337 families, of which 812 are Negro, are scheduled for displacement in Syracuse in the next three and a half years, from 1957 to 1960, because of government action. The [*Post-Standard*] newspaper also pointed out that the city now has available to it only 718 units of potential state and federal housing to accommodate those who will be uprooted.[172]

Albert C. Ettinger, a field representative of the New York State Commission for Human Rights, noted that:

In 1960 there were 1,902 Negro families living in the 15th Ward. More than half of these families had incomes of over $4,000. Assuming 20 percent of income is spent for rent—and Negroes are forced to spend nearly 25 percent of their income for private rentals in the 15th Ward—983 Negro families [out of 1,902] could have afforded to live in the outer tracts.

Ravitch and Viteritti conclude:

The old Fifteenth Ward was a community that, while segregated, offered jobs, informal mentoring, and networks of community support. All those social structures were destroyed along with the buildings that were leveled . . . .[173]

East–West Route Decisions

For the east–west interstate (I-690), the second superhighway planned through Syracuse during the years 1944–1960,[174] the state again controlled the process. The state began early, negotiating with the New York Central Railroad to purchase railroad right-of-way. The New York Central wished to give up its terminal and main track through Syracuse at the same time that the major east–west interstate was being planned, effecting an intimate connection between the freeway's final configuration and the railroad.

Thus, by the late 1950s, quite early in the history of urban interstates, major plans had been assembled for both the north–south and east–west interstates in Syracuse. Sections of the road had been completed. A 14-mile stretch with traffic circles and approach entrances, from a central street to Oneida Lake, had its formal opening in October 1959. The highway was mainly a "three-strip, 12 feet wide road (in both directions)" differing from the thruway in that approximately 3½ miles lie within the city limits.[175]

There was some opposition to city-central interstate highways. The president of an important bank considered highway construction in Syracuse too risky financially; congestion could be better addressed by widening existing streets or constructing new ones.[176] City engineer Nelson Pitts concluded—as he thought many citizens not involved in the process did—that modern highways were "speed demons" and an altogether "tortuous nightmare," unnecessary and destructive. Pitts was fired. Some opponents pointed to the negative effects of railroads in the urban core: the decline of downtown Syracuse was proof that transportation could not alter the decline of the urban central business district.

Later, some officials concluded an elevated structure spanning the downtown would reduce property values and the expressway would threaten the aesthetic improvements planned for the renewal area, including a tree-lined mall. And in 1967, the city Department of Planning expressed concerns with the "problems and potential use of the land beneath the downtown expressways." It nevertheless was still "working closely with the New York State Department of Transportation" on these problems.[177]

By the mid-1960s, the center of Syracuse was the site of high-speed divided overhead interstate highways running north–south and east–west. They replaced parts of what were once old Italian-American, Jewish-American, African-American, and other ethnic neighborhoods. Housing under those freeways was gone, its residents dispersed and displaced. Business receipts had dropped in the central business district; and the number of manufacturing facilities was down, as were employment and population. Now a major newspaper described the interstate highway network as a "Russian roulette multimillion dollar boondoggle of concrete and steel."[178]

The declines experienced by the city of Syracuse are not uniquely attributable to choices about urban freeways. Industrial relocation and economically and racially motivated suburbanization were no doubt at play in Syracuse, as in many parts of the nation. But freeway decisions influenced and reinforced these other dynamics.

Memphis, Citizens to Preserve: "We Are Through with Overton Park"

Citizens to Preserve Overton Park v. Volpe is a landmark U.S. Supreme Court case that helped establish the current framework for judicial review of administrative action in the United States. In the *Overton Park* case, the Citizens to Preserve Overton Park, the National Audubon Society, and the Sierra Club successfully challenged the federal government's approval of an Interstate 40 alignment through Overton Park.[179]

I-40 begins in Barstow, California. Coursing eastward, following in parts the old Route 66, it connects cities from Flagstaff, Arizona, to Durham, North Carolina. It is more than 2,400 miles long and terminates in Fayetteville, North Carolina. By the mid-1960s, only short sections of it remained to be completed. One of these was a 3.74-mile stretch in the central part of the Memphis urban area that includes Overton Park.

Overton Park is a 342-acre, publicly owned park located within an affluent, predominantly white residential area in midtown Memphis.[180] At the closest point (the southwest corner), the park is located approximately 2.5 miles from the heart of the central business district. In 1901, the city of Memphis acquired the acreage for Overton Park and began to manage it for multiple uses. The park includes a zoo, a nine-hole municipal golf course, nature trails, an outdoor theater, bridle path, playgrounds, a small lake, a formal garden, picnic areas, an art academy, and the Brooks Art Gallery. One hundred seventy acres of the park remains as oak-hickory forest; in 1965, this represented more than half the woodland park land in Memphis. The playgrounds, golf course, and picnic areas are in constant use. The forest is large enough to present a stopping point for many species of migratory birds in spring and fall. This also presents an opportunity for the public to enjoy bird watching in the park.[181] Named to honor the Overton family for their contributions to the city,[182] the park became renowned for its 170 acres of virgin forests and rolling green spaces, which are bisected by Lick Creek.[183]

In the mid-1950s, engineers began planning for a transcontinental route running through Memphis from Nashville on the east and from Little Rock on the west. It was planned that the route would cross the Mississippi River at Memphis. Proponents of the alignment contended that the high-speed, six-lane corridor running east–west through the heart of the city (and through Overton Park) would augment local commuter access.[184]

Memphis officials began consideration of a highway in and around Overton Park in 1953, when expressways were characterized by city engineer Will Flower as "fads." Nonetheless, Mr. Flower toured those fads in other cities and supported a Memphis link.[185] In 1955, Harland Bartholomew and Associates were employed to study possible locations of interstate highway routes in Memphis and Shelby County. Their studies were jointly financed by the city of Memphis, Shelby County, the Tennessee Department of Public Works, and the BPR. The boards of commissioners of Memphis and of Shelby County adopted the basic transportation system plan that resulted from the studies in August 1955.[186] In the plan, the east–west interstate was routed through Overton Park.

One month after Harland Bartholomew and Associates submitted the engineering studies to the state, Frank Ragsdale, chairman of the traffic advisory commission (TAC), proposed a major restructuring of the city's expressway plan. Ragsdale pointed out that the TAC had always been opposed to the east–west route through Overton Park. He added that the TAC had pushed for a circumferential route, which would allow access to the central business district while providing for dispersion of industry and the creation of an adequate truck bypass route. Ragsdale further stated that: "the city commission overruled the TAC recommendation for elimination of the east-west expressway because of pressure exerted by the downtown merchants."[187] Decrying the proposed route, Ragsdale stated that his plan would save millions in the right-of-way purchases required by the east–west route proposed by Harland Bartholomew and Associates and added: "This route would not serve anybody but Nashville . . . the only reason for it is politics and it is ridiculous. Top planners say never cut through parks and playgrounds."[188]

In 1956, the BPR approved the corridor alignment of I-40 through the park. Controversy arose almost immediately. In 1956, at a meeting in Trinity Methodist Church, citizens spoke against the route. However, according to Mrs. Anona Stoner, then-secretary of Citizens to Preserve Overton Park, many of the citizens who attended the public hearing on the interstate system that was held in Memphis on October 15, 1956, did not really understand what an expressway actually was and failed therefore to comprehend the detrimental impacts its construction would have on the park. As Richard Henry Ginn points out:

The value of any public hearing depends on how much information is available to the public before the hearings are held. Starting cold, a citizen hoping to present a case must find out what information is available, where in the bureaucratic maze of the state offices it lies, and what cooperation or opposition he is likely to encounter in digging it out.[189]

In the Memphis case, opponents were initially disorganized and were only able to put forth emotional pleas for modifying the proposed route at the time their testimony was submitted to the BPR with the state's proposal. However, expressway opponents did garner critical information from their experiences at the public hearing. As Ginn states, "The message was simple. Organization was the only means of effectively counteracting the pro-interstate forces." He adds that in the years between 1961 and 1964, opposition to the interstate ceased to be characterized by uncoordinated, sporadic attacks on the Overton Park segment of the interstate and became typified by a unified and coordinated confrontation.[190]

In 1957, opponents collected ten thousand signatures supporting their anti-freeway case.[191] Soon thereafter, at a public hearing in 1958 required by the Federal-Aid Highway Act of 1956, considerable opposition to building in the beloved park began to be formally heard.[192]

As citizen concern grew, so did the number of freeway route alternatives to alignment through the park and the studies of those alternatives, including those focused on design. At various times, transportation officials considered cut and fill, bored tunnels partially depressed, and multimode transitways.

Of the many routes that were considered as alternatives to routing the alignment through the park, two were the most serious contenders. The first alternative, which followed the park's northern boundary, would have displaced or disturbed a church, a university, and a school, in addition to other facilities.[193] The other alternative, which followed an old railroad right-of-way and northern creek beds, would have "severely impacted one of the few racially mixed areas in the city."[194]

Four design alternatives to routing the alignment through Overton Park were also outlined, including:

[1] Building the road on the land's surface; [2] constructing the road below grade level as far as the underlying water table and natural drainage constraints allowed; [3] building the road below the land's surface by overcoming water table and drainage problems; [4] hiding the road entirely as it transected the park.[195]

City officials were reasonably open to constructing the roadway below grade, but they were concerned that building the road below the water table "would risk flooding if power outages in storms stopped the electric pumps that would then be required."[196] Because of the city's high water table, I-40 could not be depressed more than 10 feet beneath the grade of the surrounding park and would have to be elevated to cross Lick Creek.[197] Given those constraints on development, only the first and second design alternatives were considered feasible. Tennessee highway officials had always preferred the first alternative, as it was "the cheapest, least complicated, and most familiar form of construction."[198] Restudies and alternative studies consistently led to the state's conclusion that the original route through the park was the most economical and the least environmentally destructive.

Between 1958 and 1964, the controversy surrounding the Overton Park alignment remained relatively quiet for two reasons: (1) local, state, and federal officials had already approved the route, thereby reducing opportunities for further discussion or objection; and (2) opponents had not yet channeled their efforts into a cohesive strategy.[199]

In May 1964, the state employed the consulting firm of Buchart-Horn to begin designing the east–west interstate. By this time, however, opponents of the Overton Park route had coalesced into a civic group—the Citizens to Preserve Overton Park (CPOP). Members of this group were much better organized in their efforts to prevent use of the park for the interstate, and retention of the Buchart-Horn firm seemed to revitalize the opposing forces.[200]

CPOP was created in 1957 in response to Memphis newspaper articles featuring maps of the proposed route through the park.[201] CPOP "was never very large," however, its members were "resourceful and imaginative in their efforts to marshal political support against I-40."[202]

When the Harland Bartholomew and Associates' chief engineer appeared before the first hearing of the city commission in September 1957, he was greeted by more than 300 citizen protesters, who had accumulated thousands of signatures on petitions opposing the route. As a result, Harland Bartholomew and Associates was instructed by the commission to restudy alternative routes.[203]

In June 1964 another group, the Memphis Park Commission, unanimously passed a resolution opposing the planned location of Interstate 40 through the park. Park opponents spent the summer garnering support from all available sources and generating reams of correspondence in opposition to the proposed route.

When the city of Memphis supplanted the city commission with a mayor and city council in 1967, CPOP became re-engaged in local politics.[204] In an attempt to make the I-40 route a central issue in the upcoming elections, CPOP sent each candidate a questionnaire regarding his stance on the roadway's alignment.[205] When this effort failed to provide the desired results, CPOP directed its efforts toward decision makers in Washington, D.C.[206] CPOP's secretary, Anona Stoner, wrote repeatedly to Secretary of Transportation Boyd and Administrator Bridwell; her correspondence eventually prompted Bridwell's first visit to Memphis.[207] On February 13, 1968, CPOP addressed the new city council.[208] The following day CPOP, along with other interested parties, took part in a lengthy meeting with Administrator Bridwell.[209]

On March 5, 1968, the city council adopted a resolution opposing the park route, but CPOP's success in having motivated the council's action was fleeting. During an April 3 meeting among the council, Administrator Bridwell, and Harland Bartholomew, the city council reversed its decision.[210] On April 4, the city council approved the I-40 route through Overton Park.

Within weeks of the city council's approval, then-Secretary of Transportation John Volpe concurred with the judgment of local officials that I-40 should be built through Overton Park. The six-lane highway would be in a right-of-way approximately 250 feet wide; it would separate the park's zoo from the remainder of the park and would take 26 acres of the park. The EIS, now required by federal law, described the benefits expected from completion of I-40. Among them was the elimination of detours and diversion of a large number of longer east–west trips through the metropolitan area on arterial streets to the interstate facility. The diversion would ameliorate badly congested peak-hour traffic conditions.[211]

That same year, the 1968 amendments to the Federal-Aid Highway Act were passed. As we noted in chapter 5, the amendments required a national policy of preservation of natural beauty of the countryside and public park and recreation lands, wildlife and waterfowl refuges, and historic sites. They reiterated the section 4(f) requirement of the Department of Transportation Act of 1966 that, except in the most unusual of circumstances, the Secretary of Transportation could not approve any program or project requiring the use of publicly owned lands unless no feasible and prudent alternative to the use of such land exists, and then only with all possible planning to minimize harm to public resources.

In September 1969, the state acquired the right-of-way inside the park. By that time about two thousand families had been relocated for the I-40 completion. Two months later, final route and design approval were announced by Secretary Volpe.[212] After 10 years of opposing the alignment in the political realm, CPOP resolved to present its case in the judicial arena.[213]

By now, local and national conservation groups had joined citizens in opposing the alignment, appearing at public hearings, leafleting, and protesting. In 1969, the coalition brought suit. The plaintiffs in the case included CPOP, the Sierra Club, and the National Audubon Society. Memphis citizens and property owners William W. Deupree, Sr., and Sunshine K. Snyder were also listed as plaintiffs.[214] The litigants began by requesting a temporary injunction preventing the Secretary of Transportation from releasing federal funds to the state's highway department for the construction of the section of I-40 through Overton Park.[215]

To be successful in their suit, the plaintiffs had to show that Secretary Volpe's decision to release funding for the roadway was invalid. To that end, they argued that the secretary was not in compliance with Department of Transportation regulations, which stated that any state highway department submitting plans for a federal-aid highway project going through a city had to hold public hearings wherein members of the public could express their opinions about the proposed project. The procedure for holding public hearings also allowed for the submission of written statements by members of the public. The procedure for submitting written statements must be described in the notice of public hearing and at the public hearing. The plaintiffs alleged that the notice of the May 1969 public hearing on I-40 failed to announce that written statements could be submitted.[216] The regulations also require that the state highway department must create a verbatim written transcript of the oral proceedings at each public hearing. Because of a recording equipment malfunction during the May 1969 meeting, the plaintiffs alleged, the transcript of the proceedings was incomplete.[217]

Concluding that the regulations had been substantially followed and that any error was harmless, the district court granted summary judgment to the defendants on those issues.[218] It came to light that all whose oral statements at the hearing were not recorded were advised by certified mail that a written statement could be filed. It was determined that forty written statements had been filed, including those filed by members of CPOP. Therefore, the plaintiffs failed to demonstrate that anyone who would have filed a statement did not because of lack of notice, nor did the plaintiffs show that any argument was omitted because of lack of notice.[219]

The plaintiffs in *Citizens to Preserve Overton Park v. Volpe* also contended that, in not supplying factual findings with respect to any feasible and prudent alternative or why design changes could not be made to reduce harm to the park, the secretary's action was arbitrary and capricious and, as such, invalid. The plaintiffs further argued that the secretary's decision to release funds was void under the Department of Transportation Act and the Federal-Aid Highway Act because Volpe had issued no formal finding. The district court disposed of these arguments by finding that the statute contains no such requirement and that the court would not imply one.[220] Sidestepping the issue of whether the secretary was required to make a determination as to a desirable alternative, or whether he had, in fact, made such a determination,[221] the district court ruled against the plaintiffs, finding no basis for concluding that the secretary had exceeded his authority (401 US 402). Granting summary judgment for the defendants, the courts rejected the plaintiffs' motion for a temporary injunction and dismissed the case.[222]

The plaintiffs then turned to the appellate court, and the Sixth Circuit Court of Appeals granted a temporary injunction preventing Secretary Volpe from releasing funds pending the outcome of their appeal.

However, the appellate court also found in favor of the defendants in the case, concluding that required procedures had been followed and that any errors were harmless. The court further found that the secretary had, in fact, made the determination required by law and that no evidence introduced by the plaintiffs disputed this.[223]

Although the plaintiffs were not successful in winning their case, they had managed to delay construction from the date of their filing until September 29, 1970. The plaintiffs then moved for a rehearing; this motion was denied on October 30, 1970. On the same date, the Tennessee Highways Department began requesting bids for the contract to construct the highway through the park; a contract was awarded on the following business day. Three days later, the plaintiffs sought a stay from the Sixth Circuit Court of Appeals until such time as the U.S. Supreme Court could consider their motion for certiorari. On November 6, Sixth Circuit Justice Stewart issued an order halting construction until the Supreme Court could rule on the plaintiffs' application for stay.[224]

The U.S. Supreme Court reversed the lower court's opinion and issued its findings on March 2, 1971.[225] In an opinion by Justice Marshall, the court reasoned that constructing a highway through a park would always be less costly and would cause less disruption to residential and commercial properties than building the highway in another location. The court found Congress' purpose in enacting the pertinent sections of the Federal-Aid Highway Act and the Department of Transportation Act was to give "paramount importance" to protecting parks.[226] Therefore, the secretary did not have discretion to approve a highway route through a park simply because factors such as cost or community impacts favor such a route.[227] The court found that the secretary could approve a highway routed through a park only in "the most unusual situations."[228]

The court lectured: "the very existence of these statutes [the Department of Transportation Act of 1966, as amended, and section 18(a) of the Federal-Aid Highway Act of 1968] indicates that protection of parkland was to be given paramount importance. The few green havens that are public parks were not to be lost unless there were truly unusual factors present in a particular case or the cost of community disruption resulting from alternative routes reaches extraordinary magnitudes. If the statutes are to have any meaning, the Secretary cannot approve the destruction of parklands unless he finds that alternative routes present unique problems."[229]

The Supreme Court remanded the case for further proceedings in the district court. The resulting trial, which took 35 days, led to the decision that Secretary Volpe did not actually decide to approve the highway or, *if he did*, he misread the law. *Overton Park* was then sent back to the agency.

Once the decision making was again in the Department of Transportation, there began a long, complex, almost comical set of findings, reversals, re-submittals, and reviews of alternative strategies for the completion of I-40. In 1972, federal and state officials prepared a combined environmental impact/section 4(f) statement on the open-cut (partially depressed) design through the park. After the required hearings, the acting Federal Highway Administrator communicated to Secretary Volpe that the FHWA had determined that the federal findings requirements had been met.

Because it had been determined that Secretary Volpe had made a proper decision as to the design of the proposed route, he had only to determine whether the Overton Park route was the only prudent and feasible route. The case had been remanded to the secretary solely for the purpose of making a route determination in compliance with section 4(f) of the Department of Transportation Act of 1966.[230]

However, in a dramatic turnabout, Secretary Volpe rejected the determination: Other locations could be characterized as prudent, and a tunnel design would be less harmful to Overton Park. Mr. Volpe, who was to become ambassador to Italy, communicated his decision on the day he left for Rome, January 19, 1973. In the words of Secretary Volpe:

> On the basis of the record before me and in light of guidance provided by the Supreme Court, I find that an Interstate highway as proposed by the State through Overton Park cannot be approved. On that record I cannot find, as the Statute requires, and as interpreted by the courts, that there are no prudent and feasible alternatives to the use of parkland nor that the broader environmental protection objectives of the NEPA and the Federal-Aid Highway Act have been met, nor that the existing proposal would comply with FHWA standards on noise.[231]

Secretary Volpe made these determinations in spite of the FHWA's finding that no feasible and prudent alternative to the park route existed.[232] Once again, Volpe did not specify a particular route that would represent a prudent and feasible alternative to the use of the park.[233]

On February 1, 1973, after Secretary Volpe only made a determination of "possible alternatives" for the state of Tennessee to consider—without deciding upon a specific alternative and without rejecting the "no build" alternative—Tennessee Department of Highways Commissioner Charles W. Speight petitioned the district court for an order requiring the secretary "to comply with terms of remand order or, alternatively, to dissolve injunction as to state defendant."[234]

The crux of the state's petition to the court was that the state was entitled either to approval of the Overton Park route or to a formal statement of which other route would be prudent and feasible, in addition to specific findings as to any legal deficiencies of the Overton Park route. The secretary's rejection of the Overton Park route and lack of determination as to an acceptable alternative left the state with no evident direction—and with no alternative proposal assured of federal funding.[235]

On May 1, 1973, the district court held that Secretary Volpe's finding was not sufficient. It further held that the new Secretary of Transportation, Claude S. Brinegar, must either specify a prudent and feasible route so the court could evaluate the correctness of the determination or find that there were no prudent and feasible alternative routes.[236] Both CPOP and the Secretary of Transportation appealed this decision.[237] The Sixth Circuit Court of Appeals reversed the decision and upheld the secretary's findings, which held that the statute did not require him to specify a prudent and feasible alternative route once he did find that one existed.[238]

Secretary Brinegar, the second of five who would face making a decision on I-40 in Memphis, ordered a review of a new Tennessee submission that included two tunnel design alternatives, a new location, and a less capital intensive alternative using transit and arterial streets. The studies were presented to Mr. Brinegar's successor, William T. Coleman, Jr., who directed preparation of an EIS that would fully consider tunnel design and "analyze location alternatives previously studied, as well as various design and construction techniques for minimizing harm to Overton Park."[239]

State and local officials opposed the tunnel alternative on the basis of construction and maintenance costs.[240] The state then proposed a "sunken Plaza roadway." In 1976 dollars, its projected cost was $33 million. The roadway would be depressed throughout the park and covered with landscaped decks.[241]

In a 1976 public hearing, more than 200 people presented their views on alternative designs, benefits, and costs of the construction through the park. The president of the Memphis Area Chamber of Commerce called the completion of the project "a key link to the Memphis economic development." But a citizen concluded that "what killed downtown in the first place were expressways." Benefits would be enjoyed only by construction companies and East Memphians who would be able to commute to downtown 5 minutes faster.[242]

A Tennessee Department of Transportation attorney concluded that a special act of Congress effectively exempting the project from NEPA would provide the quickest means to resolve the standoff and allow construction to go forward.[243]

State officials next approached the new Secretary of Transportation, Brock Adams, in March 1977. A new proposal, now referred to as "the plaza-design" was described in the meeting attended by the governor, two senators, the mayors of Memphis and Shelby County, and two members of the U.S. House of Representatives from the Memphis districts. The state was treating the decision very seriously. "Adams promised a relatively quick decision," reported the local newspaper.[244] But another group with the opposite objective also visited Mr. Adams. Included were the Sierra Club, the National Recreation and Park Association, the Mid-Memphis Improvement Association, the National Trust for Historic Preservation, Citizens to Preserve Overton Park, the National Audubon Society, Council for a Greener Memphis, the University of Tennessee Center for the Health Sciences, and a number of professionals and business people.[245]

"We Are Through with Overton Park"

Less than 6 months later, a local newspaper headline read: "We Are Through with Overton Park Officials Say, Ending Decades of Delay."[246] Brock Adams announced his decision "to reject the proposal of the State of Tennessee to build I-40 through Overton Park. This proposal . . . does not meet the standards required by the Supreme Court."

State transportation officials then laid out three options: "modify the proposal to fully address the Supreme Court standards . . . ask the Tennessee delegation to seek special federal legislation to either exempt Overton Park from [federal laws] . . . or ask them to allow a local referendum which will permit those people directly affected by I-40 to decide the future of the interstate and the park."[247]

A congressional panel then suggested that it was not out of the question to continue to pursue some plan for putting a freeway through the park. Secretary Adams himself said at an October 1977 meeting of a subcommittee of the Senate Environment and Public Works Committee, "Senator, if they (Tennessee officials) want to come in and tunnel that park and stay within that busway and ventilate it, then that project can be built." Mr. Adams "appeared to back off" from his ruling made less than one week earlier.[248]

However, many were skeptical about high cost options. The Memphis mayor pointed out: "I don't want to cut down any possibility, including a cut-and-cover tunnel . . . [but] . . . . The last cost estimate I heard for that was around $237 million."[249]

Nonetheless, state officials did put some hope in the secretary's comments and soon came back with a compromise alternative. A "nearly covered" option was proposed in November 1977. Now, rather than the 40 percent covered solution which the secretary had rejected, Commissioner Shaw and his staff suggested a 60 percent cover, which would cost about $40 million.

Meanwhile, a new sense of urgency rose. Secretary Adams was proposing a policy change at the federal level: states that had not completed their interstate segments would need to commit themselves to construction by 1982 or allocated funds would be made available for other projects, including mass transit projects. Adams rejected the partial cover idea, however, and federal funding for the route through Overton Park was thereby effectively precluded.

The idea of financing the route through the park without federal funds arose again, but Citizens to Preserve Overton Park argued that any attempt to build the road through the park, no matter how funded, would be controlled by federal law because I-40 would still be a federal interstate.

However, Senator Howard Baker of Tennessee introduced legislation that would exempt the Memphis stretch of I-40 from federal laws and allow for the partially covered tunnel alternative. By the narrowest of margins, 7–6, the Senate Public Works Committee rejected the Baker idea. Officially, the saga of Overton Park ended.[250] The committee heard testimony that suggests why the case had taken so long and why the challenge to highway administrators was so great: "Overton Park is a historic place—a battle site like Gettysburg and Yorktown. It is the first place where individual citizens used the law to stop the state and federal highway."[251]

Yet, even with Overton Park saved, the controversy over the completion of I-40 did not abate. Various bypass ideas and the use of surface streets combined with some interstate construction for a while kept the citizens of Memphis concerned about I-40. Nonetheless, 3 days prior to President Reagan's January 20, 1981, inauguration, the state of Tennessee requested that the midtown Memphis segment of I-40 be dropped from the interstate system. The committed funding for the proposed route ($300 million in federal funds) was then released to the city of Memphis to be used for other transportation-related objectives.[252]

On June 29, 2006, the fiftieth anniversary of President Dwight D. Eisenhower's signing of the highway bill clearing the way for the interstate system, the Tennessee Department of Transportation (TDOT) hosted a ceremonial event in Memphis. During the event, the TDOT unveiled a historic marker commemorating and documenting the Overton Park

Case, which continues to influence highway projects across the nation four decades after a final determination was made in the case.[253]

Present at the event were two local attorneys—Charles Newman and William M. Walsh—whose firms were on opposing sides during the I-40 litigation. Although his firm failed to prevail in the case, Mr. Walsh expressed his opinion about the lasting significance of the suit: "It was a very important case. . . . It was a warning to road planners not to design roads that go through parkland." Charles Newman, whose firm was on the winning side, noted that, in spite of several defeats at the district- and appellate-court levels, the plaintiffs carried the day because the Supreme Court "read a lot of teeth" into the highway act. Added Newman: "The outcome was always in doubt until the end."[254]

With the defeat of the route through Overton Park, I-40 was redirected onto the north loop of I-40/I-240. Completed portions of the expressway became part of Sam Cooper Boulevard. The outcome of the court case forced the TDOT to construct lengthy and expensive projects to overhaul two interchanges at the site of the intersection of I-40 and I-240.[255]

Nevertheless, according to Newman, the impacts of building the highway through Memphis' downtown area would have been far worse. He maintained: "Interstates are wonderful between cities and around cities. When they're built through cities they become Chinese walls dividing one part of the city from the other and doing a great deal of damage." Whereas some people argue that the downtown area was harmed because the loss of the Midtown–Overton route denied direct east–west expressway access to the downtown, Newman argues conversely. Citing data demonstrating that expressways "suck strength" from downtowns, he added, "I do believe the city's better off without it."[256]

The planned construction of I-40 also fomented debate in the city of Nashville, Tennessee; however, the outcome was quite different. The controversy regarding Interstate 40 in Nashville embodied several characteristics similar to those in Memphis, both cities in the state with the most miles of this interstate: impact on an urban park; early taking of homes (eleven hundred properties) and relocation of people for a route through an urban neighborhood; very limited public hearings (the major one held the day after official notice was given); redesign requests; and challenges in the federal courts. But the Nashville project was completed. The lawsuit, charging that construction of the highway would erect a physical barrier between a predominantly black area and other parts of Nashville, was unsuccessful. The route now traverses the city (see *Nashville I-40 Steering Committee v. Ellington*, 387 F. 2d 179, 6th Circuit, 1967).

Los Angeles: The Freeway with a Heart

In 1959, the California legislature created the California Freeway and Expressway System, authorizing a grid-like network of freeways overlaying the entire Los Angeles basin.[257] The goal of transportation planners at the time was that no resident of Los Angeles should ever be more than a few miles away from a freeway. The resulting dense grid feature proposed projects that, as funds dried up and public opposition began to evolve, would never be more than dotted lines on a planner's or engineer's map; such projects included the now-impossible-to-imagine Beverly Hills, Pacific Coast, and Malibu Freeways.

A young public interest lawyer in Southern California explained[258]:

Freeways that had a higher priority in terms of transportation justification were getting knocked off in Sacramento because of political clout. Beverly Hills freeway Route 2 is certainly one of those . . . Beverly Hills just boom, zapped that thing in a second. Others too, up and down the state. As these freeways of higher transportation priority got deleted, Century kept moving up. There's nobody down there in south central L.A. area—Watts, Willowbrook—the communities that the freeway transgressed have no political clout or influence or capacity to go to Sacramento to say, "We don't like this here or . . . if you're going to build it you've got to take into account the effects on our communities, etc." Of course, that's a classic situation where those with fewer resources are underrepresented in the legislative arena and the effects in this case were dramatic.

As planned, the Century Freeway roughly paralleled Century Boulevard through southern Los Angeles County, running east–west from San Bernardino, California, to the proposed Pacific Coast Freeway west of Los Angeles International Airport (LAX). Exact route location studies for the Century Freeway commenced in 1959. The eastern 34 miles were soon deleted from the project. The route of the remaining portion of the freeway, a 17-mile stretch through a densely populated corridor from the LAX area to the San Gabriel Freeway (I-605), was adopted in two stages, the western half in 1965, and the eastern half in 1968.

As it was proposed in the late 1960s, the Century Freeway was a ten-lane facility with no provisions included for high occupancy vehicle (HOV) lanes or ramp metering. More than twenty interchanges were planned to service local arterials in the ten jurisdictions the freeway traversed. Construction was to begin in 1972, and the entire route was projected to open to traffic in 1977. Building the $500 million project would displace an estimated 21,000 persons living in approximately 7,000 dwelling units in the freeway right-of-way.

Almost from its inception, the Century Freeway was controversial. During the route adoption process for the freeway's eastern end, the city of Norwalk fought successfully for termination of the freeway at I-605, eliminating 1.5 miles of roadway east to the Santa Ana Freeway (I-5). The city of Inglewood succeeded in having the western portion of the freeway routed to its south, much to the displeasure of the city of Hawthorne, whose central business district would be bisected by the proposed route. Authorities in Hawthorne refused to sign a freeway agreement for this route, which was later realigned to skirt the Hawthorne–Inglewood border.

As described previously, the abandonment of San Francisco's Embarcadero Freeway in 1966 and its subsequent elimination from the federal interstate highway system freed federal highway funds for reallocation to other interstate links in California. Amendments to the Federal-Aid Highway Act in 1968 designated the Century Freeway as Interstate 105, and funds originally earmarked for the Embarcadero were directed toward the Century Freeway.

As land acquisition for and design of the Century Freeway progressed, opponents of the freeway organized. A group of "Freeway Fighters" in Hawthorne sponsored a referendum opposing the freeway; it passed by a margin of five to one. The city of Downey sought aesthetic and noise attenuation concessions from the state highway agency (known as Caltrans) before it would approve the freeway. Meanwhile, state and federal authorities determined that the Century Freeway project was exempt from formal environmental impact statement requirements enacted in 1970, arguing that a multidisciplinary design team (in California, a recent Caltrans innovation) had developed the project with satisfactory consideration of social, economic, and environmental facts. By 1972, more than 35 percent of the needed parcels had been acquired, and 35 percent had been cleared.

Both social and economic costs of the proposed freeway were heavily borne by corridor cities such as Lynwood, predominantly a city of single-family homes bounded by South Gate on the north, Compton on the south, the Los Angeles River on the east, and Willowbrook on the west.[259]

Postwar prosperity brought thousands of residents to the area to buy homes on large lots using government-backed loans. In 1962, Lynwood was named All-American City by the National Municipal League.[260] By the late 1960s, however, as Caltrans began buying houses in the heart of the residential area for the Century Freeway, the damage to the social fabric became distressingly apparent. "About 11,000 homes and apartments were taken and the city's tax base diminished," declared Louis Heine, a retired elementary school principal who also served on the Lynwood City

Council. "Business along Long Beach Boulevard was all but destroyed by the threat of the freeway," he added.[261]

"The freeway was a huge problem," alleged Marilyn Cabaret, a 31-year Lynwood resident who served as the business-license representative in the city clerk's office in 1991. "People were frightened. Landwise, it split the town in half. The freeway has taken over 25 years to build. After people moved out of the homes in the path of the freeway, the houses sat vacant for years. Many businesses began to leave, too," she said, adding that, in the early 1970s, "Whites moved out in droves because they were afraid of the impact of integration and the freeway" (figure 6.4).[262]

In February 1972, one month prior to the planned start of construction,[263] a newly created public interest law firm, the Center for Law in the Public Interest, filed a federal lawsuit on behalf of four couples living within the proposed freeway right-of-way. Several national civil rights and environmental activist organizations (The National Association for the Advancement of Colored People, the Sierra Club, and the Environmental Defense Fund) and the Hawthorne Freeway Fighters were also parties to the suit. The city of Hawthorne was added as a plaintiff in April 1972. The suit sought to prevent the state from acquiring property until environmental impact statements were approved. The suit also alleged inadequate relocation assistance, denial of equal protection to minorities and poor residents in the corridor, inadequate public hearings, and violation of due process.

In July 1972, federal district court judge Harry Pregerson ordered the state to stop work on the Century Freeway. The preliminary injunction [*Keith v. Volpe*, 352 F. Supp. 1324 (1972)] called for preparation of a formal EIS, additional hearings focusing on noise and air pollution concerns, further studies on the availability of replacement housing for those displaced by the project, and specific assurance by the state that it could provide relocation assistance and payments to those displaced by the roadway's construction. The decision was upheld on appeal [*Keith v. Volpe*, 506 F.2d 696 (1974) *cert. denied* 95 S.Ct. 826 (1975)]. Work on the Century Freeway would be halted for the next 9 years.

New legislation, and learning about the meaning of environmental impact assessment and other legal obligations fostered by public interest lawyers, had a significant impact in cases like the Century Freeway. In California, the additional influences of a number of leaders, not popular at times with the freeway builders, were significant.

In 1974, Californians elected a new governor, Jerry Brown; in the same year, Adriana Gianturco was appointed Secretary of Transportation. Both

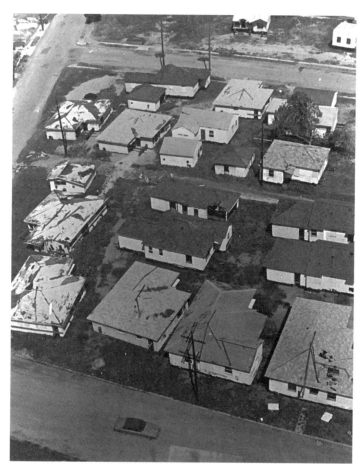

Figure 6.4
Scene of urban conditions during litigation over Century Freeway. *Source:* Century Freeway Corridor Cities Caucus, Presentation to the Honorable Drew Lewis, Secretary of Transportation, May 4, 1981.

events had an impact on Caltrans, as neither the new governor nor the new secretary were in favor of solving transportation problems strictly through the construction of more and bigger freeways. A public interest lawyer explained:

In 1974 we got a new governor and a new secretary of transportation, Adriana Gianturco, who had a very different view of freeways and building freeways. This was a period when Caltrans was going through a fairly major transition. It had all these people who had worked during the heyday of Caltrans—1950s and

1960s—building freeways up and down the state. All of a sudden the projects underway were completed and there were relatively few new ones underway and the Century Freeway was a big one that was going to be a big employer of these engineers . . . I think they saw the Century Freeway as a big boon to their work and keeping their people employed.[264]

Adriana Gianturco explained her position as follows:

We saw our freeway development in Los Angeles, as elsewhere, as being a part of a broader problem, which was: how do you provide for the movement of people and goods in an environmentally compatible, economically reasonable manner? And there was no presumption on our part that freeways were the best way to do it. If anything, the presumption was that the transportation system was too heavily dependent on highways and automobiles and that, if we were to fulfill the legislative mandate to create a balanced transportation system, it meant we needed to start devoting attention to other modes of transportation to bring them into some kind of balance with highways.[265]

As the state prepared and then circulated the EIS between 1972 and 1977, the abandoned neighborhoods in the corridor deteriorated. The mélange of vacant land and deserted buildings was the scene of numerous assaults and episodes of vandalism. Corridor cities increasingly pressured Governor Jerry Brown to complete the freeway promptly.

In December 1975, Governor Brown suggested that the proposed ten-lane facility be reduced to four lanes, indicating his opposition to construction of new major freeways in the Los Angeles area on the basis of air quality, energy, and funding constraints. Corridor cities insisted that the full ten-lane facility be constructed as proposed.

[Mayor Tom] Bradley . . . ran on a campaign of "Before my first term is over, I want to get the first dirt turned on a rapid transit system for the city of Los Angeles." [Public interest lawyers] looked at Tom Bradley and his people and said, "Here is an opportunity for you to come up with significant funds to begin a rapid transit corridor." He liked the idea . . . what he did is assemble all these local mayors and councilmen from cities, from Downey, Lynwood, Norwalk, all these people. Most of them are unsophisticated people. They've been now sold a bill of goods that the freeway is the best thing for them. They're going to have more gas stations; they're going to have more cars coming in; they're going to have small merchants; they're going to have greater numbers of people running through [the] communities; it's good for business.[266]

The state environmental process was completed in September 1977, and the EIS was then submitted to the federal government. The impact statement called for an eight-lane freeway plus a transitway. The western portion of the freeway would be routed away from Hawthorne's central business district.

The positions taken by Brown and Gianturco and Brown's view that replacement housing for the Century Freeway should be funded, at least in part, by funds formerly earmarked for transportation were not viewed favorably by the freeway construction coalition. In fact, their opinions

were extremely unpopular . . . among many interests in the state. Not in the least, of course, were the highway builders whose trust fund, the highway trust fund was . . . really the source of bread and butter for their businesses . . . and they had very much come to look upon it exactly like that. That's their money. . . . . So for Jerry [Brown] to want to hold back freeways in lieu of other types of transportation development was heresy enough. The fact that he was also talking about using some of this money to build replacement housing . . . that had been destroyed by transportation money . . . was even a more controversial measure. And then you had one third element . . . a lot of affirmative action . . . and clearly this was . . . ground breaking stuff. This was a totally different way of doing business than Caltrans had been used to.[267]

In March 1978, President Carter unveiled his National Urban Policy, in which transportation programs were considered incentives to leverage urban revitalization necessary to accomplish economic, environmental, and social goals. In October of the same year, Brock Adams, secretary of the U.S. Department of Transportation, announced his approval of the Century Freeway as proposed. On the same day, attorneys representing plaintiffs and defendants in the lawsuit announced they had reached a tentative settlement. A year later, the terms of the tentative settlement were memorialized in a consent decree.

The consent agreement contained several provisions that addressed the freeway's design and operation.[268] In addition to the transportation provisions, the consent decree contained an ambitious affirmative action program. One component of this program required contractors to hire high percentages of female and minority employees, based on demographic studies of the freeway corridor. The employment component also included apprenticeship programs for prospective construction employees. A second component required contractors to award high percentages of subcontracts to minority business enterprises (MBEs) and women-owned business enterprises (WBEs). The goals for MBE and WBE participation would be set on a project by project basis. The use of contractors and employees who resided or had businesses in the corridor was also required. The decree created the Century Freeway Affirmative Action Committee (CFAAC) to monitor and enforce their requirements. CFAAC was composed of representatives of community activist groups and parties to the consent decree and participated in project activities ranging from MBE/WBE goal setting to contractor compliance oversight.

The consent decree also included some novel provisions regarding housing. For the first time, federal highway funds not only would assist those persons actually displaced by the freeway but also would restock the supply of housing in communities that lost housing in right-of-way acquisition. The decree anticipated the construction and/or rehabilitation of 4,200 housing units in priority zones based on 6-mile intervals from the freeway routes. The California Department of Housing and Community Development, which was not a party to the lawsuit, was given lead agency status in implementing the massive housing program. The decree required phasing of freeway construction with progress on the housing program such that given percentages of housing units were available for occupancy when given percentages of freeway construction contracts had been awarded. In addition, housing contractors would have to comply with the decree's affirmative action provisions. The decree also established an independent "Office of the Advocate for Corridor Residents" to represent the interests of persons whom the freeway displaced.

On September 22, 1981, an amended consent decree, which downscaled the freeway to six lanes for general traffic and two HOV lanes, was approved. The Century Freeway would also feature ten local interchanges, ten transit stations, park and ride lots, and a 64-foot median strip. The proposed HOV connection with the Harbor Freeway was removed from the plans. The number of units to be constructed under the housing program was reduced from 4,200 units to 3,700 units. Provisions for affirmative action and the office of the advocate remained largely unchanged. At long last, ground was broken for the first Century Freeway construction project in May 1982.[269]

By 1991, the Century Freeway Housing Program had financed the construction of 1,237 rental units and 688 houses and condominiums. Another 2,500 housing units were in the planning stages. In 1991, about 60 percent of the built units were occupied by low-income families.[270]

In 1980, Los Angeles voters had passed Proposition A, which provided a one-half cent sales tax to be used partly for rail construction. The terms of the consent decree had awarded the decision regarding the type of transit system to be constructed in the median of the freeway to the Los Angeles County Transportation Commission. In June 1984, the commission voted to construct a light-rail transit line concurrent with construction of the freeway.[271]

In January 1985, then-Governor George Deukmejian praised efforts to construct the route and stated that its completion continued to be a top transportation priority. Deukmejian, however, expressed concern that the project, which was dependent upon federal funding for 92 percent of its costs, might be halted due to a congressional stalemate over how federal monies should be divided among the states. Of the $340 million in federal funding anticipated to be received by the state of California, approximately 40 percent had been earmarked for the Century Freeway. Until the matter was resolved, the Department of Transportation was withholding Highway Trust Fund money from the states.[272] At the time, only about 10 percent of the freeway had been completed. In July of the same year, however, the state transportation commission was able to approve $1.1 billion in funding for the remaining projects to be completed along the 17.3-mile corridor.[273]

During his January visit, the governor and his party also toured a condominium project that had been constructed to help replace the homes demolished to build the freeway. Constructed largely with federal funds, the three-bedroom condominiums cost approximately $85,000 apiece to build and were sold to displacees for an average of $25,000.[274]

However, in the city of Hawthorne, housing intended for predominantly minority residents of Hawthorne whose homes were being destroyed for the freeway was impeded by the city's actions. In 1984, the city council denied a needed zone change for one project (the Kornblum project) and made a second (the Cerise Avenue project) ineligible for funding under the state housing program by restricting the number of units that could be rented to low-income people to only 35 percent of the total units.[275]

The Center for Law in the Public Interest sued the city of Hawthorne in February 1985, claiming that the city had discriminated against minority and poor people by using zoning regulations to impede or halt the projects. In his September 1985 ruling, federal judge Harry Pregerson ordered the city to approve both complexes. However, one of the properties had been sold to a new owner after the city's actions, and the lawsuit delayed construction. The new property owner decided to build a conventional 32-unit project on the property; as a result, only one of the projects was constructed as replacement housing for low-income families.[276]

In June 1986, the *Los Angeles Times*, in an article entitled "Century Freeway—When It's Born, an Era Will Die," reported that after "nearly 30 years of planning, false starts and bitter litigation, the Century Freeway is finally taking shape along a 17.3-mile stretch from Los Angeles International Airport to the San Gabriel River Freeway in Norwalk." In the same article, the *Times* predicted that the Century Freeway would "almost certainly be the Los Angeles area's last major freeway, the final chapter of a phenomenal highway construction program that began with the Pasadena Freeway nearly 50 years ago." The *Times* reported that the Century Freeway, which had cost $1.8 billion as of June 1986, was "the most expensive urban freeway ever undertaken" and hypothesized that "no one will be surprised if the final price turns out to be considerably more than $2 billion."[277] One interchange alone, the proposed five-level, seven-stories-tall interchange at the junction of the Century and San Diego freeways, was projected to cost more than $200 million in 1986 dollars.[278]

In addition, the *Times* stated that the Century Freeway was "the nation's most litigated highway," with construction halted for the 9-year period from 1972 to 1981 "while the courts sorted out hundreds of issues ranging from whether the freeway was needed at all, to complex environmental challenges that fundamentally altered the way it is being built."[279]

Ronald B. Taylor extolled the distinctiveness of the planned route[280]:

There never has been anything quite like the high-flying, $135-million traffic interchange being built in South-Central Los Angeles to link the new Century Freeway with a remodeled Harbor Freeway. . . . It is the first time the state's traffic engineers have integrated three modes of transportation—light-rail trains, high-occupancy vehicles and individual cars—into one giant intersection.

The design of the Century–Harbor Interchange broke with the past. Some engineers suggested that it might become as famous as the Four Level Interchange in downtown Los Angeles, which revolutionized freeway interchange design 36 years ago. In spite of its revolutionary design features, however, it had become apparent by 1988 that the Century Freeway project had fallen far short of producing the thousands of units of affordable housing that had been promised along the 17.3-mile route of the freeway. In 1981, when construction of the Century Freeway and its light-rail line commenced, approximately 3,700 apartments and homes had been planned to replace about half the number of structures that had been demolished in its path. By 1988, only about 1,300 units had been made available.[281] The *Los Angeles Times* reported in 1988 that the Century Freeway Housing Program "was plagued by high costs, shoddy construction, high vacancy rates and strong opposition from some of the communities along the route."[282]

In that same year, as a result of the perceived deficiencies in the housing program, the Center for Law in the Public Interest proposed that the majority of the housing units remaining to be built be constructed not by the state Department of Housing and Community Development, but by a new nonprofit corporation, to be called the Century Community Housing

Corp. In documents presented by the Center for Law in the Public Interest on behalf of the plaintiffs to federal judge Harry Pregerson, the center's lawyers argued that the nonprofit group "would be able to build at least 2,500 new dwelling units in the next three years."[283]

In 1990, after the lengthy campaign to replace homes razed for the freeway, an agreement to allow local nonprofit organizations to construct and administer $55 million worth of low-cost housing had been reached. The original plan for constructing replacement housing had been established under the initial consent decree, issued 11 years prior to the date of the 1990 agreement, by federal judge Harry Pregerson. The state of California had planned to build around four thousand apartments and housing units—about half the number of structures destroyed to make way for the project—along the freeway route.[284] On June 7, 1990, the *Los Angeles Times* reported:

Under the arrangement approved by Pregerson this week, the state will commit $17.5 million of its remaining $126 million in Century Freeway housing funds. In addition, a nonprofit group called the Local Initiatives Support Corp., which has nationwide experience brokering funds for low-cost housing, will supply the rest of the financing needed to build the 500 housing units. Several local, community-based nonprofit groups, including Concerned Citizens of South-Central Los Angeles, will take responsibility for building the houses, selling some of them and managing others.[285]

On June 5, 1990, 2 days prior to the *Times* announcement about the resolution to the housing lawsuit, California voters endorsed a gasoline tax increase in order to complete the Century Freeway and dozens of other road projects in the state. In an attempt to push forward projects delayed by funding shortages, the California Transportation Commission approved $257 million for backlogged road projects throughout the state. However, a large portion of that funding was earmarked for construction on two phases of the Century Freeway.[286] "If the voters had not approved the tax increase, the delays would have continued and the 105 (Century Freeway) would have come to a screeching halt," asserted Charles J. O'Connell, a deputy district director for Caltrans in Los Angeles.[287]

In 1993—to great fanfare—the "freeway with a heart," "the intelligent freeway," "the most costly freeway ever built" finally opened. Around 1,500 people attended the 3-hour opening ceremonies. In addition to a short parade, the University of Southern California marching band, belly-dancers, American Indian storytellers, Japanese folk musicians, and the mascot for the Los Angeles Kings hockey team entertained the crowd.[288]

From inception to completion, the project devoured more than 30 years—or nearly triple the time normally required to construct a freeway. Said Rodney Slater, administrator of the Federal Highway Administration, "This project has been a long time coming, but it's been worth the wait because time has made the project about more than asphalt . . . steel, or . . . concrete. It's about *people.*"[289]

The latest in highway technology is embodied in the freeway, which has sensors buried in the pavement and linked to computers to monitor traffic flow. Closed-circuit television cameras alert highway officials to accidents that have occurred. There are meters to regulate traffic on the ramps that connect the Century Freeway to four other freeways. The Green Line fixed-rail transit system runs within the freeway median.[290]

In total, the construction of I-105 required 1,000 acres of land, 650 acres of which were reserved for landscaping.[291] The amount of land acquired and dedicated to landscaping made the Century Freeway project unique among its predecessors. In keeping with its stated goals of using minority businesses as project contractors, and in abiding by the terms of the Consent Decree, Caltrans employed scores of local contractors in the freeway's construction and landscaping and in the construction of replacement housing.

Journalist Nora Zamichow summarized[292]:

The Century Freeway sliced neighborhoods in two, tore through well-tended homes and displaced about 21,000 people living in its path. It created a wasteland roamed by vandals, a place where bodies and sofas were unceremoniously dumped. But the $2.2-billion project also has given the communities something in return. It is the only freeway that has provided housing and job training. It also has employed more women and minorities than any other transportation enterprise in California.

The low- and moderate-income housing program resulted in 15,000 jobs and constructed an assortment of homes, including apartment complexes offering after-school tutoring programs. The mandated job-training program graduated 3,426 people, 2,680 of who were placed in entry-level construction jobs.[293]

According to the Zamichow article, even officials from cities that vehemently opposed the project praised it as likely to spur economic growth and revitalize neighborhoods hit hard by the freeway construction and the economic downturn in the early 1990s. Hawthorne Mayor Steve Andersen, once a member of the Freeway Fighters, said, "The real estate community and the business community in the last six months, and from now on, will perceive the whole corridor as a good place to purchase land."[294]

Three Cities, Three Freeway Cases, Three Outcomes: A Summary of Decision Making

Although Syracuse, Memphis, and Los Angeles shared, along with several American municipalities, the influence of major forces linked to decisions about transportation, their historical responses were different from each other. Several factors are identifiable when these inner-city highway outcomes are compared.

In Syracuse, plans for an inner-city freeway were drawn up just a few years after the rise of the visionaries and the ascension of the highway engineering profession. Furthermore, in Syracuse, critical decisions were made before or relatively early in the evolution of transportation, environmental, and preservation law and policy that would now focus on mitigating environmental impacts of governmental actions, preserving historical places, relocating those affected by road building, maintaining housing stock in lower income areas, and encouraging participation of citizens who would be affected.[295] In Memphis, the influence of these law and policy changes had commenced, and citizens and grassroots environmental organizations had begun to learn how to take advantage of them and of new laws requiring public hearings. There, too, the location decisions made early in the freeway building era did not embody the visionary benefits of putting major thoroughfares through city centers: to lessen congestion, promote commerce, and clear out areas perceived as blighted. The route was designed to traverse a much-used and well-beloved city park. In Los Angeles, a new and highly effective public interest law firm helped shape the meaning of the new generation of legislation and policy initiatives. When Syracuse was considering its highways, the public interest law movement had not matured.[296]

Central to the Syracuse case was the early convergence of planning goals of "slum clearance" and redevelopment (later urban renewal) and the transportation goals of eliminating congestion and improving mobility, in major part to maintain city economic vitality—at relatively the same time as funding opportunities arose from new sources. Urban freeways were seen as vehicles to achieve both goals. Competing visions of massive inner-city road projects that emphasized their disruptive, rather than their positive, effects had not been widely disseminated. In Memphis, mobility and congestion were concerns, but when an urban park became a possible solution, the focus was less on transportation and economic goals and more on preservation and urban quality of life. The Los Angeles case was mixed. Some of the cities through which the Century Freeway was routed may have benefited from some forms of redevelopment, but others were neither interested nor in need of massive infrastructural changes. Mobility in the Los Angeles region, however, has been a major concern for many years. What's more, the aesthetic assaults that freeways could effect were clearly visible on the ground, countering the magical motorway fantasies that had abounded in previous years.

Also related to the outcome of the early highway decision making in Syracuse was "the ambiguous and rudimentary nature of the planning function" in city government during the 1940s and 1950s.[297] City planning was a relatively new profession. Highway engineering was much more entrenched and effective. As we have stressed throughout this book, highway engineers dominated discussions about the value of urban routes and decisions about where they would be placed. In fact, Syracuse's planning department was made up, until the late 1950s, mainly of engineers. Engineers were also centrally involved in our other two cases; however, their dominance was actively challenged by new and more vocal constituencies and stakeholders assisted by new laws and embryonic public interest law groups.

Syracuse did not make historic preservation a priority.[298] City officials viewed distinctive city sections as expendable or as blighted areas needing to be razed. In Memphis, in contrast, a strong historical attachment to the affected area was present. Los Angeles jurisdictions did not focus on historical preservation, but early opposition did come from cities proud of their quality of life. Also lacking in Syracuse (and related to the outcome) was an "extensive cross-city, cross-class, and interracial" alliance that brought attention (from elsewhere) to the freeway problem.[299] The city did have the Congress of Racial Equality, and the 15th Ward was quite heterogeneous, but concerns of the various groups were not yet organized into a position that could be neatly legally represented with a focus on freeways. The presence of such an alliance was at least partially a factor in Los Angeles.

Syracuse leadership at the time was willing to defer to nonlocal interests that were heavily dominated by the highway engineering profession to meet economic, fiscal, and mobility goals and to maintain fiscal solvency, a city shibboleth.[300] The city administration was mindful that continuing eligibility for state and federal funding depended on expeditious completion of arterial construction. In Memphis, the state highway bureaucracy faced strong citizen opposition, which did not make funding a project perceived as damaging to Overton Park an attractive option. In Los Angeles, the coalition of opponents simply overwhelmed concerns about the loss of highway construction funds until the negative results of no action became clear across urban neighborhoods: vandalism, crime, urban decay.

In Syracuse, the term *citizen participation* had a more narrow application than would be the case later and in other cities including in the Los Angeles region where urban freeways would be considered.[301] Evolving activism focused on racial equality and perceived insensitive urban redevelopment, which many did not even link to building of interstate routes. The Los Angeles case, in fact, was a revolutionary one: homeowners in the corridor, citizens throughout its affected cities, underrepresented workers, and business people all would have their positions heard, and most would benefit from alternatives to the early plans, which would further divide corridor cities.

In short, Syracuse planners and elected officials made or reacted to decisions when the benefits of urban freeways had not been widely questioned and when their costs were not yet apparent. In New York, Syracuse was not alone: "the people of New York entered into a devil's bargain: to secure a system closed to localism and patronage, they bought into a system closed to all but highway engineers,"[302] and later, when interstate road building was linked to the national defense interest, local authority was further eroded. Major decisions were made in Los Angeles and in Memphis somewhat after the romantic vision of futuristic urban freeways had been heavily tainted. The dominance of the highway engineer was successfully challenged in both Los Angeles and Memphis. In the former, Caltrans, a state agency with a highly professional reputation and a self-image of working for a statewide public good, found its performance seriously questioned.

As for sensitivity to effects on center city life, Syracuse was known as "the place where the trains ran through"[303]; the railroad had traversed the city's center for more than a hundred years. Trains ran literally and dramatically up and down city streets, in front of major hotels, restaurants, and bars. In addition, the new freeways ran right along the once bustling Erie Canal corridor. Major transportation infrastructure was fundamental to the central city's history and its economic progress, initially at least, inoculating the public against feeling the ill effects of such infrastructure and reducing any tendency to question its attendant impacts. No such inoculation existed for Memphis's Overton Park constituency. In Los Angeles, although freeways were part of the regional culture, sophistication about ways of mitigating their impacts in city centers had been realized by the time the Century Freeway was being planned and constructed.

Conclusion: Different City Tales

In this chapter, we have described how urban highway decisions affected cities throughout the United States in very different ways, both in the nation's most populous and economically dynamic metropolises and in smaller cities.

Controversies in many cities evolved after an earlier love affair with the urban highway concept: that vision reflected a limited experience with what the structures would be and what impacts they would have. Disagreements involved nascent concern for environmental protection and historic and neighborhood preservation and competing understandings of the destinies of cities in the period after the late 1950s and of desirable economic development futures. Some controversies were over aesthetics; some over the transportation system effects of big roads as opposed to other means of moving people. Some highly contentious cases turned on concern with racial integration and segregation.

We saw three cases in considerable detail, but we also briefly outlined disputes in several other cities. Both the longer stories and the cameos shared several important influences. Across the nation, a major shift in perception was happening, from that of urban highway as tool of blight removal and city rejuvenation to that of urban highway as destroyer of the environment and of the social fabric of affected neighborhoods. Visions of what urban transportation could be also shifted. We saw the critical effects of the modification in the legal underpinnings for decisions about infrastructure: the sea change here with individual projects challenged under the Federal-Aid Highway Act, the National Historic Preservation Act, the National Environmental Policy Act, and others, including laws that allowed the shifting of funds to alternatives to the urban freeways. The new option was especially important in some areas: There, urban roads had been attractive because early on they could bring money to the cities even if they were developed with limited city input. Before the cluster of regulatory changes, a few cities had been introduced to the urban design team, an innovation aimed at responding to some of the concerns held by the opposition. However, urban design teams, by themselves, would not be sufficient to achieve consensus on a way forward.

Traditional entrenched perspectives did remain strong in some areas and their proponents were influential, so ultimate outcomes included the partial or complete construction of urban freeways even when some indicators suggested they would be stopped. The 90 percent funding offered under the National Highway Program spoke with a strong voice.

The regulatory environment shift was felt not just upon the passage of new laws but in their interpretation by the courts and the concomitant realization by highway officials and other administrators of the need to comply with the new rules. Significantly, lawsuits that affected whether freeways would be built, and, if so, how, were supported by a growing network of freeway activists assisted by an evolving public interest law community.

On the ground we saw freeways stopped; freeways built according to traditional standards; and freeways built but modified from original plans—a smaller scale, a different design, a greater attention to landscaping and aesthetics, a higher concern for the displaced.

Next, in our final chapter, we sum up and address the extent to which persistent weaknesses in the urban development process reflected in urban freeway building have been addressed. We ask whether the visions of the various professions involved in urban transportation are beginning to come together. We describe a growing interest in removing the traditional urban freeway, physically dismantling it, and replacing it with something else. We discuss how that response is understandable and in many places attractive, although it must be done in the context of a well-ensconced existing urban pattern. We speculate on whether we are beginning to see a new direction for urban transportation in the second century of the automobile, which still remains the dominant way to move people in and through cities.

7

Conclusion and Epilogue: Urban Highways and the American City

The Road Not Taken

In the middle of the twentieth century, the construction of a new generation of high-capacity roads for American cities should have been viewed as a sophisticated synthesis of transportation planning, land-use planning, urban design, and environmental planning, guided by a strong and well-developed understanding of how cities work. If cities are a problem of "organized complexity," as Jane Jacobs argued, then their evolution must be guided by a "pattern language" commensurate with that complexity.[1] Also, planning for roads and public transit should have been completely integrated into a single process of city design. Unfortunately, this did not happen in the United States between 1930 and 1970. Instead, a narrow mode of highway planning was substituted for multimodal transportation planning, and we are still struggling with the consequences.

A nationwide highway system connecting major American cities was a logical development of modern transportation technology. It is hard to imagine the American landscape without interstate highways. But we need to make a distinction between the high-speed connecting routes *between* cities—these are the true "interstate" components of the system—and the extensions of the interstates into and around the centers of American cities. Trying to use interstate highways and other freeways so heavily as an internal mass transportation system for cities has been a major failure of public policy.

The political and economic power of the auto–oil–highway lobby, the convenience and allure of the automobile, cheap energy, the triumph of Modernist urbanism over traditional city patterns, and a funding scheme that allowed state highway engineers to dominate urban freeway planning during this crucial period—all of these contributed to the creation of a distorted transportation system that will remain resistant to change for many decades to come. Jane Jacobs and Lewis Mumford were correct in the 1960s when they resisted the urban freeway juggernaut and set forth alternatives to the massive construction of freeway mileage within American cities.

The "motorization of American cities" began long before the construction of the interstate highway system.[2] The wide-ranging mobility offered by the motor vehicle, the decline of transit, and the accelerated production of low-density suburban landscapes had already created a new urban pattern by 1956, when the interstate highway system finally received adequate funding. But the urban interstates amplified the powerful forces that were redrawing the maps of metropolitan America and laid down the armature for new layers of urban growth.

Half a century later, rising energy costs, the threat of global climate change, and intractable congestion now call into question the wisdom of such a one-sided pattern of urban transportation.[3] However, we remain "locked in" to this mode of city building through inertia, habit, congealed design standards, legislative gridlock, and the sheer political and economic power of the industries associated with freeways. This will be difficult to change.

After World War II, a vast body of knowledge about the creation of compact, mixed-use, and transit-oriented human settlements was discarded in a vehement rejection of any urban planning ideas based on the traditional city.[4] Lewis Mumford described this pervasive attitude as follows:

For most Americans, progress means accepting what is new because it is new, and discarding what is old because it is old. This may be good for a rapid turnover in business, but it is bad for continuity and stability in life. Progress, in an organic sense, should be cumulative, and though a certain amount of rubbish-clearing is always necessary, we lose part of the gain offered by a new invention if we automatically discard all the still valuable inventions that preceded it.[5]

Engineers, Modernist architects, planners, politicians, and the wider public gradually accepted the idea that the new transportation technologies of the twentieth century required radically new urban patterns that were in many ways the *inversion* or opposite of what had gone before. Motor vehicles came first; pedestrians, cyclists, and transit riders were left aside. Instead of finding creative ways to accommodate motor vehicles while preserving the many benefits of traditional city form, the old was replaced with new templates keyed to the private automobile.

Between 1955 and 1975, conflicts over urban freeways erupted in dozens of American cities, reflecting and eventually changing the legal and regulatory environment for large infrastructure projects and successfully stopping some freeway segments. The case studies of Syracuse, Memphis, and Los Angeles provide a temporal cross-section of the freeway revolts and their impacts on public policy. Syracuse embraced urban freeways early on and constructed an array of intracity connectors but paid a steep price in quality of life for this experiment in urban reconstruction. Interstate 40 through the Overton Park neighborhood of Memphis was stopped in its tracks. The Century Freeway in Los Angeles, unfolding after the earlier freeway controversies had spawned a host of new regulations and stronger concern with impacts on existing residents, was built very unlike its original traditional plan (with newly mandated transit, heavy landscaping, and extensive housing). It became the most expensive urban freeway of its time.

American urban highway development has been an iterative process, in which modifications came as highway developers learned from past mistakes—but not quickly enough to prevent negative impacts on cities, neighborhoods, and communities across the United States. Effects were many and widely felt: displacement of thousands of people and loss of affordable housing; razing of viable ethnic neighborhoods; urban air pollution; aesthetic deterioration of the urban core, loss of historical sites; removal of land from the tax rolls, reduction in the value of adjacent properties; noise pollution; and pushing out public transportation alternatives. As the negative impacts of urban highway construction became apparent, they catalyzed public disenchantment with, and opposition to, urban freeway development. This disenchantment and opposition, in turn, fostered changes in the legal and political frameworks that regulated highway development.

These changes in perception about urban highways were fed and augmented by changes in public perceptions about the environment and about civil rights during the 1960s and 1970s. As environmental protection became a more prevalent concern among mainstream American thinking, public concern about the environment changed public views about the importance of highway building and about the design and placement of the highways that were proposed.

Furthermore, the civil rights movement of the 1960s helped to bring to light the often blatant inequality of impacts on different sectors of the population related to the routine placement of urban highways through poor, often black, neighborhoods and business districts. The civil rights movement also fostered a growing demand for just treatment among the black and impoverished sectors of society, resulting in a rising wave of political protest against perceived or actual injustice. Public protests about environmental or civil rights issues created political pressure on lawmakers and resulted in a series of environmental and social justice laws meant to address and ameliorate public disquiet.

Civil rights legislation provided a basis on which to protest highway development that was perceived as discriminatory. Environmental legislation passed during the late 1960s and early 1970s allowed for litigation by freeway opponents and changed the balance of power in urban freeway controversies. The Federal-Aid Highway Act of 1962, the Department of Transportation Act of 1966, the National Historic Preservation Act of 1966, the Federal-Aid Highway Act of 1968, the National Environmental Policy Act of 1970, the Federal-Aid Highway Act of 1970, the Clean Air Act amendments of 1970, and an array of similar legislation at the state level made it impossible to build large infrastructure projects without a serious review of environmental, social, and economic impacts. These laws also provided leverage points for community organizations to successfully oppose or alter highway building projects in metropolitan areas. Community resistance became a true force, not just a temporary inconvenience in a process that marginalized local residents and got projects built.

Laws passed during the 1960s and 1970s produced a host of regulatory changes that drastically altered the playing field for urban freeway construction. By the mid-1970s, construction of urban freeways occurred (or did not occur) within a radically different and a more sophisticated legal context than it previously had. Citizens could more easily demand court review of the decisions of highway agencies; environmental impact assessment was required; relocation assistance was mandatory; and alternative modes of transportation could be sought. The highway agencies were forced to relinquish their exclusive purview over roadway, freeway, and urban highway decision making.

In spite of this impressive list of legislative milestones, however, most of the interstate highway system was completed as planned. American cities were successfully reconfigured for the motor vehicle, and that remains the starting point for any efforts to forge a new direction in transportation planning today.

Other Urban Transportation Options

Historically, policy makers decided on projects with inadequate evidence and under conditions of uncertainty. We should be cautious when criticizing the freeway builders in hindsight. But it is a useful exercise to consider other pathways for urban transportation that might have been taken during the post–World War II era. David J. St. Clair has asked:

> What would transit be now, if the motorization campaign had not taken place, if trolley coaches (along with streetcars, as well as buses where appropriate) had been used more? What would it be now if urban highway policy had not set out to restructure cities to accommodate the auto to the extent that it did? Or if transit had been viewed in the same terms as highway, that is, as a public work?[6]

Lewis Mumford had suggested in 1958 that a web of smaller arterials and "capillaries" should have been used to handle traffic flows *inside* American cities.[7] But virtually nowhere in the literature of post–World War II traffic engineering and urban planning does one find a serious appreciation of the urban boulevard or "transit boulevard" as an arterial capable of carrying large volumes of traffic while at the same time preserving a high quality of life along its edge. Similarly, the urban parkway disappeared from the technical manuals of highway engineering and city planning.[8]

The potential for transit-oriented development was also lost through public policies that treated roads as public infrastructure and transit lines as private businesses. The option of converting transit to public ownership early in the twentieth century and then supporting it with an ample stream of investment funding was lost.[9] As a result, we built our cities around an armature of wide, limited-access freeways based largely on rural design standards, creating vast swaths of "machine space" throughout our central cities, sinking ever further into automobile dependency, and creating expanses of poorly designed and environmentally destructive sprawl development on the urban fringe.[10] Such a massive investment of public funds and professional expertise should have produced a better long-term outcome.

The Genealogy of Urban Freeways

At the beginning of the twenty-first century, we can look back on the era of urban freeway building with a measure of intellectual distance, appreciating the benefits bestowed by autos and freeways while also assessing the costs. It is time for a hard look at what we have done and a reconsideration of abandoned alternatives. We have run the experiment of massive urban freeway building and the motorization of American cities. What have we learned?

The urban boulevards of the nineteenth century—developed as parts of plans for parks, residential developments, and elite urban districts—introduced segments of the urban public to the joys of unimpeded movement through the urban ambient. These boulevards, or "parkways" as they were often called, lacked true limitation of access. However, their distinct advantage was their compatibility with urban life—the patterns of sidewalks, buildings, trees, and public spaces that continue to make up the fabric of great cities such as Paris and Barcelona to this day.

Full-scale highway technology was developed in rural areas where, free of urban obstructions, highway engineers could master the science of designing roadways for efficient motor vehicle movement and reliable service. Between 1900 and 1940, landscape architects and engineers fashioned the first true limited-access parkways. The parkways were the transportation marvels of the age, selling the public and experts alike on the virtues of broad thoroughfares designed exclusively for traffic movement. During this era, there was wide professional consensus that the limited-access highway was an unqualified improvement. The Westchester County parkways in New York, along with the Long Island parkways of Robert Moses, served as influential examples of high-quality road design that was carefully integrated into the surrounding natural environment.

Inevitably, engineers and planners thought about bringing limited-access highways into the cities, and the various urban superhighway, freeway, and expressway plans of the 1920s and 1930s were born. They became powerful symbols of modernism and efficiency. Often portrayed as romantic expressions of a new machine age, urban freeways promised benefits in enhanced mobility too obvious to be questioned. On these new thoroughfares, it seemed, traffic could move smoothly through even the densest urban cores. Regional highway plans of the time often portrayed the city at the center of a radial-concentric highway network, with the central business district (CBD) encircled by one or more beltways or circumferentials. Engineers and planners also portrayed freeways leaping over the old urban fabric on elevated structures, free of the disorder and congestion below.

The expressway plans created during the late 1930s and early 1940s by municipal officials were relatively modest in scale—by later standards—with two lanes each way, design speeds of 45 mph, and often with transit rights-of-way built into the plan. However, within a decade, these local expressway plans would be eclipsed as the authority to build urban freeway systems was bestowed on state highway departments and funded by the federal government.[11] This marked a major shift in the history of urban freeway building.

Building of urban freeways turned out to be a dramatically different task than construction of rural highways or parkways. As Robert Moses started building expressways inside congested urban areas within New York City, he created some troubling precedents. The Henry Hudson Parkway used parkway design inside the city, but it preempted a large expanse of waterfront for traffic movement. The Gowanus elevated "parkway" blighted an inner-city ethnic neighborhood. In the early 1950s, the Cross Bronx Expressway wiped out a corridor of decent affordable housing. And Moses' unbuilt proposals—such as the Mid-Manhattan Expressway and the Lower Manhattan Expressway—would have done even more serious damage to the city.

At the national level, during the early 1940s, the visions of the 1930s were translated into national legislation and early planning activities. *Toll Roads and Free Roads* (1939) and *Interregional Highways* (1944) codified emerging urban freeway planning doctrines, with the assent of both leading highway engineers and city planners. The interstate highway system was created by federal legislation in 1944, although it would not receive adequate funding until 1956. In the meantime, some states and municipalities pushed ahead with urban freeway projects, among them Boston's Central Artery, Washington, D.C.'s Whitehurst Freeway, and Seattle's Alaskan Way.

With the passage of the Federal-Aid Highway Act of 1956, popularly known as the National Interstate and Defense Highways Act of 1956, financial obstacles to extensive urban freeway construction faded. Design for high volumes and high speeds replaced earlier aesthetic concerns of the parkway tradition. With the atrophy of public transit, freeways started to become the primary transportation system in many metropolitan areas, and they were repeatedly "scaled up" to accommodate the ever-growing volumes of traffic. Public officials, engineers, and planners combined freeway building with urban renewal to restructure vast areas of the central city. Residents of low-income and minority neighborhoods surrounding the CBD paid a disproportionate price for this restructuring in the form of freeway blight, displacement, and the disruption of older, transit- and pedestrian-based urban patterns. Reacting against extensive urban freeway construction, coalitions of freeway opponents eventually stopped or obstructed freeways in many cities during the 1960s and forced highway planners to confront the damage they were causing in central cities.

During the 1960s, planners, architects, and landscape architects mounted a sustained critique of conventional freeway planning doctrine, calling for the application of urban design expertise to highway building projects. The legitimacy of highway engineers as *de facto* city planners was sharply questioned. Research on urban freeways accelerated, lively debates transpired, and imaginative plans were drawn up. But planners and designers never really penetrated the highway policy network. Their approach to freeway planning exerted some influence—some freeway segments were modified or deleted—but the mass production of urban freeways sized and engineered for traffic service proceeded. The belated application of urban design to urban freeways was a form of technological "barn-door closure," to use Langdon Winner's evocative phrase.[12] It came far too late to redirect the program.

Professions and the Dilemmas of Urban Freeway Planning

Urban freeway planning shows that different professions approach urban problems with different assumptions, characteristic methodologies, views of the existing city, and prescriptions for good city form. Although some professional specialization is necessary to cope with the complexity of modern city building, specialization can also spawn a narrowness that obscures the organized complexity of the city. Professional worldviews—as embodied in methodologies, recurring solutions, standards, and habitual ways of framing a problem—can congeal into distorted views of urban life. As Lisa Peattie observed of development planners:

Representations were not simply the way the planners presented a world, intimately known, in order to achieve some particular effect on an audience; the planners to a substantial degree experienced the city through their own representations of it.[13]

Professionals see the world through lenses provided by their professional cultures. These make action possible but also limit what can be seen and imagined. Narrow professional worldviews can produce plans with unexpected and undesirable outcomes.

Highway engineers developed a carefully codified set of urban freeway planning concepts and images. This technical literature was presented as a rational system for traffic movement, not a blueprint for urban form, but it still programmed a new city pattern. It was, in fact, a most powerful form of city planning. Engineers valued their image as apolitical experts, even as they proved to be skilled political actors. Compared with the other professions involved, engineers used an abstract, mechanistic, quantity-oriented conception of space—space as a plane upon which traffic movements occurred in predictable patterns, as with plumbing systems or electrical circuits. Economic models based on narrow, neoclassical theories ignored qualitative variables or, indeed, variables that could not be easily measured using conventional techniques. Engineering texts often offered clear rules for successful technical performance. Aggregate statistics, computer models, and aerial views of projects emphasized the big metropolitan picture rather than the detail of urban neighborhoods and streets.[14] Asked to build an enormous network of highways in a short time, engineers sought to simplify and standardize the production of highway mileage, not convert it into a complicated urban design project requiring careful molding of each urban segment to fit local needs.[15]

Highway planning methods usually projected existing trends out into the future, rather than questioning those trends in the light of more encompassing standards for "good city form."[16] Reams of data about traffic movement created an illusion of "objectivity" and scientific legitimacy, pushing aside more comprehensive assessments of urban conditions. Economics-based models downplayed or ignored land use, urban design, and cultural and aesthetic variables and favored current preference—however ill-informed and irrational—over considered judgments of the long-term public interest. All too often, transportation models and technical analyses simply ratified a "City Inevitable"[17] in which sprawl land-use patterns required more freeways, and more freeways made it possible to build more sprawl land-use patterns.

City planners saw the conscious shaping of urban form as their domain, but planning was a relatively new profession with a weak research base, and it lacked support from powerful private constituencies.[18] During this crucial period, planners produced few persuasive, workable responses to the proposed construction of urban expressways in central cities. Land-use planners called attention to the critical connection between transportation and land use, argued for a balance of transportation modes, and warned against dividing of stable neighborhoods. But they still accepted the engineers' basic premise—that cities had to be rebuilt for the automobile—and drew the new freeway systems on their maps. The urban design wing of the planning profession strove to develop options that were more sensitive to the central city urban context, but the research of the 1960s intersected with the highway planning process only during its later phases, when it was impossible to deflect the program from its initial course. Very few of the imaginative alternatives were ever built.

The city planning profession was fragmented into segments based on traditional zoning-driven land use, social science, and urban design.[19] Land-use planners often portrayed urban space as a fairly coarse array of land uses and associated activities or as the legal space of zoning districts defining allowable height, bulk, density, and use. Social science–oriented planners tended to view the city through the lens of aggregate statistics and mathematical relationships, searching for variables to explain patterns of urban change. Urban designers inherited the cognitive training, language, and skills of architecture and landscape architecture, viewing the city as an array of three-dimensional forms, textures, and activities. These diverse viewpoints never coalesced into a unified policy on the form of central cities.

In theory, urban planners were supposed to be the guardians of a comprehensive vision, synthesizing all of the disparate elements of city form. But, as historian Mark Foster has observed, between 1900 and 1940 "city officials and urban planners failed to develop anything approaching a consensus over what constituted an ideal urban form. They were not only divided over whether to encourage centralization or decentralization, but over what factors actually influenced urban growth in any given direction."[20] The earlier tradition of "civic design" had been whittled away by the critiques of City Efficient planners, Modernist architects, and enthusiasts of machine-age technology.[21] To many it seemed that nothing from the past could be updated and applied in the reconstruction of the modern city and that not much of the old city was worth saving. The regional planning visions of organizations such as the Regional Planning Association of America had no enduring political constituency and were left behind in the post–World War II rush to construct the publicly subsidized but privately built world of suburban sprawl. Reductive and simplistic visions of the city of the future filled the void left by the absence of a compelling vision of a compact, multimodal "regional city."[22]

Architects also staked a claim to the design of the urban environment and generated scores of plans for rebuilt cities. From their drafting boards emerged bold schemes for totally redesigned urban centers, with transportation channels ingeniously built into the architectural forms.[23] But architects were locked out of the freeway policy loop, with most of their professional practice limited to work on individual buildings for specific clients. During the freeway controversies, architects reenacted many of their traditional conflicts with engineers. To many architects, engineering work seemed crudely utilitarian, untouched by art or social conscience. Architects were trained to think in terms of form concepts: volumes, spaces, symbolic meanings, historical allusions, architectural theories, and, for some, social and cultural factors influencing design. But architects were more skilled at the drafting board than in the ways of entering into the bureaucratic and political competition that decided urban outcomes, especially when it concerned peripheral domains such as freeways, traditionally the bailiwick of engineers.

Landscape architects had fewer pretensions than the other actors in this story. They produced pioneering designs during the parkway era but played a more limited role in the post–World War II era as right-of-way improvers rather than lead actors in freeway location and design. This exclusion was rectified somewhat during the 1960s, when landscape architects joined multidisciplinary teams working on the integration of freeways with existing urban form. Landscape architects contributed a heightened concern for the shape, texture, and character of spaces created by urban freeways. Their professional concern for urban design and environmental quality helped to bring these neglected dimensions back into the urban freeway debates of the 1960s and after.

To sum up, the era of urban freeway building exposed persistent weaknesses in the urban development process. Even today, the professions responsible for the built environment tend to speak different languages. At times they work at cross purposes. Urban design often gets lost in the single-focused concern with traffic movement, two-dimensional land-use planning, or architectural prowess. Engineers are pressured to achieve functional efficiency, planners to maintain orderly land-use patterns, and architects and landscape architects to satisfy their clients. As a result, we have sprawling suburbs and rebuilt downtowns that, although tenaciously planned, do not add up to a coherent urban whole.

Changing Lanes: New Directions for the Twenty-First Century

The United States is overdue for a transportation policy that integrates transportation, land use, urban design, and environmental planning into a reliable system for the creation of high-quality human settlements at all scales. For 60 years we have been pursuing the chimera of massive urban freeway building at great financial expense and with troubling results on the ground. Instead of producing the gleaming, healthy, modernized cities portrayed in the utopias of the 1930s, automobile dependency has helped to produce a polarized urban landscape of troubled inner cities combined with vast tracts of fragmented sprawl on the urban edge. Can the balance now swing back toward the other transportation modes—transit, walking, and cycling—integrated into compact, mixed-use, and environmentally sustainable regions, cities, and towns?

We cannot go back and redo the public policies, business strategies, and personal choices that created the existing form of American cities. But we can change direction and move toward more sustainable forms of multimodal transportation. Certainly, improvements in automotive technology have reduced the pollution and energy consumption of motor vehicles, and, given the inertia of existing transportation modes, innovation in this area has had modest success. But we also need to change the bias toward the motor vehicle that is so deeply embedded in our urban patterns. We now have better templates for land development on the urban fringe,[24] combined with retrofit strategies for infill sites and existing neighborhoods.[25] New Urbanists have produced an outpouring of literature and built examples that demonstrate the feasibility of creating compact, walkable, sustainable, and transit-oriented urban form. But design ideas do not implement themselves, and reshaping the automobile-dependent city is going to be a prolonged struggle.

Although not a panacea for our transportation problems, transit-oriented development does provide an alternative to more freeway building within many metropolitan areas. Transit systems are less destructive of the urban fabric, as they can be placed on narrow rights-of-way, located underground, or operated within existing street rights-of-way (e.g., streetcars, trolley buses, conventional buses, and segments in bus rapid-transit systems). Also, there is a necessary interconnection between transit and well-designed, walkable city streets. Transit systems must be embedded within healthy pedestrian environments in order to work well, as most transit trips begin and end on foot. And transit stations need to be surrounded by high-density, mixed-use centers in order to generate sufficient ridership. Whereas urban freeways have broken up neighborhoods and channeled thousands of cars onto city streets, reducing the quality of life in the corridors where they have been built, well-designed modern transit systems can reinforce the creation of safe, well-inhabited, walkable urban neighborhoods—one of the fundamental constituents of a good city.

Epilogue

Cities across the nation have proposed, approved, or begun demolition of urban highways and are planning to replace them with housing, parks, bicycle paths, commercial buildings, office space, tunnels, urban boulevards, and traditional city streets. Two factors are propelling urban freeway removal. First, many highways constructed during the postwar era are approaching the end of their useful lives (typically considered to be approximately 40 years); and, second, there is an increasing perception that urban centers afford important redevelopment potential.

The Central Artery (Boston, Massachusetts)

With "The Big Dig," the under-grounding of the I-93 freeway (the Central Artery), the city of Boston took freeway revolts to a higher level by dismantling an existing freeway instead of simply stopping one from being developed. Boston's Central Artery/Tunnel Project, according to the Highway Division of the Massachusetts Department of Transportation, "has been recognized as the largest, most complex, and technologically challenging highway project in the history of the United States." The immense project has significantly reduced traffic congestion and improved mobility. It has also helped to improve the city's environment and created a foundation for ongoing economic growth in one of America's oldest, most historic, and most congested cities. The project replaced Boston's crumbling six-lane elevated Central Artery (I-93) with the current eight- to ten-lane state-of-the-art subterranean highway along with two new bridges spanning the Charles River. It also reconnected downtown Boston to the waterfront and resulted in the creation of more than 300 acres of open land.[26]

Harbor Drive (Portland, Oregon)

When the city of Portland decided to demolish the Harbor Drive freeway and replace it with a 37-acre park more than 30 years ago, it became the first city in the United States to introduce the concept of freeway demolition. The Harbor Drive freeway (U.S. Route 99W) was a 3-mile-long, six-lane, ground-level highway running alongside the Willamette River. The freeway, which was constructed in 1942, connected an industrial neighborhood, Lake Oswego, and areas south of downtown Portland. It carried 25,000 vehicles per day. By 1968, a movement to enhance open space adjacent to the waterfront had been initiated. Portland's 1968 Downtown Waterfront Plan recommended removing the Harbor Drive freeway and developing the land as a 37-acre waterfront park, thereby beautifying the area. After Harbor Drive was closed and removed to make way for the construction of the Tom McCall Waterfront Park in May 1974, no noticeable congestion-related impacts were documented on the surrounding surface streets.[27]

Riverfront Parkway (Chattanooga, Tennessee)

Riverfront Parkway, a four-lane freeway in Chattanooga, Tennessee, was constructed in the 1960s to carry industrial truck traffic along the Tennessee River. However, in the late 1960s, Chattanooga's manufacturing base withered, and thousands of jobs were eliminated. With the loss of the heavy industrial traffic, the freeway no longer served the purpose for which it had been constructed. Moreover, it was determined that the development and configuration of roads constructed to move traffic into and out of the city had hurt downtown Chattanooga's business environment and had hastened the once-vibrant city center's decline, in addition to dividing the city from its waterfront. In a further blow to the city's image, the federal government pronounced Chattanooga's air to be the most polluted in the nation. In the 1980s, the city initiated a rigorous effort to improve its image, including efforts to improve the quality of its downtown and restore its connection to the river.[28]

Reconfiguring the Riverfront Parkway restored pedestrian access to the river by providing an easier street to cross and restored an urban streetscape that enriched and expanded Chattanooga's downtown. Redesign of the Riverfront Parkway acted as a catalyst for, and key component of, Chattanooga's 21st Century Riverfront Plan. The redesign process involved extensive public involvement: It included a series of meetings and a community design session wherein residents, key property owners, city officials, and Tennessee Department of Transportation representatives collaborated to conceptualize a plan to modify the freeway more closely to match the city's needs. Upon completion, Riverfront Parkway was transformed into a two-lane parkway featuring pedestrian crossings facing Chattanooga's Ross Landing Park, the Tennessee Aquarium, and the Bluff View Arts District, which greatly enhanced public safety.[29]

The Park East Freeway (Milwaukee, Wisconsin)

The Park East Freeway, a mile-long elevated spur that connected I-43 to Milwaukee's downtown, represented one segment of a 1970s-era plan to circle Milwaukee's central business district with an expressway. In 2003, in part to encourage redevelopment and reinvestment in the area surrounding the freeway, the city replaced the aging spur with McKinley Avenue, a landscaped, six-lane, at-grade boulevard fully integrated with the surrounding street grid. The expressway loop plan had elicited heavy opposition from elected officials and community activists when it began; as a result, its development had been stopped before the expressway could be extended to Lake Michigan, and the freeway was underutilized. The spur not only divided the northern part of downtown from the rest of the central city but also created a visual and a physical barrier and lowered property values on the surrounding land. Using federal Intermodal Surface Transportation Efficiency Act (ISTEA) funding and local Tax Increment Financing, demolition began in 2002 and was completed in 2003.

The freeway's removal converted approximately 26 acres of right-of-way into developable land. The 64-acre redevelopment area, which includes the former right-of-way in addition to the surrounding land, created three new neighborhoods on twenty-eight traditional city blocks: the Lower Water Street District (office and residential in addition to the existing residential); the Upper Water Street District (higher density residential); and the McKinley Avenue District (office, retail, and entertainment) (figures 7.1 and 7.2).[30]

The Central Freeway (San Francisco, California)

Opened in 1959, the Central Freeway was envisioned as the first section of two crosstown highways planned ultimately to connect the Golden Gate Bridge to the Bay Bridge. Because of a citizen-initiated "freeway revolt," only 1.75 miles of the originally planned route were built. Extending west from Highway 101, the freeway was constructed as a six-lane elevated structure that transitioned to a four-lane, two-level structure and ultimately to a north–south one-way couplet, Franklin and Gough Streets. At its peak service level, the freeway carried approximately 100,000 vehicles a day. The 1989 Loma Prieta Earthquake damaged the freeway, resulting in the demolition of the segment north of Fell Street. Caltrans began planning a seismic retrofit of the remaining freeway; however, local officials and citizens, encouraged by the perceived benefits from the freeway's partial removal, began to consider and propose alternatives to the existing freeway, including a depressed freeway with an at-grade intersection at Market Street. In 1996, the segment between Mission Street and Fell Street was closed for 4 months to demolish the upper, eastbound deck. Gridlock predicted by Caltrans staff, local politicians, and the media did not materialize. During the segment's closure, Hayes Valley residents near the freeway became accustomed to lower levels of traffic, noise, fumes, and vibrations. In 1999, with both freeway retrofit and removal initiatives appearing on the ballot, voters rejected the freeway's retrofit and approved the removal of the freeway and its replacement with a surface boulevard. Octavia Boulevard, which opened in 2005, features four center lanes serving through traffic, two side local lanes, landscaped dividers, and two on-street parking lanes. At the boulevard's northern end lies the newly revitalized commercial Hayes Street corridor, enhanced by a new local park. Nearly one thousand housing units were planned for development on the land made available through the freeway's removal.[31]

Likewise in San Francisco, the Embarcadero Freeway, which we also discuss in chapter 6, was planned to connect the Golden Gate Bridge with

(a)

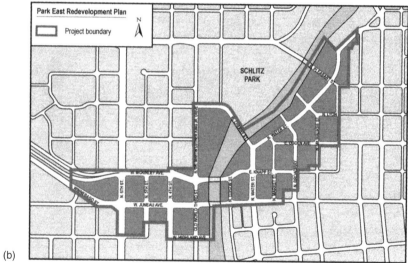

(b)

Figure 7.1
Aerial view of Park East Redevelopment Plan showing demolition area (a) and map of surface streets within the Park East Redevelopment Plan project boundaries (b). *Source:* City of Milwaukee, Department of City Planning, 2004.

Figure 7.2
Rendering of McKinley Avenue, the boulevard that will replace the demolished Park East Freeway in Milwaukee. *Source:* Park East Redevelopment Plan rendering courtesy of Graef, Anhalt, Schloemer & Associates, Inc. Milwaukee, WI, 2003.

the Bay Bridge. However, only 1.2 miles of the freeway were built before construction came to a halt. The city demolished this freeway spur during the 1990s, replacing it with a waterfront boulevard and a new trolley line. Removal of the freeway spur allowed the construction of thousands of new housing units and the development of millions of square feet of office space. Freeway removal also allowed for creation of the new neighborhoods of Rincon Hill and South Beach. The area on which these neighborhoods were developed had been underused land because it was blocked from the waterfront by the freeway.[32]

Other Freeway Removals

There are also midrange alternatives to removing or rebuilding old urban freeways that soften their impacts and meet at least some of the objectives of traffic movement. The West Side Highway in Manhattan, described in chapter 6, provides such an example. This elevated freeway along the Hudson River collapsed and was closed in 1973. After its closure, 53 percent of the traffic that had used the freeway simply vanished.[33]

Subsequent to the demise of the proposed Westway, construction of the replacement West Side Highway (the "NY 9A Reconstruction Project") began in April 1996 and was completed in August 2001. The new highway makes use of the surface streets that existed prior to the construction of the elevated West Side Highway. Most of the highway has four lanes in either direction, whereas smaller sections contain only three lanes. The new West Side Highway handles an average of approximately 95,000 vehicles per day.[34] The new highway permits trucks, which the former elevated highway did not allow. In conjunction with the Henry Hudson Parkway, the West Side Highway creates a verdant boulevard along the Hudson River all along the western length of Manhattan.[35,36]

As noted in chapter 6, Baltimore's "highway to nowhere" displaced almost three thousand residents when it was built more than four decades ago. The "highway to nowhere" is currently being demolished. The city plans to replace the highway with a light-rail public transit station and parking lots. City decision makers and citizens hope that the freeway's removal and its replacement with public transportation facilities will help to relieve social problems in the area and make the blighted area more attractive to its growing downtown biomedical industry.[37]

New Haven's Route 34, commonly known as the Oak Street Connector, is a short segment of highway that conducts visitors to a Walgreens and a parking garage. Its construction razed a neighborhood, displaced hundreds of people, and physically divided the city. Now, with financial assistance from the federal government in the amount of $16 million, New Haven is demolishing the Oak Street Connector.[38]

In some cases, cities are "removing" the concrete barriers that freeways form through their downtowns by "capping" or "decking" them. Using this method, the freeway is covered in greenery and turned into a greenbelt, park, and/or pedestrian-friendly development instead of being demolished. This "gray-to-green metamorphosis" is under way or being considered in major cities from Los Angeles and Dallas to St. Louis and Cincinnati, as they strive to find a means to revitalize portions of their downtowns.[39]

Environmentalists, developers, and citizens alike embrace the concept for dissimilar reasons. Environmentalists urge the introduction of more trees and grass to offset carbon emissions and to promote walkable neighborhoods, thereby reducing reliance on cars; the development community is eager for space to develop in prime downtown areas; and citizens are in favor of the development of parks and other amenities they can reach on foot.[40]

Capping freeways is not a new concept—the idea dates back to the 1930s.[41] It is currently gaining in popularity because, as we have noted, many of the urban freeways constructed during the mid-twentieth century are now reaching the end of their useful lives, and available land in newly resurgent downtowns has become a valuable commodity. Furthermore, the demand for greenbelts, parks, and public spaces in concretized urban areas has become urgent.[42]

In Dallas, the Woodall Rodgers Park Foundation is spearheading efforts to build a 5-acre park on the eight-lane Woodall Rodgers Freeway north of downtown, between U.S. Route 75 and Interstate 35E. If the project goes forth, traffic would be channeled to a tunnel. Capping the freeway is part of a larger plan to revitalize the city's core and to connect all parts of a 68-acre cultural district that includes museums, restaurants, residential towers, and a new opera hall and performing arts center (figure 7.3).[43]

In Los Angeles and neighboring Santa Monica there exist several proposals to cap obsolete sections of the Hollywood Freeway (Route 101) in Hollywood and downtown Los Angeles and to cap I-10 in Santa Monica with parks and mixed-use developments. The Los Angeles area's density makes the creation of parkland difficult, and old freeways offer spaces that can be used for this purpose. One plan encompasses 100 acres of land and calls for the creation of a 15- to 20-acre park. This plan would also connect city hall and Little Tokyo with Union Station, Chinatown, and Olvera Street. Another plan calls for the creation of a park and school on 40 acres of the Hollywood Freeway running through a primarily residential area. In Santa Monica, an old section of I-10 is being proposed as a link between the civic center and the area near the Santa Monica Pier.[44]

In Cincinnati, freeways separated the downtown from the riverfront near the junction of I-75 and I-71. Several exits have been consolidated to create Fort Washington Way and to open about 16 acres of space for development and 40 acres of space for a park located adjacent to the Ohio River. In St. Louis, designs and proposals are being called for to connect

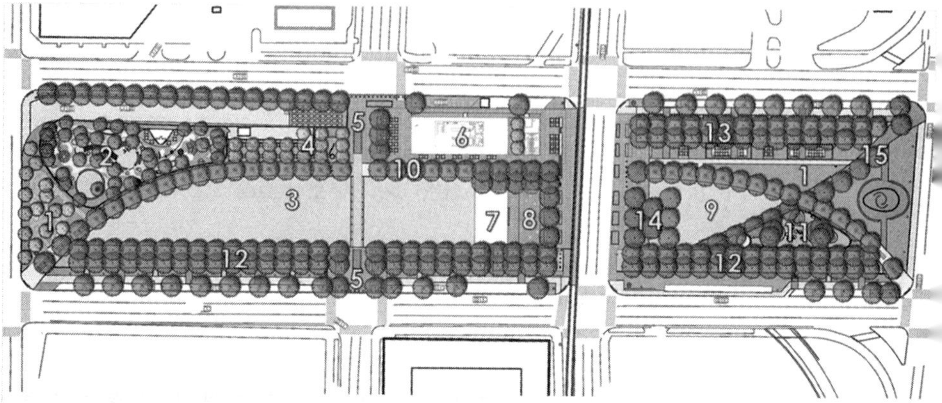

1. Botanical Garden & Courtyard
2. Children's Garden
3. Great Lawn
4. Reading & Games Courtyard
5. Hart Plaza & Boulevard
6. Café & Nancy Collins Fisher Pavilion
7. Muse Family Performance Stage
8. Grand Plaza & Water Garden
9. East Lawn
10. Chase Promenade
11. "My Best Friend's" Park
12. Jane's Lane
13. Groves at Uptown
14. Groves at East Lawn
15. Groves at Pearl Crossing

Figure 7.3
Illustration of Woodall Rodgers Freeway decking proposal, showing the proposed 5-acre Klyde Warren Park and parts of the 68-acre cultural district. *Source:* Woodall Rodgers Park Foundation, "Site Plan." http://www.woodallrodgerspark.org/PictureGallery.aspx?cid=1

the Gateway Arch grounds and the downtown area over I-70, which currently divides the two areas. City to River, a nonprofit citizen group, has proposed removal of a section of the interstate that is no longer needed, as traffic has been redirected to a new bridge built north of the Gateway Arch. Turning that portion of I-70 into a 1.4-mile boulevard and parkway would create valuable real estate close to the Gateway Arch, linking downtown hotels, casinos, sports stadiums, and the city's historic riverfront.[45]

In addition to those freeways already removed and those with fairly advanced plans for removal or major alteration, many cities are contemplating taking down aging, underused, or otherwise undesirable urban freeways or portions thereof. Among these are the following: Syracuse's I-81 (discussed in chapter 5 of this book)[46]; the South Bronx's Sheridan Expressway[47]; Hartford's I-84[48]; New Orleans' I-10 along Claiborne Avenue[49]; Rochester's Inner Loop[50]; Trenton's Route 29[51]; Washington, D.C.'s Whitehurst Expressway, its Southeast Freeway, and its Rock Creek and Potomac Parkway[52]; Cleveland's Shoreway Freeway[53]; Akron's Inner Belt Freeway[54]; Nashville's Downtown Loop[55]; Baltimore's Jones Falls Expressway[56]; the Niagara Gorge's Robert Moses Parkway[57]; Buffalo's Route 5[58]; and Chicago's Lakeshore Drive.[59]

What the federal government provided for, it can also help take down. In October 2010, the U.S. Department of Transportation (DOT) and the U.S. Department of Housing and Urban Development (HUD) jointly announced the award of more than $20 million in grants targeting urban freeway removal projects in three cities—New Orleans' Claiborne Expressway, New York City's Sheridan Expressway, and New Haven's Downtown Crossing. In all three cases, funds will be used to remove these elevated urban freeways and replace them with walkable boulevards. Although federal funding has previously been allocated for other freeway-to-boulevard conversion projects, the allocation of these grants does represent an important shift in focus on the part of DOT and HUD: This is the first time federal funds have been specifically targeted toward the removal of elevated urban highways.[60]

The urban freeway removal movement is not limited to the United States. Cities that are removing urban freeways in other nations include Seoul, South Korea; Paris, France; Vancouver, Canada; and Toronto, Canada. One excellent example of the rejuvenating effects of urban freeway removals is found in Madrid. In the Spanish capital, a park called Madrid Río is nearly complete. More than 6 miles long, the park has been constructed on top of a system of tunnels dug to entomb sections of a highway—the M-30 Ring Road. The park provides green space and tree cover (approximately eight thousand pine trees were planted) and contains amenities such as areas for socializing and chess playing, pedestrian and bicycle paths, a children's wading pool, splashing fountains, ball fields, art studios, a dance theater, a tile-paved plaza large enough to hold 100,000 people, and views of the royal palace. The park also features a boathouse, boating lanes in the river, and a public beach on the river.[61]

The Madrid highway internment project also reconnects formerly cut-off neighborhoods to the center of the city, restores a long-lost section of the Manzanares River, and rejuvenates a previously neglected section of the capital. The park represents only a portion of a larger $4.5 billion project, which will also construct dozens of new metro and light-rail stations linking widely disparate, disconnected, and often poor districts on the outskirts of Madrid to the downtown area.[62]

We can also look to Canadian cities such as Vancouver, British Columbia, which continues to thrive even though it has no massive internal freeway system and has invested instead in more modest arterials and transit systems supported by high-density, mixed-use development. Thus, there are hopeful signs that an alternative mode of city building will take hold.

However, we should take care not to regard the removal of urban freeways as a solution for city ills. Urban freeway removal as a manifestation of "New Urbanism" is, at this time, more of a design concept than an economic development strategy or a vehicle for city regeneration. The challenges faced by American cities (from changing patterns of wealth development and industrial relocation to major shifts in global migration trends) are complex; they require a combination of strategic undertakings to resolve them. The aging of our population and the gentrification of some urban areas are encouraging some in-migration into the central business district, but some urban populations continue to decline (Syracuse's population dropped dramatically since 1950; that of Memphis grew significantly), and the construction of housing units and commercial interests on the relatively small acreages of developable lands reclaimed through freeway demolition are unlikely to result in large movements of residents back into cities. Moreover, some form of more traditional urban transit will always be essential to a city's prosperity. As Bill Bryant, president of the Port of Seattle Commission argues: "I hope the city of the future includes solid middle-class jobs, family-wage jobs, and that cities will find a way to be compatible with manufacturing, fishing and industrial sectors." He adds, "That requires trains and trucks."[63]

Hopeful signs are only small changes in a much vaster urban landscape where urban freeways remain the dominant transportation elements. Most American cities are still completely dependent on urban highway systems that were envisioned during the 1930s and 1940s and built during the 1950s and 1960s. In the suburbs and exurbs, life without access to a car is almost impossible. Many cities continue to widen and expand their freeways, rebuilding old intersections with large flyovers and multilevel interchanges. New beltways are proposed for the distant urban fringe. So it remains to be seen whether we will continue to build ourselves further and further into automobile dependency and urban fragmentation. Alternatively, we can chart a new direction, taking advantage of modern technologies where appropriate but not allowing them to displace time-tested urban patterns (that remain valid today) or to ruin the natural environment. It has taken us more than half a century to build our way into this predicament. It may take nearly as long to find a way out.

Notes

Introduction

1. Oscar Handlin and John Burchard, eds., *The Historian and the City* (Cambridge, Mass.: MIT Press, 1963).

Chapter 1

1. Jeffrey Brown, "Statewide Transportation Planning: Lessons from California," *Transportation Quarterly* 56, no. 2 (Spring 2002): 51–62.

2. Lewis Mumford *The Highway and the City* (New York: Harcourt, Brace & World, Inc., 1963), 247.

3. Lawrence Halprin, *Freeways* (New York: Reinhold Publishing Corporation, 1966), 23.

4. State of California, Department of Public Works, Division of Highways. *Statistical supplement portion of the annual report to the Governor of California by the Director of Public Works* (California: State of California, 1966).

5. Mark H. Rose, "Rebuilding America: Express Highways and Visions of Reform 1890–1941." In Mark H. Rose, *Interstate: Express Highway Politics, 1939–1989. Revised edition.* (Knoxville, Tenn.: University of Tennessee Press, 1990), 6.

6. Ibid., 7.

7. Quoted in Helen Leavitt, *Superhighway—Superhoax* (Garden City, N.Y.: Doubleday & Co., 1970), 3.

8. For an example, see Michael Hough, *Out of Place: Restoring Identity to the Regional Landscape* (New Haven: Yale University Press, 1990), 68–76.

9. Bruce E. Seely, *Building the American Highway System: Engineers as Policy Makers* (Philadelphia: Temple University Press, 1987); American Association of State Highway Officials, *AASHO: The First Fifty Years, 1914–1964* (Washington, D.C.: AASHO, 1965).

10. The standard history is Mel Scott, *American City Planning since 1890* (Berkeley: University of California Press, 1969). Two earlier reviews of professional

progress are Henry V. Hubbard, "Planning the City and the Region—Then and Now," *American City* 43 (September 1930): 99–100; and John T. Howard, "Planning Is a Profession," *Journal of the American Institute of Planners* 20, no. 2 (Spring 1954): 58–59.

11. As late as 1981, Kevin Lynch asserted that "we have no adequate contemporary normative theory about the form of cities. There is dogma and there is opinion, but there is no systematic effort to state general relationships between the form of a place and its value." Kevin Lynch, *A Theory of Good City Form* (Cambridge, Mass.: MIT Press, 1981), 99.

12. For some perspectives on this issue see Robert Gutman, *Architectural Practice: A Critical View* (Princeton: Princeton Architectural Press, 1988); Bernard Michael Boyle, "Architectural Practice in America, 1865-1965: Ideal and Reality," in *The Architect: Chapters in the History of the Profession*, ed. Spiro Kostof (New York: Oxford University Press, 1977), 309–344; and Andrew Saint, *The Image of the Architect* (New Haven: Yale University Press, 1983).

13. For a typology of actors in the larger urban transportation planning process, see Delbert A. Taebel and James V. Cornehls, *The Political Economy of Urban Transportation* (Port Washington, N.Y.: Kennikat Press, 1977), chap 1. They offer the following cast of characters: (1) automobile monopolists, (2) automobile apologists, (3) social engineers, (4) trust-busters, (5) transit technicians, (6) balancers, and (7) ecologists.

14. Historian of science Larry Laudan argues that we should study "entire systems of thought" rather than unit ideas. "Individual concepts, particular propositions, which are components of these larger complexes, do not—indeed cannot—stand alone, and as a result we generally should not appraise or evaluate concepts on a piecemeal basis . . . it follows that the intellectual historian—in so far as he wants to explain the evolving vicissitudes of belief—must take [research traditions] as his fundamental units for historical analysis." Larry Laudan, *Progress and Its Problems: Toward a Theory of Scientific Growth* (Berkeley: University of California Press, 1977), 182.

15. Frank Fischer and Carmen Sirianni, eds., *Critical Studies in Organization and Bureaucracy* (Philadelphia: Temple University Press, 1984).

16. Norman T. Newton, *Design on the Land: The Development of Landscape Architecture* (Cambridge, Mass.: Belknap Press of Harvard University Press, 1971). Also see Francesco Dal Co, "From Parks to the Region: Progressive Ideology and the Reform of the American City," in *The American City: From the Civil War to the New Deal*, trans. Barbara Luigia La Penta (Cambridge, Mass.: MIT Press, 1979).

17. Sometimes, these served as precursors of later highway schemes. Burnham's "Civic Center" location is occupied today by a freeway interchange—he was right about its centrality in the circulation system of Chicago. See Harold M. Mayer and Richard C. Wade, *Chicago: Growth of a Metropolis* (Chicago: University of Chicago Press, 1969), 442.

18. For example, see Andrew Wright Crawford, "Fairmount Parkway—A Notable Correction of William Penn's Plan," *American City* 29 (July 1923): 18–20.

19. The basic idea is probably as old as cities themselves and seems to develop naturally in cities with "organic" form. Roads from the hinterland penetrate to the market center; ring roads are built to provide access between the radials.

20. Daniel H. Burnham and Edward H. Bennett, *Report on a Plan for San Francisco* (San Francisco: Sunset Books, 1905; facsimile reprinted, Berkeley: Urban Books, 1971).

21. Peter Marcuse, "Housing Policy and City Planning: The Puzzling Split in the United States, 1893-1931," in *Shaping an Urban World: Planning in the 20th Century*, ed. Gordon Cherry (New York: St. Martin's Press, 1980), 23–58.

22. For a City Efficient critique of the fading City Beautiful tradition, see George B. Ford, "Digging Deeper into City Planning," *American City* 6 (1912): 557–562.

23. Scott, *American City Planning*, chap. 4; Norman Johnston, "Harland Bartholomew: Precedent for the Profession," *Journal of the American Institute of Planners* 39, no. 2 (March 1973): 115–124; and M. Christine Boyer, *Dreaming the Rational City: The Myth of American City Planning* (Cambridge, Mass.: MIT Press, 1983), chap. 5.

24. Marc A. Weiss, *The Rise of the Community Builders* (New York: Columbia University Press, 1987), and Robert Fitch, "Planning New York," in *The Fiscal Crisis of American Cities*, ed. Roger E. Alcaly and David Mermelstein (New York: Vintage Books, 1976), 246–284. For a contemporary view, see Lawrence Veiller, "Protecting Residential Districts," *American City* 10 (June 1914): 525–529.

25. John Friedmann and Clyde Weaver, *Territory and Function: The Evolution of Regional Planning* (Berkeley: University of California Press, 1979). On the *Regional Plan of New York and Its Environs*, see David A. Johnson, "Regional Planning for the Great American Metropolis: New York between the World Wars," in *Two Centuries of American Planning*, ed. Daniel Schaffer (Baltimore: Johns Hopkins University Press, 1988), 167–196.

26. Scott, *American City Planning*, 192, 237–247.

27. On the role of planning during the 1920s, see Guy Alchon, *The Invisible Hand of Planning: Capitalism, Social Science, and the State in the 1920s* (Princeton: Princeton University Press, 1985). Alchon argues that "In the 1920s the Hooverian vision of a society managed by enlightened private groups contributed powerfully to the mutual legitimation of technocratic professionals and business planners" (p. 167). The goal was "to depoliticize authority, remove political issues from political processes, and to encourage the determination of public policy within the administrative precincts of technocratic and managerial elites" (p. 171).

28. Seely, *Building the American Highway System*. See also Martin J. Schiesl, *The Politics of Efficiency: Municipal Administration and Reform in America: 1880–1920* (Berkeley: University of California Press, 1977).

29. Seely, *Building the American Highway System*; and Public Works Historical Society, "Interstate Highway Research Project: Analysis," Draft Report Submitted for Comment to the AASHTO Task Force (June 1988), 4–10.

30. Seely, *Building the American Highway System*. For a history of highway legislation, see Gary T. Schwartz, "Urban Freeways and the Interstate System," *Southern California Law Review* 49 (March 1976): 406–513.

31. Ibid., 406–513.

32. During the 1920s, the Bureau of Public Roads made important contributions to the advancing science of highway planning, particularly in the areas of projecting future traffic flows, designing comprehensive highway systems, and scheduling projects in a logical sequence. For a review of pioneering highway planning research of the 1920s, see Robert E. Heightchew, Jr., "TSM: Revolution or Repetition?" in *Urban Transportation: Perspectives and Prospects*, ed. Herbert S. Levinson and Robert A. Weant (Westport, Conn.: Eno Foundation for Transportation, 1982), 62–70. Heightchew argues that much of this knowledge was lost and had to be reinvented later.

33. Louis Ward Kemp, "Aesthetes and Engineers. The Occupational Ideology of Highway Design." *Technology and Culture* 27 (October 1986): 759–797; 762.

34. For a review of traffic issues of the 1920s, see Mark S. Foster, *From Streetcar to Superhighway, American City Planners and Urban Transportation 1900–1940* (Philadelphia: Temple University Press, 1981); and Paul Barrett, *The Automobile and Urban Transit: The Formation of Public Policy in Chicago, 1900–1930* (Philadelphia: Temple University Press, 1983). Journals of urbanism from this period such as *American City* published numerous articles about automobile congestion and ways to relieve it.

35. This transition is described in David W. Jones, *Urban Transit Policy: An Economic and Political History* (Englewood Cliffs, N.J.: Prentice-Hall, 1985).

36. See Blaine A. Brownell, "Urban Planning, the Planning Profession, and the Motor Vehicle in Early Twentieth-Century America," in *Shaping an Urban World: Planning in the 20th Century*, ed. Gordon E. Cherry (New York: St. Martin's Press, 1980), 59–77; and Mark S. Foster, *From Streetcar to Superhighway, American City Planners and Urban Transportation, 1900–1940* (Philadelphia: Temple University Press, 1981), chap. 5. The line between city planning and engineering was less distinct in the 1920s than it is now. Harland Bartholomew, the most prolific planning consultant of the 1920s, used the label "planning engineer," as did other physical planners.

37. For example, see Warson Randolph, "Street Widening in New Bedford, Mass.," *American City* 10 (May 1914): 471–473; and "Two Notable Examples of Street Widening in New York City," *American City* 36 (March 1927): 340–343.

38. The magazine *American City* carried many articles on viaduct construction between World Wars I and II. On viaduct building during the 1930s, see Albert C. Rose, *Historic American Roads: From Frontier Trails to Superhighways* (New York: Crown Publishers, 1976), 102.

39. For example, "Speed and Safety at a Bridge Approach," *American City* 42 (February 1930), 161; "Proposed Approaches to Hudson River Bridge," *American City* 40 (June 1929): 100.

40. See Gordon M. Sessions, *Traffic Devices: Historical Aspects Thereof* (Washington, D.C.: Institute of Traffic Engineers, 1971).

41. "Raised Sidewalks and Traffic Separation Urged for Chicago," *American City* 35 (September 1926): 334–336.

42. For an informative review of some of these proposals, see Robert E. Heightch-ew, Jr., "TSM: Revolution or Repetition?" in *Urban Transportation: Perspectives and Prospects*, ed. Herbert S. Levinson and Robert A. Weant (Westport, Conn.: Eno Foundation for Transportation, 1982), 62–70.

43. See Norma Evenson, *Le Corbusier: The Machine and the Grand Design* (New York: Braziller, 1969). Some useful interpretive essays can be found in Russell Walden, ed., *The Open Hand: Essays on Le Corbusier* (Cambridge, Mass.: MIT Press, 1977). Le Corbusier did not invent the idea of radically transforming cities for the automobile, but he was certainly a skilled publicist for the idea. See Jean-Louis Cohen, "Le Corbusier and Media: A Dialogue with Jean-Louis Cohen," *Design Book Review* no. 14 (Spring 1988): 15–18.

44. See Carol Willis, "Skyscraper Utopias: Visionary Urbanism in the 1920s," in *Imagining Tomorrow*, ed. Joseph J. Corn (Cambridge, Mass.: MIT Press, 1986), 164–187.

45. Manfredo Tafuri, "The Disenchanted Mountain: The Skyscraper and the City," in *The American City: From the Civil War to the New Deal*, ed. Giorgio Ciucci, Francesco Dal Co., Mario Maniéri-Elia, and Manfredo Tafuri, trans. Barbara Luigia La Penta (Cambridge, Mass.: MIT Press, 1979), 389–528.

46. The book-length treatment is in Fritz Malcher, *The Steadyflow Traffic System*, Harvard City Planning Series, Vol. 9 (Cambridge, Mass.: Harvard University Press, 1935), published after Malcher's death in 1933. See also Fritz Malcher, "Express Highways Combined with the 'Steadyflow' System," *American City* 44 (January 1931): 152–155; Fritz Malcher, "Planning Arterial Highways to Meet Modern Needs," *American City* 42 (January 1930): 158; and "Will 1932 Witness the Beginning of a New Epoch in Highway Design and Construction?" *American City* 46 (January 1932): 104–105.

47. Fritz Malcher, "A Traffic Planner Imagines a City," *American City* 44 (March 1931): 134–135.

48. Detroit Rapid Transit Commission, *Proposed Super-Highway Plan for Greater Detroit* (Detroit: Detroit Rapid Transit Commission, 1924); Subcommittee on Two Level Streets and Separated Grades of the Committee on Traffic Regulation and Public Safety of the City Council of the City of Chicago, *A Memorandum and Preliminary Report with Reference to Elevated Through Highways for the Chicago Metropolitan Area* (Chicago, 1928).

49. Turner, Daniel L. "The Detroit Super-Highway Project," *American City* 32 (April 1925): 373–376.

50. For a critical review of the plan, see Robert Fitch, "Planning New York," in *The Fiscal Crisis of American Cities*, ed. Roger E. Alcaly and David Mermelstein (New York: Vintage Books, 1976), 246–284. Fitch argues that Moses' sometimes acrimonious conflicts with the Regional Plan Association over rapid transit, bridge design, and other issues did not prevent him from using their proposed freeway corridors for his own projects. According to Fitch, the plan proposed "Slab City" at the center and "Spread City" in the suburbs, accelerating the shift of capital into unproductive real estate ventures and pushing industry out of the

central city. The purpose was "to transform the class character of neighborhoods in the interest of real-estate values" (p. 252).

51. Committee on the Regional Plan of New York and Its Environs, *Regional Plan of New York and Its Environs. Vol. 1, The Graphic Regional Plan: Atlas and Description* (New York: Committee on the Regional Plan of New York and Its Environs, 1929).

52. See the renderings in Thomas Adams, *The Building of the City* (New York: Committee on the Regional Plan of New York and Its Environs, 1931).

Chapter 2

1. U.S. Department of Commerce, Bureau of the Census; U.S. Department of Transportation, Bureau of Public Roads. Cited in John B. Rae, *The Road and Car in American Life* (Cambridge, Mass.: MIT Press, 1971), Table 3.4, "Private Automobile Registrations and Population, 1900-1969."

2. For a review of many of these improvements, see John Nolen and Henry V. Hubbard, *Parkways and Land Values*, Harvard City Planning Studies, Vol. 11 (Cambridge, Mass.: Harvard University Press, 1937).

3. "160-Mile Elevated Super-Highway System Proposed for Chicago," *Roads and Streets* 76 (December 1933): 433–437.

4. Bruce E. Seely, *Building the American Highway System, Engineers as Policy Makers*. (Philadelphia: Temple University Press, 1987), chap. 7.

5. Ibid., 157.

6. Ibid., 156–164.

7. David W. Jones, Jr. *Urban Transit Policy, An Economic and Political History* (Englewood Cliffs, N.J.: Prentice-Hall, 1985), 64–72.

8. Ibid., 64–72. See also Seely, *Building the American Highway System*, Part II, "The Golden Age of Highway Building, 1921-36."

9. Mel Scott, *American City Planning Since 1890: A History Commemorating the Fiftieth Anniversary of the American Institute of Planners* (Berkeley: University of California Press, 1969), 280–283. Financial pressures, along with divisions within the planning fraternity, led to the termination of the quarterly *City Planning* in 1934, but the American City Planning Institute replaced it with a more modest publication, *The Planners' Journal* in 1935. See Donald A. Krueckeberg, "The Story of the Planners' Journal," *Journal of the American Planning Association* 46 (January 1980): 9–10.

10. See Blaine A. Brownell, "Urban Planning, the Planning Profession, and the Motor Vehicle in Early Twentieth Century America," in *Shaping an Urban World: Planning in the 20th Century*, ed. Gordon E. Cherry (New York: St. Martin's Press, 1980), 59–77; Peter Marcuse, "Housing Policy and City Planning The Puzzling Split in the United States, 1893-1931," in *Shaping an Urban World: Planning in the 20th Century*, ed. Gordon Cherry (New York: St. Martin's Press, 1980), 23–58; and M. Christine Boyer, *Dreaming the Rational City: The Myth of American City Planning* (Cambridge, Mass.: MIT Press, 1983). As Marc Weiss

has shown, city planners and the "community builder" sector of the real estate profession worked hand in hand to design, legislate, and implement zoning and subdivision regulations for the protection of property values in residential neighborhoods; see Marc Weiss, *Rise of the Community Builders* (New York: Columbia University Press, 1987). Planning had no accreditation or licensing procedures comparable to those of medicine, law, or architecture. Harvard opened the first separate School of City Planning in 1929; prior to that date, planning was an appendage of architecture or landscape architecture departments.

11. Karl B. Lohmann, *Principles of City Planning* (New York: McGraw-Hill, 1931). Lohmann taught at The University of Illinois and frequently shared the classroom with Harland Bartholomew.

12. Ibid., 76–77.

13. Clarence Stein, "The Case for New Towns," *The Planners' Journal* 5, no. 2 (March–June 1939): 39–41.

14. "Townless Highways," *American City*, 42 (May 1930): 94–96.

15. On the Regional Planning Association of America and its urban form proposals, see Carl Sussman, ed., *Planning the Fourth Migration: The Neglected Vision of the Regional Planning Association of America* (Cambridge, Mass.: MIT Press, 1976); and Francesco Dal Co, "From Parks to the Region: Progressive Ideology and the Reform of the American City," in *The American City: From the Civil War to the New Deal*, trans. Barbara Luigia La Penta (Cambridge, Mass.: MIT Press, 1979) [Italian original, 1973].

16. For example, see Robert Whitten, "The Economic Utilization of Land in City Building," *American City* 30 (May 1924): 527–530. Whitten argued that "The suburban or satellite town offers our only hope of substantial relief from the increasing congestion incident to the evergrowing bulk of the great city."

17. John Ihlder, "Rehabilitation of Blighted Areas: The Part of City Planning," *City Planning* 6, no. 2 (April 1930): 106.

18. Harland Bartholomew, "A Program to Prevent Economic Disintegration in American Cities," in *Proceedings of the Twenty-Fourth National Conference on City Planning Held in Pittsburgh, Pennsylvania 14–16 November 1932* (Philadelphia: William Fell, 1932), 1.

19. Harland Bartholomew, "Is City Planning Effectively Controlling City Growth in the United States," *American City* 45 (July 1931): 128.

20. Ibid., 127.

21. Scott, *American City Planning*, 282–283.

22. Harold S. Buttenheim, "Trends in Present-Day City Planning in the United States," *City Planning* 7, no. 2 (April 1931): 109.

23. For a catalog of urban design concepts from the 1920s and 1930s, see Werner Hegemann, *City Planning Housing*, Vol. 3, *A Graphic Review of Civic Art, 1922–1937*, ed. William W. Forster and Robert C. Weinberg (New York: Architectural Book Publishing Co., 1938). For an earlier compendium, see Werner Hegemann and Elbert Peets, *The American Vitruvius: An Architects' Handbook of Civic Art*, reprint ed. (New York: Princeton Architectural Press, 1988) [originally published in 1922 by The Architectural Book Publishing Company, New York].

24. Boston, City Planning Board, *Report on a Thoroughfare Plan for Boston,* Robert Whitten, Consultant (Boston, 1930).

25. Ibid., 82.

26. Robert Whitten, "The Prevention of Blight in Residential Areas Adjacent to Expressways," in *Proceedings of the Twenty-Third National Conference on City Planning Held in Rochester, New York 22–24 July 1931* (Philadelphia: William Fell, 1931), 157–178.

27. Eugene S. Taylor, "A Comprehensive System of Elevated Superhighways," *City Planning* 7, no. 2 (April 1931): 118.

28. See "Badly Needed Drives Built on Made Land in New Park Project," *Roads and Streets* 68 (May 1928): 229–232. These plans are discussed in Chicago Plan Commission, *The Outer Drive* (Chicago, 1929).

29. See Mark Foster, *From Streetcar to Superhighway: American City Planners and Urban Transportation, 1900–1940* (Philadelphia: Temple University Press 1981); and Paul Barrett, *The Automobile and Urban Transit: The Formation of Public Policy in Chicago, 1900–1930* (Philadelphia: Temple University Press, 1983).

30. Automobile Club of Southern California, Engineering Department, *Traffic Survey: Los Angeles Metropolitan Area Nineteen Hundred Thirty-seven* (Los Angeles, 1937).

31. Los Angeles, Transportation Engineering Board, *A Transit Program for the Los Angeles Metropolitan Area* (Los Angeles, 1939).

32. For a more detailed commentary on these plans, see David Jones, "The California Innovation" *California's Freeway Era in Historical Perspective* (Berkeley: Institute of Transportation Studies, 1989), chap. 7.

33. Richard Schermerhorn, Jr., "A Practical Program for the Protection and Development of Roadside Beauty," *American City* 42 (March 1930): 140. As an example of an urban highway design by a landscape architect, see Charles Downing Lay, "Proposed Scheme for High-Speed Trunk Highway Through a Suburban or City District," *Architectural Record* 73, no. 1 (January 1933): 15.

34. Robert Fishman, *Urban Utopias in the Twentieth Century* (Cambridge, Mass.: MIT Press, 1977).

35. Norma Evenson, *Le Corbusier: The Machine and the Grand Design* (New York: Braziller, 1969).

36. For a later elaboration of these ideas, see Frank Lloyd Wright, *The Living City* (New York: Horizon Press, 1958). Also, see Giorgio Ciucci, "The City in Agrarian Ideology and Frank Lloyd Wright: Origins and Development of Broadacres," in *The American City: From the Civil War to the New Deal,* trans. Barbara Luigia La Penta (Cambridge, Mass.: MIT Press, 1979).

37. Eliel Saarinen, "Architecture and City Planning," *City Planning* 1, no. 3 (October 1925): 143–155.

38. Robert Caro, *The Power Broker: Robert Moses and the Fall of New York* (New York: Knopf, 1974; Vintage, 1975).

39. Ibid., 339–340.

40. Ibid., 341–344.

41. Robert Fitch, "Planning New York," in *The Fiscal Crisis of American Cities*, ed. Roger E. Alcaly and David Mermelstein (New York: Vintage Books, 1976), 246–284; and David A. Johnson, "The Emergence of Metropolitan Regionalism: An Analysis of the 1929 Regional Plan of New York and Its Environs." Ph.D. dissertation, Cornell University, 1974.

42. Lewis Mumford, *The Culture of Cities* (New York: Harcourt, Brace and Company, 1938), 489.

43. See Allyn R. Jennings, "New York Strides Ahead in Park and Parkway Improvements," *American City* 52 (July 1937): 43–45; and "New York's West Side Improvement," *American City* 52 (November 1937): 52.

44. Caro, *The Power Broker*, 525–540.

45. For an alternative interpretation, see Kenneth T. Jackson, "Robert Moses and the Planned Environment: A Re-Evaluation," in *Robert Moses: Single-Minded Genius*, ed. Joann P. Krieg (Interlaken, N.Y.: Heart of the Lakes Publishing, 1989), 21–30. Jackson argues that the topography of the area, not racism on the part of Moses, offers an alternative explanation for the lack of amenities along the Hudson River at 125th Street. He also asserts that "blacks did not live along the western reaches of 125th Street until long after these decisions were reached."

46. Caro, *The Power Broker*, 563–566.

47. At the time, of course, the parkway replaced a landscape of shacks and railroad tracks and was seen as a clear improvement.

48. "Pattern for the Future," *Architectural Forum* 78 (May 1943): 4.

49. Caro, *The Power Broker*, 520–525.

50. Robert Moses, "The Comprehensive Parkway System of the New York Metropolitan Region," *Civil Engineering* 9, no. 3 (March 1939): 160–162.

51. Robert Whitten. "The Expressway in the Region," *City Planning* 8, no. 1 (January 1932): 27.

52. Elizabeth M. Herlihy, "Boston's Master Highway Plan," in *Proceedings of the Twenty-Third National Conference on City Planning Held at Rochester, New York 22–24 June 1931* (Philadelphia: William Fell, 1931), 81–84.

53. For an early critical study of the doctrines of the Chicago School, see Milla A. Alihan, *Social Ecology* (New York: Columbia University Press, 1938). For another, see M. Gottdiener, *The Social Production of Urban Space* (Austin, Tex.: University of Texas Press, 1985).

54. As Rexford Tugwell discovered in his battle with Robert Moses over the planning of New York City, comprehensive planning was a blunt lance in jousts with disciplined, highly organized interest groups and political operators, each trying to capture a piece of the public works budget. See Mark Gelfand, "Rexford G. Tugwell and the Frustration of Planning in New York City," *Journal of the American Planning Association* 51 (Spring 1985): 151–160.

Chapter 3

1. U.S. Congress, House, Committee on Roads, *Toll Roads and Free Roads*, Report prepared by U.S. Bureau of Public Roads, 76th Cong., 1st sess., 1939, H. Doc. 272; and U.S. Congress, House, Committee on Roads, *Interregional Highways*, Report prepared by U.S. Interregional Highway Committee, 78th Cong., 2d sess., 1944, H. Doc. 379.

2. David R. Jones, Jr., *California's Freeway Era in Historical Perspective* (Berkeley: Institute of Transportation Studies, 1989): 200; Brian Taylor, "When Finance Leads Planning: Urban Planning, Highway Planning, and Metropolitan Freeways in California," *Journal of Planning Education and Research* 20 (Winter 2000): 196–214.

3. Jones, *California's Freeway Era*, 200.

4. Bruce E. Seely, *Building the American Highway System: Engineers as Policy Makers* (Philadelphia: Temple University Press, 1987): chaps. 7–8.

5. Mark Gelfand, *A Nation of Cities: The Federal Government and Urban America, 1933–1965* (New York: Oxford University Press, 1975); and Jeffrey L. Meikle, *Twentieth Century Limited: Industrial Design in America, 1925–1939* (Philadelphia: Temple University Press, 1979).

6. Folke T. Kihlstedt, "Utopia Realized: The World's Fairs of the 1930s," in *Imagining Tomorrow: History, Technology, and the American Future*, ed. Joseph J. Corn (Cambridge, Mass.: MIT Press, 1986): 97–118; Meikle, *Twentieth Century Limited*, chap. 9, "A Microcosm of the Machine-Age World."

7. Norman Bel Geddes, *Magic Motorways* (New York: Random House, 1940), 4.

8. Ibid., 4.

9. Ibid., 238.

10. Ibid., 209.

11. Ibid., 209–211.

12. Ibid., 211.

13. Ibid., 215–219.

14. Ibid., 218–219.

15. See Carol Willis, "Skyscraper Utopias, Visionary Urbanism in the 1920s," in *Imagining Tomorrow: History, Technology, and the American Future*, ed. Joseph J. Corn (Cambridge, Mass: MIT Press, 1986), 164–187. Also note similarities with Fritz Malcher's *The Steadyflow Traffic System*, Harvard City Planning Studies, 9 (Cambridge, Mass: Harvard University Press, 1935).

16. Norman Bel Geddes, *Magic Motorways*, 242–244. Bel Geddes mentions several earlier plans for grade separations and multilevel streets, including the 1937 plan for Los Angeles put forth by the Automobile Club of Southern California (p. 234).

17. Ibid., 240.

18. Ibid., 238.

19. Frank T. Sheets, "The Development of Primary Roads during the Next Quarter Century," *American Highways* 18 (October 1939): 34.

20. Meikle, *Twentieth Century Limited*, 208–209. Bel Geddes was invited to the White House for an informal dinner in March 1939; see Mark H. Rose, *Interstate: Express Highway Politics, 1941–1956* (Lawrence, Kans.: The Regents Press of Kansas, 1979), 11.

21. Bel Geddes, *Magic Motorways*, 281.

22. On this issue, see James Holston, *The Modernist City: An Anthropological Critique of Brasilia* (Chicago: University of Chicago Press, 1989); and Manfredo Tafuri, *Architecture and Utopia: Design and Capitalist Development*, trans. Barbara Luigia La Penta (Cambridge, Mass.: MIT Press, 1976).

23. One need not accept the "conspiracy" explanation of the decline of American transit in order to posit a strong connection between the power of automobile interests and pro-highway transportation policy. Here, we only observe that the Futurama vision meshed well with the needs of corporate capital. For an analysis of the role of the automobile lobby in shaping federal transportation policy, see David J. St. Clair, *The Motorization of American Cities* (New York: Praeger, 1986).

24. Seely, *Building the American Highway System*, 170–171. On Roosevelt's conflicts with Robert Moses during Roosevelt's tenure as chairman of the Taconic State Park Commission, see Robert Caro, *The Power Broker: Robert Moses and the Fall of New York* (New York: Knopf, 1974; Vintage, 1975), 287–293.

25. Seely, *Building the American Highway System*, 169–171. Also discussed in Gary T. Schwartz, "Urban Freeways and the Interstate System," *Southern California Law Review* 49 (March 1976): 422.

26. Jonathan Gifford argues that the report seriously underestimated the economic feasibility of toll highways, possibly in order to cast doubt on toll proposals and advance the bureau's own agenda of freeways constructed using the existing federal–state partnership. See Jonathan L. Gifford, "An Analysis of the Federal Role in the Planning, Design and Deployment of Rural Roads, Toll Roads and Urban Freeways." Ph.D. dissertation, University of California at Berkeley, 1983: 113–128.

27. The need for urban freeways had been documented by surveys sponsored by the bureau during the late 1930s. On Roosevelt's view of the urban–rural issue, see Seely, *Building the American Highway System*, 170. With strong rural interests in Congress, urban interstates had no political future unless they were advanced as part of a national system with large rural components.

28. "[T]he construction of transcity connections of the main rural highways and other express routes into the center of the cities ranks first in the list of highway projects worthy of consideration by the Congress. Possibly no other work that might be done would so profitably provide employment coincident with the centers of present unemployment." U.S. Congress, *Toll Roads and Free Roads*, 95.

29. Ibid., 90.

30. Ibid., 91.

31. "In the larger cities generally only a major operation will suffice—nothing less than the creation of a depressed or an elevated artery (the former usually to be preferred) that will convey the massed movement pressing into, and through, the heart of the city, under or over the local cross streets without interruption by their conflicting traffic." U.S. Congress, *Toll Roads and Free Roads*, 93. However, these new federal trunk highways would handle only a portion of the city commuter traffic; other urban highways could have to be constructed to handle the remainder.

32. The works of the Chicago sociologists are not cited directly in *Toll Roads and Free Roads*, but the report's intellectual roots are visible. See Robert E. Park, Ernest W. Burgess, and Roderick D. McKenzie, *The City* (Chicago: University of Chicago Press, 1967 [originally published 1925]. See also Milla A. Alihan, *Social Ecology* (New York: Columbia University Press, 1938); and M. Gottdiener, *The Social Production of Urban Space* (Austin, Tex.: University of Texas Press, 1985), chap. 2.

33. See James F. Short, Jr., ed., *The Social Fabric of the Metropolis: Contributions of the Chicago School of Urban Sociology* (Chicago: University of Chicago Press, 1971). As Short correctly points out, the Chicago sociologists discussed cooperation as well as competition in their analyses of urban life.

34. Richard M. Hurd, *Principles of City Land Values* (New York: The Record and Guide, 1903). For Homer Hoyt's "sector theory" of urban growth, a modification of the concentric ring theory, see Homer Hoyt, *Structure and Growth of Residential Neighborhoods in American Cities* (Washington, D.C.: USGPO, 1939).

35. For an interesting contemporary critique of the literature on urban "blight," see Philip V. I. Darling, "Some Notes on Blighted Areas," *Planners' Journal* 9, no. 1 (January–March 1943): 9–18.

36. See St. Clair, *Motorization of American Cities*, for an analysis of the role of the automobile lobby in shaping American transportation policy. As St. Clair acknowledges, consumer choice of the automobile as the most convenient mode of transportation played a crucial role in the transformation, but it is not an adequate explanation by itself.

37. For a critique of technological determinism in urban geography, see Gottdiener, *The Social Production of Urban Space*, 44–45.

38. We borrow the concept of the "City Inevitable" from D. A. Hart, *Strategic Planning in London The Rise and Fall of the Primary Road Network* (Oxford: Pergamon, 1976).

39. See, for example, John F. Bauman, "The Paradox of Post-War Urban Planning: Downtown Revitalization versus Decent Housing for All," in *Two Centuries of American Planning*, ed. Daniel Shaffer (Baltimore: Johns Hopkins University Press, 1988): 231–264; and John F. Bauman, *Public Housing, Race, and Renewal: Urban Planning in Philadelphia, 1920–1974* (Philadelphia: Temple University Press, 1987).

40. U.S. Congress, *Toll Roads and Free Roads*, 99.

41. But the report did acknowledged that "the nature of the facilities required will depend upon conditions peculiar to each city." U.S. Congress, *Toll Roads and Free Roads*, 92.

42. Ibid., 96.

43. Ibid., 97.

44. The freeway system eventually built in Baltimore is, in fact, a radial-concentric system, but with the circumferential or belt line approximately 6–8 miles from the center. Ironically, given its choice as an example in *Toll Roads and Free Roads*, in 1968 Baltimore would become the site of one of the first urban design concept teams assembled to correct the deficiencies of earlier freeway planning theories. (See chapter 6 for more detail on the Baltimore design team and its conflicts with Baltimore officials.)

45. U.S. Congress, *Toll Roads and Free Roads*, 99.

46. U.S. Congress, *Interregional Highways*.

47. The first meeting of the Interregional Highways Committee was held June 24, 1941. Herbert S. Fairbank, of the Public Roads Administration, was appointed secretary of the committee. The introduction to *Interregional Highways* explained that a "small staff was supplied by the Public Roads Administration," and the "research and writing of this report are the work primarily of Mr. Fairbank, assisted by this staff." The list of staff personnel is a "Who's Who" of highway engineering in the 1940s, 1950s, and 1960s, including names such as E. H. Holmes, Joseph Barnett, O. K. Normann, D. W. Loutzenheiser, and David R. Levin.

48. U.S. Congress, *Interregional Highways*, 3–4.

49. The report states that there would be 2,123 miles within the municipal limits of cities of 10,000 or more population and 2,347 miles within the limits of cities of less than 10,000 population. U.S. Congress, *Interregional Highways*, 51.

50. Ibid., 52.

51. *Interregional Highways* renders the diagram as follows: The central business district is the focal point of the metropolitan area, the location of large office buildings, retail stores, and civic and cultural buildings. Moving outward, there is a "secondary business area" that gradually blends in with a "large area of mixed land uses and rundown buildings," referred to as the "slum area." The next ring, larger than the slum area, is the "blighted area," which is in danger of becoming a full-fledged slum if not rehabilitated. The outermost ring contains "newer residential areas" of suburban and even exurban subdivisions extending out to the city limits and beyond. U.S. Congress, *Interregional Highways*, 53.

52. Ibid., 54. This theme was probably emphasized by Harland Bartholomew, who described the dangers of excessive decentralization in his writings of the early 1930s. See Harland Bartholomew, "A Program to Prevent Economic Disintegration in American Cities," *Proceedings of the National Conference on City Planning, Pittsburgh, Pennsylvania, 14–16 November 1932* (Philadelphia: William Fell Co., 1932): 1–16.

53. U.S. Congress, *Interregional Highways*, 56.

54. Ibid., 56.

55. Ibid., 61.

56. Ibid., 62. The committee noted, however, that these wedges were also highly desirable for "other purposes of city planning" such as parks, playgrounds, or new residential communities.

57. Ibid., 65.

58. Ibid., 69.

59. Ibid., 70.

60. Ibid., 71–73. In a "small city" the interregional highway bypasses the city to one side, with only a service road providing direct access to the city. In a "medium size city," the interregional route penetrates to the city center, passing along one side of the central business district. In addition to this main route, an "interregional circumferential" is provided to one side of the city, allowing long-distance through traffic to bypass the central core. Other "secondary circumferentials" may be provided to allow traffic to enter or leave the main interregional route from other main arterials without having to do so near the central business district.

61. The other circumferentials are placed just inside the edge of the city's built-up area along all four compass points; these routes distribute traffic laterally from one route to another and "to the several quarters of the city." On the north side of the city, apparently the sector experiencing suburban growth, *two* circumferentials are recommended: the "interregional circumferential" out beyond existing suburban developments, and a local or "city circumferential" closer to the center along the edge of some older residential neighborhoods.

62. U.S. Congress, *Interregional Highways*, 75.

63. Ibid., 76.

64. Ibid., 70. The report also stated that "the closest possible cooperation is needed between highway, housing, and city planning authorities" (p. 65).

65. Seely, *Building the American Highway System*, 181.

66. Federal-Aid Highway Act of 1944, 58 Stat. 842. The hearings on the act are in U.S. Congress, House, Roads Committee, *Hearings on H.R. 2426: Federal-Aid for Post-War Highway Construction*, 2 vols., 78th Congress, 2d session, 1944.

67. The "deferred" 2,300 miles of urban routes were finally specified in 1955 in U.S. Bureau of Public Roads, *General Location of National System of Interstate Highways* (Washington, D.C.: USGPO, 1955). As Schwartz writes, "These designations served to convert the urban Interstates from somewhat vague and abstract policy into quite specific plans." Schwartz, "Urban Freeways," 438.

68. Jonathan Gifford argues that three cardinal principles guided the Bureau of Public Roads in its administration of the interstate system. First, the *uniformity principle*: uniform high standards for the entire system, minimizing special modifications for freeways in urban areas. This meant that the urban freeways would be designed for high speeds, often with sweeping curves cutting across the old urban grain. Second, the *limited system*: focusing the federal effort on a concen-

trated, limited system of highways—in urban areas, a few large highways rather than a more complex mix of arterials adapted to specific urban conditions. Third, the *traffic service principle*: designing the new interregional highways to accommodate even peak hour traffic for the entire 20-year design life of the highways. See Gifford, "Analysis of the Federal Role," 155–177.

69. Harry W. Alexander, "Bringing Interregional Thoroughfares to the Hearts of the Cities," *American City* 60 (February 1945): 59.

70. Jones, "California's Freeway Era," 200. Jones writes: "Tasking highway departments to play a principal role in the metropolitan arena—*the* principal role, as it turned out—was a conclusive event. . . . Freeways displaced parkways as the focal technology of urban road programs; transit development was displaced from the metropolitan agenda; and planning for transportation was severed from planning for adjacent land use. This was the significance of the battery of highway legislation adopted in 1941, 1943, 1945, and 1947."

71. See V. G. Iden, "Elevated Highway Design for Speed, Safety and Beauty," *American City* 53 (May 1938): 46–48; "Elevated Highways Only Solution to Traffic Congestion." *Architect and Engineer* 137 (April 1939): 50–52; Frederick Hamilton, "El-Way to Ease San Francisco Traffic," *Architect and Engineer* 154 (September 1943): 27–29; and "Elevated Highways Versus Depressed Highways," *American City* 55 (October 1940): 61–62.

72. William J. Cox, "By-Passing Cities in the Vertical Plane," *American City* 60 (October 1945): 95.

73. Robert Moses, "Parks, Parkways, Express Arteries, and Related Plans for New York City After the War," *American City* 58 (December 1943): 53. See also Robert Moses, "Public Building to Come," *American Highways* 22, no. 3 (July 1943): 22–23: "I do not advocate rejecting, tearing down and rebuilding everything in the country, nor long-range academic planning of works which do not commend themselves to the average citizen and taxpayer."

74. G. Donald Kennedy, "Highways, the Framework of the City and Regional Plan," in *New Architecture and City Planning*, ed. Paul Zucker (New York: Philosophical Library, 1944), 413–424. See also William R. McConochie, "Planning Post-War Highways in Cities," *Traffic Engineering* 15, no. 8 (May 1945): 319.

75. Paul Oppermann, Discussion of Charles Gordon, "Transportation as an Element in Urban Rehabilitation," in *Proceedings of the National Conference on Planning, Boston, Massachusetts 15–17 May 1939* (Chicago: American Society of Planning Officials, 1939), 25.

76. The pages of *American City* during the late 1930s and 1940s contained numerous articles on replanning blighted areas. See for example, Marjorie Sewell, "How Blighted Areas in Philadelphia and Boston Might Be Transformed," *American City* 58 (October 1943): 47–49; "Replanning an Obsolete Square Mile," *American City* 58 (December 1943): 46; or "Huge Model Visualizes Committee's Plans for 'Toledo Tomorrow,'" *American City* 60 (July 1945): 72–74.

77. Magali S. Larson, "Emblem and Exception: The Historical Definition of the Architect's Professional Role," in *Professionals and Urban Form*, ed. Judith R.

Blau, Mark La Gory, and John S. Pipkin (Albany, N.Y.: State University of New York Press, 1983), 74.

78. See Jose Louis Sert and C.I.A.M., *Can Our Cities Survive?* (Cambridge, Mass: Harvard University Press, 1942); and Sigfried Giedion, *Space Time and Architecture*, The Charles Eliot Norton Lectures for 1938–39 (Cambridge, Mass.: Harvard University Press, 1941).

79. Richard Polenberg, *One Nation Divisible: Class, Race, and Ethnicity in the United States Since 1938* (New York: Penguin, 1980).

Chapter 4

1. See David Jones, "The California Innovation," in *California's Freeway Era in Historical Perspective* (Berkeley: Institute of Transportation Studies, 1989), chap. 8.

2. G. T. Schwartz, "Urban Freeways and the Interstate System," *Southern California Law Review* 49, no. 2 (January, 1976): 406–513: 424.

3. AASHO Staff and BPR Staff, "A History of the Interstate System," in *AASHO: The First Fifty Years, 1914–1964* (Washington, D.C.: AASHO. 1965), 184.

4. Alan Altshuler, *The City Planning Process: A Political Analysis* (Ithaca, N.Y.: Cornell University Press, 1965).

5. Ibid., p. 28.

6. Mark Gelfand, *A Nation of Cities: The Federal Government and Urban America, 1933–1965* (New York: Oxford University Press, 1975), 224.

7. Altshuler, *City Planning Process*, 29.

8. Altshuler notes that by 1960, "the land-use forecasts made by the city planners and suburban nonplanners had proven virtually worthless"; Altshuler, *City Planning Process*, 32.

9. Jerome A. Cohn, "Urban Background to the Interstate Highway Program: The Planning and Politics of Highways in Syracuse, 1944-1960." Ph.D. dissertation, Syracuse University, 1978.

10. Schwartz, "Urban Freeways," 425.

11. See Jonathan L. Gifford, "An Analysis of the Federal Role in the Planning, Design and Deployment of Rural Roads, Toll Roads and Urban Freeways." Ph.D. dissertation, University of California at Berkeley, 1983, p. 190. Required features included design to accommodate traffic that would exist 20 years after construction, access control, and a minimum design speed in urban areas of 40 mph, 50 mph desirable. Other design standards covered curvature, gradients, lane width, and divided highways.

12. Highway Research Board, Committee on Controlled Access in Urban Areas, "Controlled Access Expressways in Urban Areas: A Symposium," *Highway Research Board Bulletin*, no. 25 (July 1950): 30; Thomas H. MacDonald, "Highway Development under the New Federal Legislation," *American Highways* 25 (April 1946): 8, 22; Thomas H. MacDonald, "The Highway Improvement Program in

Relation to the Conventional Public Works Concept," *American Highways* 26 (January 1947): 10, 28. For a lengthier treatment of this theme, see Nathan L. Smith, "Blighted Areas and Traffic," *Traffic Quarterly* 1, no. 4 (October 1947): 312–324.

13. In 1949, the BPR was transferred from the Federal Works Administration to the Department of Commerce, entirely separate from the federal government's housing and redevelopment programs. Mark Gelfand contends that the bureau's interest in urban redevelopment was actually "part of an unsuccessful attempt by the Federal Works Agency to wrest administration of the proposed urban redevelopment program away from the HHFA [Housing and Home Finance Administration]." When that project dissolved, the bureau dropped its advocacy of freeways as tools for the restructuring the central city and returned to the primary mission, expediting traffic. See Gelfand, *Nation of Cities*, 226.

14. Thomas H. MacDonald, "The Case for Urban Expressways," *American City* 62, no. 6 (June 1947): 92–93.

15. Ibid., 92.

16. Ibid., 93.

17. Ibid.

18. Joseph Barnett, "Express Highway Planning in Metropolitan Areas," reprinted from *American Society of Civil Engineers Proceedings*: March, May, September, November, 1946, and January, April 1947 (Washington, D.C., June 1947). This booklet includes discussion of Barnett's essay by sixteen commentators, mostly civil engineers. As mentioned earlier, at this time the Bureau of Public Roads was called the Public Roads Administration and was located in the Federal Works Agency.

19. Ibid., 11.

20. Ibid., 13. Barnett's criteria for urban freeways, in abbreviated form, are as follows: (a) fit traffic needs; (b) free flowing and safe; (c) make the driver's path direct and simple, the required actions natural; (d) flexible, giving driver a wide choice of destinations; (e) adaptable to future changes; (f) integration with the city plan; (g) wide distribution to the street system; (h) stage construction should be practicable; (i) maintain traffic adequately; (j) minimize disruption to existing facilities; (k) leave important structures intact; (l) connect with the larger system; (m) cost in line with service; (n) nominal maintenance costs; and (o) pleasing in appearance.

21. Joseph Barnett, "Importance of Planning and Building Urban Road Systems and Requirements Therefor," *American Planning and Civic Annual* (1949): 68–69.

22. Barnett, "Express Highway Planning," 15.

23. Ibid., 19–21.

24. Ibid., 30.

25. Ibid., 31.

26. Ibid., 58.

27. Ibid., 52–57. Herrold's role in the debates over freeway planning in Minneapolis–St. Paul is discussed in Altshuler, *The City Planning Process.*

28. Ibid., 54.

29. Ibid., 57.

30. Charles M. Noble, "Highway Planning in Metropolitan Areas," *American Planning and Civic Annual* (1948): 104.

31. For example, in his American Institute of Planners President's Report for 1949, Frederick Adams wrote that "we are still too lacking in agreement among ourselves on basic planning objectives, without which we cannot hope for public acceptance of comprehensive planning as a recognized professional field. . . . I believe we suffer from timidity and inarticulateness in our dealings with the public at large and especially with our friends in the sister professions—who do not seem to suffer from a like backwardness." Frederick J. Adams, "President's Report for 1949," *Journal of the American Institute of Planners* 16, no. 1 (Winter 1950): 2–5.

32. Noble, "Highway Planning in Metropolitan Areas," 111.

33. Excerpts from Mr. Timby's statement, given November 30, 1967. Hearings before the Subcommittee on Roads, of the Committee on Public Works, United States Senate, 90th Congress, 1st Session on Urban Highway Planning, Location and Design (November 14, 15, 16, 28, 29 and 30, 1967): 174–175.

34. David Lagesse, "The Road Warriors. Building the Highways that Changed a Nation," *U.S. News & World Report, Special Issue, Master Builders.* January 26, 2012. Available at: http://www.usnews.com/usnews/doubleissue/builders/articles/30interstate.htm.

35. See Harland Bartholomew, "The Location of Interstate Highways in Cities," *American Planning and Civic Annual* (1949): 73–78.

36. American Institute of Planners, Committee on Urban Transportation, *Urban Freeways* (New York: American Transit Association, 1947).

37. See, for example, the statement by Henry Churchill in American Institute of Planners, *Urban Freeways,* 25. Also see Leslie Williams, "Planning Public Transportation on Urban Expressways," *Proceedings of the Highway Research Board* (1945): 363–375; Earl Van Storch, "Housing Development and Express Highways," *Highway Research Board Bulletin,* no. 10 (1947): 35.

38. American Institute of Planners, *Urban Freeways,* 15.

39. Ibid., 22–23.

40. See Jones, "The California Innovation," 221–223 and 233–235. The idea of using expressways for transit rights-of-way lived on during the following decade. See "Put Public Transit on Expressway Malls, *American City* 67 (March 1952): 143. Chicago made use of the idea more than other cities; see "The Congress Street Superhighway," *American City* 67 (September 1952): 145; and Harold M. Mayer and Richard C. Wade, *Chicago: Growth of a Metropolis* (Chicago: University of Chicago Press, 1969), 440–448.

41. Walter Blucher, "Moving People," *Virginia Law Review* 36 (1950): 849.

42. Henry S. Churchill, "The Place of Land-Use Control in Traffic Control," *Traffic Quarterly* 1 (October 1947): 370.

43. Peter P. Hale, "The City Means Nothing to Traffic," *Traffic Quarterly* 2 (April 1948): 175–182.

44. This edition, a revision of Ladislas Segoe's pioneering edition of 1941, was supervised by Howard Menhinick, director of the Department of Regional Studies, Tennessee Valley Authority. Menhinick was on the staff of the Harvard University School of City Planning for 8 years prior to joining the Tennessee Valley Authority.

45. Harold M. Lewis, *Planning the Modern City*, Vol. 1 (New York: John Wiley & Sons, 1949), 148.

46. S. E. Sanders and A. J. Rabuck, *New City Patterns* (New York: Reinhold Publishing Corporation, 1946).

47. In their schematics, the overall urban pattern is star-shaped, with a single central business district and secondary business districts approximately 6 miles from the center along the wedges extending outward from the center.

48. For the argument that only fragments of the city can be planned within the American urban context, see Manfredo Tafuri, "The Disenchanted Mountain: The Skyscraper and the City," in Giorgio Giucci, Francesco Dal Co, Mario Manieri-Elia and Manfredo Tafuri, eds., *The American City. From Civil War to New Deal* (Cambridge, Mass.: MIT Press, 1979), 483. On the building of modernist fragments within American central cities, see any good urban history; for example, Harold M. Mayer and Richard C. Wade, *Chicago: Growth of a Metropolis* (Chicago: University of Chicago Press, 1969). The pages of *American City* during the late 1940s and early 1950s contained numerous examples: see the cover for August 1950 and in the same issue Joseph M. Darst, "St. Louis Rebuilds," *American City* 65 (August 1950): 100–101.

49. New York, City Planning Commission, *Selected Measures for the Partial Relief of Traffic Congestion in New York City*, prepared by Gano Dunn, W. Earle Andrews, and Gilmore D. Clarke (1946).

50. For other Moses plans of this era, see Robert Moses, *Arterial Plan for Pittsburgh*, prepared for the Pittsburgh Regional Planning Association (November 1939); see also chapter 6 of this volume.

51. Christopher Tunnard, "Cities by Design," *Journal of the American Institute of Planners* 17, no. 3 (Summer 1951): 142–150.

52. Ibid., 143.

53. Ibid., 145.

54. Ibid., 146.

55. Ibid., 149.

56. Ibid. Tunnard saw little hope that the architects would come to the rescue: "the architect, who once was the guardian of urban esthetics, has given up trying."

57. This research can be tracked through the voluminous pages of the publications of the Highway Research Board.

58. Robert E. Heightchew, Jr., "TSM: Revolution or Repetition?" in *Urban Transportation: Perspectives and Prospects*, ed. Herbert S. Levinson and Robert A. Weant (Westport, Conn.: Eno Foundation for Transportation, 1982), 62–70.

59. See Robert Emmanuel Barkley, "Origin-Destination Surveys and Traffic Volume Studies," Highway Research Board Bibliography No. 11, December 1951. Part I provides a review of the literature; part II provides an annotated bibliography.

60. For example, extrapolation of automobile ownership figures into the future.

61. See Louis Ward Kemp, "Aesthetes and Engineers: The Occupational Ideology of Highway Design," *Technology and Culture* 27 (October 1986): 766–767.

62. Ibid., 778–780.

63. Ibid., 765–766.

64. For signs of an early critique along these lines, see William W. Forster, Review of "Controlled Access Expressways in Urban Areas: A Symposium," *Highway Research Board Bulletin*, no. 25 (1950), in *Journal of the American Institute of Planners* 17, no. 3 (Summer 1951): 156–158. Forster pointed out that "we are given an optimistic picture of increased land values resulting from parkway construction. While this certainly applies to parkways built on land of previous low values, it does not necessarily follow that expressways will always benefit lands of established high values. In such cases the over-all city or regional value may become the justifying factor."

65. As Louis Ward Kemp points out, engineer Howard Bevis argued that "social or non-user benefits should be excluded from consideration until such time as the technology is sufficiently advanced to provide precise measures for both these types of benefits and for social costs." Howard Bevis, "The Application of Benefit-Cost Ratios to an Expressway System," *Proceedings of the Highway Research Board* 35 (1956): 66, quoted in Kemp, "Aesthetes and Engineers," 765.

66. Excluding hard-to-calculate costs also reduced the chances of political conflict over highway location. See Kemp, "Aesthetes and Engineers," 766.

67. For a more detailed history of these technical changes in highway design, see Kemp, "Aesthetes and Engineers," and Jones, "The California Innovation."

68. Kemp, "Aesthetes and Engineers," 769.

69. Ibid., 769.

70. Ibid., 773.

71. For a later description, see W. A. Bugge and W. Brewster Snow, "The Complete Highway," in *The Highway and the Landscape*, ed. W. Brewster Snow (New Brunswick, N.J.: Rutgers University Press, 1959).

72. Kemp, "Aesthetes and Engineers," 773–775.

73. Ibid., 773.

74. For a review of the statements, see Norman T. Newton, *Design on the Land: The Development of Landscape Architecture* (Cambridge, Mass.: Belknap Press of Harvard University Press, 1971).

75. Robert Mitchell and Chester Rapkin, *Urban Traffic: A Function of Land Use* (New York: Columbia University Press, 1954).

76. Ibid., 7.

77. J. L. Sert, "Centers of Community Life," in *The Heart of the City: Toward the Humanisation of Urban Life*, ed. J. Tyrwhitt, J. L. Sert, and E. N. Rogers (New York: Pellegrini and Cudahy, 1952), 11.

78. W. J. Holford, "The Commercial Core of London," in *The Heart of the City: Toward the Humanisation of Urban Life*, ed. J. Tyrwhitt, J. L. Sert, and E. N. Rogers (New York: Pellegrini and Cudahy, 1952), 97–98.

79. Robert C. Weinberg, Review of *The Heart of the City*, ed. J. Tyrwhitt, J. L. Sert, and E. N. Rogers, in *Journal of the American Institute of Planners* 19, no. 1 (Winter 1953): 46.

80. For Gruen's own account, see Victor Gruen, *The Heart of Our Cities* (New York: Simon and Schuster, 1964). See also David L. Browning, "Legacy of a Planning Legend: The Victor Gruen Plan for a Greater Fort Worth Tomorrow," *Crit*, no. 12 (Winter 1983): 5–9.

81. Browning, "Legacy of a Planning Legend," 8–9.

82. "How to Rebuild Cities Downtown," *Architectural Forum* 102, no. 6 (June 1955): 122. The roundtable was held in St. Louis. It represented "merchandising, banking, real estate, office management, entertainment, transportation management, highway planning, parking, government, architecture, planning, building, public education." Among the participants: Architects: George Hellmuth, John Merrill, Oskar Stonorov; Government: Carl Feiss; Planning: Walter Blucher, Ernest J. Bohn; Transportation: Walter McCarter, Robert B. Mitchell, Wilbur S. Smith.

83. Ibid., 128.

84. Ladislas Segoe, "Rochester's Traffic Strainer," *American City* 69 (April 1954): 133; Seward H. Mott and Buford Hayden "Providing for Automotive Services in Urban Land Development," *Traffic Quarterly* 7, no. 3 (July 1953): 374–375; "Atlanta, Ga. Is On the Way to Traffic Relief," *American City* 70 (April 1955): 138.

85. Richard Dewey, a professor of sociology and anthropology at the University of Illinois, noted that "Nothing seems quite so dear to the heart of planners as the picture, real or imaginary, of magnificent freeways cutting through a maze of city buildings (often at several levels), stretching from rural-urban fringe areas to the city's very heart. . . . In my opinion, the problems involving the suburbs which the metropolitan-area planner must face are intensified by the construction of the high-speed freeways. In a sense these freeways are new and shiny funnels, the spouts of which are placed in our already overfilled urban bottles." "A Critical Look at Freeways to Downtown Areas," *American City* 70 (January 1955): 153–154.

86. The literature on urban freeways in the *Journal of the American Institute of Planners* between 1946 and 1956 is remarkably sparse, considering the importance of the subject.

87. Jones, "The California Innovation," 200.

88. U.S. Department of Commerce, Bureau of Public Roads, *General Location of National System of Interstate Highways* (Washington, D.C.: USGPO, 1955). Gary Schwartz points out that General J. S. Bragdon, President Eisenhower's advisor

on the interstate highway issue, was suspicious "that the Bureau undertook the 1955 designation process partly in order to commit the urban Interstates before the [1956 Highway Act] was passed, and partly to enhance the System's congressional popularity." Schwartz, "Urban Freeways," 435.

89. See David Brodsly, *L.A. Freeway, An Appreciative Essay* (Berkeley: University of California Press, 1981) for an explanation of the form of the Los Angeles freeway system, which followed the earlier transportation patterns defined by the trail, railroad, streetcar, and early highway patterns.

90. For a legislative history of the interstate system, see Mark Rose, *Interstate*. The "defense" justification involved the provision of efficient evacuation routes from cities in the event of war; see David J. St. Clair, *The Motorization of American Cities* (New York: Praeger, 1986). See also Michael R. Fein, *Paving the Way: New York Road Building and the American State, 1880–1956* (Lawrence, Kan.: The University Press of Kansas).

91. See Jones, "The California Innovation," 200. For contemporary articles on New York freeways, see Bertram D. Tallamy, "The Development of Expressways in New York State," *Traffic Quarterly* 7, no. 3 (July 1953): 291–302. Also see Charles H. Sells, "New York State Prepares for City Arterial Routes," *American Highways* 23, no. 4 (October 1944): 5; and "New York State's Answer to Urban Traffic Problems," *American City* 63 (July 1948): 72–74.

92. Tracy B. Augur, "Highways for New Urban Patterns," *Highway Research Board Bulletin*, no. 113 (1956): 54–58. For a contemporary explanation for the lack of well-documented city planning research, see Martin Meyerson, "Research and City Planning," *Journal of the American Institute of Planners* 20, no. 4 (Fall 1954): 201–205. Meyerson pointed out that (1) "In virtually no place is there money or time for any but the most immediately practical of studies, with pressure for as rapid and simple an undertaking as possible"; and (2) "A further limitation of research is that at present no methodology has been developed which can handle the multiplicity of factors with which city planning deals."

93. We borrow the term "mass production" as applied to urban freeways from Jones, "The California Innovation," 246.

Chapter 5

1. Daniel Moynihan, "Policy vs. Program in the '70s," *The Public Interest* (Summer 1970): 90, 93–94, as cited in Gary T. Schwartz, "Urban Freeways and the Interstate System," *Southern California Law Review* 49 (March 1976): 406–513, see 406.

2. Schwartz, "Urban Freeways and the Interstate System," 406.

3. Ibid., 412–413.

4. U.S. Congress, House, Committee on Roads, *Toll Roads and Free Roads*, Report prepared by U.S. Bureau of Public Roads, 76th Cong., 1st sess., 1939, H. Doc. 272 Available at: http://www.fhwa.dot.gov/reports/routefinder/index.htm.

5. The AASHO defines an expressway as "a divided arterial highway for through traffic with full or partial control of access and generally with grade separations at

intersections. A significant distinction between a major street and an expressway is the distance between crossings and access connections . . . an expressway has relatively few, if any." American Association of State Highway Officials, *A Policy on Arterial Highways in Urban Areas* (Washington, D.C.: AASHO, 1957), 70.

6. U.S. Congress, House, Committee on Roads, *Interregional Highways*, Report prepared by U.S. Interregional Highway Committee, 78th Cong., 2d sess., 1944, H. Doc. 379. Available at: http://www.fhwa.dot.gov/reports/routefinder/index.htm.

7. U.S. Department of Transportation, Federal Highway Administration, *Highway History*, http://www.fhwa.dot.gov/highwayhistory/data/page01.cfm.

8. Schwartz, "Urban Freeways and the Interstate System," 416.

9. Raymond A. Mohl, "Ike and the Interstates: Creeping Toward Comprehensive Planning," *Journal of Planning History* 2 no. 3 (August 2003): 237–262, see 240.

10. Ibid., 240.

11. This approach was supposed to allow local interests to secure a special audience for particular construction and routing. Mark H. Rose, *Interstate: Express Highway Politics 1939–1989* (Knoxville: University of Tennessee Press, 1970), 26.

12. In Syracuse, for example, concern over possible economic decline was recognized by the Metropolitan Development Association, which wrote in May 1965, "The twenty year period which ended in the mid-1950s was one of small but vastly troubling decline for the city." *Central Syracuse Bulletin*, May 8, 1965.

13. Schwartz, "Urban Freeways and the Interstate System," 423.

14. Ibid., 425. The planning process for this "picture book" was completed in just 8 months. See B. D. Taylor, "When Finance Leads Planning: Urban Planning, Highway Planning, and Metropolitan Freeways in California," *Journal of Planning Education and Research* 20, no. 2 (2000): 196–214.

15. American Association of State Highway Officials, *A Policy on Arterial Highways in Urban Areas* (Washington, D.C.: AASHO, 1957), 71.

16. Schwartz, "Urban Freeways and the Interstate System," 426.

17. Rose, *Interstate*, 31.

18. Schwartz, "Urban Freeways and the Interstate System," 426.

19. *Urban Transportation Planning in the United States. An Historical Overview, Revised Edition*, November 1992. Prepared by Edward Weiner, Office of Economics, Office of the Assistant Secretary for Policy and International Affairs, Office of the Secretary of Transportation, Washington, D.C. Distributed in cooperation with Technology Sharing Program, U.S. Department of Transportation, Washington, D.C.

20. Highway Revenue Act of 1956, Ch.462, Sections 202–206, 209, 70 Stat. pp. 387–401.

21. Schwartz, "Urban Freeways and the Interstate System," 438.

22. Lewis Mumford, *The Highway and the City* (New York: Harcourt, Brace and World, 1963), 244–248.

23. Arie Rip, "Controversies as Informal Technology Assessment," *Knowledge: Creation, Diffusion, Utilization* 8, no. 2 (December 1986): 349–371.

24. Frank H. Malley and Milton Breivogel "Urban Freeways," *Journal of the American Planning Association* 14, no. 4 (1948): 23–26.

25. American Association of State Highway Officials, *A Policy on Arterial Highways in Urban Areas* (Washington, D.C.: AASHO, 1957).

26. Ibid., 67.

27. Ibid., 6–7.

28. Ibid, 254.

29. Ibid., 46.

30. Ibid., 388, 430–434.

31. Ibid., 139–143.

32. Schwartz, "Urban Freeways and the Interstate System," 444–447.

33. Ibid., 446–447.

34. Feiss mentioned this in his testimony before Congress in 1967; see U.S. Senate, Committee on Public Works, Subcommittee on Roads, *Urban Highways*, Hearings on Urban Highway Planning, Location, and Design, Part 1, 90th Cong., 1st sess., November 1967, 124.

35. Edward T. Chase, "The Hundred Billion Dollar Question: Will the New National Highway Program Be Used to Attack the Desperate Metropolitan Crisis or to Compound It?" *Architectural Forum* 107 (July 1957): 135.

36. James W. Rouse, "The Highways and Urban Growth," in "The New Highways: Challenge to the Metropolitan Region," *Urban Land Institute Technical Bulletin*, no. 31 (November 1957): 26. Rouse, of course, later achieved fame as an innovative real estate developer.

37. J. Douglas Carroll, Jr., "Highways and the Future Demand and Supply of Metropolitan Transportation," in "The New Highways: Challenge to the Metropolitan Region," *Urban Land Institute Technical Bulletin*, no. 31 (November 1957): 65–74, see 73.

38. Luther Gulick, "The New Highway Program Requires Metropolitan Cooperation," in "The New Highways: Challenge to the Metropolitan Region," *Urban Land Institute Technical Bulletin*, no. 31 (November 1957): 88–89.

39. Grady Clay, "Main Street 1969: Miracle Miles or a Big Mess?" *Journal of the American Institute of Planners* 23, no. 3 (1957): 131–133. Clay later became editor of *Landscape Architecture* and the author of several books on the cultural geography of cities. Jonathan L. Gifford also maintains that the cities were placed in a subordinate role throughout the urban freeway planning process; see Jonathan L. Gifford, "An Analysis of the Federal Role in the Planning, Design and Deployment of Rural Roads, Toll Roads and Urban Freeways." Ph.D. dissertation, University of California at Berkeley, 1983: 225.

40. American Association of State Highway Officials and American Municipal Association, Joint Committee on Highways, *The Sagamore Conference on Highways and Urban Development: Guidelines for Action* (1958), Foreword.

41. Ibid., 5.

42. Ibid., 9–10.

43. Joseph Barnett, "Factors Influencing Location and Design of Urban Expressways from the Highway Engineer's Viewpoint." Paper presented at the Sagamore Conference on Highways and Urban Development, 5–9 October 1958: 1.

44. Lawrence Halprin, *Freeways* (New York: Reinhold Publishing, 1966). Halprin prefaced his text with the following statement:.

I backed into the design of freeways. My practice is a generalized one in environmental planning and I came to freeway problems with no particular background in their solution. I had been asked several years ago by the California State Division of Highways to help in the urban design problems of several freeways. Since there was little or no information available at that time on the subject, I requested authority to make a general survey of design principles before tackling the particular freeway problems.

45. Ibid., 5 (Prologue).

46. Ibid., 12.

47. Ibid., 17.

48. Ibid., 24.

49. Ibid.

50. See John H. Mollenkopf, *The Contested City* (Princeton: Princeton University Press, 1983); Chester Hartman, *The Transformation of San Francisco* (Totowa, N.J.: Rowman & Allanheld, 1984).

51. See Robert Fitch, "Planning New York," in *The Fiscal Crisis of American Cities*, ed. Roger E. Alcaly and David Mermelstein (New York: Vintage Books, 1976), 246–284; and J. F. Bauman, *Public Housing, Race, and Renewal Urban Planning in Philadelphia, 1920–1974* (Philadelphia: Temple University Press, 1987), 185–191.

52. Quigg Newton, "Planning Comes of Age," *Journal of the American Institute of Planners* 23, no. 4 (1957): 189. Newton was then president of the University of Colorado and had been mayor of Denver from 1947 to 1955.

53. Catherine Bauer, "Do Americans Hate Cities?" *Journal of the American Institute of Planners* 23, no. 1 (Winter 1957): 2–8.

54. Ibid., 2.

55. Ibid., 6.

56. Richard A. Miller, "Expressway Blight," *Architectural Forum* 111 (October 1959): 159–163.

57. Ibid., The Central Artery has been demolished and the highway placed underground.

58. For one contemporary interpretation of these events, see James Bailey, "How S.O.M. Took On the Baltimore Road Gang," *Architectural Forum* 130 (March 1969): 40–45. Bailey's report was criticized by leading members of the Baltimore urban design concept team in a subsequent letter, "Stating the Facts," *Architectural Forum* 130 (June 1969): 6.

59. "Urbane Freeway," *Architectural Forum* 129 (September 1968): 68–73.

60. "Team Concepts for Urban Highways and Urban Design," *Highway Research Record*, no. 220 (1968).

61. Lowell K. Bridwell, "Remarks Before Pennsylvania Department of Highway Seminar, February 28, 1968, Harrisburg," *Highway Research Record*, no. 220 (1968), 2.

62. Andrew F. Euston, "Design Concepts for the Future," *Highway Research Record*, no. 220 (1968): 5.

63. Ibid., 6.

64. Milton Pikarsky, "Joint Development Concept: Chicago Crosstown Expressway," *Highway Research Record*, no. 220 (1968): 17.

65. Archibald C. Rogers, "The Urban Freeway: An Experiment in Team Design and Decision-Making," *Highway Research Record*, no. 220 (1968): 20.

66. Congress, House, *Federal-Aid Highway Act of 1962*, Public Law 87–866, 87th Cong. 2d sess., 1962, H.R. 12135.

67. U. S. Department of Transportation, 1980. As cited in *Urban Transportation Planning in the United States. An Historical Overview, Revised Edition*, November 1992. Prepared by Edward Weiner, Office of Economics, Office of the Assistant Secretary for Policy and International Affairs, Office of the Secretary of Transportation, Washington, D.C. Distributed in cooperation with Technology Sharing Program, U.S. Department of Transportation, Washington, D.C.

68. Melvin R. Levin and Norman A. Abend. *Bureaucrats In Collision: Case Studies in Area Transportation* Planning (Cambridge, Mass.: The MIT Press, 1971). In 1969, looking back on the actual effect of the Highway Act of 1962, planner Thomas Morehouse asked whether the 1962 act had fulfilled the "promise of bringing highways into harmony with the urban environment." He concluded that it had not:.

[T]he Bureau absorbed the 1962 requirement in such a way as to leave the existing program structure and modes of operation intact, avoid any additional delays, in highway construction schedules, satisfy the state highway departments, and yet meet the formal requirements of the law.

In a rejoinder to Morehouse, transportation planner J. Douglas Carroll argued that the act had produced more effective, cooperative planning. He accused planners critical of the highway program of using "their energies and position more for the purpose of generating invective and criticism than to develop constructive and useful solutions to these thorny design and policy questions."

Planner Robert Einsweiler responded to Morehouse by suggesting that the reasons for planners' ineffectiveness extended far beyond the intransigence of the highway agencies: "If one probes more deeply, however, he can find established laws, availability of personnel, capability of personnel, methods of funding, amounts of funding, attitudes of local governments toward metropolitan intervention, and other arguments as the real basis for why things are as they are." See Thomas A. Morehouse, "The 1962 Highway Act: A Study in Artful Interpretation," *Journal of the American Institute of Planners* 35, no. 3 (May 1969): 160–168; J. Douglas Carroll, Jr., "Comments on Morehouse Interpretation." *Journal of the American Institute of Planners* 35, no. 4 (July 1969): 290; and Robert C. Einsweiler, "The 1962 Highway Act," *Journal of the American Institute of Planners* 35, no. 4 (July 1969): 291–292.

69. *Urban Transportation Planning in the United States. An Historical Overview, Revised Edition,* November 1992. Prepared by Edward Weiner, Office of Economics, Office of the Assistant Secretary for Policy and International Affairs, Office of the Secretary of Transportation, Washington, D.C. Distributed in cooperation with Technology Sharing Program, U.S. Department of Transportation, Washington, D.C.

70. Catherine Bauer Wurster, "Architecture and the Cityscape: Notes on the Primitive State of Urban Design in America," *AIA Journal* 35, no. 3 (March 1961): 36, 38.

71. Hearings before the Committee on Government Operations, U.S. Senate, 89th Congress, Second Session, on S. 3010, A Bill to Establish a Department of Transportation and for Other Purposes, March 2, 1966.

72. Partial statement of Walter G. Baskerville, Sr., President of the Upper Mississippi Towing Corp. of Minneapolis, Minn. Hearings on the creation of a federal Department of Transportation before the Subcommittee of a Committee on Government Operations, House of Representatives, 89th Congress, 2nd Session, on HR 13200, a Bill to Establish a Department of Transportation, and for Other Purposes (May 3, 1966).

73. Partial statement of Charles E. Shumate, President of the American Association of State Highway Officials and Chief Engineer of the Colorado Department of Highways, Hearings on the creation of a federal Department of Transportation before the Subcommittee of a Committee on Government Operations, House of Representatives, 89th Congress, 2nd Session, on HR 13200, a Bill to Establish a Department of Transportation, and for Other Purposes (April 26, 1966).

74. Partial Statement of Morris Ketchum, Jr., FAIA, President of the American Association of Architects. Hearings on the creation of a federal Department of Transportation before the Subcommittee of a Committee on Government Operations, House of Representatives, 89th Congress, 2nd Session, on HR 13200, a Bill to Establish a Department of Transportation, and for Other Purposes (April 27, 1966).

75. Message from the President of the United States transmitting the proposal to Congress. Hearings on the creation of a federal Department of Transportation before the Subcommittee of a Committee on Government Operations, House of Representatives, 89th Congress, 2nd Session, on HR 13200, a Bill to Establish a

Department of Transportation, and for Other Purposes. (March 29–30, 1966):42, 43.

76. Congress, Senate, Committee on Public Works, Subcommittee on Roads, *Urban Highways*, Hearings on Urban Highway Planning, Location, and Design, Part 1. 90th Cong., 1st sess., November 1967.

77. As described by Slayton, Urban America was created in 1965 as a fusion of the National Planning and Civic Federation and Action, two older organizations concerned with urban affairs.

78. U.S. Congress, Senate, Committee on Public Works, Subcommittee on Roads, *Urban Highways*, Hearings on Urban Highway Planning, Location, and Design, Part 1. 90th Cong., 1st sess., November 1967: 11.

79. Ibid., 13.

80. Ibid., 11.

81. Ibid., 23.

82. Ibid., 25.

83. Ibid., 27.

84. Ibid., 39.

85. Ibid., 56.

86. Ibid., 62–63. Lowell Bridwell, the Federal Highway Administrator, would accuse McHarg of "stupidity and prejudice" for making these remarks. See Lowell K. Bridwell, "Remarks Before Pennsylvania Department of Highways Seminar, February 28, 1968, Harrisburg." *Highway Research Record*, no. 220 (1968): 2.

87. U.S. Congress, *Urban Highways*, 125.

88. Ibid., 133.

89. Ibid., 46–48.

90. Ibid., 115.

91. Ibid., 156.

92. Ibid.

93. Ibid., 161.

94. Ibid., 165.

95. Ibid., 302.

96. Ibid., 304.

97. Ibid., 307–308. Downs also submitted a paper titled "Uncompensated Non-Construction Costs Which Urban Highways and Urban Renewal Impose Upon Residential Households."

98. For a somewhat testy defense of the highway planning process, see the remarks of Federal Highway Administrator Frances C. Turner in "The Case for Highway Planning," *Transportation Law Journal* 4, no. 2 (July 1972): 167–175. Turner claimed that critics of highway planning "simply do not know what they are talking about. . . . The transportation land-use planning process as we know it today is probably the most outstanding and successful of all planning pro-

grams." In 1964, one consulting engineer contended that "the movement to establish 'planning' as a profession unto itself carries with it ominous implications . . . it is the responsibility of the engineering profession to return planning to its proper place as an integral part of the total engineering operation," James M. Abernathey, "Some Ethical Implications of Professional Planning," *American Society of Civil Engineers: Journal of Professional Practice* 90, no. PP2 (May 1964): 23–29, see 23. For the argument that "civil engineers are logical and wise choices for leadership roles in urban planning," see Harold L. Michael, "Interdisciplinary Education for Urban Planning," *American Society of Civil Engineers: Journal of Professional Practice* 90, no. PP1 (January 1964): 29–33.

99. Drummond Ayres, Jr., "Washington, 'White Roads Through Black Bedrooms,'" *New York Times*, December 31, 1967: *The Week in Review*, 97

100. Excerpts from the statement of Senator Edwin Muskie before the Subcommittee on Parks and Recreation of the Committee on Interior and Insular Affairs, United States Senate, in the Second Session of the 89th Congress, June 8, 1966: 10.

101. Ibid., 32.

102. Ibid., 32.

103. Ibid., 11–17.

104. U. S. Department of Transportation, 1980. As cited in *Urban Transportation Planning in the United States. An Historical Overview, Revised Edition*, November 1992. Prepared by Edward Weiner, Office of Economics, Office of the Assistant Secretary for Policy and International Affairs, Office of the Secretary of Transportation, Washington, D.C. Distributed in cooperation with Technology Sharing Program, U.S. Department of Transportation, Washington, D.C.

105. Alan Leiserson, Legal Services Director, Tennessee Department of Environment and Conservation, telephone conversation on June 23, 2010, 1:50 PM CDT. According to Mr. Leiserson, the Overton Park case was based strictly on NEPA. The laws controlling highway development in Tennessee now include:

Tennessee Water Quality Act, 1971 and 1977 amendments

Tennessee Code Annotated 69–3-101 et seq.

Aquatic Resource Alterations (Streams and Wetlands)

Rule Citation: Series 1200 1200–4-7-.01 et seq.

106. Text of Governor Sargent's transportation policy announcement made February 11, 1970. As appended in "Study Design for a Balanced Transportation Development Program for the Boston Metropolitan Region," Systems Design Concepts, Inc. (1970).

107. See Kathleen Armstrong, "Litigating the Freeway Revolt: Keith v. Volpe," *Ecology Law Quarterly* 2 (1972): 761–799; and John Barry Kelly, II, "Challenging Highways: Widening the Access to Judicial Review," *Catholic University Law Review* 20, no. 1 (1970): 143–156.

108. Oscar S. Gray, "Environmental Requirements of Highway and Historic Preservation Legislation" *Catholic University Law Review* 20, no. 1 (1970): 45–

67; Peter G. Koltnow, "Changing Highway Priorities: Construction, Economy, and Environmental Improvement," *Catholic University Law Review* 20, no. 1 (1970): 119–131.

109. Hearings before the House of Representatives, Subcommittee on Roads of the Committee on Public Works, Washington, D.C., on H.R. 16000, which authorized completion of the Interstate System with the district of Columbia. Hearing date: Tuesday, April 2, 1968.

110. Ibid., 4–13. Excerpts from the statement of Mr. Charles Cassell, Black United Front.

111. Ibid., 13–18. Excerpts from the statement of Reginald Booker, Chairman, Emergency Committee on the Transportation Crisis.

112. Frank H. Malley and Milton Breivogel, "Urban Freeways" Abstract of papers published in the *Journal of the American Institute of Planners* (Fall 1948): 23.

113. Joseph F. C. DiMento, "Artere urbane: tre diversi esperimenti nelle città americane," *Storia Urbana* 122 (gennaio-marzo, 2009): 69–92. Translated into English as: "Urban Freeways: Three Different City Tales."

Chapter 6

1. Gary T. Schwartz, "Urban Freeways and the Interstate System," *Southern California Law Review* 49, no. 2 (March 1976): 167–264, see 183.

2. Ibid., 425. The planning process for this "picture book" was completed in just 8 months. See B. D. Taylor, "When Finance Leads Planning: Urban Planning, Highway Planning, and Metropolitan Freeways in California," *Journal of Planning Education and Research* 20, no. 2 (Winter 2000): 196–214.

3. U.S. Department of Commerce, Bureau of Public Roads, National System of Interstate Highways. Available at http://www.ajfroggie.com/roads/yellowbook/.

4. G. Fellman, B. Brandt, and R. Rosenblatt, "Dagger in the Heart of Town," *Transaction* 7, no. 11 (September 1970): 38–47.

5. B. Kelley, *The Pavers and the Paved* (New York: Donald W. Brown Inc., 1971), 93.

6. Among the cases where race was explicitly recognized as a factor, as opposed to being an underlying motivation suspected by some observers, were Atlanta, Baltimore, Detroit, and Nashville.

7. Quoted in Kelley, *The Pavers and the Paved*, 93. In the United States the cities were Atlanta, Baltimore, Boston, Charleston, West Virginia, Cleveland, Detroit, Indianapolis, Memphis, Nashville, Newark, New Orleans, New York, Philadelphia, Pittsburgh, San Francisco, and Washington, D.C.

8. Judy B. Rosener, "A Cafeteria of Techniques and Critiques," *Public Management* 57 (December 1975): 16–19.

9. Dean W. Hestermann et al., "Impacts of a Consent Decree on 'The Last Urban Freeway': Interstate 105 in Los Angeles County," *Transportation Research, Part A, Policy and Practice* 27, no. 4 (July 1993): 299–313.

10. J. DiMento, J. Baker, R. Detlefson, D. van Hengel, D. Hestermann, and B. Nordenstam, "Court Intervention, The Consent Decree, and the Century Freeway" (Caltrans, Research Technical Agreement, September 1991). Interview II27.

11. Andrew M. Giguere, "'. . . and never the twain shall meet': Baltimore's East–West Expressway and the Construction of the 'Highway to Nowhere.'" A thesis presented to the faculty of the College of Arts and Sciences of Ohio University in partial fulfillment of the requirements for the degree Master of Arts, June 2009: 74–104. The proposals included: The Advisory Engineers Plan (1942); The Advisory Engineers Plan (1944); The Robert Moses Plan (1944); the Smith Plan (1945); The Child's Report (1946); The 1949 Plan; The 1957 Plan; and the Expressway Consultants 10-D Plan (1961).

12. Ibid., 110.

13. Ibid., 101, 117.

14. Ibid., 117.

15. Ibid., 255.

16. Ibid., 126.

17. Ibid., 126.

18. Ibid., 166.

19. Ibid., 172.

20. Ibid., 178–179.

21. Ibid., 214.

22. Ibid., 213.

23. Ibid., 214.

24. Ibid., 11.

25. Ibid., 217–220.

26. Ibid., 11.

27. James Dilts, "City Hopes To Start Corridor Road Soon," *Baltimore Sun* (1971): C22, as cited in Giguere, ". . . and never the twain shall meet": 12.

28. *Architects and Planners in the Middle of a Road War: The Urban Design Concept Team in Baltimore, 1966–1971*. Unpublished manuscript, awaiting journal approval.

29. I-695 I-95 Inner Belt Expressway Unbuilt. Available at: http://www.boston roads.com/roads/inner-belt/.

30. Ibid. See also Massachusetts Department of Public Works, *Master Highway Plan for the Boston Metropolitan Area*, 1948.

31. Robert J. Samuelson, "Cambridge and the Inner Belt Highway: Some Problems are Simply Insoluble," *The Harvard Crimson* (June 2, 1967). Available at: http://www.thecrimson.com/article/1967/6/2/cambridge-and-the-inner-belt -highway/.

32. Ibid., np.

33. Ibid., np.

34. I-695 I-95 Inner Belt Expressway Unbuilt. Available at http://www.boston roads.com/roads/inner-belt/.

35. Ibid., np.

36. Ibid., np.

37. Ibid., np.

38. Allan K. Sloan, *Citizen Participation in Transportation Planning: the Boston Experience*. (Pensacola, Florida: Ballinger Publication Company, 1974).

39. Ibid., 135.

40. Boston Redevelopment Authority, *Boston Transportation Planning Review*, 1972.

41. I-695 I-95 Inner Belt Expressway Unbuilt. Available at http://www.boston roads.com/roads/inner-belt/.

42. Raymond A. Mohl, "Interstating Miami," *Tequesta: The Journal of the Historical Association of Southern Florida* 68 (2008): 5–40, 11.

43. Wilber M. Smith was a licensed professional engineer who became the first state traffic engineer in the state of South Carolina while working for the South Carolina Department of Highways. After leaving the Department of Highways to study traffic engineering at Yale, he founded Wilbur Smith & Associates with his brother, James M. Smith. Originally largely an engineering firm, the firm now incorporates infrastructure planning and economics in its professional roster.

44. Mohl, "Interstating Miami," 5.

45. Ibid., 12.

46. Ibid., 12.

47. Ibid., 13.

48. Ibid., 15.

49. Ibid., 14–16.

50. Ibid., 5.

51. Richard O. Baumbach and William E. Borah, *The Second Battle of New Orleans: A History of the Vieux Carre Riverfront-Expressway Controversy*. Published for the Preservation Press, National Trust for Historic Preservation in the United States (Tuscaloosa, Ala.: University of Alabama Press, 1981), 3.

52. Ibid., 53.

53. "Council Kills Motion to Re-Examine Studies," *Times Picayune* (June 17, 1966): 1–1.

54. Baumbach and Borah, *The Second Battle of New Orleans*.

55. Ibid.

56. Ibid.

57. Daniel Samuels wrote in his thesis at the University of New Orleans that North Claiborne was "the locus of cultural and economic life for New Orleanians of African descent." He added:

I thought it would be interesting to look back at the newspaper accounts from the 1960s about the pitched battle that must have been fought over the decision to erase a place of vital importance to a community that has done so much to shape the city's character.

What I found was nothing. There was no dramatic public battle. I'm sure people objected, but in those days they were easily ignored. It also seems that many area residents didn't know what was going to happen until the demolition and tree "removal" process began in August 1966. The city's planning commission, according to Samuels, had already concluded that the North Claiborne area showed "existence of severe blight"—they should see it now!—and apparently the thinking was that no one would be harmed or damaged by running a highway through here. (From "No one who mattered, anyway." Rob Walker, "Under the Freeway."

Available at: http://books.google.com/books?id=FHiiDuAg0bIC&pg=PT104 &lpg=PT104&dq=Rob+Walker+%22Under+the+Freeway%22&source=bl &ots=ZXBowPfxfA&sig=yxgdkQNe1ybH0TUA5pG8spseSRs&hl=en&sa= X&ei=Gs-qT5nBLdCl2AWz1-HAAg&ved=0CE0Q6AEwAA#v=onepage&q&f =false.

58. Anthony Flint, *Wrestling with Moses: How Jane Jacobs Took on New York's Master Builder and Transformed the American City* (New York: Random House, 2009).

59. Ibid., xvi.

60. Ibid.

61. Ibid.

62. Ibid.

63. Ibid.

64. Ibid., 165.

65. Ibid.

66. Ibid., 174.

67. Ibid., 175–176.

68. *New York Times* (June 5, 1984): B1, col. 3.

69. Kevin Sack, "New York Told to Repay Westway Fund," *New York Times* (August 11, 1990).

70. Sierra Club v. U.S. Army Corps of Engineers. 614 F. Supp. 1475 (1985) United States District Court, S.D. New York.

71. Henry Malcolm Steiner, *Conflict in Urban Transportation: The People Against the Planners* (Lanham, Md.: Lexington Books, 1978).

72. James E. Vance, Jr., *Geography and Urban Evolution in the San Francisco Bay Area* (Berkeley: Institute of Governmental Studies, University of California at Berkeley, 1964).

73. San Francisco, City Planning Commission, "The Master Plan of the City and County of San Francisco: Summary" (San Francisco, January 1946).

74. See William H. Lathrop, Jr., "The San Francisco Freeway Revolt," *Transportation Engineering Journal of the American Society of Civil Engineers* 97 (February 1971): 133–144.

75. Ibid., 134–136.

76. Ibid.

77. FAHA Hearings, Hearings before the Subcommittee on Roads of the Committee on Public Works, U.S. Senate, 90th Congress (1967), November 29, 1967, Statement by John F. Shelley, Mayor of San Francisco, Presented by Maurice Shean, Federal Legislative Representative for the City and County of San Francisco, California.

78. *New York Times* (June 4, 1989): 35, col. 6.

79. The Federal Highway Administration (FHWA), the Washington State Department of Transportation and the City of Seattle released the Final Environmental Impact Statement for the project in July 2011. The FHWA signed the Record of Decision in August 2011. Washington State Department of Transportation (2011). Available at http://www.wsdot.wa.gov/Projects/Viaduct/.

80. The project's Environmental Assessment was released by the FHWA and Washington State Department of Ttransportation in June 2008. The Finding of No Significant Impact was signed by the FHWA in February 2009. Ibid.

81. Ibid.

82. Zachary M. Schrag, "The Freeway Fight in Washington, D.C.: The Three Sisters Bridge in Three Administrations," *Journal of Urban History* 30, no. 5 (July 2004): 648–673.

83. Ibid., 656.

84. The following, according to the group's Web site, is the Committee of 100 mission statement: "The Committee of 100 advocates responsible planning and land use in Washington, D.C. Our work is guided by the values inherited from the L'Enfant Plan and McMillan Commission, which give Washington its historic distinction and natural beauty, while responding to the special challenges of 21st century development. We pursue these goals through public education, research and civic action, and we celebrate the city's unique role as both the home of the District's citizens and the capital of our nation." The Committee of 100 on the Federal City, "Mission." Available at http://www.committeeof100.net/Who-We-Are/index.html.

85. Schrag "The Freeway Fight in Washington, D.C.," 657.

86. Excerpted from the statement of Frederic Heutte, Executive Committee, Catholic Interracial Council of Washington, D.C., before the Subcommittee on Roads of the Committee on Public Works of the House of Representatives (April 2, 1968): 61.

87. Available at http://www.committeeof100.net/Who-We-Are/history.html. Also see: Richard Striner, Ph.D., "The Committee of 100 on the Federal City Its History and Its Service to the Nation's Capital." Available at: http://www.com mit teeof100.net/Who-We-Are/history.html.

88. Ibid. See also Schrag, "The Freeway Fight in Washington, D.C."

89. 658.

90. Ibid., 660.

91. Ibid., 661.

92. Bob Levey and Jane Freundel Levey. "END OF THE ROADS; In the Interstate Era, Congress ruled Washington like a fiefdom. Then a fight over some freeways inspired a biracial, neighborhood-level movement to fight the federal power." *The Washington Post* (November 26, 2000) Final Edition, Magazine Section, W10. Available at: http://www.washingtonpost.com/wp-srv/metro/endofroads.pdf.

93. Ibid.

94. Ibid.

95. Schrag, "The Freeway Fight in Washington, D.C.," 668.

96. Mark H. Rose, *Interstate: Express Highway Politics 1939–1989* (Knoxville, TN: University of Tennessee Press, 1990). In 1968, the Hawaii Department of Transportation (DOT) proposed a 6.5-mile-long Interstate H-4 through downtown Honolulu. It would have run east from Interstate H-1 along the Honolulu waterfront. However, opposition to an elevated waterfront freeway stopped the Hawaii DOT from proceeding with the project. In Portland and Denver, the states' governors deleted objectionable interstate routes. In both cases, local and state political leaders took advantage of the Federal-Aid Highway Act of 1973 to use funds saved by eliminating interstate routes to finance public transit projects.
  In western Philadelphia, in order to complete the blue route, I-476, the Pennsylvania Department of Transportation made compromises on design that cost $75 million. The 21.5-mile section, under construction since 1967, was opened on December 9, 1991. *New York Times* (December 21, 1991).
  In Richmond, Virginia, controversy arose over an interstate circumferential route around the city. The political aspects, some described as racial, of the controversy came to a head when an anti-freeway activist and Petersburg Mayor Hermanze Fauntleroy asked then-Secretary of Transportation Neil Goldschmidt for a "community impact analysis." *Washington Post* (December 8, 1980): B3. The project was also delayed by concerns of historical preservationists. However, by the mid-1980s, much of the route, including the depressed sections, was completed. Symbolic of the extended and acrimonious dispute surrounding it, however, the beltway that was supposed to be incised from Richmond's suburbs abruptly terminates 27 miles short of its ultimate target. See Glenn Frankel, "Richmond's Beltway Battle: Black Richmonders Fight White Suburbanites Over Concrete Noose" *Journal of Urban History* 30, no. 5, (July 2004): 674–706.

97. Joseph F. DiMento, "Stent (or Dagger?) in the Heart of Town: Urban Freeways in Syracuse 1944-1967," *Journal of Planning History* 8, no. 2 (May 2009): 133–161.

98. U.S. Census Bureau, June 2007. Note: In the *American Community Survey Demographic and Housing Estimates: 2006–2008* report, the city's population for the period was estimated to be 137,701.

99. Roscoe C. Martin et al., "Decisions in Syracuse," *Metropolitan Action Studies* no. 1 (Bloomington, Ind.: Indiana University Press, 1961).

100. Syracuse–Onondaga County Post-War Planning Council, *Postwar Perspective, A Report to the People of the City of Syracuse and the County of Onondaga, 1944* (draft, Sergei Grimm, 1944): TR-7, as cited in Joseph F. C. DiMento, "Stent (or Dagger) in the Heart of Town: Urban Freeways in Syracuse, 1944-1967," *Journal of Planning History* 8, no. 2 (May 2009): 140–141.

101. Plans called for a divided highway with two traffic lanes.

102. Syracuse–Onondaga County Post-War Planning Council, *Postwar Perspective* (draft, Sergei Grimm, 1944): TR-9, as cited in DiMento, "Stent (or Dagger) in the Heart of Town," 142.

103. Syracuse–Onondaga County Post-War Planning Council, *Postwar Perspective* (draft, Sergei Grimm, 1944): 64–67, as cited in DiMento, "Stent (or Dagger) in the Heart of Town," 142.

104. Concern over possible economic decline was recognized by the Metropolitan Development Association, which wrote in May 1965, "The twenty year period that ended in the mid-1950s was one of small but vastly troubling decline for the city." *Central Syracuse Bulletin* (May 8, 1965).

105. J. A. Cohn, "Urban Background to the Interstate Highway Program: The Planning and Politics of Highways in Syracuse: 1944–1960." Ph.D. thesis, Syracuse University, 1978: 35.

106. City Planning Commission, Annual Report of the City Planning Commission 1946 (Syracuse, N.Y.: City of Syracuse): 4, as cited in DiMento, "Stent (or Dagger) in the Heart of Town," 142.

107. "Report on Arterial Routes in the Syracuse Urban Area" (State of New York, Department of Public Works, 1947): n.n., as cited in DiMento, "Stent (or Dagger) in the Heart of Town," 142.

108. "City Planning Commission Highlights of 1957" (Syracuse, N.Y.: City of Syracuse, 1957): 8, as cited in DiMento, "Stent (or Dagger) in the Heart of Town," 142.

109. "City Planning Commission Highlights of 1957" (Syracuse, N.Y.: City of Syracuse, 1957): 7, as cited in DiMento, "Stent (or Dagger) in the Heart of Town," 142.

110. Cohn, "Urban Background to the Interstate Highway Program." This position was very common in the United States. "Expressways were universally seen as keeping downtowns viable by connecting them with expanding, largely residential suburbs." Brian Taylor, "When Finance Leads Planning: Urban Planning, Highway Planning, and Metropolitan Freeways in California," *Journal of Planning Education and Research* 20, no.2 (Winter 2000): 196–214; see 198.

111. "Syracuse Tackles Its Future," *Fortune* (May 1943).

112. New York State Department of Public Works, "Report on Arterial Routes in the Syracuse Urban Area, Prepared by the Department of Public Works," September 18, 1947; Charles H. Sells, Superintendent, Claude A. Bonaparte, Deputy Superintendent, Bertram D. Tallamy, Chief Engineer, [and] Division of Construction. All other authors were engineers except for the state architect, Cornelius J. White.

113. Ibid.

114. Ibid., 6.

115. Ibid., 13.

116. Ibid., 28. Congestion evidently came from both cars and traffic agencies: a later report noted that existing governmental organization was not the best structure to cope with current traffic demands; eleven agencies had a "finger in the pie" of traffic management.

117. Syracuse City Planning Commission, "Report of the New York State Department of Public Works—Report on Arterial Routes in the Syracuse Urban Area" (Syracuse, N.Y.: City of Syracuse, 1948).

118. Ibid., 40: "[With] five interchanges on . . . the existing east-west Thruway and similar access to the prospective north-south thruway, Syracuse becomes the primary distribution center for New York State, particularly for industries making extensive use of highway transport."

119. Ibid ., 111.

120. City Planning Commission, *Annual Report of the City Planning Commission 1946* (Syracuse, N.Y.: City of Syracuse, 1946), 4.

121. Report of the City Planning Commission on N.Y.S. Department of Public Works' Arterial Route Plan for Syracuse Urban Area., 1948, 1.

122. Ibid., 2.

123. Ibid., 2, Grimm letter in the report.

124. Arterial Route Memo, Proposals for City Hall Area and East–West Route, Nd. 1953.

125. Ibid., 3.

126. Economic Research Council of Metropolitan Syracuse. Syracuse, although located in a "slowly growing" eastern U.S. region, was growing rapidly; its general growth rate approximated that of the nation as a whole.

127. Such as Moses' attempts in Baltimore and New Orleans, briefly described earlier; and see Jeffrey Brown, "A Tale of Two Visions: Harland Bartholomew, Robert Moses, and the Development of the American Freeway," *Journal of Planning History* 4, no. 1 (February 2005): 3–32, see 23.

128. Harold S. Buttenheim, as noted in Cohn, "Urban Background to the Interstate Highway Program."

129. This was, in part, based on advocacy in the 1939 *Toll Roads and Free Roads* BPR Report. Brown, "A Tale of Two Visions," 15.

130. Cohn, "Urban Background to the Interstate Highway Program," 83.

131. Walter Carroll, "47-Ton Punch Flattens 15ᵗʰ Ward Structures," *Post-Standard* (August 11, 1954).

132. Walter Carroll, "Negroes Lack of Housing . . . Modern Ghetto Threat to Peace and Progress." *Post-Standard* (January 21, 1954). For the history of the ward, see Marvin L. Simner, *Growing Up Jewish in the 15th Ward: Recollections from the 1920s through the 1950s* (London and Ontario: Phylmar Associates, 2006).

133. Walter Carroll, "Builders Offer 15ᵗʰ Ward Solution," *Post-Standard* (January 31, 1954): A11–1.

134. Ibid., 11–13.

135. Ibid.

136. This fiscal conservatism was criticized in a 1957 American Society of Planning Officials report: "Syracuse lags behind many cities of its own size with respect to a record of accomplishments. The city's highway construction program is now only getting under way." Understanding the historical rationale for a "complete reliance on a pay-as-you-go plan," the report said, "no justification now exists for its continuation" (p. 16). Dennis O'Harrow, Reginald R. Isaacs, and Frank M. Kubota, "City of Syracuse Planning, Housing and Urban Renewal" (report, American Society of Planning Officials May 1957): 22. This quietly critical report speculated that the perception that urban renewal programs are "far-fetched" came from a "failure of public officials to demonstrate the practical advantages of urban renewal."

137. Brown, "A Tale of Two Visions," 3–32.

138. Ibid. Also see "Area Earmarked for Purchase and Resale by City," *Post-Standard* (June 4, 1954). One area under construction for the arterial system had become "less feasible" due to the expensive commercial development along that axis.

139. "Public Housing Needed as 15ᵗʰ Ward Solution, State Housing Head Says," *Post-Standard* (June 23, 1954).

140. "New Public Housing Seen Inevitable," *Herald Journal* (June 23, 1954).

141. "Stichman OKs Public Housing for 15ᵗʰ Ward. Plan Lauded as One of Best . . . City Hits Proposals to Shift Site to Suburbs," *Post-Standard* (December 10, 1954).

142. "Possibility Looms of New Site for Housing Project," *Post-Standard* (December 10, 1954). Also see "15ᵗʰ Ward Housing Site May Change," *Herald Journal* (December 14, 1954).

143. "Possibility Looms for New Site for Housing Project," *Post-Standard*, December 10, 1954. Also see "15ᵗʰ Ward Housing Site May Change," *Herald Journal* (December 14, 1954).

144. Urban Renewal Plan, Survey Area Number 2, October 8, 1954 (City of Syracuse, City Planning Commission, 1954): 10.

145. "Townsend Street Site Abandoned Due to Land Problem," *Post-Standard* (April 7, 1955).

146. "Sub-standard Dwellings Torn Down in Area," *Post-Standard* (November 14, 1954).

147. Ken Jackson, *Syracuse City Eagle* (Vol. 4, Issue 36, 2007). Cover story, September 6 to 12, 2007. "Que Reunion Recalls the 15th Ward: What Urban Renewal Didn't Destroy."

148. Ibid.

149. Ibid.

150. Memories of Syracuse's 15th Ward. The Films of the SU Public Memory Project. Available through kphillip@syr.edu.

151. Diane Ravitch and Joseph P. Viteritti, *Making Good Citizens Education and Civil Society* (New Haven and London: Yale University Press, 2001), 99.

152. "Federal Aid," *Post-Standard* (September 5, 1954).

153. "Syracuse is Assured U.S. Aid in Slum Plan," *Herald Journal* (May 28, 1955).

154. City Planning Commission, *Annual Report 1955, Syracuse* (Syracuse, N.Y.: City of Syracuse, 1955).

155. Ibid., 7. By federal law, the city was the local urban renewal agency and the mayor the chief executive, with state law noting the agents were city departments and commissions.

156. In April 1955, Governor Harriman vetoed the Hughes–Schoeneck legislation that would have made possible the use of state housing and clearance loans for the local contribution to urban renewal ("Urban Renewal Battle: Mead Fought Harriman for City Slum Program," *Post-Standard*, February 6, 1956). But a 1956 state law established a revolving fund for buying land in advance of authorization of construction of an arterial project, thus making it "feasible to reduce the City and State cost of the arterial right-of-way passing through clearance and redevelopment areas" (the land is re-conveyed for the arterial at a written-down cost); Syracuse-Onondaga Planning Agency, "Clearance, Redevelopment, Urban Renewal," n.d., 3.

157. *Urban renewal*, at the time, was a new and confusing term; it appeared as "something far-fetched and not to be taken into account in the every-day thinking.' This was a time of "general confusion both in Syracuse and elsewhere relative to the several phases or states of planning physical improvements. The terms *general, specific, comprehensive, detail planning, preliminary design, detail design, construction or contract drawings* befuddle non-technical people"; Syracuse-Onondaga County Planning Agency, "Clearance Redevelopment, Urban Renewal," 6.

158. Ibid., 1, 3.

159. Ibid., R 104.

160. "Linking of Arterial to Slum Clearing 'Needs Exploring,'" *Post-Standard* (June 2, 1955).

161. "55 East and West Side Blocks to Be Taken by City," *Post-Standard* (October 16, 1955).

162. "Renewal Sites Tied to Artery," *Syracuse Herald American* (October 16, 1955).

163. "Mead Akin to DeWitt Clinton and Urban Renewal to Erie Canal," *Post-Standard* (January 21, 1956).

164. "Proposal to Move 15th Ward Families to West End Site Urged at Parley," *Post-Standard* (March 6, 1954). See also "East-West Project Outlined," *Herald Journal* (March 6, 1954).

165. "Grimm Calls for Dynamic City Planning," *Herald Journal* (February 28, 1955).

166. Cohn, "Urban Background to the Interstate Highway Program," 64. Russian-born Grimm's early work was described in a presentation to traffic engineers in 1944; therein he took two relatively innovative positions: (1) in planning traffic facilities in relation to future land use, "origin and destination data may prove to be . . . misleading"; and (2) Syracuse's studies "allowed us to get away from the too narrow concept of a road with sidewalks and trees, to a much broader concept of depressed or elevated routes." Sergei N. Grimm, "Fitting Traffic and Transportation Services into the City Plan," 1944 Proceedings of the Institute of Traffic Engineers, Chicago, October 2–4, 1944.

167. "Expressway Approved By Public Hearing," October 3, 1956. A newspaper article with no identifying details other than these; accessed in the archives of the Onondaga Historical Association.

168. Cohn, "Urban Background to the Interstate Highway Program," 35.

169. See P. Siskind, "Shades of Black and Green: The Making of Racial and Environmental Liberalism in Nelson Rockefeller's New York," *Journal of Urban History* 34, no. 2 (January 2008): 243–265. See also W. E. Pritchett and M. H. Rose, "Introduction: Politics and the American City, 1940-1990," *Journal of Urban History* 34, no. 2 (January 2008): 209–220 on the "dramatic, upward shift in the locus of authority for shaping the urban economy" (p. 210); and M. R. Fein, *Paving the Way: New York Road Building and the American State 1880–1956* (Lawrence, Kans.: University Press of Kansas, 2008). Before the move back from control by the "imperious-federal and state officials" (Siskind, "Shades of Black and Green," 210), Syracuse's highways were virtually completed.

170. *Post-Standard* (April 6, 1958), quoted in *Post-Standard* (April 6, 2008): B-2, col. 1.

171. Memories of Syracuse's 15th Ward. The Films of the SU Public Memory Project. Available through kphillip@syr.edu.

172. "Only 718 Units in Housing for Uprooted," *Post-Standard* (May 5, 1957): 5.

173. Ibid., 5.

174. Sometimes known as Interstate Connection 570.

175. "City-Wide Celebration to Mark Oswego Boulevard Opening," The Automobile Club of Syracuse, *Official Bulletin*, 24, no. 11 (October 1959).

176. Cohn, "Urban Background to the Interstate Highway Program," 4.

177. Syracuse, N.Y. City Planning Commission, *Annual Report 67*, SU: 5.

178. Cohn, "Urban Background to the Interstate Highway Program," 4.

179. Citizens to Preserve Overton Park, 401 U.S. 402.

180. Peter L. Strauss, "Revisiting Overton Park: Political and Judicial Controls Over Administrative Actions Affecting the Community," *UCLA Law Review* 39 UCLALR 1251, 1252 (1991–1992): 1261.

181. Richard Henry Ginn, "Interstate 40 Through Overton Park: A Case Study of Location Decision-Making." A Thesis Presented to the Graduate Council of The University of Tennessee in Partial Fulfillment of the Requirements for the Degree Master of Science in Planning, December 1970.

182. "Overton Park: The Evolution of a Park Space," Memphis Park Commission, City of Memphis, Public Construction Office (Prepared for Ritchie Smith Associates, Overton Park Master Plan); John Linn Hopkins (September 1, 1987): 35.

183. Ibid., 37.

184. Peter L. Strauss, *Administrative Law Stories: Citizen's to Preserve Overton Park v. Volpe*, Columbia Law School Public Law and Legal Theory Working Paper Number 5–85 (Fall 2004): 3, as cited in Nicole Meyer, Sarah Kaplan, and Michelle Green, *Citizens to Preserve Overton Park A Case Study*, Chicago-Kent College of Law, Public Interest Law and Policy (Fall 2009): 5.

185. "I-40 Issue Traces Trail of Controversy to '53," *Commercial Appeal* (Memphis, Tenn.) (October 1, 1977).

186. Ginn, "Interstate 40 Through Overton Park," 26.

187. Ginn, "Interstate 40 Through Overton Park," 36; citing Frank Ragsdale, president of Memphis Transit Authority, telephone interview, September 10, 1970.

188. Ginn, "Interstate 40 Through Overton Park," 23. Ginn's source: "News item in the Memphis Press-Scimitar, September 11, 1958."

189. Ibid. Citing A. Q. Mowbray, *Road to Ruin* (Philadelphia and New York: J. B. Lippincott Company, 1969), 106.

190. Ibid.

191. "I-40 Issue Traces Trail of Controversy to '53," *Commercial Appeal* (Memphis, Tenn.) (October 1, 1977).

192. *Bon Air EIS* (Memphis, Tenn.: City of Memphis, 1972), 1–8. SU.

193. Strauss, *Administrative Law Stories: Citizen's to Preserve Overton Park v. Volpe*, 4, as cited in Meyer, Kaplan, and Green, *Citizens to Preserve Overton Park*, 10.

194. Ibid., 10.

195. Ibid., 4, citing Strauss, *Administrative Law Stories: Citizen's to Preserve Overton Park v. Volpe*, 1261.

196. Ibid., 10–11, citing Strauss, *Administrative Law Stories: Citizen's to Preserve Overton Park v. Volpe*, 13.

197. Ibid., 11, citing Strauss, *Administrative Law Stories: Citizen's to Preserve Overton Park v. Volpe*, 13.

198. Ibid., 11, citing Strauss, *Administrative Law Stories: Citizen's to Preserve Overton Park v. Volpe*, 13.

199. Ginn, "Interstate 40 Through Overton Park," 38.

200. Ibid., 44.

201. Strauss, *Administrative Law Stories: Citizen's to Preserve Overton Park v. Volpe*, 19, as cited in Meyer, Kaplan, and Green, *Citizens to Preserve Overton Park A Case Study*, 13.

202. Strauss, *Administrative Law Stories: Citizen's to Preserve Overton Park v. Volpe*, 19.

203. Ibid., 13.

204. Ibid., 13.

205. Ibid., 14.

206. Ibid., 14.

207. Ibid., 14.

208. Ibid., 14.

209. Ibid., 14.

210. Ibid., 14–15.

211. *Bon Air EIS*, 1–7.

212. *Bon Air EIS*, 1–11.

213. Meyer, Kaplan, and Green, *Citizens to Preserve Overton Park*, 15.

214. *Citizens to Preserve Overton Park, Inc. v. Volpe*, 309 F. Supp. 1189, 1191 (W.D. Tenn. 1970), as cited in Meyer, Kaplan, and Green, *Citizens to Preserve Overton Park A Case Study*, 15.

215. *Citizens to Preserve Overton Park, Inc. v. Volpe*, 309 F. Supp. at 1191, as cited in Meyer, Kaplan, and Green, *Citizens to Preserve Overton Park*, 19.

216. 23 USC Section 128(a); *Citizens to Preserve Overton Park*, 309 F. Supp. at 1192.

217. Ibid., 1192.

218. *Citizens to Preserve Overton Park, Inc. v. Volpe*, 432 F. 2d 1307, 1312 (6th Cir. 1970) at 1193–1194.

219. Ibid., 1193–1194.

220. *Citizens to Preserve Overton Park*, 309 F. Supp. at 1194.

221. Meyer, Kaplan, and Green, *Citizens to Preserve Overton Park*, 23.

222. Ibid., 23.

223. *Citizens to Preserve Overton Park*, 309 F. Supp. at 1312, 1313.

224. Meyer, Kaplan, and Green, *Citizens to Preserve Overton Park*, 26.

225. *Citizens to Preserve Overton Park*, 401 U.S. 402.

226. Ibid., 412–413.

227. Ibid., 412.

228. Ibid., 411.

229. Ibid.

230. 494 F.2d 1212: Citizens to Preserve Overton Park, Inc., et al., Plaintiff-appellant, v. Claude S. Brinegar, Secretary, United States Department of Transportation, Defendant-appellant, and Charles W. Speight, Commissioner, Tennessee Department of Highways, defendant-appellee Available at: http://law.justia.com/cases/us-court-of-appeals/F2/494/1212/112646/ (p. 4).

231. *Citizens to Preserve Overton Park, Inc. v. Brinegar*, 494 F.2d 1212, 1213–1214 (6th Cir. 1974) *rev'g*, 357 F. Supp. 846 (W.D. Tenn. 1973), *cert. denied sub nom.*, *Citizens to Preserve Overton Park v. Smith*, 421 U.S. 991 (1975), as cited in Meyer, Kaplan, and Green, *Citizens to Preserve Overton Park*, 31.

232. Ibid., 52 n. 220.

233. Ibid. at 52.

234. Citizens to Preserve Overton Park, Inc., et al., Plaintiff-appellant, v. Claude S. Brinegar, Secretary, United States Department of Transportation, Defendant-appellant, and Charles W. Speight, Commissioner, Tennessee Department of Highways, defendant-appellee, United States Court of Appeals, Sixth Circuit - 494 F.2d 1212, pp. 7–8. Available at: Available at: http://law.justia.com/cases/us-court-of-appeals/F2/494/1212/112646/.

235. Ibid., 7–8.

236. *Citizens to Preserve Overton Park, Inc. v. Brinegar*, 494 F.2d at 1214.

237. Ibid., 1214.

238. Ibid., 1216.

239. *Bon Air EIS*, 1–13.

240. "All 8 Plans for Overton X-Way Called Harmful to Environment," *Memphis Press Scimitar* (July 8, 1976).

241. "Completion of X-Way Urged as Hearing Opens," *Memphis Press Scimitar* (August 18, 1976).

242. Ibid.

243. Ibid.

244. "Brock Adams Inherits Overton Park Problem," *Commercial Appeal* (Memphis, Tenn.) (March 27, 1977).

245. "Foes Expect I-40 Park Route Defeat," *Commercial Appeal* (Memphis, Tenn.) (October 4, 1977).

246. "We Are Through with Overton Park Officials Say, Ending Decades of Delay," *Commercial Appeal* (Memphis, Tenn.) (October 4, 1977).

247. "State Won't Abandon I-40 Plans, Shaw Says," *Commercial Appeal* (Memphis, Tenn.) (October 4, 1977).

248. "Adams Shifts Ruling, Would Allow Tunnel Under Overton Park," *Commercial Appeal* (Memphis, Tenn.) (October 9, 1977): SU.

249. "Adams' Retrenchment Maintains Slight Hope for I-40's Completion," *Commercial Appeal* (Memphis, Tenn.) (May 12, 1978): SU.

250. "Baker Grasping 'Last Straw' for Overton Park Freeway," CP 5–4-789; "Baker's I-40 Proposal Defeated," *Commercial Appeal* (Memphis, Tenn.) (May 12, 1978).

251. H. Vogel, "Interstate Expressway versus Parkland," *Environmental Policy and Law* 5 (1979): 186 SU.

252. Strauss, *Administrative Law Stories: Citizen's to Preserve Overton Park v. Volpe*, 53, as cited in Meyer, Kaplan, and Green, *Citizens to Preserve Overton Park: A Case Study*, 35.

253. Tom Charlier, "Justices' 1971 Ruling Protects Parkland from Interstate Intrusion," June 29, 2006. Available at: http://www.harrisshelton.com/articles/article_CA_overtoncourtcase062906.pdf.

254. Ibid.

255. Ibid.

256. Ibid.

257. Except where otherwise cited, materials in this section draw from, *inter alia*, D. Hestermann, J. DiMento, D. van Hengel, and B. Nordenstam, "Impacts of a Consent Decree on 'the Last Urban Freeway': Interstate 105 in Los Angeles County," *Transportation Research Part A: Policy and Practice* 27, no. 4 (July 1993): 299–313.

258. Joseph DiMento et al., Public Policy Research Organization of the University of California at Irvine, excerpted from a personal interview conducted on July 24, 1989.

259. Marilyn Tower Oliver, "Optimism Amid Diversity, Adversity. Lynwood: A Lot of Friendly People Live in This Multicultural Community, Which Looks Forward to the 1993 Completion of the Century Freeway," *Los Angeles Times* (March 3, 1991). Available at: http://articles.latimes.com/keyword/century-freeway.

260. Ibid.

261. Ibid.

262. Ibid.

263. Nora Zamichow, "After Decades of Debate, Century Freeway to Open. Transit: $2.2-Billion Project Has Torn Apart Lives and Communities but Also Brought Job Training and Housing," *Los Angeles Times* (October 10, 1993). Available at: http://articles.latimes.com/keyword/century-freeway.

264. J. DiMento et al., Excerpted from a personal interview with John Phillips, July 24, 1989.

265. Joseph DiMento, Public Policy Research Organization of the University of California at Irvine, excerpted from an interview with Adriana Gianturco (1991): II-40.

266. Zamichow, "After Decades of Debate, Century Freeway to Open."

267. Joseph DiMento et al., Public Policy Research Organization of the University of California at Irvine. Anonymous respondent, "Court Intervention, the Consent Decree, and the Century Freeway" (1991): II-41.

268. Zamichow, "After Decades of Debate, Century Freeway to Open." Eight lanes for general traffic; a two-lane transitway (two HOV lanes were expected to be constructed first, with possible future conversion to a light-rail facility); six or more transit stations with park and ride lots; seventeen interchanges with local streets; ramp metering, and HOV bypass lanes; direct connection from the Century Freeway's transitway to a proposed bus or rail transit facility on the Harbor Freeway; an intersecting freeway leading to downtown Los Angeles; priority access into Los Angeles International Airport for Century Freeway transitway users; a promise by defendants to consider providing two of the eight general-purpose lanes for additional HOV use prior to the Century Freeway's opening; and heavy landscape and noise attenuation.

269. Hestermann et al., "Impacts of a Consent Decree on 'The Last Urban Freeway.'"

270. Kim Kowsky, "Poor Win Housing Fight. Hawthorne: Complex Eyed for Military Use Belongs to Poor and Century Freeway Refugees, Judge Rules," *Los Angeles Times* (September 1, 1991). Available at: http://articles.latimes.com/keyword/century-freeway.

271. Hestermann et al., "Impacts of a Consent Decree on 'The Last Urban Freeway.'"

272. Victor Merina, "Century Freeway Tour Pleases Deukmejian," *Los Angeles Times* (January 24, 1985). Available at http://articles.latimes.com/keyword/century-freeway.

273. "State Approves Funds to Complete Century Freeway," *Los Angeles Times* (July 7, 1985). No author given. Available at: http://articles.latimes.com/keyword/century-freeway.

274. Merina, "Century Freeway Tour Pleases Deukmejian."

275. Gerald Faris, "1 Century Freeway Housing Project to Be Built, but 2nd Falls Through," *Los Angeles Times* (April 27, 1986). Available at: http://articles.latimes.com/keyword/century-freeway.

276. Ibid.

277. Ray Hebert, "Century Freeway—When It's Born, an Era Will Die," *Los Angeles Times* (June 22, 1986). Available at: http://articles.latimes.com/keyword/century-freeway.

278. Ibid.

279. Ibid.

280. Ronald B. Taylor, "Soaring Interchange on Century Freeway to Be One of a Kind," *Los Angeles Times* (December 10, 1989). Available at: http://articles.latimes.com/keyword/century-freeway.

281. William Trombley, "New Housing Plan Urged for Century Freeway Route," *Los Angeles Times* (July 25, 1988). Available at: http://articles.latimes.com/keyword/century-freeway.

282. Ibid.

283. Ibid.

284. Ibid.

285. Ibid.

286. Virginia Ellis, "State Speeds Up Funding of Southland Road Work Prop. 111: Transportation Commission Allocates Money To Be Raised by Higher Gasoline Taxes for the Century Freeway and Other Projects," *Los Angeles Times* (June 14, 1990). Available at: http://articles.latimes.com/keyword/century-freeway. Most of the early funding went to the southern portion of the state, with the biggest allotments—totaling $118.5 million—earmarked for construction on two phases of the Century Freeway in Los Angeles County and on state Routes 30 and 330 in San Bernardino County.

287. Ibid.

288. Nora Zamichow, "Century Freeway Opening Is a Road Rally. Transit: Part Carnival, Part Sporting Event Mark Debut of $2.2-Billion Project," *Los Angeles Times* (October 15, 1993). Available at: http://articles.latimes.com/keyword/century-freeway.

289. Ibid.

290. Ibid.

291. Holly Crawford, The Road: The Century Freeway Project, 1991. Art and poetry project exhibited at the South Bay Contemporary Museum of Art, the Museum of Art in Downey, the City of Benecia Art Gallery, and the California Department of Housing and Community Development, Inglewood Office. Available at: http://www.art-poetry.info/id16.html.

292. Zamichow, "After Decades of Debate, Century Freeway to Open."

293. Ibid.

294. Ibid.

295. See Raymond A. Mohl, "Stop the Road: Freeway Revolts in American Cities," *Journal of Urban History* 30 (July 2004): 674–706. Mohl contrasts Miami's "virtually completed" urban freeway prior to shifts in law and policy with Baltimore; see 698.

296. Nor had the devolution of highway decision making returned, at least in part, to local actors. See Mark H. Rose, "Reframing American Highway Politics, 1956-1995," *Journal of Planning History* 2 (August 2003): 212–236, see 220.

297. Cohn, "Urban Background to the Interstate Highway Program," 278. On the relatively weak roles of planners and the dominant influence of engineers in urban freeway development, see also Alan Altshuler, "The Interstate Freeway," in A. A. Altshuler, *The City Planning Process: A Political Analysis* (Ithaca, N.Y.: Cornell University Press, 1965); Brown, "A Tale of Two Visions"; and Frederick Warren Howell, *The History of Planning in Syracuse, New York* (New York: Cornell University, 1956). See also Martin Roscoe et al., *Decisions in Syracuse* (Garden City, N.Y.: Anchor Books, Doubleday & Company, 1965); and Raymond A.

Mohl, "Stop the Road: Freeway Revolts in American Cities," *Journal of Urban History* 30 (July 2004): 674–706.

298. Ada Louise Huxtable, "Ugly Cities and How they Grow," *New York Times* (March 15, 1964). Available at http://select.nytimes.com/gst/abstract.html?res=F 70612F8395415738DDDAC0994DB405B848AF1D3&scp=1&sq=Ugly+cities+ and+How+They+Grow&st=p.

299. Mohl, "Stop the Road: Freeway Revolts in American Cities," 676.

300. Although Syracuse was not alone in this deference, other cities took a more active stance, for example, San Francisco and Boston. A few in the city themselves recognized an alternative. In 1956, the chairman of the city planning commission noted: "We have waited for the state to plan what in the State's opinion is 'best' for us. Cleveland has done its own detailed planning of . . . and then advised State and Federal agencies what the city needs." "Cleveland Praised for Planning," *Herald Journal* November 9, 1956. A newspaper article with no details other than these; accessed in archives of the Onondaga Historical Association.

301. Syracuse, New York, City Planning Commission, *Some Data for Preparation of the Administrative Organization for Urban Renewal*, January 23, 1956. "*Citizen Participation* . . . is thoroly [sic] provided for through committees and groups under the Planning commission. . . . Some interested groups meet in the commission offices for briefing and discussion on specific problems."

302. Michael R. Fein, *Paving the Way: New York Road Building and the American State 1800–1956* (Lawrence, Kans.: University Press of Kansas, 2008), 4, 167.

303. Cohn, "Urban Background to the Interstate Highway Program," 256, quoting Chase. SU.

Chapter 7

1. Christopher Alexander et al., *A Pattern Language: Towns, Building, Construction* (New York: Oxford University Press, 1977).

2. David J. St. Clair, *The Motorization of American Cities* (New York: Praeger, 1986), 173; David W. Jones, *Mass Motorization and Mass Transit: An American History and Policy Analysis* (Bloomington, Ind.: Indiana University Press, 2008).

3. Michael Bernick and Robert Cervero, *Transit Villages in the 21st Century* (New York: McGraw-Hill, 1997); Robert Cervero, *The Transit Metropolis: A Global Inquiry* (Washington, D.C.: Island Press, 1998); Peter Calthorpe and William Fulton, *The Regional City: Planning for the End of Sprawl* (Washington, D.C.: Island Press, 2001).

4. Daniel Solomon, *Global City Blues* (Washington, D.C.: Island Press, 2003); Malcolm Millais, *Exploding the Myths of Modern Architecture* (London: Frances Lincoln Limited, 2009).

5. Lewis Mumford, *The Highway and the City* (New York: Mentor, 1963), 245.

6. St. Clair, *The Motorization of American Cities*.

7. Lewis Mumford, "The Highway and the City," *Architectural Record* (April 1958): 179–182.

8. Allan B. Jacobs, Elizabeth Macdonald, and Yodan Rofé, *The Boulevard Book: History, Evolution, Design of Multiway Boulevards* (Cambridge, Mass.: MIT Press, 2002).

9. Jones, *Mass Motorization and Mass Transit.*

10. Andres Duany, Elizabeth Plater-Zyberk, and Jeff Speck, *Suburban Nation: The Rise of Sprawl and the Decline of the American Dream* (New York: North Point Press, 2001); Douglas Kelbaugh, *Repairing the American Metropolis* (Seattle: University of Washington Press, 2002).

11. Brian D. Taylor, "Public Perceptions, Fiscal Realities, and Freeway Planning: The California Case," *Journal of the American Planning Association* 61, no.1 (Winter 1995): 43–56; Brian Taylor, "When Finance Leads Planning: Urban Planning, Highway Planning, and Metropolitan Freeways in California," *Journal of Planning Education and Research* 20, no. 2 (Winter 2000): 196–214; Jones, *Mass Motorization and Mass Transit.*

12. Langdon Winner, *Autonomous Technology: Technics Out of Control as a Theme in Political Thought* (Cambridge, Mass.: MIT Press, 1977).

13. Lisa Peattie, *Planning: Rethinking Ciudad Guayana* (Ann Arbor, Mich.: University of Michigan Press, 1987), 111.

14. See Yale Rabin, "Federal Urban Transportation Policy and the Highway Planning Process in Metropolitan Areas," *Annals of the American Academy of Political and Social Science* 451 (September 1980): 21–35.

15. For a sympathetic exploration of the engineering profession and a defense of engineering solutions, see Samuel C. Florman, *The Civilized Engineer* (New York: St. Martin's Press, 1987); *The Existential Pleasures of Engineering* (New York: St. Martin's Press, 1976). Florman argues that "society has a disconcerting way of unexpectedly changing its standards of taste. . . . We have highways running all over creation because engineers never dreamed that one day people would decide that highways were ugly and unpleasantly noisy" (*Existential Pleasures*, 37).

16. Kevin Lynch, *A Theory of Good City Form* (Cambridge, Mass.: MIT Press, 1981).

17. Douglas A. Hart, *Strategic Planning in London: The Rise and Fall of the Primary Road Network* (Oxford, England: Pergamon, 1976).

18. This was the case, except for the real estate industry's support for planning to preserve property values through the careful segregation of land uses. See Marc A. Weiss, *The Rise of the Community Builders* (New York: Columbia University Press, 1987).

19. There may be other ways to draw these lines, depending upon one's analytical purpose, but these three subgroups are clearly discernible, and they persist to this day.

20. Mark Foster, "City Planners and Urban Transportation: The American Response," *Journal of Urban History* 5, no. 3 (May 1979): 367.

21. Jeffrey Brown, "From Traffic Regulation to Limited Ways: The Effort to Build a Science of Transportation Planning," *Journal of Planning History* 5, no. 1 (February 2006): 3–34.

22. Calthorpe and Fulton, *The Regional City*.

23. Some of these could be construed as anti-urban schemes, however, despite their elevated pedestrian plazas and walkways. For a critical appraisal of these architectural designs for central cities, see Kenneth Frampton, *Modern Architecture: A Critical History* (New York: Oxford University Press, 1980).

24. Jonathan Barnett, *Redesigning Cities: Principles, Practice, Implementation* (Chicago: American Planning Association, 2003).

25. Ellen Dunham-Jones and June Williamson, *Retrofitting Suburbia: Urban Design Solutions for Redesigning Suburbia* (New York: John Wiley & Sons, 2009); Galina Tachieva, *The Sprawl Repair Manual* (Washington, D.C.: Island Press, 2010).

26. Massachusetts Department of Transportation, Division of Highways, "The Central Artery/Tunnel Project—The Big Dig." Available at: http://www.massdot .state.ma.us/highway/TheBigDig.aspx.

27. Washington State Department of Transportation, "6 Case Studies in Urban Freeway Removal," *Seattle Urban Mobility Plan*, 2008. Available at: http://www .seattle.gov/transportation/docs/ump/06%20SEATTLE%20Case%20studies %20in%20urban%20freeway%20removal.pdf.

28. Ibid.

29. Ibid.

30. Ibid.

31. Ibid.

32. Ibid.

33. Charles Siegel, "Removing Urban Freeways" (March 19, 2007). Available at: http://www.planetizen.com/node/23300.

34. 9A West Side (Joe DiMaggio) Highway: Historic Overview. Available at: http://www.nycroads.com/roads/west-side/.

35. The 550-acre Hudson River Park—the largest park constructed in the city since Central Park—is sited on the west side of the highway from West 72nd to the Battery. A bicycle path runs the length of the highway. The new highway also incorporates special lighting that brings to mind the city's past while enhancing the beauty of the new roadway. Low-profile barrier curbs and 19-foot-wide raised medians enhance the boulevard concept by permitting the planting of more and larger trees closer to the road. The medians also enhance pedestrian safety at road crossings, protect vegetation from vehicles and from wintertime salting of the roadway, and provide an attractive entrance to the waterfront park. "9A West Side (Joe Dimaggio) Highway Historic Overview." Available at: http://www .nycroads.com/roads/west-side/.

36. The West Side Highway runs just west of the former site of the World Trade Center (WTC). As a result, the highway played a major role in the aftermath of

the September 11, 2001, attack on the WTC. Three huge segments of the tower that crashed down onto the highway were used in iconic photographs of the tragedy. Emergency vehicles and personnel traveled down the West Side Highway and were greeted by cheering crowds on their return. Finally, nearly all of the debris from the WTC was trucked up the West Side Highway to be shipped off by barge. "West Side Highway." Available at: http://en.wikipedia.org/wiki/West_Side_High way.

37. Ibid.

38. Ibid.

39. Haya El Nasser, "Urban Parks Take Over Downtown Freeways," *USA TODAY*. Available at: http://www.usatoday.com/news/nation/2010-05-05-urban -parks_N.htm.

40. Ibid.

41. Ibid.

42. Ibid.

43. Ibid.

44. Ibid.

45. El Nasser, "Urban Parks Take Over Downtown Freeways."

46. Onondaga Citizens League, "Rethinking I-81," 2009. Available at: http:// onondagacitizensleague.org/pdfs/OCLRethinkingI81_9print.pdf. The elevated segment of Interstate 81 traversing the center of the city is approaching the end of its projected life. Alternatives to the freeway are being studied. In 2009, the Onondaga Citizens League issued a report entitled "Rethinking I-81." The report petitions for the I-81 alternatives study to include "a pedestrian-friendly boulevard in the European tradition" as one of the alternatives to be considered. According to the report, "As it now stands, I-81 is a visual and physical barrier between downtown Syracuse and the growing educational and medical institutions of University Hill—the economic engines of the region."

47. Environmental groups and neighborhood residents have been promoting the removal of the Sheridan Expressway and the restoration of the Bronx River, along which it runs, as a park. Despite widespread citizen support, it is not yet certain whether the Sheridan Expressway will be removed. The New York State Department of Transportation was expected to reach a final decision in 2012. The Southern Bronx River Watershed Alliance is encouraging the Department of Transportation to take into consideration the economic, environmental, and quality of life benefits to local residents that would ensue from replacing the Sheridan Expressway with parks, affordable housing, and commercial development. New York City is also beginning a study of the traffic impacts, economic opportunities, and community benefits that may result from the expressway's removal. Southern Bronx River Watershed Alliance, "Replacing Sheridan can be good for all," Letter to the editor of the *Hunts Point Express*, dated May 4, 2011. Available at: http:// www.southbronxvision.org/.

48. The Preservation Institute, "Removing Freeways—Restoring Cities." Available at: http://www.preservenet.com/freeways/FreewaysPlansProposals.html. In

Hartford, the Aetna Viaduct, an elevated portion of I-84 that cuts through the center of the city, reached the end of its projected life in 2005. The city proposed repairing the freeway; however, citizens groups began to appeal for its removal. The city has obtained funding for a study of alternatives, one of which calls for converting the freeway into a boulevard.

49. The New Orleans cases are discussed in chapter 6. The city of New Orleans constructed an elevated portion of Interstate 10 along Claiborne Avenue in a pre-dominantly black residential and commercial neighborhood. The once-thriving commercial district experienced serious decline subsequent to its completion. Smart Mobility, Inc., and Waggoner & Ball Architects, "Restoring Claiborne Avenue. Alternatives for the Future of Claiborne Avenue. Claiborne Corridor Alternatives Report," July 15, 2010. The Claiborne expressway, which failed to improve traffic flow to the extent predicted by its developers, is now showing signs of deterioration. In addition to the city's master plan, the Unified New Orleans Plan (the blueprint for Katrina recovery) also proposes the expressway's removal. James Gill, "Reviving a New Orleans neighborhood's heart," *Times-Picayune* (August 01, 2010). Available at: http://www.nola.com/opinions/index .ssf/2010/08/reviving_a_new_orleans_neighbo.html.

50. The Inner Loop of Rochester, New York, completely encircles downtown Rochester. In 1990, the city completed its "Vision 2000 Plan" for downtown, which included the removal of the Inner Loop. The city's plans to "demote the moat" are strongly supported by residents of the city. The Preservation Institute, "Freeway Removal Plans and Proposals" Available at: http://www.preservenet. com/freeways/FreewaysPlansProposals.html.

51. Ibid. In Trenton, New Jersey, a major initial goal of the Route 29 freeway was to remove truck traffic from local streets; however, truck traffic was banned from the freeway prior to its completion. Responding to complaints from the city, the state Department of Transportation is planning to remove the Route 29 freeway and replace it with a boulevard and local city streets. The freeway's removal will result in 18 acres of land being opened for development.

52. Ibid. Washington, D.C., officials are deliberating on plans to remove the ¾-mile-long Whitehurst Freeway, which divides the Georgetown area from the waterfront. The freeway would be replaced with a boulevard. District officials are also discussing the removal of other elevated freeways: the Southeast Freeway, near the Capitol, and a portion of the Rock Creek and Potomac Parkway, near the Lincoln Memorial.

53. Ibid. The Cleveland, Ohio, *Connecting Cleveland 2020* plan calls for the Shoreway freeway to be converted to a boulevard. Demolition of the freeway would remove the obstruction between Cleveland and its Lake Erie waterfront.

54. Ibid. In Akron, Ohio, officials have proposed removing the Innerbelt freeway to foster economic development in the area formerly occupied by the freeway.

55. Ibid. Nashville's 50-year plan, adopted in 2004, calls for the gradual removal of the eight-mile Downtown Loop, which is composed of three interstates—Interstate 65, Interstate 40, and Interstate 24. The Downtown Loop would be re-

placed with boulevards, mixed-use communities, and parks, reconnecting adjacent neighborhoods to the downtown area.

56. Ibid. In 2005, the late Walter Sondheim, a civic leader who campaigned for the revitalization of downtown Baltimore through projects like Charles Center and the redevelopment of the Inner Harbor, proposed eliminating the segment of the Jones Falls Expressway leading into downtown. He advocated its replacement with an extension of President Street. City officials have articulated some backing for this project, which will probably be implemented around 2020, when the contemporary elevated structure will be obsolescent.

57. The Preservation Institute, "Removing Freeways—Restoring Cities." In 2000, the Niagara Heritage Partnership called for the state of New York to remove the 6.5-mile-long section of the Robert Moses Parkway connecting Niagara Falls, New York, and Lewiston, New York. The partnership further proposed that that portion of the Niagara Gorge's shore be restored with native vegetation, and that one lane of the parkway, furthest from the river, be left as a bicycle and hiking path. Their proposal was rapidly endorsed by the Sierra Club and the Audubon Society, in addition to dozens of other groups. The Niagara Heritage Partnership believes that implementation of this proposal would create a nature reserve in the spirit of iconic landscape architect Frederick Law Olmsted's original plan for Niagara Falls while helping to revitalize the city.

58. Ibid. The New York State Department of Transportation is proposing the expansion of Route 5, which runs along Buffalo's waterfront; however, some citizens are calling for the freeway's removal and its replacement with an urban boulevard.

59. A grassroots coalition called The Campaign for a Clear and Free Lakefront is proposing the removal of Lakeshore Drive, an eight-lane superhighway, from the Grant Park area. Ultimately, the coalition proposes the removal of Lakeshore Drive from the entire waterfront, creating open space along the lakefront. The Campaign for a Free and Clear Lakefront, "Forever Free and Clear? Or Forever Stuck in Traffic?" Available at: http://foreverfreeandclear.org/.

60. Congress for the New Urbanism, "Highway to Boulevard Concept Comes of Age With Today's Joint HUD-DOT Announcement," 2010. Available at: http://www.cnu.org/cnu-news/2010/10/highway-boulevard-concept-comes-age-todays-joint-hud-dot-announcement.

61. Michael Kimmelman, "In Madrid's Heart, Park Blooms Where a Freeway Once Blighted," *New York Times* (December 26, 2011). Available at: http://www.nytimes.com/2011/12/27/arts/design/in-madrid-even-maybe-the-bronx-parks-replace-freeways.html?_r=2&partner=rss&emc=rss.

62. Ibid.

63. William Yardley, "Seattle Ponders (Some More) the Wisdom of Replacing a Roadway," *New York Times* (April 10, 2001): 17.

Bibliography

The bibliography is structured as follows: The first section contains books; edited books; conference proceedings; discussion papers; planning reviews, reports, and studies; and dissertations. The "Articles" section contains journal and newspaper articles, official bulletins, and book reviews. Interview transcripts comprise the following section. The "U. S. Government Materials" section contains documents produced by executive departments and commissions at the federal level. It also contains Congressional documents and reports and Congressional hearing materials in addition to governmental and quasi-governmental reports produced by state agencies or departments. The "Internet Articles" section includes bibliographic data and url addresses of various articles or documents gleaned from the World Wide Web. The final section, "Miscellany," contains materials that did not fit in any other category.

Abbott, Andrew. *The Building of the City*. New York: Committee on the Regional Plan of New York and Its Environs, 1931.

Abbott, Andrew. *Outline of Town and City Planning: A Review of Past Efforts and Modern Aims*. New York: Russell Sage, 1935.

Abbott, Andrew. *The System of Professions: An Essay on the Division of Expert Labor*. Chicago: University of Chicago Press, 1988.

Adams, Thomas. *The Building of the City*. New York: Committee on the Regional Plan of New York and Its Environs, 1931.

Adler, Seymour. *The Political Economy of Transit in the San Francisco Bay Area, 1945–1963. Redundancy in Public Transit*. vol. 3. Berkeley: Institute of Urban and Regional Development, University of California at Berkeley, 1980.

Agg, Thomas R. *The Construction of Roads and Pavements*. New York: McGraw-Hill, 1940.

Alchon, Guy. *The Invisible Hand of Planning: Capitalism, Social Science, and the State in the 1920s*. Princeton, N.J.: Princeton University Press, 1985.

Alexander, Christopher. From a Set of Forces to a Form. In *The Man-Made Object*, ed. Gyorgy Kepes, 96–107. New York: Braziller, 1966.

Alexander, Christopher, Hajo Neis, Artemis Anninou, and Ingrid King. *A New Theory of Urban Design*. New York: Oxford University Press, 1987.

Alexander, Christopher, Sara Ishikawa, and Murray Silverstein. *A Pattern Language: Towns, Building, Construction*. New York: Oxford University Press, 1977.

Alihan, Milla A. *Social Ecology*. New York: Columbia University Press, 1938.

Allor, David J., Elizabeth D. Byrne, and Robin Corathers. "The Development of the Practitioner's Art: Ladislas Segoe, 1921–1968." Paper presented at the First National Conference on American City Planning History, March 13–15, 1986, Columbus, Ohio.

Alonso, William. Cities and City Planners. In *The Professions in America*, ed. Kenneth S. Lynn, 170–185. Boston: Houghton Mifflin, 1965.

Alonso, William, and Paul Starr. *The Politics of Numbers*. New York: Russell Sage Foundation, 1987.

Altshuler, Alan. *The City Planning Process: A Political Analysis*. Ithaca, N.Y.: Cornell University Press, 1965.

Altshuler, Alan. *Urban Transportation Policy*. Cambridge, Mass.: MIT Press, 1980.

Altshuler, Alan, with James P. Womak and John R. Pucher. *The Urban Transportation System: Politics and Policy Innovation*. Cambridge, Mass.: MIT Press, 1979.

American Association of State Highway Officials. *A Policy on Arterial Highways in Urban Areas*. Washington, D.C.: AASHO, 1957.

American Association of State Highway Officials. *AASHO: The First Fifty Years, 1914–1964*. Washington, D.C.: AASHO, 1965.

American Association of State Highway Officials. *A Policy on Arterial Highways in Urban Areas*. Washington, D.C.: AASHO, 1973.

American Association of State Highway Officials and American Municipal Association, Joint Committee on Highways. *The Sagamore Conference on Highways and Urban Development: Guidelines for Action*, 1958.

American Association of State Highway Officials, National Association of Counties, and National League of Cities. *Highways and Urban Development*. The Second National Conference on Highways and Urban Development, Williamsburg, Virginia, 1965.

American Association of State Highway Officials (AASHO) Staff and Bureau of Public Roads (BPR) Staff. A History of the Interstate Program. In *AASHO: The First Fifty Years, 1914–1964*. Washington, D.C.: AASHO, 1965.

American Highway Users Alliance. *What Freeways Mean to Your City*. Washington, D.C.: American Highway Users Alliance, 1956.

American Highway Users Alliance. Freeways in the Urban Setting: The Hershey Conference. Washington, D.C.: American Highway Users Alliance, 1962.

American Highway Users Alliance. *Urban Freeway Development in Twenty Major Cities*. Washington, D.C.: American Highway Users Alliance, 1964.

American Institute of Planners, Committee on Urban Transportation. *Urban Freeways*. New York: American Transit Association, 1947.

Amir, Shaul. "Conservation Kills a Highway: The Hudson River Expressway Controversy." Conflict in Locational Decisions, Discussion Paper No. 4. Philadelphia: Wharton School of Finance and Commerce, University of Pennsylvania, 1970.

Andreski, Stanislav. *Social Science as Sorcery*. New York: St. Martin's Press, 1972.

Appleyard, Donald. Understanding Professional Media: Issues, Theory, and a Research Agenda. In *Human Behavior and Environment: Volume Two*, ed. Irwin Altman and Joachim F. Wohlwill, 43–88. New York: Plenum Press, 1977.

Appleyard, Donald, Kevin Lynch, and John R. Myer. *The View from The Road*. Cambridge, Mass.: MIT Press, 1964.

Arnold, Bion J. *Report on the Improvement and Development of the Transportation Facilities of San Francisco*. San Francisco, 1913.

Aronowitz, Stanley. *Science as Power: Discourse and Ideology in Modern Society*. Minneapolis, Minn.: University of Minnesota Press, 1988.

Automobile Club of Southern California Archives. *Traffic Survey: Los Angeles Metropolitan Area Nineteen Hundred Thirty-seven*. Los Angeles, 1937.

Banham, Reyner. *Theory and Design in the First Machine Age*. 2nd ed. Cambridge, Mass.: MIT Press, 1960.

Banham, Reyner. *Megastructure: Urban Futures of the Recent Past*. New York: Harper & Row, 1976.

Barnett, Jonathan. *The Elusive City: Five Centuries of Design, Ambition and Miscalculation*. New York: Harper & Row, 1986.

Barnett, Jonathan. *Redesigning Cities: Principles, Practice, Implementation*. Chicago: American Planning Association, 2003.

Barnett, Joseph. *Express Highway Planning in Metropolitan Areas: With Discussion*. Reprinted from the Proceedings of the American Society of Civil Engineers: March, May, September, November 1946 and January, April 1947. Washington, D.C.: Bureau of Public Roads, June 1947.

Barnett, Joseph. "Factors Influencing Location and Design of Urban Expressways from the Highway Engineer's Viewpoint." Paper presented at the Sagamore Conference on Highways and Urban Development, October 5–9, 1958.

Barrett, Paul. *The Automobile and Urban Transit: The Formation of Public Policy in Chicago, 1900–1930*. Philadelphia: Temple University Press, 1983.

Bartelsmeyer, Ralph R. A Highway Engineer's Experiences in Urban Area Development. In *Proceedings of the 41st Annual Meeting of the American Institute of Planners Held in New York, New York 26–30 October 1958*, 39–42. Washington, D.C.: American Institute of Planners, 1958.

Bartholomew, Harland. A Program to Prevent Economic Disintegration in American Cities. In *Proceedings of the Twenty-Fourth National Conference on City Planning Held in Pittsburgh, Pennsylvania 14–16 November 1932*, 1–16. Philadelphia: William Fell, 1932.

Bartholomew, Harland. *Land Uses in American Cities*. Cambridge, Mass.: Harvard University Press, 1955.

Baum, Howell S. *Planners and Public Expectations.* Cambridge, Mass.: Schenk-man Publishing Co, 1983.

Bauman, John F. Visions of a Post-War City. In *Introduction to Planning History*, ed. Donald Krueckeberg, 170–189. New Brunswick, N.J.: Center for Urban Policy Research, Rutgers University, 1983.

Bauman, John F. *Public Housing, Race, and Renewal: Urban Planning in Philadelphia, 1920–1974.* Philadelphia: Temple University Press, 1987.

Bauman, John F. The Paradox of Post-War Urban Planning: Downtown Revitalization versus Decent Housing for All. In *Two Centuries of American Planning*, ed. Daniel Shaffer, 231–264. Baltimore: Johns Hopkins University Press, 1988.

Baumbach, Richard O., and William E. Borah. *The Second Battle of New Orleans: A History of the Vieux Carre Riverfront-Expressway Controversy. Published for the Preservation Press. National Trust for Historic Preservation in the United States. University.* Tuscaloosa, Ala.: University of Alabama Press, 1981.

Bel Geddes, Norman. *Magic Motorways.* New York: Random House, 1940.

Bender, Thomas. The Cultures of Intellectual Life: The City and the Professions. In *New Directions in American Intellectual History*, ed. John Higham and Paul K. Conkin, 181–195. Baltimore: Johns Hopkins University Press, 1979.

Berman, Marshall. *All That Is Solid Melts into Air.* New York: Simon & Schuster, 1982.

Bernick, Michael, and Robert Cervero. *Transit Villages in the 21ˢᵗ Century.* New York: McGraw-Hill, 1997.

Billington, David P. *The Tower and the Bridge: The New Art of Structural Engineering.* New York: Basic Books, 1983.

Bishop, Bruce, Clarkson H. Oglesby, and Gene E. Willeke. The Making of the Plan. In *Planning for the Future of American Cities: Proceedings of the Joint Conference on City, Regional, State and National Planning Held in Cincinnati, Ohio 20–22 May 1935*, 50–55. Chicago: American Society of Planning Officials, 1935.

Blau, Judith R., Mark LaGory, and John S. Pipkin, eds. *Professionals and Urban Form.* Albany, N.Y.: State University of New York Press, 1983.

Blumenfeld, Hans. In *The Modern Metropolis: Its Origins, Growth, Characteristics, and Planning*, ed. Paul D. Spreiregen. Cambridge, Mass.: MIT Press, 1971.

Blythe, D. K. Highway Planning in Metropolitan Areas. In *Urban Survival and Traffic*, ed. T. E. H. Williams, 18–25. London: E. & F. N. Spon, 1962.

Boston, City Planning Board. *Report on a Thoroughfare Plan for Boston.* Boston: Robert Whitten, Consultant, 1930.

Boston Redevelopment Authority. "Central Artery." *Boston Transportation Planning Review*, 1972.

Bottles, Scott L. *Los Angeles and the Automobile: The Making of the Modern City.* Berkeley: University of California Press, 1987.

Boudon, Raymond. *The Analysis of Ideology.* trans. Malcolm Slater. Cambridge, England: Polity Press, 1989.

Bouman, Martin J. Freeways in Urban Areas. In Bergstrom, Donald E., Carl Moskowitz and Harry Parker, et. al. eds. *Proceedings of the 17th Annual Western Section Meeting of the Institute of Traffic Engineers Held in Portland, Oregon 13–15 July 1964*: 41–49. Institute of Traffic Engineers, 1964.

Boyer, M. *Christine. Dreaming the Rational City: The Myth of American City Planning*. Cambridge, Mass.: MIT Press, 1983.

Boyle, Bernard Michael. Architectural Practice in America, 1865–1965: Ideal and Reality. In *The Architect: Chapters in the History of the Profession*, ed. Spiro Kostof, 309–344. New York: Oxford University Press, 1977.

Bridges/Burke Architects. *Interstate 90 Urban Design Report*. Seattle, 1969.

Brodsly, David. *L.A. Freeway: An Appreciative Essay*. Berkeley: University of California Press, 1981.

Brown, Lawrence A. *Innovation Diffusion: A New Perspective*. London: Methuen, 1981.

Brownell, Blaine A. Urban Planning, the Planning Profession, and the Motor Vehicle in Early Twentieth Century America. In *Shaping and Urban World: Planning in the 20th Century*, ed. Gordon E. Cherry, 59–77. New York: St. Martin's Press, 1980.

Bruce-Biggs, B. *The War Against the Automobile*. New York: E.P. Dutton, 1977.

Buel, Ronald. *Dead End: The Automobile and Mass Transportation*. Englewood Cliffs, N.J.: Prentice-Hall, 1972.

Bugge, W. A., and W. Brewster Snow. The Complete Highway. In *The Highway and the Landscape*, ed. W. Brewster Snow, 3–32. New Brunswick, N.J.: Rutgers University Press, 1959.

Burby, John. *The Great American Motion Sickness*. Boston: Little, Brown & Co, 1971.

Bureau of Government Research, New Orleans, Louisiana. *Vieux Carre Historic District Demonstration Study, Summary Report: Evaluation of the Effects of the Proposed Riverfront Expressway*. New Orleans, December 1968.

Burnham, Daniel H., and Edward H. Bennett. *Plan of Chicago*. New York: Da Capo Books, 1971 [originally published 1909].

Burnham, Daniel H., and Edward H. Bennett. *Report on a Plan for San Francisco* [facsimile reprint]. Berkeley: Urban Books, 1971 [original: San Francisco: Sunset Books, 1905].

California Division of Highways. *San Francisco Panhandle Parkway & Crosstown Tunnel*. San Francisco, March 1964.

California Division of Highways. *Technical Report: Golden Gate Freeway, Interstate Highway Route 480*. San Francisco, March 1965.

Calthorpe, Peter. *The Next American Metropolis*. New York: Princeton Architectural Press, 1993.

Calthorpe, Peter, and William Fulton. *The Regional City: Planning for the End of Sprawl*. Washington, D.C.: Island Press, 2001.

Caro, Robert. *The Power Broker: Robert Moses and the Fall of New York.* New York: Knopf, 1974; Vintage, 1975.

Carroll, J. Douglas, Jr. Adapting Urban Environments to Travel Technology or the Reverse. In *Urban Survival and Traffic,* ed. T. E. H. Williams, 38–45. London: E. & F. N. Spon, 1962.

Cervero, Robert, and Michael Bernick. *Transit Villages in the 21ˢᵗ Century.* New York: McGraw-Hill, 1997.

Cervero, Robert. *Suburban Gridlock.* New Brunswick, N.J.: Center for Urban Policy Research, Rutgers University, 1986.

Cervero, Robert. *The Transit Metropolis.* Washington, D.C.: Island Press, 1998.

Charles A. Maguire and Associates. *Master Highway Plan for the Boston Metropolitan Area.* Boston, 1948.

Chicago Area Transportation Study. Final Report. Vol. 1, *Survey Findings.* Chicago, December 1959.

Chicago Area Transportation Study, Vol. 2, *Data Projections.* Chicago, July 1960.

Chicago Area Transportation Study, Vol. 3, *Transportation Plan.* Chicago, April 1962.

Chicago, Committee on Traffic and Public Safety. *Limited Ways for the Greater Chicago Traffic Area.* Chicago, December 1932.

Chicago, Department of Superhighways. *A Comprehensive Superhighway Plan for the City of Chicago.* Prepared by Charles E. De Leuw, William R. Matthews, and A. J. Schafmayer, Chicago, 1939.

Chicago Plan Commission. *The Outer Drive.* Chicago, 1929.

Choay, Françoise. *The Modern City: Planning in the 19th Century.* trans. Marguerite Hugo and George R. Collins. New York: Braziller, 1969.

Cincinnati, City Planning Commission. *The Cincinnati Metropolitan Master Plan and The Official City Plan of the City of Cincinnati.* General Consultants, Ladislas Segoe and Tracy B. Augur, Cincinnati, 1948.

Ciucci, Giorgio. The City in Agrarian Ideology and Frank Lloyd Wright: Origins and Development of Broadacres. In *The American City: From the Civil War to the New Deal.* trans. Barbara Luigia La Penta. Cambridge, Mass.: MIT Press, 1979, 267–270.

Ciucci, Giorgio, Francesco Dal Co, Mario Manieri-Elia, and Manfredo Tafuri. *The American City: From the Civil War to the New Deal.* trans. Barbara Luigia La Penta. Cambridge, Mass.: MIT Press, 1979.

Clarke, Gilmore D. The Parkway Idea. In *The Highway and the Landscape.* ed. W. Brewster Snow., 33–55. New Brunswick, N.J.: Rutgers University Press, 1959.

Clawson, Marion. *New Deal Planning: The National Resources Planning Board.* Baltimore: Johns Hopkins University Press, 1981.

Cohn, Jerome A. "Urban Background to the Interstate Highway Program: The Planning and Politics of Highways in Syracuse, 1944–1960." Ph.D. dissertation, Syracuse University, 1978.

Colean, Miles. *Renewing Our Cities.* New York: Twentieth Century Fund, 1953.

Collins, George R. *Visionary Drawings of Architecture and Planning: 20th Century through the 1960s.* Cambridge, Mass.: MIT Press, 1979.

Colquhoun, Alan. "On Modern and Post-Modern Space." In Joan Ockman, ed., *Architecture, Criticism, Ideology.* Princeton: Princeton Architectural Press, 1985: 103–117.

Colquhoun, Alan. *Modernity and the Classical Tradition: Architectural Essays, 1980–1987.* Cambridge, Mass.: MIT Press, 1989.

Committee on the Regional Plan of New York and Its Environs. *The Graphic Regional Plan: Atlas and Description.* vol. 1. Regional Plan of New York and Its Environs. New York: Regional Plan of New York and Its Environs, 1929.

Connolly, William E. *The Terms of Political Discourse.* Oxford: Martin Robertson, 1983.

Corn, Joseph J., ed. *Imagining Tomorrow: History, Technology, and the American Future.* Cambridge, Mass.: MIT Press, 1986.

Corn, Joseph J., and Brian Horrigan. *Yesterday's Tomorrows: Past Visions of the American Future.* New York: Summit Books, 1984.

Cottingham, Phoebe H. "Decision Rules in a Public Bureaucracy: An Examination of Highway Planning." Ph.D. dissertation, University of California at Berkeley, 1969.

Creighton, Roger L. Integrated Transportation Planning: Surveys, Objectives, Forecasts, and Details. In *Proceedings of the 43rd Annual Conference of the American Institute of Planners Held in Philadelphia, Pennsylvania 23–27 October 1960,* 97–101. Washington, D.C.: American Institute of Planners, 1960.

Crowther, Geoffrey. *Traffic in Towns: A Study of the Long Term Problems of Traffic in Urban Areas. Great Britain, Ministry of Transport.* London: H.M. Stationery Office, 1963.

Curtis, William J. R. *Modern Architecture since 1900.* 2nd ed. Englewood Cliffs, N.J.: Prentice-Hall, 1987.

Cutler, Phoebe. *The Public Landscape of the New Deal.* New Haven: Yale University Press, 1985.

Cutler, William W., III, and Howard Gillette, Jr., eds. *The Divided Metropolis: Social and Spatial Dimensions of Philadelphia, 1800–1975.* Westport, Conn.: Greenwood Press, 1980.

Dal Co, Francesco. From Parks to the Region: Progressive Ideology and the Reform of the American City. In *The American City: From the Civil War to the New Deal.* trans. Barbara Luigia La Penta. Cambridge, Mass.: MIT Press, 1979, 143–292. [Italian original, 1973].

Danielson, Michael N. *Federal-Metropolitan Politics and the Commuter Crisis. Metropolitan Politics Series, No. 2.* New York: Columbia University Press, 1965.

Davies, Richard O. *The Age of Asphalt: The Automobile, the Freeway, and the Condition of Metropolitan American.* Philadelphia: J.B. Lippincott, 1975.

Davis, Harmer E., and W. Norman Kennedy. Some Aspects of Urban Transport Planning. In *Urban Survival and Traffic*, ed. T. E. H. Williams, 163–172. London: E. & F. N. Spon, 1962.

de Boer, Enne. *Transport Sociology: Social Aspects of Transport Planning*. Oxford: Pergamon Press, 1986.

Dear, Michael, and A. J. Scott, eds. *Urbanization and Urban Planning in Capitalist Society*. New York: Methuen, 1981.

DeMars, Vernon. Guides to City Form. In *Proceedings of the 42nd Annual Meeting of the American Institute of Planners Held in Seattle, Washington 26–30 July 1959*, 140–148. Washington, D.C.: American Institute of Planners, 1959.

Detroit Transportation Board. *Detroit Expressway and Transit System*. Prepared by W. Earle Andrews, Ladislas Segoe, and De Leuw Cather and Company, 1945.

DiMento, Joseph. *Court Intervention, the Consent Decree, and the Century Freeway, Final Report*. University of California at Irvine, Public Policy Research Organization. Published by Caltrans. September 1991.

Doig, Jameson W. *Metropolitan Transportation Politics and the New York Region. Metropolitan Politics Series, No. 6*. New York: Columbia University Press, 1966.

Dowall, David. "Theories of Urban Form and Land Use: A Review." Working Paper No. 295. Institute of Urban and Regional Development, University of California, Berkeley, 1978.

Duany, Andres, Elizabeth Plater-Zyberk, and Jeff Speck. *Suburban Nation: The Rise of Sprawl and the Decline of the American Dream*. New York: North Point Press, 2000.

Dunham-Jones, Ellen, and June Williamson. *Retrofitting Suburbia: Urban Design Solutions for Redesigning Suburbia*. New York: John Wiley & Sons, 2009.

Dunn, James A. *Miles to Go*. Cambridge, Mass.: MIT Press, 1981.

Dyckman, John W. Three Crises of American Planning. In *Planning Theory in the 1980s*, ed. Robert W. Burchell and George Sternlieb, 279–295. New Brunswick, N.J.: Center for Urban Policy Research, Rutgers University, 1978.

Eckbo, Garrett. Metropolitan Design: Form and Content in Urban Areas. In *Proceedings of the 42nd Annual Meeting of the American Institute of Planners Held in Seattle, Washington 26–30 July 1959*, 135–139. Washington, D.C.: American Institute of Planners, 1959.

Edelman, Murray. *The Symbolic Uses of Politics*. Urbana, Ill.: University of Illinois Press, 1967.

Edelman, Murray. *Political Language: Words That Succeed and Policies That Fail*. New York: Academic Press, 1977.

Elder, Charles D., and Roger W. Cobb. *The Political Uses of Symbols*. New York, London: Longman, 1983.

Esherick, Joseph. Architectural Education in the Thirties and Seventies: A Personal View. In *The Architect: Chapters in the History of the Profession*, ed. Spiro Kostof, 238–279. New York: Oxford University Press, 1977.

Evenson, Norma. *Le Corbusier: The Machine and the Grand Design.* New York: Braziller, 1969.

Fein, Michael R. *Paving the Way: New York Road Building and the American State, 1880–1956.* Lawrence: University Press of Kansas, 2008.

Fainstein, Norman I., and Susan S. Fainstein, eds. *Urban Policy Under Capitalism.* Beverly Hills: Sage, 1982.

Fainstein, Susan, Norman Fainstein, Richard Child Hill, Dennis R. Judd, and Michael Peter Smith. *Restructuring the City: The Political Economy of Urban Redevelopment.* New York and London: Longman, 1983.

Fein, Albert. *A Study of the Profession of Landscape Architecture: Technical Report.* Washington, D.C.: American Society of Landscape Architects, 1972.

Fein, M. R. *Paving the Way: New York Road Building and the American State 1880–1956.* Lawrence: University Press of Kansas, 2008.

Feyerabend, Paul. *Against Method.* London: Verso, 1975.

Fischer, Frank, and Carmen Sirianni, eds. *Critical Studies in Organization and Bureaucracy.* Philadelphia: Temple University Press, 1984.

Fisher, Howard T. Radials and Circumferentials—An Outmoded Urban Concept? In *Urban Survival and Traffic*, ed. T. E. H. Williams, 46–59. London: E. & F. N. Spon, 1962.

Fishman, Robert. *Urban Utopias in the Twentieth Century.* Cambridge, Mass.: MIT Press, 1977.

Fitch, James Marston. The Profession of Architecture. In *The Professions in America*, ed. Kenneth S. Lynn, 231–241. Boston: Houghton Mifflin, 1965.

Fitch, Robert. Planning New York. In *The Fiscal Crisis of American Cities*, ed. Roger E. Alcaly and David Mermelstein, 246–284. New York: Vintage Books, 1976.

Flink, James. *The Car Culture.* Cambridge, Mass.: MIT Press, 1975.

Flint, Anthony. *Wrestling with Moses: How Jane Jacobs Took on New York's Master Builder and Transformed the American City.* New York: Random House, 2009.

Florman, Samuel C. *The Existential Pleasures of Engineering.* New York: St. Martin's Press, 1976.

Florman, Samuel C. *Blaming Technology: The Irrational Search for Scapegoats.* New York: St. Martin's Press, 1981.

Florman, Samuel C. *The Civilized Engineer.* New York: St. Martin's Press, 1987.

Fogelson, Robert. *The Fragmented Metropolis.* Cambridge, Mass.: Harvard University Press, 1967.

Foglesong, Richard E. *Planning the Capitalist City: The Colonial Era to the 1920s.* Princeton, N.J.: Princeton University Press, 1986.

Ford Motor Co. *Freedom of the American Road.* Dearborn, Mich.: Ford Motor Co., 1956.

Forester, John. *Planning in the Face of Power*. Berkeley: University of California Press, 1989.

Foster, Mark S. *From Streetcar to Superhighway: American City Planners and Urban Transportation, 1900–1940*. Philadelphia: Temple University Press, 1981.

Frampton, Kenneth. *Modern Architecture: A Critical History*. New York: Oxford University Press, 1980.

Frieden, Bernard J., and Lynne B. Sagalyn. *Downtown, Inc.: How America Rebuilds Cities*. Cambridge, Mass.: MIT Press, 1989.

Friedland, Roger. *Power and Crisis in the City*. London: MacMillan, 1982.

Friedman, Lawrence M. *Government and Slum Housing: A Century of Frustration*. Chicago: Rand McNally, 1968.

Friedmann, John. *Planning in the Public Domain: From Knowledge to Action*. Princeton, N.J.: Princeton University Press, 1987.

Friedmann, John, and Clyde Weaver. *Territory and Function: The Evolution of Regional Planning*. Berkeley: University of California Press, 1979.

Funigiello, Philip J. *The Challenge to Urban Liberalism: Federal-City Relations during World War II*. Knoxville, Tenn.: University of Tennessee Press, 1978.

Gakenheimer, Ralph. *Transportation Planning as Response to Controversy: The Boston Case*. Cambridge, Mass.: MIT Press, 1976.

Gans, Herbert J. Toward a Human Architecture: A Sociologist's View of the Profession. In *Professionals and Urban Form*, ed. Judith R. Blau, Mark LaGory, and John S. Pipkin, 303–319. Albany, N.Y.: State University of New York Press, 1983.

Garrison, William L., et al. *Studies of Highway Development and Geographic Change*. Seattle: University of Washington Press, 1959.

Geison, Gerald, ed. *Professions and Professional Ideologies in America*. Chapel Hill, N.C.: University of North Carolina Press, 1983.

Gelfand, Mark. *A Nation of Cities: The Federal Government and Urban America, 1933–1965*. New York: Oxford University Press, 1975.

Gerckens, Laurence C. Historical Development of American City Planning. In *The Practice of Local Government Planning*, 2nd ed., ed. Frank S. So and Judith Getzels, 20–59. Washington, D.C.: International City Management Association, 1988.

Giedion, Sigfried. *Space, Time and Architecture. The Charles Eliot Norton Lectures for 1938–39*. Cambridge, Mass.: Harvard University Press, 1941.

Giedion, Siegfried. *Mechanization Takes Command*. New York: Norton, 1948.

Giedion, Sigfried. *Space, Time and Architecture*. 3rd ed. Revised and enlarged. Cambridge, Mass.: Harvard University Press, 1954.

Gifford, Jonathan L. "An Analysis of the Federal Role in the Planning, Design and Deployment of Rural Roads, Toll Roads and Urban Freeways." Ph.D. dissertation, University of California at Berkeley, 1983.

Giguere, Andrew M. ". . . and never the twain shall meet": Baltimore's East–West Expressway and the Construction of the "Highway to Nowhere." A thesis presented to the faculty of the College of Arts and Sciences of Ohio University in partial fulfillment of the requirements for the degree Master of Arts, June 2009.

Gillette, Howard, Jr., and Zane L. Miller, eds. *American Urbanism: A Historiographical Review*. New York: Greenwood Press, 1987.

Gilman, W. C. & Co. *St. Louis Metropolitan Area Transportation Study, 1957-'70-'80*. August 1959.

Ginn, Richard Henry. "Interstate 40 Through Overton Park: A Case Study of Location Decision-Making." A Thesis Presented to the Graduate Council of The University of Tennessee in Partial Fulfillment of the Requirements for the Degree Master of Science in Planning, December 1970.

Giulano, Genevieve. Land Use Impacts of Transportation Investments: Highways and Transit. In *The Geography of Urban Transportation*, ed. Susan Hanson, 247–279. New York: Guilford Press, 1986.

Gonen, Amiram. The Spadina Expressway in Toronto: Decision and Opposition. In *Conflict in Locational Decisions, Paper No. 5*. Philadelphia: Wharton School of Finance and Commerce, University of Pennsylvania, 1970.

Goodwin, Marshall H., Jr. "California's Growing Freeway System." Ph.D. dissertation, University of California at Los Angeles, 1969.

Gordon, Charles. Transportation as an Element in Urban Rehabilitation. With a Discussion by Paul Oppermann and L. Deming Tilton. In *Proceedings of the National Conference on Planning Held in Boston, Massachusetts 15–17 May 1939*, 24–28. Chicago: American Society of Planning Officials, 1939.

Gottdiener, M. *The Social Production of Urban Space*. Austin, Tex.: University of Texas Press, 1985.

Gottdiener, M., and Ph. Alexandros Lagopoulos, eds. *The City and the Sign: An Introduction to Urban Semiotics*. New York: Columbia University Press, 1986.

Gouldner, Alvin W. *The Dialectic of Ideology and Technology*. New York: Oxford University Press, 1976.

Grimm, Sergei N. Fitting Traffic and Transportation Services into the City Plan. In *Proceedings of the Institute of Traffic Engineers, Chicago, October 2–4, 1944*. New York: Institute of Traffic Engineers, 1945.

Gropius, Walter. *Rebuilding Our Communities*. Chicago: Paul Theobald, 1945.

Gruen, Victor. *The Heart of Our Cities*. New York: Simon and Schuster, 1964.

Gutfreund, Owen D. *Twentieth-Century Sprawl: Highways and the Reshaping of the American Landscape*. New York: Oxford University Press, 2004.

Gutman, Robert. *Architectural Practice: A Critical View*. Princeton, N.J.: Princeton Architectural Press, 1988.

Hall, Peter. *Great Planning Disasters*. Berkeley: University of California Press, 1980.

Hall, Peter. *Cities of Tomorrow: An Intellectual History of Urban Planning and Design in the Twentieth Century*. Oxford: Basil Blackwell, 1988.

Halprin, Lawrence. *Freeways*. New York: Reinhold, 1966.

Hammer, Philip. What's Up Ahead for Downtown. In *Proceedings of the 42nd Annual Meeting of the American Institute of Planners Held in Seattle, Washington 26–30 July 1959*, 12–27. Washington, D.C.: American Institute of Planners, 1959.

Hancock, John. The New Deal and American Planning: The 1930s. In *Two Centuries of American Planning*, ed. Daniel Schaffer, 197–230. Baltimore: Johns Hopkins University Press, 1988.

Handlin, Oscar, and John Burchard, eds., *The Historian and the City*. Cambridge, Mass.: MIT Press, 1963.

Hanson, Susan, ed. *The Geography of Urban Transportation*. New York: Guilford Press, 1986.

Harland Bartholomew and Associates. *A Major Street Plan for Oakland, California*. St. Louis, 1927.

Harland Bartholomew and Associates. *Plans for Major Traffic Thoroughfares and Transit*. St. Louis and Lower East Side, New York City, 1932.

Harland Bartholomew and Associates. *A Report on Freeways and Major Streets in Oakland, California*. St. Louis, 1947.

Hart, Douglas A. *Strategic Planning in London: The Rise and Fall of the Primary Road Network*. Oxford: Pergamon, 1976.

Hartman, Chester. *The Transformation of San Francisco*. Totowa, N.J.: Rowman & Allanheld, 1984.

Harvard University, Graduate School of Design, Landscape Architecture Research Office. *Highway Esthetics: Functional Criteria for Planning and Design*. June 1968.

Harvey, David. *Social Justice and the City*. Baltimore: Johns Hopkins University Press, 1973.

Harvey, David. *The Limits to Capital*. Chicago: University of Chicago Press, 1982.

Harvey, David. *Consciousness and the Urban Experience*. Baltimore: Johns Hopkins University Press, 1985.

Harvey, David. *The Urbanization of Capital: Studies in the History and Theory of Capitalist Urbanization*. Baltimore: Johns Hopkins University Press, 1985.

Harvey, David. *The Condition of Postmodernity*. London: Basil Blackwell, 1989.

Haskell, Thomas L. Deterministic Implications of Intellectual History. In *New Directions in American Intellectual History*, ed. John Higham and Paul K. Conkin, 132–148. Baltimore: Johns Hopkins University Press, 1979.

Hebden, Norman, and Wilbur S. Smith. *State-City Relationships in Highway Affairs*. New Haven, Conn.: Yale University Press, 1950.

Hebert, Richard. *Highways to Nowhere: The Politics of City Transportation*. New York: Bobbs-Merrill, 1972.

Hegemann, Werner. *Report on a City Plan for the Municipalities of Oakland and Berkeley*. Oakland: Kelley Davis Co, 1915.

Hegemann, Werner. *City Planning Housing*. vol. 1. Historical and Sociological. New York: Architectural Book Publishing Co., 1936.

Hegemann, Werner. *City Planning Housing*. vol. 2. Political Economy and Civic Art, ed. Ruth Nanda Anshen. New York: Architectural Book Publishing Co., 1937.

Hegemann, Werner. *City Planning Housing*. vol. 3. A Graphic Review of Civic Art, 1922–1937, ed. William W. Forster and Robert C. Weinberg. New York: Architectural Book Publishing Co., 1938.

Hegemann, Werner, and Elbert Peets. *The American Vitruvius: An Architects' Handbook of Civic Art*. New York: Princeton Architectural Press, 1988 [originally published in 1922 by The Architectural Book Publishing Company, New York].

Heightchew, Robert E., Jr. TSM: Revolution or Repetition? In *Urban Transportation: Perspectives and Prospects*, ed. Herbert S. Levinson and Robert A. Weant, 62–70. Westport, Conn.: Eno Foundation for Transportation, 1982.

Herlihy, Elizabeth M. Boston's Master Highway Plan. In *Proceedings of the Twenty-Third National Conference on City Planning Held in Rochester, New York 22–24 June 1931*, 81–84. Philadelphia: William Fell, 1931.

Hickock, Beverly. *Development of the Interstate Highway Program, 1916 to Date: A Selective, Partially Annotated Bibliography*. Berkeley: Institute of Transportation Studies, University of California at Berkeley, 1980.

Highways and Transportation Committee, American Society of Planning Officials. Highways and Transportation in Relation to Each Other and to Other Planned Development. In *Proceedings of the National Conference on Planning Held in San Francisco, California 8–11 July 1940*, 42–69. Chicago: American Society of Planning Officials, 1940.

Hodge, David. Social Impacts of Urban Transportation Decisions. In *The Geography of Urban Transportation*, ed. Susan Hanson, 301–327. New York: Guilford Press, 1986.

Hogentogler, C. A., E. A. Willis, and J. A. Kelley. Intangible Economics of Highway Transportation. In *Proceeding of the Highway Research Board* [13th Annual, Dec. 7–8 1933], Part I, 189–204. Washington, D.C.: Highway Research Board, 1934.

Holford, W. J. The Commercial Core of London. In *The Heart of the City: Towards the Humanisation of Urban Life*, ed. J. Tyrwhitt, J. L. Sert, and E. N. Rogers, 97–98. New York: Pellegrini and Cudahy, 1952.

Hollinger, David A. Historians and the Discourse of Intellectuals. In *New Directions in American Intellectual History*, ed. John Higham and Paul K. Conkin, 42–63. Baltimore: Johns Hopkins University Press, 1979.

Holmes, E. H. Urban Highways and the Federal-Aid Highway Act of 1956. In *Proceedings of the 41st Annual Meeting of the American Institute of Planners Held in New York, New York 26–30 October 1958*, 43–46. Washington, D.C.: American Institute of Planners, 1958.

Holston, James. *The Modernist City: An Anthropological Critique of Brasilia*. Chicago: University of Chicago Press, 1989.

Hornbeck, Peter L., and Garland A. Okerland. *Visual Values for the Highway User*. Washington, D.C.: USGPO, 1973.

Horwood, Edgar M., and Ronald R. Boyce. *Studies of the Central Business District and Urban FreewayDevelopment.* Seattle: University of Washington Press, 1959.

Hough, Michael. *Out of Place: Restoring Identity to the Regional Landscape.* New Haven, Conn.: Yale University Press, 1990.

Howell, Frederick Warrren. *The History of Planning in Syracuse, New York.* New York: Cornell University Press, 1956.

Hoyt, Homer. *Structure and Growth of Residential Neighborhoods in American Cities.* Washington, D.C.: USGPO, 1939.

Hubbard, Theodora K., and Henry V. Hubbard. *Our Cities To-Day and To-Morrow.* Cambridge, Mass.: Harvard University Press, 1929.

Hurd, Richard M. *Principles of City Land Values.* New York: The Record and Guide, 1903.

Institute of Traffic Engineers. *System Considerations for Urban Freeways.* Washington, D.C.: Institute of Traffic Engineers, 1967.

Jackson, Kenneth. *The Crabgrass Frontier: The Suburbanization of the United States.* New York: Oxford University Press, 1985.

Jackson, Kenneth T. Robert Moses and the Planned Environment: A Re-Evaluation. In *Robert Moses: Single-Minded Genius,* ed. Joann P. Krieg, 21–30. Interlaken, N.Y.: Heart of the Lakes Publishing, 1989.

Jacobs, Allan. *Making City Planning Work.* Chicago: American Society of Planning Officials, 1978.

Jacobs, Allan B, Elizabeth Macdonald, and Yodan Rofé. *The Boulevard Book: History, Evolution, Design of Multiway Boulevards.* Cambridge, Mass.: MIT Press, 2002.

Jacobs, Jane. *The Death and Life of Great American Cities.* New York: Vintage, 1961.

Jameson, Fredric. Architecture and the Critique of Ideology. In *Architecture Criticism Ideology,* ed. Joan Ockman, 51–87. Princeton, N.J.: Princeton Architectural Press, 1985.

Jellicoe, G. A. *Motopia: A Study in the Evolution of Urban Landscape.* New York: Praeger, 1961.

Johnson, David A. "The Emergence of Metropolitan Regionalism: An Analysis of the 1929 Regional Plan of New York and Its Environs." Ph.D. dissertation, Cornell University, 1974.

Johnson, David A. Regional Planning for the Great American Metropolis: New York between the World Wars. In *Two Centuries of American Planning,* ed. Daniel Schaffer, 167–196. Baltimore: Johns Hopkins University Press, 1988.

Joint Committee on Highways of the American Municipal Association and the American Association of State Highway Officials. *Guidelines for Action.* Sagamore Conference on Highways and Urban Development, Syracuse University, 1958.

Jones, David W., Jr. Urban Highway Investment and the Political Economy of Fiscal Retrenchment. In *Current Issues in Transportation Policy*, ed. Alan Altshuler, 65–82. Lexington, Mass: D. C. Heath, Lexington Books, 1979.

Jones, David W., Jr. *Urban Transit Policy: An Economic and Political History.* Englewood Cliffs, N.J.: Prentice-Hall, 1985.

Jones, David W., Jr. *California's Freeway System in Historical Perspective.* Manuscript in ITS Library, University of California at Berkeley, 1989.

Jones, David W., Jr. The California Innovation. In *California's Freeway Era in Historical Perspective.* Berkeley: Institute of Transportation Studies, 1989.

Jones, David W., Jr. *Mass Motorization and Mass Transit: An American History and Policy Analysis.* Bloomington, Ind.: Indiana University Press, 2008.

Jordy, William H. *The Impact of European Modernism in the Mid-Twentieth Century.* vol. 4. American Buildings and Their Architects. Garden City, N.Y.: Anchor Press/Doubleday, 1976.

Judd, Dennis R. *The Politics of American Cities: Private Power and Public Policy.* Boston: Little, Brown & Company, 1979.

Kansas City, City Plan Commission. *Expressways: Greater Kansas City.* Kansas City, March 1951.

Kelbaugh, Douglas. *Repairing the American Metropolis.* Seattle: University of Washington Press, 2002.

Keller, Mollie. The Best Laid Plans: Robert Moses and the Making of Metroland. In *Robert Moses: Single-Minded Genius*, ed. Joann P. Krieg, 203–211. Interlaken, N.Y.: Heart of the Lakes Publishing, 1989.

Kellett, John R. *The Impact of Railways on Victorian Cities.* London: Routledge & Kegan Paul, 1969.

Kelley, Ben. *The Pavers and the Paved.* New York: Donald W. Brown, 1971.

Kelman, Steven. Cost-Benefit Analysis and Environmental, Safety, and Health Regulation: Ethical and Philosophical Considerations. In *Ethics in Planning*, ed. Martin Wachs, 233–245. New Brunswick, N.J.: Center for Urban Policy Research, Rutgers University, 1985.

Kennedy, G. Donald. Highways, the Framework of the City and Regional Plan. In *New Architecture and City Planning*, ed. Paul Zucker, 413–424. New York: Philosophical Library, 1944.

Kihlstedt, Folke T. Utopia Realized: The World's Fairs of the 1930s. In *Imagining Tomorrow: History, Technology, and the American Future*, ed. Joseph J. Corn, 97–118. Cambridge, Mass.: MIT Press, 1986.

Kress, Gunther, and Robert Hodge. *Language as Ideology.* London: Rouledge & Kegan Paul, 1979.

Kress, Gunther, and Robert Hodge. *Social Semiotics.* Ithaca, N.Y.: Cornell University Press, 1988.

Krieg, Joann P., ed. *Robert Moses: Single-Minded Genius.* Interlaken, N.Y.: Heart of the Lakes Publishing, 1989.

Krueckeberg, Donald A., ed. *Introduction to Planning History in the United States*. New Brunswick, N.J.: Center for Urban Policy Research, Rutgers University, 1983.

Krueckeberg, Donald A., ed. *The American Planner: Biographies and Recollections*. New York: Methuen, 1983.

Kuhn, Thomas S. *The Structure of Scientific Revolutions*. 2nd ed. Chicago: University of Chicago Press, 1970 [first edition published 1962].

Kurylo, Walter. "A Study of the Federal-Aid Highway Program with Special Emphasis on Its Major Budgetary and Planning Aspects." Ph.D. dissertation, The American University, 1959.

Labatut, Jean, and Wheaton J. Lane, eds. *Highways in Our National Life*. Princeton, N.J.: Princeton University Press, 1950.

LaCapra, Dominick, ed. *Modern European Intellectual History: Reappraisals and New Perspectives*. Ithaca, N.Y.: Cornell University Press, 1982.

LaCapra, Dominick, ed. *Rethinking Intellectual History: Texts, Contexts, Language*. Ithaca, N.Y.: Cornell University Press, 1983.

Lang, Jon. *Creating Architectural Theory*. New York: Van Nostrand Reinhold, 1987.

Larson, Magali Sarfatti. *The Rise of Professionalism: A Sociological Analysis*. Berkeley: University of California Press, 1977.

Laudan, Larry. *Progress and Its Problems: Towards a Theory of Scientific Growth*. Berkeley: University of California Press, 1977.

Larson, Magali Sarfatti. Emblem and Exception: The Historical Definition of the Architect's Professional Role. In *Professionals and Urban Form*, ed. Judith R. Blau, Mark La Gory, and John S. Pipkin, 49–86. Albany, N.Y.: State University of New York Press, 1983.

Leavitt, Helen. *Superhighway—Superhoax*. Garden City, N.Y.: Doubleday & Co, 1970.

Lees, Andrew. *Cities Perceived: Urban Society in European and American Thought, 1820–1940*. New York: Columbia University Press, 1985.

Levin, Melvin R., and Norman A. Abend. *Bureaucrats in Collision: Case Studies in Area Transportation Planning*. Cambridge, Mass.: MIT Press, 1971.

Lewis, Eugene. *Public Entrepreneurship: Toward a Theory of Bureaucratic Political Power*. Bloomington, Ind.: Indiana University Press, 1980 [Midland Books, 1984].

Lewis, Harold MacLean. *Planning the Modern City*. 2 vols. New York: John Wiley & Sons, 1949.

Forestier-Walker, Llewelyn-Davies Weeks. *Bor: Architects and Planning Consultants, and Ove Arup & Partners: Consulting Engineers. Motorways in the Urban Environment*. London: British Road Federation, 1971.

Logan, John R., and Harvey L. Molotch. *Urban Fortunes: The Political Economy of Place*. Berkeley: University of California Press, 1987.

Lohmann, Karl B. *Principles of City Planning*. New York: McGraw-Hill, 1931.

Los Angeles Metropolitan Parkway Engineering Committee. *Interregional, Regional, Metropolitan Parkways*. Los Angeles: Metropolitan Parkway Engineering Committee, 1946.

Los Angeles and the Regional Planning Commission. *Freeways for the Region*. Los Angeles, 1943.

Los Angeles and the Transportation Engineering Board. *A Transit Program for the Los Angeles Metropolitan Area*. Los Angeles, 1939.

Los Angeles, Traffic Commission, Committee on Los Angeles Plan of Major Highways. *A Major Traffic Street Plan for Los Angeles*. Prepared by Frederick Law Olmsted, Harland Bartholomew, and Charles Henry Cheney. Los Angeles, May 1924.

Lowi, Theodore. *The End of Liberalism*. 2nd ed. New York: W. W. Norton, 1979.

Lubove, Roy. *Community Planning in the 1920s: The Contribution of the Regional Planning Association of America*. Pittsburgh: University of Pittsburgh Press, 1963.

Lupo, Alan, Frank Colcord, and Edmund P. Fowler. *Rites of Way: The Politics of Transportation in Boston and the U.S. City*. Boston: Little, Brown and Company, 1971.

Lynch, Kevin. *The Image of the City*. Cambridge, Mass.: MIT Press, 1960.

Lynch, Kevin. Quality in City Design. In *Who Designs America?* ed. Laurence B. Holland, 120–157. Garden City, N.Y.: Doubleday, Anchor Books, 1966.

Lynch, Kevin. *What Time Is This Place?* Cambridge, Mass.: MIT Press, 1972.

Lynch, Kevin. *Managing the Sense of a Region*. Cambridge, Mass.: MIT Press, 1976.

Lynch, Kevin. *A Theory of Good City Form*. Cambridge, Mass.: MIT Press, 1981.

MacIntyre, Alasdair. Utilitarianism and the Presuppositions of Cost-Benefit Analysis: An Essay on the Relevance of Moral Philosophy to the Theory of Bureaucracy. In *Ethics in Planning*, ed. Martin Wachs, 216–232. New Brunswick, N.J.: Center for Urban Policy Research, Rutgers University, 1985.

MacKaye, Benton. *The New Exploration: A Philosophy of Regional Planning*. Urbana, Ill.: University of Illinois Press, 1962 [originally published 1928].

Malcher, Fritz. *The Steadyflow Traffic System. Harvard City Planning Studies*. vol. 9. Cambridge, Mass.: Harvard University Press, 1935.

Mallamo, J. Lance. "Building the Roads to Greatness: Robert Moses and Long Island's State Parkways. In *Robert Moses: Single-Minded Genius*, ed. Joann P. Krieg, 159–167. Interlaken, N.Y.: Heart of the Lakes Publishing, 1989.

Manieri-Elia, Mario. Toward an 'Imperial City': Daniel H. Burnham and the City Beautiful Movement. In *The American City: From the Civil War to the New Deal*. trans. Barbara Luigia La Penta. Cambridge, Mass.: MIT Press, 1979 [Italian original, 1973].

Marcuse, Peter. Housing Policy and City Planning: The Puzzling Split in the United States, 1893–1931. In *Shaping an Urban World: Planning in the 20th Century*, ed. Gordon Cherry, 23–58. New York: St. Martin's Press, 1980.

Martin, Roscoe C., Frank J. Munger, Jesse Burkhead, Guthrie S. Birkhead, Harold Herman, Herbert M. Kagi, Lewis P. Welch, and Clyde J. Wingfield. Decisions in Syracuse. In *Metropolitan Action Studies, no. 1*. Bloomington, Ind.: Indiana University Press, 1961.

Mayer, Harold M., and Richard C. Wade. *Chicago: Growth of a Metropolis*. Chicago: University of Chicago Press, 1969.

McClintock, Miller. Of Things to Come. In *Proceedings of the National Planning Conference Held in Detroit, Michigan 1–3 June 1937*, 34–38. Chicago: American Society of Planning Officials, 1937.

McCroskey, Theodore, Charles A. Blessing, and J. Ross McKeever. *Surging Cities*. Boston: Greater Boston Development Committee, 1948.

McHarg, Ian. *Design with Nature*. Garden City, N.Y.: Doubleday/Natural History Press, 1969.

McLean, Mary, ed. *Local Planning Administration*. 3rd ed. Chicago: International City Managers' Association for the Institute for Training in Municipal Administration, 1959.

McShane, Clay. Urban Pathways: The Street and Highway, 1900–1940. In *Technology and the Rise of the Networked City in Europe and America*, ed. Joel A. Tarr and Gabriel Dupuy, 67–87. Philadelphia: Temple University Press, 1988.

Meikle, Jeffrey L. *Twentieth Century Limited: Industrial Design in America, 1925–1939*. Philadelphia: Temple University Press, 1979.

Meinig, Donald W., ed. *The Interpretation of Ordinary Landscapes*. New York: Oxford University Press, 1979.

Menhinick, Howard, ed. *Local Planning Administration*. 2nd ed. Chicago: International City Manager's Association, 1948.

Mertins, Herman, Jr., and David R. Miller. Urban Transportation Policy: Fact or Fiction? In *Urban Transportation Policy: New Perspectives*, ed. David R. Miller, 19–35. Lexington, Mass.: Lexington Books, D.C. Heath and Company, 1972.

Meyer, J. R., J. F. Kain, and M. Wohl. *The Urban Transportation Problem*. Cambridge, Mass.: Harvard University Press, 1965.

Millais, Malcolm. *Exploding the Myths of Modern Architecture*. London: Frances Lincoln Limited, 2009.

Miller, David R., ed. *Urban Transportation Policy: New Perspectives*. Lexington, Mass.: D. C. Heath, Lexington Books, 1972.

Miller, Robert. The Long Island Motor Parkway: Prelude to Robert Moses. In *Robert Moses: Single-Minded Genius*, ed. Joann P. Krieg, 151–158. Interlaken, N.Y.: Heart of the Lakes Publishing, 1989.

Mitchell, Robert B. The Relationships Between Urban Highways and Land Development. In *Proceedings of the 41st Annual Meeting of the American Institute of*

Planners Held in New York, New York 26–30 October 1958, 47–50. Washington, D.C.: American Institute of Planners, 1958.

Mitchell, Robert B., and Chester Rapkin. *Urban Traffic: A Function of Land Use.* New York: Columbia University Press, 1954.

Mollenkopf, John H. *The Contested City.* Princeton, N.J.: Princeton University Press, 1983.

Monkkonen, Eric H. *American Becomes Urban: The Development of U.S. Cities and Towns, 1780–1980.* Berkeley: University of California Press, 1988.

Moses, Robert. *Arterial Plan for Pittsburgh.* Prepared for the Pittsburgh Regional Planning Association, November 1939.

Moses, Robert et al. *Portland Improvement.* New York: William E. Rudge's Sons, 1943.

Mowbray, A. Q. *Road to Ruin.* Philadelphia and New York: J. B. Lippincott Company, 1969.

Muller, Peter O. Transportation and Urban Form: Stages in the Spatial Evolution of the American Metropolis. In *The Geography of Urban Transportation*, ed. Susan Hanson, 24–48. New York: Guilford Press, 1986.

Mumford, Lewis. *The Culture of Cities.* New York: Harcourt, Brace and Company, 1938.

Mumford, Lewis. *City Development: Studies in Disintegration and Renewal.* New York: Harcourt, Brace and Co, 1945.

Mumford, Lewis. *The City in History.* New York: Harcourt, Brace & World, 1961.

Mumford, Lewis. *The Highway and the City.* New York: Mentor, 1963.

Mumford, Lewis. *The Urban Prospect.* New York: Harcourt Brace Jovanovich, 1968.

Mumphrey, Anthony J. "The New Orleans Expressway Controversy: An Analytic Account." Conflict in Locational Decisions, Discussion Paper No. 1. Philadelphia: Wharton School of Finance and Commerce, University of Pennsylvania, 1970.

Mumphrey, Anthony J., John E. Seley, and Julian Wolpert. "A Decision Model for Locating Controversial Facilities." Conflict in Locational Decisions, Discussion Paper No. 11. Philadelphia: Wharton School of Finance and Commerce, University of Pennsylvania, 1971.

Murphey, Murray G. The Place of Beliefs in Modern Culture. In *New Directions in American Intellectual History*, ed. John Higham and Paul K. Conkin, 151–165. Baltimore: Johns Hopkins University Press, 1979.

National Capital Planning Commission. *A Policies Plan for the Year 2000.* Washington, D.C., 1961.

National Capital Planning Commission. *Worthy of the Nation: The History of Planning for the National Capital.* Washington, D.C.: Smithsonian Institution, 1977.

Nervi, Pier Luigi. *Steel Elevated Freeways*. Oakland, Calif.: Kaiser Steel Corporation, 1962.

New York, City Planning Commission. *Selected Measures for the Partial Relief of Traffic Congestion in New York City*. Prepared by Gano Dunn, W. Earle Andrews, and Gilmore D. Clarke, 1946.

Newton, Norman T. *Design on the Land: The Development of Landscape Architecture*. Cambridge, Mass.: Belknap Press of Harvard University Press, 1971.

Nolen, John, and Henry V. Hubbard. *Harvard City Planning Studies*. vol. 9. Parkways and Land Values. Cambridge, Mass.: Harvard University Press, 1937.

O'Harrow, Dennis. *Plan Talk and Plain Talk*. ed. Marjorie S. Berger. Washington, D.C.: APA Planners Press, 1981.

O'Harrow, Dennis, Reginald R. Isaacs, and Frank M. Kubota. *City of Syracuse Planning, Housing and Urban Renewal*. Report to the American Society of Planning Officials, May 1957.

Olsson, Gunnar. *Birds in Egg: Eggs in Bird*. London: Pion, 1980.

Owen, Wilfred. *The Metropolitan Transportation Problem*. Washington, D.C.: The Brookings Institution, 1956.

Park, Robert E., Ernest W. Burgess, and Roderick D. McKenzie. *The City*. Chicago: University of Chicago Press, 1925.

Patton, Phil. *Open Road: A Celebration of the American Highway*. New York: Simon & Schuster, 1986.

Pavlos, Elliott A. Chicago's Crosstown: A Case Study in Urban Expressways. In *Urban Transportation Policy: New Perspectives*, ed. David R. Miller, 57–65. Lexington, Mass.: Lexington Books, D.C. Heath and Company, 1972.

Peattie, Lisa. *Planning: Rethinking Ciudad Guayana*. Ann Arbor, Mich.: University of Michigan Press, 1987.

Pells, Richard H. *Radical Visions and American Dreams: Culture and Social Thought in the Depression Years*. New York: Harper & Row, Harper Torchbooks, 1973.

Pells, Richard H. *The Liberal Mind in a Conservative Age: American Intellectuals in the 1940s and 1950s*. New York: Harper & Row, 1985.

Perloff, Harvey. *Education for Planning: City, State, and Regional*. Baltimore: Johns Hopkins University Press for Resources for the Future, 1957.

Perrucci, Robert, and Joel Gerstl. *Profession Without Community: Engineers in American Society*. New York: Random House, 1969.

Perry, David C. The Moses Model of Governance. In *Robert Moses: Single-Minded Genius*, ed. Joann P. Krieg, 69–78. Interlaken, N.Y.: Heart of the Lakes Publishing, 1989.

Philpott, Thomas Lee. *The Slum and the Ghetto: Neighborhood Deterioration and Middle-Class Reform, Chicago, 1880–1930*. New York: Oxford University Press, 1978.

Pillsbury, Warren A. *The Economic and Social Effects of Highway Improvement: An Annotated Bibliography.* Charlottesville, Va.: Virginia Council of Highway Investigation and Research, 1961.

Plane, David A. Urban Transportation: Policy Alternatives. In *The Geography of Urban Transportation,* ed. Susan Hanson, 386–414. New York: Guilford Press, 1986.

Plotkin, Sidney. *Keep Out: The Struggle for Land Use Control.* Berkeley: University of California Press, 1987.

Plowden, Stephen. *Towns against Traffic.* London: Andre Deutsch, 1972.

Plowden, Stephen. *Taming Traffic.* London: Andre Deutsch, 1980.

Polenberg, Richard. *One Nation Divisible: Class, Race, and Ethnicity in the United States Since 1938.* New York: Penguin, 1980.

Public Works Historical Society. "Interstate Highway Research Project: Analysis." Draft Report Submitted for Comment to the AASHTO Task Force, June 1988.

Pushkarev, Boris S., and Jeffery M. Zupan. *Public Transportation and Land Use Policy.* Bloomington, Ind.: University of Indiana Press, 1977.

Rae, John B. *The Road and Car in American Life.* Cambridge, Mass.: MIT Press, 1971.

Rapoport, Amos. *Human Aspects of Urban Form.* Oxford: Pergamon, 1977.

Ravetz, Alison. *Remaking Cities: Contradictions of the Recent Urban Environment.* London: Croom Helm, 1980.

Ravitch, Diane, and Joseph P. Viteritti. *Making Good Citizens Education and Civil Society.* New Haven, Conn.: Yale University Press, 2001.

Reiner, Thomas A., and Michael A. Hindery. City Planning: Images of the Ideal and the Existing City. In *Cities of the Mind: Images and Themes of the City in the Social Sciences,* ed. Lloyd Rodwin and Robert M. Hollister, 133–147. New York: Plenum Press, 1984.

Riddick, Winston Wade. "The Politics of National Highway Policy, 1953–1966." Ph.D. dissertation, Columbia University, 1973.

Robinson, John. *Highways and Our Environment.* New York: McGraw-Hill, 1971.

Rodwin, Lloyd, and Robert M. Hollister. *Cities of the Mind: Images and Themes of the City in the Social Sciences.* New York: Plenum Press, 1984.

Rose, Albert C. *Historic American Roads: From Frontier Trails to Superhighways.* New York: Crown Publishers, 1976.

Rose, Mark H. *Interstate: Express Highway Politics, 1941–1956.* Lawrence, Kans.: The Regents Press of Kansas, 1979.

Rose, Mark H. *Interstate: Express Highway Politics 1939–1989.* Knoxville, Tenn.: University of Tennessee Press, 1990.

Saalman, Howard. *Haussmann: Paris Transformed.* New York: Braziller, 1971.

Saarinen, Eliel. *The City: Its Growth, Its Decay, Its Future.* New York: Reinhold Publishing Corporation, 1943.

Saint, Andrew. *The Image of the Architect.* New Haven, Conn.: Yale University Press, 1983.

San Francisco, City Planning Commission. *Shoreline Development: A Portion of the Master Plan of San Francisco, Preliminary Report.* September 1943.

San Francisco, City Planning Commission. *The Master Plan of the City and County of San Francisco: Summary.* January 1946.

San Francisco, City Planning Commission. *Transportation Plan for San Francisco.* Prepared by De Leuw Cather and Company, and Ladislas Segoe and Associates, 1948.

San Francisco, Department of Public Works. *A Report on the San Francisco City-wide Traffic Survey.* Prepared by Miller McClintock, 1937.

San Francisco, Department of Public Works. *San Francisco Western Freeway: Phase I, Determination of Need.* Prepared by Wilbur Smith & Associates, December 1957.

San Francisco, Department of Public Works. *San Francisco Western Freeway: Phase II, Route Location and Economic Study.* Prepared by Wilbur Smith & Associates, September 1958.

San Francisco, Department of Public Works and Department of City Planning. *Trafficways in San Francisco—A Reappraisal.* November 1960.

San Francisco, Technical Committee of the Mayor's Administrative Transportation Council. *Traffic.* San Francisco: Transit and Thoroughfare Improvements for San Francisco, 1947.

Sanders, S. E., and A. J. Rabuck. *New City Patterns.* New York: Reinhold Publishing Corporation, 1946.

Savitch, H. V. *Post-Industrial Cities: Politics and Planning in New York, Paris, and London.* Princeton, N.J.: Princeton University Press, 1988.

Sayer, Andrew. *Method in Social Science: A Realist Approach.* London: Hutchinson, 1984.

Sayer, Derek. *The Violence of Abstraction.* Oxford: Basil Blackwell, 1987.

Schaffer, Daniel, ed. *Two Centuries of American Planning.* Baltimore: Johns Hopkins University Press, 1988.

Schiesl, Martin J. *The Politics of Efficiency: Municipal Administration and Reform in America: 1880–1920.* Berkeley: University of California Press, 1977.

Schneider, Kenneth R. *Autokind v. Mankind.* New York: W. W. Norton, 1971.

Schorr, Philip. *Planned Relocation.* Lexington, Mass.: Lexington Books, D.C. Heath and Company, 1975.

Schultz, Stanley K. *Constructing Urban Culture: American Cities and City Planning, 1800–1920.* Philadelphia: Temple University Press, 1989.

Schuyler, David. *The New Urban Landscape: The Redefinition of City Form in Nineteenth-Century America.* Baltimore: Johns Hopkins University Press, 1986.

Scott, Mel. "Western Addition District Redevelopment Study." San Francisco City Planning Commission, November 1947.

Scott, Mel. *American City Planning since 1890*. Berkeley: University of California Press, 1969.

Scott, Mel. *The San Francisco Bay Area: A Metropolis in Perspective*. 2nd ed. Berkeley: University of California Press, 1985.

Scully, Vincent. *American Architecture and Urbanism*. New York: Praeger, 1969.

Seely, Bruce E. *Building the American Highway System: Engineers as Policy Makers*. Philadelphia: Temple University Press, 1987.

Segal, Howard P. *Technological Utopianism in American Culture*. Chicago: University of Chicago Press, 1985.

Segoe, Ladislas. *Local Planning Administration*. Chicago: International City Managers' Association for the Institute for Training in Municipal Administration, 1941.

Seley, John E. "Development of a Sophisticated Opposition: The Lower Manhattan Expressway." Conflict in Locational Decisions, Discussion Paper No. 7. Philadelphia: Wharton School of Finance and Commerce, University of Pennsylania, 1970.

Seley, John E. "Spatial Bias: The Kink in Nashville's I-40." Conflict in Locational Decisions, Discussion Paper No. 3. Philadelphia: Wharton School of Finance and Commerce, University of Pennsylvania, 1970.

Seley, John E. *The Politics of Public-Facility Planning*. Lexington, Mass.: Lexington Books, D.C. Heath and Co, 1983.

Sert, Jose Luis. Centers of Community Life. In *The Heart of the City: Towards the Humanisation of Urban Life*, ed. J. Tyrwhitt, J. L. Sert, and E. N. Rogers. New York: Pellegrini and Cudahy, 1952, 3–16.

Sert, Jose Luis, and C.I.A.M. *Can Our Cities Survive?* Cambridge, Mass.: Harvard University Press, 1942.

Sessions, Gordon M. *Traffic Devices: Historical Aspects Thereof*. Washington, D.C.: Institute of Traffic Engineers, 1971.

Shanor, Rebecca Read. *The City That Never Was*. New York: Viking, 1988.

Sharpe, William, and Leonard Wallock eds. *Visions of the Modern City*. Proceedings of the Heyman Center for the Humanities. New York: Columbia University, 1983.

Shirvani, Hamid. *The Urban Design Process*. New York: Van Nostrand Reinhold, 1985.

Short, James F., Jr., ed. *The Social Fabric of the Metropolis: Contributions of the Chicago School of Urban Sociology*. Chicago: University of Chicago Press, 1971.

Silver, Christopher. *Twentieth-Century Richmond: Planning, Politics, and Race*. Knoxville, Tenn.: University of Tennessee Press, 1984.

Sloan, Allan K. *Citizen Participation in Transportation Planning: The Boston Experience*. Pensacola, Fla.: Ballinger, 1974.

Smithson, Alison, and Peter Smithson. *Urban Structuring*. New York: Reinhold, 1967.

Snow, W. Brewster. *The Highway and the Landscape*. New Brunswick, N.J.: Rutgers University Press, 1959.

Soderberg, C. Richard. The American Engineer. In *The Professions in America*, ed. Kenneth S. Lynn, 203–230. Boston: Houghton Mifflin, 1965.

Soja, Edward W. *Postmodern Geographies: The Reassertion of Space in Critical Social Theory*. London: Verso, 1989.

Solomon, Daniel. *ReBuilding*. New York: Princeton Architectural Press, 1992.

Solomon, Daniel. *Global City Blues*. Washington, D.C.: Island Press, 2003.

Sontag, Susan. *Illness as Metaphor*. New York: Random House, Vintage Books, 1978.

St. Clair, David J. *The Motorization of American Cities*. New York: Praeger, 1986.

Steiner, Henry Malcolm. *Conflict in Urban Transportation: The People Against the Planners*. Lanham, Md.: Lexington Books, 1978.

Stilgoe, John R. *Metropolitan Corridor: Railroads and the American Scene*. New Haven, Conn.: Yale University Press, 1983.

Stimpson, Catharine R., Elsa Dixler, Martha J. Nelson, and Kathryn B. Yatrakis, eds. *Women and the American City*. Chicago: University of Chicago Press, 1981.

Stone, Tabor R. *Beyond the Automobile: Reshaping the Transportation Environment*. Englewood Cliffs, N.J.: Prentice-Hall, 1971.

Subcommittee on Two Level Streets and Separated Grades of the Committee on Traffic Regulation and Public Safety of the City Council of the City of Chicago. *A Memorandum and Preliminary Report with Reference to Elevated Through Highways for the Chicago Metropolitan Area*. Chicago, 1928.

Susman, Warren I. *Culture as History: The Transformation of American Society in the Twentieth Century*. New York: Pantheon, 1984.

Sussman, Carl, ed. *Planning the Fourth Migration: The Neglected Vision of the Regional Planning Association of America*. Cambridge, Mass.: MIT Press, 1976.

Swierchek, Chad. *Interstate Highways or Freeways in Omaha*. Lincoln, Neb.: University of Nebraska, 2008. Available at: http://segonku.unl.edu/~nswiercek/ih.fo.htm.

Szanton, Peter. *Not Well Advised*. New York: Russell Sage Foundation and Ford Foundation, 1981.

Tachieva, Galina. *The Sprawl Repair Manual*. Washington, D.C.: Island Press, 2010.

Taebel, Delbert A., and James V. Cornehls. *The Political Economy of Urban Transportation*. Port Washington, N.Y.: Kennikat Press, 1977.

Tafuri, Manfredo, and Francesco Dal Co. *Architecture and Utopia: Design and Capitalist Development*. trans. Barbara Luigia La Penta. Cambridge, Mass.: MIT Press, 1976 [Italian original, 1973].

Tafuri, Manfredo, and Francesco Dal Co. *Modern Architecture*. 2 vols. trans. Robert Erich Wolf. New York: Rizzoli, 1976.

Tafuri, Manfredo, and Francesco Dal Co. The Disenchanted Mountain: The Skyscraper and the City, in *The American City: From the Civil War to the New Deal*, 389–528, trans. Barbara Luigia La Penta. Cambridge, Mass.: MIT Press, 1979.

Tafuri, Manfredo, and Francesco Dal Co. *The Sphere and the Labyrinth: Avant-Gardes and Architecture from Piranesi to the 1970s*. trans. Pellegrino d'Acierno and Robert Connolly. Cambridge, Mass.: MIT Press, 1987 [Italian original, 1980].

Taylor, S. S. (Sam). Space Age City Traffic. In *Proceedings of the Institute of Traffic Engineers, Held in New York, New York, 14–17 Sept. 1959*, 30–41.Washington, D. C.: Institute of Traffic Engineers, 1959.

Thomas, June Manning, and Marsha Ritzdorf, eds. *Urban Planning and the African American Community*. Thousand Oaks, Calif.: Sage Publications, 1997.

Thompson, J. Michael. *Motorways in London*. London: Duckworth, 1969.

Thompson, John B. *Studies in the Theory of Ideology*. Berkeley: University of California Press, 1984.

Trancik, Roger. *Finding Lost Space: Theories of Urban Design*. New York: Van Nostrand Reinhold, 1986.

Traffic Studies in Relation to City Planning. In *Proceeding of the National Conference on Planning Held in Minneapolis, Minnesota 20–22 June, 1938*, 28–40. Chicago: American Society of Planning Officials, 1938.

Tripp, Alker. *Road Traffic and Its Control*. 2nd ed. London: Edward Arnold & Co, 1950.

Tunnard, Christopher, and Boris Pushkarev. *Man-Made America: Chaos or Control?* New Haven, Conn.: Yale University Press, 1963.

Tunnard, Christopher, and Boris Pushkarev. *Man-Made America: Chaos or Control?* Foreword by Wolf Von Eckhardt. New York: Harmony Books, 1981 [originally published 1963].

Tyrwhitt, J., J. L. Sert, and E. N. Rogers. *The Heart of the City: Towards the Humanisation of Urban Life*. New York: Pellegrini and Cudahy, 1952.

U.S. Congress, Congressional Budget Office. *Highway Assistance Programs: A Historical Perspective*. Washington, D.C.: USGPO, 1978.

U.S., Federal Highway Administration. *America's Highways, 1776–1976*. Washington, D.C.: USGPO, 1976.

U.S., Federal Highway Administration, Office of Research, Environmental Design and Control Division. *A Study of Social, Economic, and Environmental Impacts and Land Use Planning Related to Urban Highway Tunnel Location: An Annotated Bibliography*. Prepared by Planning Environment International, in Association with JRB Associates, June 1975.

Urban Design Concept Associates. *Project Description*. Baltimore, December 1969.

Urban Land Institute. *New Highways: Challenge to the Metropolitan Region.* Technical Bulletin No. 31. Selected papers prepared as background for a symposium sponsored by Connecticut Mutual Life Insurance Co., September 1957. Washington, D.C.: Urban Land Institute, 1958.

Vance, James E., Jr. *Geography and Urban Evolution in the San Francisco Bay Area.* Berkeley: Institute of Governmental Studies, University of California, 1964.

Vance, James E., Jr. Focus on Downtown. In *Internal Structure of the City*, ed. Larry S. Bourne, 112–120. New York: Oxford University Press, 1971.

Vance, James E., Jr. *This Scene of Man.* New York: Harper & Row, 1977.

Vance, James E., Jr. *Capturing the Horizon: The Historical Geography of Transportation.* New York: Harper & Row, 1986.

Wachs, Martin, ed. *Ethics in Planning.* New Brunswick, N.J.: Center for Urban Policy Research, Rutgers University, 1985.

Walden, Russell, ed. *The Open Hand: Essays on Le Corbusier.* Cambridge, Mass.: MIT Press, 1977.

Walker, Mabel L. *Urban Blight and Slums. Harvard City Planning Studies.* vol. 12. Cambridge, Mass.: Harvard University Press, 1938.

Walker, Robert. *The Planning Function in Urban Government.* Chicago: University of Chicago Press, 1941.

Warner, Sam Bass, Jr. Slums and Skyscrapers: Urban Images, Symbols, and Ideology. In *Cities of the Mind: Images and Themes of the City in the Social Sciences*, ed. Lloyd Rodwin and Robert M. Hollister, 181–195. New York: Plenum Press, 1984.

Washington State University, Highway Research Section, Engineering Research Division. *A Study of the Social.* Pullman, Wash.: Economic and Environmental Impact of Highway Transportation Facilities on Urban Communities, 1968.

Weigold, Marilyn E. *Pioneering in Parks and Parkways: Westchester County, New York, 1895–1945. Essays in Public Works History, Essay No. 9.* Chicago: Public Works Historical Society, 1980.

Weiner, Edward. *Urban Transportation Planning in the United States: An Historical Overview.* New York: Praeger, 1987.

Weiss, Marc A. *The Rise of the Community Builders.* New York: Columbia University Press, 1987.

White, Hayden. *Tropics of Discourse: Essays in Cultural Criticism.* Baltimore: Johns Hopkins University Press, 1978.

Whitt, J. Allen. *Urban Elites and Mass Transportation.* Princeton, N.J.: Princeton University Press, 1982.

Whitten, Robert. The Prevention of Blight in Residential Areas Adjacent to Expressways. In *Proceedings of the Twenty-Third National Conference on City Planning Held in Rochester, New York 22–24 July 1931*, 157–178. Philadelphia: William Fell, 1931.

Whyte, William H. *The Last Landscape.* Garden City, N.Y.: Doubleday & Co., Anchor Books, 1970.

Wilbur Smith and Associates. *Future Highways and Urban Growth*. New Haven, Conn.: Under Commission from the Automobile Manufacturers Association, 1961.

Wilbur Smith and Associates. *Transportation and Parking for Tomorrow's Cities*. New Haven, Conn.: Under Commission from the Automobile Manufacturers Association, 1966.

Williams, T. E. H. *Urban Survival and Traffic*. London: E. & F. N. Spon, 1962.

Willis, Carol. Skyscraper Utopias: Visionary Urbanism in the 1920s. In *Imagining Tomorrow: History, Technology, and the American Future*, ed. Joseph J. Corn, 164–187. Cambridge, Mass.: MIT Press, 1986.

Wilson, William H. Moles and Skylarks. In *Introduction to Planning History*, ed. Donald Krueckeberg, 88–121. New Brunswick, N.J.: Center for Urban Policy Research, Rutgers University, 1983.

Wilson, William H. *The City Beautiful Movement: Creating the North American Landscape*. Baltimore, Md.: Johns Hopkins University Press, 1994.

Winner, Langdon. *Autonomous Technology: Technics-Out-of-Control as a Theme in Political Thought*. Cambridge, Mass.: MIT Press, 1977.

Winner, Langdon. *The Whale and the Reactor: A Search for Limits in an Age of High Technology*. Chicago: University of Chicago Press, 1986.

Wirt, Frederick M. *Power in the City: Decision Making in San Francisco*. Berkeley: University of California Press, 1974.

Wolfe, Alan. *America's Impasse: The Rise and Fall of the Politics of Growth*. Boston: South End Press, 1981.

Wood, Gordon S. Intellectual History and the Social Sciences. In *New Directions in American Intellectual History*, ed. John Higham and Paul K. Conkin, 27–41. Baltimore: Johns Hopkins University Press, 1979.

Wright, Frank Lloyd. *The Living City*. New York: Horizon Press, 1958.

Yago, Glenn. *The Decline of Transit: Urban Transportation in German and U.S. Cities, 1900–1970*. New York: Cambridge University Press, 1984.

Zettel, Richard M., and Paul W. Shuldiner. *Freeway Location Conflicts in California*. Research Report No. 29. Berkeley: Institute of Transportation and Traffic Engineering, University of California at Berkeley, 1959.

Articles

Abernathey, James M. "Some Ethical Implications of Professional Planning." *American Society of Civil Engineers: Journal of Professional Practice* 90 (no. PP2) (May 1964): 23–29.

Abrams, Charles. "Downtown Decay and Revival." *Journal of the American Institute of Planners* 27 (1) (February 1961): 3–9.

"A Critical Look at Freeways to Downtown Areas." *American City* 70 (January 1955): 153–154.

Adams, Arthur H. "Los Angeles County Is Ready with Limited Access Highway Plans." *American City* 60 (September 1945): 96–97.

Adams, Frederick J. "President's Report for 1949." *Journal of the American Institute of Planners* 16 (1) (Winter 1950): 2–5.

"Adams Shifts Ruling, Would Allow Tunnel Under Overton Park." *Commercial Appeal*. Memphis, Tenn. (October 9, 1977).

"Adams' Retrenchment Maintains Slight Hope for I-40's Completion." *Commercial Appeal*. Memphis, Tenn. (May 12, 1978).

Adler, Seymour. "The Dynamics of Transit Innovation in Los Angeles." *Environment and Planning. D, Society & Space* 4 (3) (September 1986): 321–335.

Alexander, Christopher. "A City Is Not a Tree." *Architectural Forum* 122 (April 1965): 58–62 and (May 1965): 58–61.

Alexander, Harry W. "Bringing Interregional Thoroughfares to the Hearts of the Cities." *American City* 60 (February 1945): 59.

"All 8 Plans for Overton X-Way Called Harmful to Environment." *Press Scimitar* (July-8–1776).

Alonso, William. "The Unplanned Paths of Planning Schools." *Public Interest* (82) (Winter 1986): 58–71.

Altshuler, Alan. "The Goals of Comprehensive Planning." *Journal of the American Institute of Planners* 31 (3) (August 1965): 186–195.

American Institute of Planners and Institute of Traffic Engineers. "Professional Responsibility of City Planners and Traffic Engineers in Urban Transportation." *Journal of the American Institute of Planners* 27 (1) (February 1961): 70–73.

American Society of Civil Engineers, Committee on Highway Planning and Economics of the Highway Division. "Revolution in Urban Highway Planning." *American Society of Civil Engineers: Journal of Transportation Engineering* 97 (no. TE1) (February 1971): 145–151.

Ames, ArDee. "An End to Highway Aid." *Nation's Cities* 2 (August 1964): 6.

Ames, ArDee. "Urban Renewal and Transportation." *Nation's Cities* 2 (December 1964): 10–13.

Amir, Shaul. "Highway Location and Public Opposition." *Environment and Behavior* 4 (December 1972): 413–436.

"A 'Motor-Safe' Residential District." *American City* 53 (April 1938): 87.

Andrews, W. Earle. "Urban Arterial Developments Which Benefit the Community." *Highway Research Board Bulletin* (no. 190) (1958): 25–28.

Appleyard, Donald. "The Major Published Works of Kevin Lynch: An Appraisal." *Town Planning Review* 49 (October 1978): 551–557.

Appleyard, Donald. "The Environment as a Social Symbol." *Journal of the American Institute of Planners* 45 (2) (April 1979): 143–153.

"Area Earmarked for Purchase and Resale by City." *Post-Standard*. Syracuse, N.Y. (June 4, 1954).

Armstrong, Kathleen. "Litigating the Freeway Revolt: Keith v. Volpe." *Ecology Law Quarterly* 2 (Winter 1972): 761–799.

"Arresting the Highwaymen: Editorial." *Architectural Forum* 110 (April 1959): 93.

"A Safety Intersection on the Lincoln Highway." *American City* 42 (January 1930): 129.

Ascher, Charles S. "Some of Today's Planning Ideas Are Five Centuries Old." *American City* 67 (June 1952): 139.

"Atlanta, Ga. Is On the Way to Traffic Relief." *American City* 70 (April 1955): 138.

"A Traffic Planner Imagines a City." *American City* 44 (March 1931): 134–135.

Augur, Tracy B. "Highways for New Urban Patterns." *Highway Research Board Bulletin* (no. 113) (1956): 54–58.

"Auto Speedway or Parkway?" *American City* 64 (July 1949): 88–90.

Automobile Club of Syracuse. "City-Wide Celebration to Mark Oswego Boulevard Opening." *Official Bulletin* 24 (no. 11) (October 1959).

Ayres, Drummond, Jr. "Washington, 'White Roads Through Black Bedrooms.'" *New York Times* (December 31, 1967).

Bacon, Edmund N. "A Case Study in Urban Design." *Journal of the American Institute of Planners* 26 (3) (August 1960): 224–235.

Bacon, Edmund N. "Urban Redevelopment and Highway Planning." *Highway Research Board Bulletin* (no. 64) (1952): 9–12.

Bailey, James. "How S.O.M. Took on the Baltimore Road Gang." [Reply: N. A. Owings and others, *Architectural Forum* 130 (June 1969): 6.] *Architectural Forum* 130 (March 1969): 40–45.

"Baker Grasping 'Last Straw' for Overton Park Freeway." "Baker's I-40 Proposal Defeated." *Commercial Appeal.* Memphis, Tenn. (May 12, 1978).

"Baltimore Public Receives Master Transportation Plan." *American City* 65 (February 1950): 151.

Barkan, Benedict G. "Latest Methods of Determining Urban Highway Routes." *American Society of Civil Engineers, Journal of the Urban Planning and Development Division* 93 (no. UP4) (December 1967): 5–18.

Barkley, Robert Emmanuel. "Origin-Destination Surveys and Traffic Volume Studies." Highway Research Board Bibliography No. 11, December 1951.

Barnett, Joseph. "Arterial Routes and Urban Development." *Landscape Architecture* 38 (July 1948): 145–147.

Barnett, Joseph. "Importance of Planning and Building Urban Road Systems and Requirements Therefor." *American Planning and Civic Annual* (1949), 67–72.

Barnett, Joseph. "Urban Freeways and Center City Planning and Design." *American Society of Civil Engineers, Journal of the Urban Planning and Development Division* 93 (no. UP4) (December 1967): 257–277. Discussions by Norman Cooper and George F. Stevenson, *American Society of Civil Engineers, Journal of the Urban Planning and Development Division* 94 (no. UP1) (August 1968): 96–98.

Bartholomew, Harland. "The Principles of City Planning." *American City* 26 (May 1922): 457–461.

Bartholomew, Harland. "Is City Planning Effectively Controlling City Growth in the United States." *American City* 45 (July 1931): 127–128.

Bartholomew, Harland. "St. Louis Plans New Major Streets." *American City* 57 (November 1942): 62–63.

Bartholomew, Harland. "The Location of Interstate Highways in Cities." *American Planning and Civic Annual* (1949): 73–78.

"Basic Plan to Vitalize Fort Worth District." *American City* 71 (June 1956): 132.

Bassett, Edward M. "The Freeway: A New Kind of Thoroughfare." *American City* 42 (February 1930): 95.

Bassett, Howard M. "A New Type of Protected Trafficway Being Built in Westchester County, N.Y." *American City* 48 (March 1933): 59–60.

Bauer, Catherine. "Review of *City Development: Studies in Disintegration and Renewal*, by Lewis Mumford." *Journal of the American Institute of Planners* 11 (3) (July-August-September 1945): 36–40.

Bauer, Catherine. "Do Americans Hate Cities?" *Journal of the American Institute of Planners* 23 (1) (Winter 1957): 2–8.

Beesley, M. E., and J. F. Kain. "Urban Form, Car Ownership and Public Transport." *Urban Studies (Edinburgh, Scotland)* 1 (November 1964): 174–203.

Bergman, Leonard A. "New York State to Build Highways Through Cities as Check on Decentralization." *Civil Engineering (New York, N.Y.)* 16 (November 1946): 477.

Bevis, Howard. "The Application of Benefit-Cost Ratios to an Expressway System." *Proceedings of the Highway Research Board* 35 (1956): 66.

Bibbins, J. "Rowland. "The Battle of the Streets." *American City* 29 (October 1923): 364–368.

Birch, Eugenie L. "Advancing the Art and Science of Planning: Planners and Their Organizations, 1909–1980." *Journal of the American Planning Association* 46 (January 1980): 22–49.

Bishop, Bruce, Clarkson H. Oglesby, and Gene E. Willeke. "The Planning Profession's Responsibility to the People: Good Plans." *Journal of the American Institute of Planners* 14 (4) (Fall 1948): 13–16.

Bishop, Bruce, Clarkson H. Oglesby, and Gene E. Willeke. "Community Attitudes Toward Freeway Planning: A Study of California's Planning Procedures." *Highway Research Record* 305 (1970): 41–52.

Black, Alan. "The Chicago Area Transportation Study: A Case Study of Rational Planning." *Journal of Planning Education and Research* 10 (3) (1990): 27–37.

Blessing, Charles A. "The Architect and the Planner." *Journal of the American Institute of Architects* 35 (3) (March 1961): 85–89.

Blucher, Walter H. "Planning for the Post-War Period." *American Highways* 21 (3) (July 1942): 12–16.

Blucher, Walter H. "Order or Confusion in City Transportation Planning?" *Traffic Engineering* 15 (1) (October 1944): 7–9.

Blucher, Walter H. "Moving People." *Virginia Law Review* 36 (1950): 849–857.

Blumenfeld, Hans. "Are Land Use Patterns Predictable?" *Journal of the American Institute of Planners* 25 (2) (May 1959): 61–66.

Blumenfeld, Hans. "The Urban Pattern." *Annals of the American Academy of Political and Social Science* 352 (March 1964): 74–83.

Blumenfeld, Hans. "The Role of Design." *Journal of the American Institute of Planners* 33 (5) (September 1967): 304–310.

Bollong, J. W. A. "Discussion of 'Order or Confusion in City Transportation Planning.'" *Traffic Engineering* 15 (1) (October 1944): 9–10.

Bor, Walter, and John Roberts. "Urban Motorways Impact." *Town Planning Review* 43 (October 1972): 299–321.

Boyer, M. Christine. "The Tragedy of American City Planning." *Crit* (no. 17) (Fall 1986): 41–48.

Breivogel, Milton. "Urban Freeways: Paper Abstract." *Journal of the American Institute of Planners* 14 (4) (Fall 1948): 24–26.

Bressi, Todd W. "Freeway With a Fringe on Top." *Planning* 55 (7) (July 1989): 8–11.

Browning, David L. "Legacy of a Planning Legend: The Victor Gruen Plan for a Greater Fort Worth Tomorrow." *Crit* (no. 12) (Winter 1983): 5–9.

Bridwell, Lowell K. "Remarks Before Pennsylvania Department of Highways Seminar, February 28, 1968, Harrisburg." *Highway Research Record* 220 (1968): 1–4.

"Brock Adams Inherits Overton Park Problem." *Commercial Appeal*. Memphis, Tenn. (March 27, 1977).

Brooks, Michael P. "Four Critical Junctures in the History of the Urban Planning Profession: An Exercise in Hindsight." *Journal of the American Planning Association* 54 (2) (Spring 1988): 241–248.

Brown, Denise Scott. "Team 10, Perspecta 10, and the Present State of Architectural Theory." *Journal of the American Institute of Planners* 33 (1) (January 1967): 42–50.

Brown, Denise Scott. "An Alternate Proposal That Builds on the Character and Population of South Street." *Architectural Forum* 135 (October 1971): 42–44.

Brown, Jeffrey. "A Tale of Two Visions: Harland Bartholomew, Robert Moses, and the Development of the American Freeway." *Journal of Planning History* 4 (1) (February 2005): 3–32.

Brown, Jeffrey. "From Traffic Regulation to Limited Ways: The Effort to Build a Science of Transportation Planning." *Journal of Planning History* 5 (1) (February 2006): 3–34.

Brown, Jeffrey. "Statewide Transportation Planning: Lessons from California." *Transportation Quarterly* 56 (2) (2002): 51–62.

Brown, Jeffrey R., Eric A. Morris, and Brian D. Taylor. "Planning for Cars in Cities: Planners, Engineers, and Freeways in the 20th Century." *Journal of the American Planning Association* 75 (2) (Spring 2009): 161–177.

Brown, Ralph E., Jr. "Planning's Role in Standards for Future Highways." *American Society of Civil Engineers: Journal of Transportation Engineering* 97 (no. TE2) (May 1971): 227–236.

Browning, Clyde E. "Review Article: Recent Studies of Central Business Districts." *Journal of the American Institute of Planners* 27 (1) (February 1961): 82–87.

Browning, David L. "Legacy of a Planning Legend: The Victor Gruen Plan for a Greater Fort Worth Tomorrow." *Crit* (no. 12) (Winter 1983): 5–9.

Bruce-Briggs, B. "Mass Transportation and Minority Transportation." *Public Interest* (40) (Summer 1975): 43–74.

Brummitt, Wyatt B. "The Superhighway." *American City* 40 (January 1929): 85–88.

Buttenheim, Harold S. "Trends in Present-Day City Planning in the United States." *City Planning* 7 (2) (April 1931): 100–115.

Campaglia, Muriel. "In the Path of the Interstates." *City* 4 (1) (June/July 1970): 25–31.

Canty, Donald. "Fight to Tame the Urban Freeway Takes a Positive New Turn." *Architectural Forum* 119 (October 1963): 68–73.

Carroll, J. "Highways and the Future Demand and Supply of Metropolitan Transportation." The New Highways: Challenge to the Metropolitan Region. Urban Land Institute Technical Bulletin (no. 31) (November 1957): 65–74.

Carroll, J. "Douglas, Jr., Roger L. Creighton, and John R. Hamburg. "Transportation Planning for Central Areas." *Journal of the American Institute of Planners* 27 (1) (February 1960): 26–34.

Carroll, J. "Comments on Morehouse Interpretation." *Journal of the American Institute of Planners* 35 (4) (July 1969): 290.

Carroll, Walter. "47-Ton Punch Flattens 15th Ward Structures," *Post-Standard.* Syracuse, N.Y. (August 11, 1954).

Carroll, Walter. "Builders Offer 15th Ward Solution," *Post-Standard.* Syracuse, N.Y. (January 31, 1954): A 11–1.

Chapin, W. S. "What Can Be Done About Traffic Congestion? Part II: Urban Parkways and Expressways." *Civil Engineering* 16 (April 1946): 151–153.

Chase, Edward T. "The Hundred Billion Dollar Question: Will the New National Highway Program Be Used to Attack the Desperate Metropolitan Crisis or to Compound It?" *Architectural Forum* 107 (July 1957): 135.

Cheney, Charles H. "Traffic Street Plan and Boulevard System Adopted for Portland, Oregon." *American City* 25 (July 1921): 47–51.

Churchill, Henry S. "The Place of Land-Use Control in Traffic Control." *Traffic Quarterly* 1 (October 1947): 367–372.

Churchill, Henry S. "Planning in a Free Society." *Journal of the American Institute of Planners* 20 (4) (Fall 1954): 189–191.

Claire, William H. "Dual-Purpose Land Development." *Journal of the American Institute of Planners* 19 (4) (Fall 1953): 227–229.

Clark, Frederick P. "'Limited Motorways,' or 'Freeways.'" *American City* 51 (January 1936): 53–56.

Clarke, Gilmore D. "Modern Motor Arteries." *American City* 43 (July 1930): 107–108.

Clarke, Gilmore D. "Modern Motor Ways." *Architectural Record* 74 (6) (December 1933): 430–439.

Clarkeson, John. "Urban Expressway Location." *Traffic Quarterly* 7 (April 1953): 252–260.

Clay, Grady. "Main Street 1969: Miracle Miles or a Big Mess." *Journal of the American Planning Association* 23 (3) (1957): 131–134.

Clay, Grady. "The Tiger Is Through the Gate." *Landscape Architecture* 49 (2) (Winter 1958–1959): 79–82.

Colcord, Frank C., Jr. "Transportation and the Political Culture." *Highway Research Record* 356 (1971): 32–42.

"Comments on Educating Planners." *Journal of the American Institute of Planners* 36 (4) (July 1970): 220–228.

"Comments on the Demonstration Cities Program." *Journal of the American Institute of Planners* 32 (6) (November 1966): 366–376.

"Completion of X-Way Urged as Hearing Opens." *Press Scimitar*. Memphis, Tenn. (August 18, 1976).

"Conference on Freeways in the Urban Setting." *American Institute of Architects Journal* 38 (November 1962): 27–42.

Cookingham, L. P. "The Kansas City Story." *American City* 73 (September 1958): 170.

Corbett, Harvey Wiley. "Different Levels for Foot, Wheel and Rail." *American City* 31 (July 1924): 2–6.

Cortelyou, S. V. "Streets Cross Over Depressed Highways: Arroyo Seco Has Six Mile Double Lane Arterial." *Architect and Engineer* 127 (October 1936): 48–50.

"Council Kills Motion to Re-Examine Studies." *Times Picayune* (June 17, 1966): 1–1.

Courtney, John M. "Joint Development and Multiple Use of Highway Rights of Way: A Concept Team Approach." *Urban Law Annual* (1970): 39–55.

Cox, William J. "By-Passing Cities in the Vertical Plane." *American City* 60 (October 1945): 95.

Crane, David A. "The City Symbolic." *Journal of the American Institute of Planners* 26 (4) (November 1960): 280–292.

Crane, David A. "Review of *The Image of the City*, by Kevin Lynch." *Journal of the American Institute of Planners* 27 (2) (May 1961): 152–155.

Crane, David A. "The Public Art of City Building." *Annals of the American Academy of Political and Social Science* 352 (March 1964): 84–94.

Crawford, Andrew Wright. "Fairmount Parkway—A Notable Correction of William Penn's Plan." *American City* 29 (July 1923): 18–20.

Creighton, Roger L. "Urban Expressways: Joint Planning of Transportation and Land Use." *American Society of Civil Engineers: Journal of the City Planning Division* 85 (no. CP1) (June 1959): 1–5.

Cron, Frederick W. "Can Engineers Co-operate? Yes!" *Landscape Architecture* 49 (2) (Winter 1958–59): 82–83.

Crosby, W. W. "Freeways Versus Highways." *Planners' Journal* 3 (3) (May-June 1937): 62.

Darling, Philip V. I. "Some Notes on Blighted Areas." *Planners' Journal* 9 (1) (January-March 1943): 9–18.

Darst, Joseph M. "St. Louis Rebuilds." *American City* 65 (August 1950): 100–101.

Davis, Mike. "Urban Renaissance and the Spirit of Postmodernism." *New Left Review* (151) (May/June 1985): 106–113.

de Neufville, Judith Innes, and Stephen E. Barton. "Myths and the Definition of Policy Problems." *Policy Sciences* 20 (3) (1987): 181–206.

Dewey, Richard. "A Critical Look at Freeways to Downtown Areas." *American City* 70 (January 1955): 153–154.

Dill, Malcolm H. "The Cincinnati Metropolitan Master Plan." *Journal of the American Institute of Planners* 14 (1) (Winter 1948): 19–28.

Dilts, James. "City hopes to start corridor road soon." *Baltimore Sun* (1971): C22.

DiMento, Joseph F. C. "Stent (or Dagger) in the Heart of Town: Urban Freeways in Syracuse, 1944–1967." *Journal of Planning History* 8 (2) (May 2009): 133–161.

Dix, Gerald. "Little Plans and Noble Diagrams." *Town Planning Review* 49 (July 1978): 329–352.

Dixon, John M. "Last Hitch in the Inner Belt." *Architectural Forum* 124 (May 1966): 68–71.

Downer, Jay. "County Park Development and Regional Planning." *American City* 32 (May 1925): 509–512.

Downs, Myron D. "Redevelopment Plans for Cincinnati's River Front." *American City* 55 (February 1940): 50.

"Downtown Snarl: A Case for Sorting, Stacking, and Storing." *Architectural Forum* 119 (October 1963): 78–83.

"Downtown Traffic Jams." *American City* 70 (July 1955): 143.

Draper, Earle S. "The TVA Freeway." *American City* 49 (February 1934): 47–48.

Durden, Dennis, and Duane F. Marble. "The Role of Theory in CBD Planning." *Journal of the American Institute of Planners* 27 (1) (February 1961): 10–16.

Duhl, Leonard J. "Planning the Physical Environment." *Highway Research Board Bulletin* (no. 190) (1958): 20–24.

Dunhill, Priscilla. "Expressway Named Destruction." *Architectural Forum* 126 (March 1967): 54–59. Replies by Mark Lowrey and Mrs. D. F. Tobin. *Architectural Forum* 126 (May 1967): 11.

Dunhill, Priscilla. "Reconciling the Conflict of Highways and Cities." *Reporter* 8 (February) (1968): 21–23.

Dunhill, Priscilla. "The Freeway versus the City." *Architectural Forum* 128 (January 1968): 72–77.

Dyckman, John W. "What Makes Planners Plan?" *Journal of the American Institute of Planners* 27 (2) (May 1961): 164–167.

Dyckman, John W. "New Ideas in Planning." *Journal of the American Institute of Planners* 28 (1) (February 1962): 63–65.

Dyckman, John W. "The European Motherland of American Urban Romanticism." *Journal of the American Institute of Planners* 28 (4) (November 1962): 277–281.

Dyckman, John W. "The Scientific World of the City Planners." *American Behavioral Scientist* 6 (6) (February 1963): 46–50.

Dyos, H. J. "Some Social Costs of Railway Building in London." *Journal of Transport History* 3 (1) (May 1957): 23–30.

"Cleveland Praised for Planning." *Herald Journal.* Syracuse, N.Y. (November 9, 1956).

"East-West Project Outlined." *Herald Journal.* Syracuse, N.Y. (March 6, 1954).

Einsweiler, Robert C. "The 1962 Highway Act." *Journal of the American Institute of Planners* 35 (4) (July 1969): 291–292.

"Elevated Highways Only Solution to Traffic Congestion." *Architect and Engineer* 137 (April 1939): 50–52.

"Elevated Highways Versus Depressed Highways." *American City* 55 (October 1940): 61–62.

"Eleventh Hour Rescue Plans Fail: Road Will Screen San Francisco Shrine." *Architectural Forum* 105 (November 1956): 17.

Elliott, Ward. "The Los Angeles Affliction: Suggestions for a Cure." *Public Interest* (38) (Winter 1975): 119–128.

Emery, George F.. "Urban Expressways." *American Planning and Civic Annual* (1947): 123–129.

Ericksen, E. "Gordon. "The Superhighway and City Planning: Some Ecological Considerations with Reference to Los Angeles." *Social Forces* 28 (4) (May 1950): 429–434.

Euston, Andrew F. "Design Concepts for the Future." *Highway Research Record* 220 (1968): 5–10.

Evans, Henry K. "Traffic Planning in San Francisco." *Traffic Quarterly* 3 (1) (Jan. 1949): 31–37.

Ewing, Reid. "Is Los Angeles-Style Sprawl Desirable?" *Journal of the American Planning Association* 63 (1) (Winter 1997): 107–126.

"Express Highways Combined with the 'Steadyflow' System." *American City* 44 (January 1931): 152–155.

"Expressway Approved by Public Hearing." *Post-Standard*. Syracuse, N.Y. (October 3, 1956). A newspaper article with no details other than these, accessed in the archives of the Onondaga Historical Association. Also quoted in *Post-Standard*. Syracuse, N.Y. (April 6, 2008): B-2, col. 1.

"Expressway Plan for Cleveland." *American City* 60 (January 1945): 81.

Fagin, Henry. "Comprehensive Metropolitan Transportation Planning." *Highway Research Board Bulletin* (no. 293) (1961): 33–39.

Fainstein, Norman I., and Susan S. Fainstein. "Is State Planning Necessary for Capital? The US Case." *International Journal of Urban and Regional Research* 9 (4) (December 1985): 485–507.

Feiss, Carl. "Urban Redevelopment and Highway Planning." *Highway Research Board Bulletin* (no. 38) (1951): 31–38.

Feiss, Carl. "Review of *The View from The Road*, by Donald Appleyard, Kevin Lynch, and John R. Myer." *Journal of the American Institute of Architects* 43 (5) (May 1965): 67–68.

Feiss, Carl. "The Foundations of Federal Planning Assistance." *Journal of the American Planning Association* 51 (Spring 1985): 175–184.

Fellman, Gordon. "Neighborhood Protest of an Urban Highway." *Journal of the American Institute of Planners* 35 (March 1969): 118–122.

"15th Ward Housing Site May Change." *Herald Journal*. Syracuse, N.Y. (December 14, 1954).

"55 East and West Side Blocks to Be Taken by City." *Post-Standard*. Syracuse, N.Y. (October 16, 1955).

Filler, Martin. "Moses and Megalopolis." *Art in America* 69 (November 1981): 124–133.

Fisch, Fred W. "Urban Arterial Route Program in New York State." *Traffic Quarterly* 2 (1) (January 1948): 44–52.

Fitch, Robert. "New York 2000: The Secret Life of Urban Real Estate." *Village Voice* (November 17, 1987), 26.

Fitzpatrick, W. W. "One Method of Lessening Street Congestion in Large Cities." *American City* 28 (April 1923): 409.

Fleming, Major General Philip B. "Public Works Planning in War and Peace." *American Highways* 22 (1) (January 1943): 4–6.

"Foes Expect I-40 Park Route Defeat." *Commercial Appeal*. Memphis, Tenn. (October 4, 1977).

Ford, George B. "Digging Deeper into City Planning." *American City* 6 (1912): 557–562.

Forster, William W. "Controlled Access Expressways in Urban Areas: A Symposium." *Highway Research Board Bulletin* (no. 25) (1950), in *Journal of the American Institute of Planners* 17 (3) (Summer 1951): 156–158.

Foster, Mark S. "City Planners and Urban Transportation: The American Response." *Journal of Urban History* 5 (3) (May 1979): 365–396.

Fowler, Charles Evan. "Detroit's Struggle with the Traffic Problem." *American City* 30 (June 1924): 612–615.

Frankel, Glenn. "Richmond's Beltway Battle: Black Richmonders Fight White Suburbanites Over Concrete Noose." *Journal of Urban History* 30 (5) (July 2004): 674–706.

Frederick, Joseph C. "Aesthetic Considerations in Urban Arterial Route Planning." *Highway Research Record* 23 (1963): 22–35.

"Freeways: Role? Necessity? Cost? Location? Impact?" *Commonwealth* 37 (5) (January 1961).

"Freeways in the Urban Setting: Report of Conference at Hershey, Pennsylvania." *Landscape Architecture* 53 (October 1962): 73–79.

Fried, Marc, and Peggy Gleicher. "Some Sources of Residential Satisfaction in an Urban Slum." *Journal of the American Institute of Planners* 27 (4) (November 1961): 305–315.

"Future of the Profession." *Landscape Architecture* 53 (1) (October 1962): 25–26.

Garrison, W. L. "Impacts of Technological Systems on Cities." *Built Environment* 6 (2) (1980): 120–130.

Garrison, W. L. "Rexford G. Tugwell and the Frustration of Planning in New York City." *Journal of the American Planning Association* 51 (Spring 1985): 151–160.

Gelfand, Mark. "Rexford G. Tugwell and the Frustration of Planning in New York City." *Journal of the American Planning Association* 51 (Spring 1985): 151–160.

Gettys, W. E. "Human Ecology and Social Theory." *Social Forces* 18 (1940): 469–476.

Goist, Park Dixon. "Lewis Mumford and 'Anti-Urbanism.'" *Journal of the American Institute of Planners* 35 (5) (September 1969): 340–347.

Goist, Park Dixon. "Seeing Things Whole: A Consideration of Lewis Mumford." *Journal of the American Institute of Planners* 38 (6) (November 1972): 379–391.

Goldfarb, Lawrence A. "Review of *Urban Design: The Architecture of Towns and Cities*, by Paul D. Spreiregen." *Journal of the American Institute of Planners* 33 (1) (January 1967): 62–64.

Goldstein, Sidney. "Economic and Social Impact Considerations in Highway Programs." *Urban Law Annual* (1970): 3–19.

Gordon, Peter, and Harry W. Richardson. "Are Compact Cities a Desirable Planning Goal?" *Journal of the American Planning Association* 63 (1) (Winter 1997): 95–106.

Gottdiener, M. "Space as a Force of Production." *International Journal of Urban and Regional Research* 11 (3) (September 1987): 405–416.

Gray, Oscar S. "Environmental Requirements of Highway and Historic Preservation Legislation." *Catholic University Law Review* 20 (1) (1970): 45–67.

Grier, George W. "Social Impact Analysis of an Urban Freeway System." *Highway Research Record* 305 (1970): 63–74.

"Grimm Calls for Dynamic City Planning." *Herald Journal*. Syracuse, N.Y. (February 28, 1955).

"Guidelines for Urban Freeway Design Developed in Joint Conference of Officials with Design Professions." *Architectural Record* 132 (1) (July 1962): 12.

Gulick, Luther. "The New Highway Program Requires Metropolitan Cooperation." In "The New Highways: Challenge to the Metropolitan Region," *Urban Land Institute Technical Bulletin* (no. 31) (November 1957): 85–92.

Gutman, Robert. "Review of *Cities and Space: The Future Use of Urban Land*, edited by Lowdon Wingo, Jr." *Journal of the American Institute of Planners* 31 (3) (August 1965): 274–277.

Gutman, Robert. "Educating Architects: Pedagogy and the Pendulum." *Public Interest* (80) (Summer 1985): 67–91.

Hale, Peter P. "The City Means Nothing to Traffic." *Traffic Quarterly* 2 (2) (April 1948): 175–182.

Hamburg, John R., and Roger L. Creighton. "Predicting Chicago's Land Use Pattern." *Journal of the American Institute of Planners* 25 (2) (May 1959): 67–72.

Hamilton, Frederick. "El-Way to Ease San Francisco Traffic." *Architect and Engineer* 154 (September 1943): 27–29.

Hancock, John. "Planners in the Changing American City, 1900–1940." *Journal of the American Institute of Planners* 33 (5) (September 1967): 290–304.

Handler, A. "Benjamin. "What Is Planning Theory?" *Journal of the American Institute of Planners* 23 (3) (1957): 144–150.

Hansen, Walter G. "How Accessibility Shapes Land Use." *Journal of the American Institute of Planners* 25 (May 1959): 73–76.

Harris, Britton. "Plan or Projection: An Examination of the Use of Models in Planning." *Journal of the American Institute of Planners* 26 (4) (November 1960): 265–272.

Harris, Chauncy D., and Edward L. Ullman. "The Nature of Cities." *Annals of the American Academy of Political and Social Science* 242 (November 1945): 7–17.

Hartman, Chester. "Relocation: Illusory Promises and No Relief." *Virginia Law Review* 57 (1971): 745–817.

Hazen, Joseph C., Jr. "Highways and the City." *American Highways* 36 (3) (July 1957): 11–12.

Heintzelman, Walter G. "The City and the Engineer." *American Society of Civil Engineers: Journal of Engineering Issues* 97 (no. PP1) (October 1971): 55–63.

Henard, E. "The Cities of the Future." *American City* 4 (January 1911): 27–31.

Herrold, George H. "Trade or Traffic In City Centers." *Journal of the American Institute of Planners* 11 (Summer 1945): 35.

Herzlinger, Regina. "Costs, Benefits, and West Side Highway." *Public Interest* (55) (Spring 1979): 77–98.

Hestermann Dean, W., et al. "Impacts of a consent decree on 'the last urban freeway': Interstate 105 in Los Angeles county." *Transportation Research Part A, Policy and Practice* 27 (4) (July 1993): 299–313.

Hewes, L. I. "Metropolitan Highway Problems." *Civil Engineering (New York, N.Y.)* 9 (12) (December 1939): 715–718.

Highway Research Board, Committee on Controlled Access in Urban Areas. "Controlled Access Expressways in Urban Areas: A Symposium." *Highway Research Board Bulletin* (no. 25) (July 1950).

"Highways into Cities." *Architectural Forum* 106 (February 1957): 98.

Hill, David R. "Lewis Mumford's Ideas on the City." *Journal of the American Planning Association* 51 (Autumn 1985): 407–421.

Hill, David R. "Jane Jacobs' Ideas on Big, Diverse Cities: A Review and Commentary." *Journal of the American Planning Association* 54 (3) (Summer 1988): 302–314.

Hill, G. S. "Proposed Solution of San Francisco-Oakland Bay Area Motor Vehicle Traffic Problem." *Architect and Engineer* 202 (July 1955): 7.

Hillenbrand, Bernard F. "The Road Program—Opportunity and Challenge." *American Highways* 35 (4) (October 1956): 12.

Holleran, Leslie G. "Problems in the Separation of Highway Grade Crossings." *American City* 38 (March 1928): 75–77.

Holmos, E. E., Jr. "Architects and Highway Planning." *Progressive Architecture* 42 (December 1961): 68.

"Hooking into the Interstate System." *American City* 72 (April 1957): 132–133.

Hoppenfeld, Morton. "The Role of Design in City Planning." *Journal of the American Institute of Planners* 26 (2) (May 1960): 98–103.

Hoppenfeld, Morton. "The City Planning Standpoint." *Journal of the American Institute of Architects* 38 (November 1962): 32–35.

Horvath, Ronald J. "Machine Space." *Geographical Review* 64 (April 1964): 167–188.

Horwood, Edgar M. "Freeway Impact on Municipal Land Planning Effort." *Highway Research Board Bulletin* (no. 268) (1960): 1–12.

Houghteling, Joseph C. "Confessions of a Highway Commissioner." *Cry California* 1 (2) (Spring 1966): 29–32.

"How a Highway Program Is Sold at the Local Level." *American Highways* 35 (4) (October 1956): 22–24.

"How to Rebuild Cities Downtown." *Architectural Forum* 102 (June 1955): 122.

Howard, John T. "In Defense of Planning Commissions." *Journal of the American Institute of Planners* 17 (2) (Spring 1951): 89–94.

Howard, John T. "Planning Is a Profession." *Journal of the American Institute of Planners* 20 (2) (Spring 1954): 58–59.

Howard, John T. "Metropolitan Planning and the Federal Highway Program." *American City* 72 (June 1957): 225.

Howser, Theron R. "A Plan for a City Built to Fit the Automobile." *American City* 49 (July 1934): 56–57.

Hoyt, Homer. "Changing Land-Use Patterns as a Basis for Long-Range Highway Planning." *Highway Research Board Bulletin* (no. 64) (1952): 1–8.

Hubbard, Henry V. "Planning the City and the Region—Then and Now." *American City* 43 (September 1930): 99–100.

"I-40 Issue Traces Trail of Controversy to '53." *Commercial Appeal.* Memphis, Tenn. (October 1, 1977).

Iden, V. G. "Elevated Highway Design for Speed, Safety and Beauty." *American City* 53 (May 1938): 46–48.

Ihlder, John. "Rehabilitation of Blighted Areas: The Part of City Planning." *City Planning* 6 (2) (April 1930): 106–118.

"In the Path of the Interstates." *City* 4 (1) (June/July 1970): 25–31.

Innes, Judith. "The Power of Data Requirements." *Journal of the American Planning Association* 54 (Summer 1988): 275–278.

"Is Super-Congestion Inevitable." *American City* 36 (June 1927): 800–805.

Ives, Howard S. "Role and Progress of the Landscape Engineer in a Highway Organization." *Highway Research Record* 23 (1963): 2–6.

Jackson, J. B. "Highway Planning." *Landscape Architecture* 47 (4) (July 1957): 504.

Jacobs, Allan, and Donald Appleyard. "An Urban Design Manifesto." *Journal of the American Planning Association* 53 (Winter 1987): 112–120.

James, Henry. "The Building of the City: A Review." *Regional Plan Association Bulletin* (no. 6) (February 15, 1932): 1–12.

James, L. Douglas. "The Civil Engineer Can Improve His Public Image." *American Society of Civil Engineers: Journal of Professional Practice* 93 (no. PP1) (December 1967): 11–15. Discussion by Alan C. Twort, *American Society of Civil Engineers: Journal of Professional Practice* 94 (no. PP1) (June 1968): 37–38. Closure by L. Douglas James, *American Society of Civil Engineers. Journal of Professional Practice* 95 (no. PP1) (July 1969): 89.

Jennings, Allyn R. "New York Strides Ahead in Park and Parkway Improvements." *American City* 52 (July 1937): 43–45.

Johnson, Walter K. "The 1962 Highway Act: Its Long Term Significance." *Urban Law Annual* (1970): 57–64.

Johnston, Norman J. "Harland Bartholomew: Precedent for the Profession." *Journal of the American Institute of Planners* 39 (2) (March 1973): 115–124.

"Joint Development and Multiple Uses: Integrated Transportation Corridors." *Catholic University Law Review* 20 (1) (1970): 93–117.

Jordy, William H. "The Symbolic Essence of Modern European Architecture of the Twenties and Its Continuing Influence." *Journal of the Society of Architectural Historians* 22 (October 1963): 177–187.

Kain, John F., and John R. Meyer. "Transportation and Poverty." *Public Interest* (18) (Winter 1970): 75–87.

Kassabaum, George E. "The Highway Hangup." *Journal of the American Institute of Architects* 51 (May 1969): 44.

Kelly, John Barry, II. "Challenging Highways: Widening the Access to Judicial Review." *Catholic University Law Review* 20 (1) (1970): 143–156.

Kelly, John F. "Residences and Freeways." *American Highways* 36 (3) (July 1957): 5.

Kemp, Louis Ward. "Aesthetes and Engineers: The Occupational Ideology of Highway Design." *Technology and Culture* 27 (October 1986): 759–797.

Kendrick, Boyce L. "The Bumpy Road to a Better Highway." *Journal of the American Institute of Architects* (February 1969): 70–77.

Kennedy, G. "A National System of Interstate Highways." *American Highways* 23 (3) (July 1944): 7.

Klein, Norman. "Baltimore Urban Design Concept Team." *Highway Research Record* 220 (1968): 11–16.

Kleniewski, Nancy. "Triage and Urban Planning: A Case Study of Philadelphia." *International Journal of Urban and Regional Research* 10 (4) (December 1986): 563–579.

Koltnow, Peter G. "Changing Highway Priorities: Construction, Economy, and Environmental Improvement." *Catholic University Law Review* 20 (1) (1970): 119–131.

Kostritsky, George E. "The New Expressway Image." *Journal of the American Institute of Architects* 38 (November 1962): 41–42.

Krader, Lawrence. "Research Needs in the Behavioral Sciences Relative to Highway Planning." *Highway Research Board Bulletin* (no. 256) (1960): 5–8.

Krueckeberg, Donald A. "The Story of the Planner's Journal." *Journal of the American Planning Association* 46 (January 1980): 5–21.

Lash, Michael. "Community Conflict and Highway Planning: The Case of a Town That Didn't Want a Freeway." *Highway Research Record* 69 (1963): 1–17.

Lathrop, William H., Jr. "The San Francisco Freeway Revolt." *Transportation Engineering Journal* 97 (February 1971): 133–144.

Lay, Charles Downing. "Proposed Scheme for High-Speed Trunk Highway Through a Suburban or City District." *Architectural Record* 73 (1) (January 1933): 15.

Lay, Charles Downing. "New Towns for High-Speed Roads." *Architectural Record* 78 (5) (November 1935): 352–354.

"Le Corbusier and Media: A Dialogue with Jean-Louis Cohen." *Design Book Review* (no. 14) (Spring 1988): 15–18.

Lee, Douglass B. "Requiem for Large-Scale Models." *Journal of the American Institute of Planners* 39 (3) (May 1973): 163–178.

Lee, James E. "The Role of the Planner in the Present: A Problem in Identification." *Journal of the American Institute of Planners* 24 (3) (1958): 151–157.

Lee, James E. "Planning and Professionalism." *Journal of the American Institute of Planners* 26 (1) (February 1960): 25–30.

Levin, David R. "Limited-Access Highways in Urban Areas." *American City* 59 (February 1944): 77.

Levin, David R. "Expressways and the Central Business District." *American Planning and Civic Annual* (1954): 131–148.

"Linking of Arterial to Slum Clearing 'Needs Exploring.'" *Post-Standard*. Syracuse, N.Y. (June 2, 1955).

Linville, Jack. "Troubled Urban Interstates." *Nation's Cities* 8 (12) (December 1970): 8–11.

Lochner, Harry W. "The Integration of Expressways With Other Urban Elements." *Traffic Quarterly* 7 (3) (July 1953): 346–352.

Lynch, Kevin, and Lloyd Rodwin. "A Theory of Urban Form." *Journal of the American Institute of Planners* 24 (4) (1958): 201–214.

MacBride, Dexter. "The Impact of Modern Freeways Upon the Community and Individual." *Architect and Engineer* 205 (May 1956): 23.

MacDonald, Thomas H. "Looking Toward the Highway Future." *American Highways* 16 (1) (January 1937): 4–7.

MacDonald, Thomas H. "Highways and the National Defense." *American Highways* 19 (4) (October 1940): 11–14.

MacDonald, Thomas H. "The City's Place in Post-War Highway Planning." *American City* 58 (February 1943): 42–44.

MacDonald, Thomas H. "The Case for Urban Expressways." *American City* 62 (6) (June 1947): 92–93.

MacDonald, Thomas H. "The Highway Improvement Program in Relation to the Conventional Public Works Concept." *American Highways* 26 (January 1947): 10, 28.

MacDonald, Thomas H. "The Interstate System in Urban Areas." *American Planning and Civic Annual* (1950): 114–119.

Malcher, Fritz. "Planning Arterial Highways to Meet Modern Needs." *American City* 42 (January 1930): 158.

Malcher, Fritz. "A Traffic Planner Imagines a City." *American City* 44 (March 1931): 134–135.

Malcher, Fritz. "Express Highways Combined with the 'Steadyflow' System." *American City* 44 (January 1931): 152–155.

Malcher, Fritz. "Will 1932 Witness the Beginning of a New Epoch in Highway Design and Construction?" *American City* 46 (January 1932): 104–105.

Bibliography 325

Malley, Frank H. "Urban Freeways: Paper Abstract." *Journal of the American Institute of Planners* 14 (4) (Fall 1948): 23–24.

Malley, Frank H., and Milton Breivogel. "Urban Freeways." *Journal of the American Planning Association* 14 (4) (1948): 23–26.

Manheim, Marvin. "The Impacts of Highways on Environmental Values." *Highway Research Record* 305 (1970): 26–27.

Marris, Peter. "The Social Implications of Urban Redevelopment." *Journal of the American Institute of Planners* 28 (3) (August 1962): 180–186.

Mashaw, Jerry L. "The Legal Structure of Frustration: Alternative Strategies for Public Choice Concerning Federally Aided Highway Construction." *University of Pennsylvania Law Review* 122 (1973): 1–96.

Mayer, Harold M. "Moving People and Goods in Tomorrow's Cities." *Annals of the American Academy of Political and Social Science* 242 (November 1945): 116–128.

McClintock, Miller. "Street Traffic—Past and Future." *American City* 43 (September 1930): 115–116.

McConochie, William R. "Planning Post-War Highways in Cities." *Traffic Engineering* 15 (8) (May 1945): 319.

McConochie, William R. "Public Transit on Freeways." *American City* 75 (May 1960): 106–108.

McMahon, L. E., and A. I. Bourquin. "Detroit's Evolution of an Expressway System." *Landscape Architecture* 44 (October 1953): 4–10.

McMonagle, J. Carl. "Urban Planning Problems." *Highway Research Board Bulletin* (no. 6) (1946): 33–40.

McVoy, Arthur D. "Pedestrian-Way Business Districts." *American City* 72 (March 1957): 136–138.

"Mead Akin to DeWitt Clinton and Urban Renewal to Erie Canal." *Post-Standard*. Syracuse, N.Y. (January 21, 1956).

Melamed, A. "Review of *The Death and Life of Great American Cities*, by Jane Jacobs." *Journal of the American Institute of Planners* 28 (2) (May 1962): 136–139.

Metzenbaum, James. "Planning the Main Thoroughfares and Open Spaces for an Entire Region." *American City* 37 (November 1927): 580–582.

Meyerson, Martin. "Research and City Planning." *Journal of the American Institute of Planners* 20 (4) (Fall 1954): 201–204.

Meyerson, Martin, and Robert B. Mitchell. "Changing City Patterns." *Annals of the American Academy of Political and Social Science* 242 (November 1945): 149–162.

Michael, Harold L. "Interdisciplinary Education for Urban Planning." *American Society of Civil Engineers: Journal of Professional Practice* 90 (no. PP1) (January 1964): 29–33. Discussion by Felix A. Wallace and Sergei Grimm, *American Society of Civil Engineers: Journal of Professional Practice* 91 (no. PP1) (January

1965): 33–36. Closure by Harold L. Michael, *American Society of Civil Engineers: Journal of Professional Practice* 91 (no. PP2) (September 1965): 79–80.

Miller, Richard A. "Expressway Blight." *Architectural Forum* 111 (October 1959): 59–63.

Miltoun, Francis. "The Auto-Strade (Automobile Toll Highways) of Italy." *Roads and Streets* 68 (April 1928): 194–196.

"Milwaukee Visualizes a Terminal Area for Air-Water-Rail Transportation." *American City* 43 (July 1930): 143.

Minderman, Earl. "Chicago's New Lake-Front Highway." *American City* 57 (June 1942): 41–42.

Mitchell, Robert B., ed. "Building the Future City." *Annals of the American Academy of Political and Social Science* 352 (November 1945).

Mitchell, Robert B. "The New Frontier in Metropolitan Planning." *Journal of the American Institute of Planners* 27 (3) (August 1961): 169–175.

Mitchell, Robert B., ed. Urban Revival: Goals and Standards. *Annals of the American Academy of Political and Social Science* 352 (March 1964).

Mocine, Corwin R. "The Planning Profession's Responsibility to the People: Guidance." *Journal of the American Institute of Planners* 14 (4) (Fall 1948): 16–20.

Mocine, Corwin R. "Urban Physical Planning and the 'New Planning.'" *Journal of the American Institute of Planners* 32 (4) (July 1966): 234–237.

Mohl, Raymond A. "Ike and the Interstates: Creeping Toward Comprehensive Planning." *Journal of Planning History* 2 (3) (August 2003): 237–262.

Mohl, Raymond A. "Interstating Miami: Urban Expressways and the Changing American City." *Tequesta: The Journal of the Historical Association of Southern Florida* 68 (2008): 193–226.

Montgomery, Roger. "Spoons in the Morning, Cities in the Afternoon." *Landscape* 18 (2) (Spring-Summer 1969): 3–38.

Morehouse, Thomas A. "Author's Reply to Carroll and Einsweiler." *Journal of the American Institute of Planners* 35 (6) (November 1969): 416.

Morehouse, Thomas A. "The 1962 Highway Act: A Study in Artful Interpretation." *Journal of the American Institute of Planners* 35 (3) (May 1969): 160–168.

Morris, Robert L. "Evaluating the Requirements for a Downtown Circulation System." *Highway Research Board Bulletin* 347 (1962): 211–221.

Moses, Robert. "The Comprehensive Parkway System of the New York Metropolitan Region." *Civil Engineering (New York, N.Y.)* 9 (3) (March 1939): 160–162.

Moses, Robert. "Parks, Parkways, Express Arteries, and Related Plans for New York City After the War." *American City* 58 (December 1943): 53–58.

Moses, Robert. "Public Building to Come." *American Highways* 22 (3) (July 1943): 22–23.

Moses, Robert. "New Super-Highways: Blessing or Blight?" *Harper's* (December 1956): 27–31.

"Motor Age Highways." *American City* 44 (February 1931): 144.

Mott, George Fox, ed. Urban Change and the Planning Syndrome. *Annals of the American Academy of Political and Social Science* 405 (January 1973).

Mott, Seward H., and Buford Hayden. "Providing for Automotive Services in Urban Land Development." *Traffic Quarterly* 7 (3) (July 1953): 367–379.

Moynihan, Daniel P. "New Roads and Urban Chaos." *Reporter* 14 (April 1960): 13.

Moynihan, Daniel P. "The War Against the Automobile." *Public Interest* (3) (Spring 1966): 10–26.

Moynihan, Daniel P. "Policy vs. Program in the '70s." *Public Interest* 90 (Summer 1970): 93–94.

Mumford, Lewis. "The Highway and the City." *Architectural Record* 123 (April 1958): 179–182.

Murphy, Raymond. "The Central Business District and Its Implications for Highway Planning." *Highway Research Board Bulletin* 221 (1959): 29–32.

Murphy, Raymond E., J. E. Vance, Jr., and Bart J. Epstein. "Internal Structure of the CBD." *Economic Geography* 31 (1) (January 1955): 21–46.

Myhra, David. "Rexford Guy Tugwell: Initiator of America's Greenbelt New Towns, 1935 to 1936." *Journal of the American Institute of Planners* 40 (3) (May 1974): 176–188.

"New Highways: Number One Enemy? Ten Specialists View (with Some Alarm) the Highway Program." *Landscape Architecture* 49 (2) (Winter 1958–59): 79–98.

"New Public Housing Seen Inevitable." *Herald Journal.* Syracuse, N.Y. (June 23, 1954).

"New Through-Traffic Parkway in New York City." *American City* 50 (July 1935): 79.

Newton, Quigg. "Planning Comes of Age." *Journal of the American Institute of Planners* 23 (4) (1957): 185–191.

"New York to Have a $13,500,000 Elevated Express Highway." *American City* 35 (1926): 8–10.

"New York's West Side Improvement." *American City* 52 (November 1937): 52.

Noble, Charles M. "Highway Planning in Metropolitan Areas." *American Planning and Civic Annual* (1948): 104–112.

"Non-Blight Elevated Expressways." *American City* 77 (September 1962): 157.

Norton, Perry, Jr. "The Expressway Dilemma." *Journal of the American Institute of Planners* 14 (Fall 1948): 36.

Novick, David. "The Civil Engineer in the Multidisiplinary Design Team." *American Society of Civil Engineers: Journal of Engineering Issues* 98 (no. PP2) (April 1972): 221–226.

Nunn, Douglas. "Community Acceptance of Highway Corridor Development." *American Society of Civil Engineers: Journal of Engineering Issues* 101 (no. EI3) (July 1975): 337–350.

Obrand, Michael. "Protecting Public Parks from Highway Intrusion." *Hastings Law Journal* 23 (1973): 449–465.

Ogburn, Charlton, Jr. "The Motorcar vs. America." *American Heritage* 21 (4) (June 1970): 104–110.

Oglesby, Clarkson H., Bruce Bishop, and Gene E. Willeke. "A Method for Decisions Among Freeway Location Alternatives Based on User and Community Preferences." *Highway Research Record* 305 (1970): 1–15.

O'Leary, Jeremiah D., Jr. "Evaluating the Environmental Impact of an Urban Expressway." *Traffic Quarterly* 23 (3) (July 1969): 341–351.

Olson, Sherry. "Baltimore Imitates the Spider." *Annals of the Association of American Geographers. Association of American Geographers* 69 (4) (December 1979): 557–574.

Olson, Sherry. "Urban Metabolism and Morphogenesis." *Urban Geography* 3 (1982): 87–109.

"160-Mile Elevated Super-Highway System Proposed for Chicago." *Roads and Streets* 76 (December 1933): 433–437.

"On Freedom, Freeways, and Flexibility: The Private Correspondence of Messrs Wolfe and Mumford." *Journal of the American Institute of Planners* 27 (1) (February 1961): 74–77.

"Only 718 Units in Housing for Uprooted." *Syracuse Post-Standard* (May 5, 1957).

Oppermann, Paul. "A Planner's View of Express Highways." *Highway Research Board Bulletin* (no. 10) (1947): 19–26.

Orton, Lawrence M. "Bankrupt Principles of Urban Growth." *American City* 76 (October 1961): 101–103.

Osborn, Michelle. "The Crosstown is Dead, Long Live the Crosstown: Philadelphia's Controversial Crosstown Expressway." *Architectural Forum* 135 (October 1971): 38–41.

"Outstanding Road Construction in Wayne County, Michigan." *American City* 44 (January 1931): 85–88.

"Panel Discussion on Expressways and the Central Business District." *American Planning and Civic Annual* (1954): 131–148.

Pastier, John. "To Live and Drive in L.A." *Planning* 51 (2) (February 1986): 21–25.

"Pattern for the Future: Gowanus Elevated Parkway." *Architectural Forum* 78 (May 1943): 4.

Perin, Constance. "A Noiseless Secession from the Comprehensive Plan." *Journal of the American Institute of Planners* 33 (5) (September 1967): 336–347.

Perloff, Harvey S. "Regional Research and Highway Planning." *Highway Research Board Bulletin* (no. 190) (1958): 14–19.

Perry, Clarence A. "Planning a Neighborhood Unit." *American City* 41 (September 1929): 124–127.

Peters, James. "Interstates: Nearing the End of the Road." *Planning* 47 (December 1981): 12–15.

"Philadelphia Embarks on Vast Improvement Program." *American City* 65 (May 1950): 130–131.

"Philadelphia's Long Look at Oncoming Traffic." *American City* 72 (June 1957): 183.

Pikarsky, Milton. "Joint Development Concept: Chicago Crosstown Expressway." *Highway Research Record* 220 (1968): 17–19.

"Pittsburgh Begins to Rebuild." *American City* 54 (March 1939): 49.

"Planners Appraise the Profession." *American City* 77 (July 1962): 136.

"Planning Arterial Highways to Meet Modern Needs." *American City* 42 (January 1930): 158.

"Planning for City Superhighways." *Traffic Engineering* 11 (4) (August 1940): 62–64.

"Planning for Metropolitan Transportation." *Journal of the American Institute of Planners* 18 (2) (Spring 1952): 75–79.

"Planning Idea: Take to the Streets, Relocation Housing without Resident Removal." *Progressive Architecture* 49 (August 1968): 148–150.

"Possibility Looms of New Site for Housing Project." *Post-Standard.* Syracuse, N.Y. (December 10, 1954).

Powell, Charles U. "Varying Treatment of Arterial Parkways." *American City* 48 (May 1933): 36–38.

"Proposed Approaches to Hudson River Bridge." *American City* 40 (June 1929): 100.

Pouncey, G. "Andrew. "Harland Bartholomew: September 14, 1889—December 2, 1989." *Planning History Present* 3 (2) (1990): 1.

"Pressures in the Process of Administrative Decision: A Study of Highway Location." *University of Pennsylvania Law Review* 108 (February 1960): 534–586.

Preston, Richard E. "The Zone in Transition: A Study of Urban Land Use Patterns." *Economic Geography* 42 (3) (July 1966): 236–260.

Pritchett, W. E., and M. H. Rose. "Introduction: Politics and the American City, 1940–1990." *Journal of Urban History* 34 (2) (January 2008): 209–220.

"Proposal to Move 15th Ward Families to West End Site Urged at Parley." *Post-Standard.* Syracuse, N.Y. (March 6, 1954).

"Proposed Approaches to Hudson River Bridge." *American City* 40 (June 1929): 100.

"Public Housing Needed as 15th Ward Solution, State Housing Head Says." *Post-Standard.* Syracuse, N.Y. (June 23, 1954).

Purdy, Lawson. "The Housing of the Very Poor." *American City* 39 (July 1928): 128–129.

Pushkarev, Boris. "Highway Location as a Problem of Urban and Landscape Design." *Highway Research Record* 23 (1963): 7–18.

Pushkarev, Boris. "Review of *The View from the Road*, by Donald Appleyard, Kevin Lynch, and John R. Myer." *Journal of the American Institute of Planners* 31 (August 1965): 267–268.

"Put Public Transit on Expressway Malls." *American City* 67 (March 1952): 143.

Quinn, James A. "The Burgess Zonal Hypothesis and Its Critics." *American Sociological Review* 5 (1940): 210–218.

Rabin, Yale. "Federal Urban Transportation Policy and the Highway Planning Process in Metropolitan Areas." *Annals of the American Academy of Political and Social Science* 451 (September 1980): 21–35.

"Raised Sidewalks and Traffic Separation Urged for Chicago." *American City* 35 (September 1926): 334–336.

Randolph, Warson. "Street Widening in New Bedford, Mass." *American City* 10 (May 1914): 471–473.

Randolph, Warson. "Two Notable Examples of Street Widening in New York City." *American City* 36 (March 1927): 340–343.

Rannells, John. "Transportation Planning." *Journal of the American Institute of Planners* 26 (3) (August 1960): 186–194.

Rannells, John. "Approaches to Analysis." *Journal of the American Institute of Planners* 27 (1) (February 1961): 17–25.

Rannells, John. "Introduction to Frustrations and Fruitions: Conference on Freeways in the Urban Setting." *Journal of the American Institute of Architects* 38 (November 1962): 28.

Rappaport, Dr. "Ing. Ph. A. "New Highway Design and Construction in Germany." *American City* 49 (October 1934): 69.

Rappaport, Dr. "New Methods of Highway Control and Development in Germany." *American City* 49 (February 1934): 52.

Ravetz, Alison. "Changing Attitudes: The Idea of Value in the Inner City." *Built Environment* 4 (3) (1978): 177–182.

Ravitz, Mel J. "The Sociologist as a Participant in an Urban Planning Program." *Journal of the American Institute of Planners* 20 (2) (Spring 1954): 76–80.

"Redevelopment Plan for Cincinnati's Blighted Riverfront." *American City* 62 (January 1947): 78–79.

Redmond, W. R. "Public Attitudes Towards Transportation." *American Society of Civil Engineers: Journal of Engineering Issues* 99 (no. PP1) (January 1973): 77–83.

Reid, Paul M. "Cooperation Between the Planner and the Traffic Engineer." *Proceedings of the Institute of Traffic Engineers* (1957): 64–67.

"Renewal Sites Tied to Artery." *Syracuse Herald American*. Syracuse, N.Y. (October 16, 1955).

"Renewing Our Cities: San Francisco Decides to Fight Blight." *Architectural Forum* 102 (June 1955): 12.

"Research to Emphasize Urban Problems." *American City* 75 (July 1960): 11.

Riedesel, G. A., and C. John. "Cook. "Desirability Rating and Route Selection." *Highway Research Record* 305 (1970): 16–25.

Rip, Arie. "Controversies as Informal Technology Assessment." *Knowledge: Creation, Diffusion, Utilization* 8 (2) (December 1986): 349–371.

Roeseler, W. G. "Kansas City's Downtown Story." *American City* 71 (April 1956): 123–124.

Rogers, Archibald C. "The Urban Freeway: An Experiment in Team Design and Decision-Making." *Highway Research Record* 220 (1968): 20–28.

Rosener, Judy B. "A Cafeteria of Techniques and Critiques." *Public Management* 57 (December 1975): 16–19.

Rouse, James W. "The Highways and Urban Growth." The New Highways: Challenge to the Metropolitan Region. *Urban Land Institute Technical Bulletin* (no. 31) (November 1957): 25–30.

Row, Arthur T. "Transportation in the Center City Development Plan for Philadelphia." *Highway Research Board Bulletin* (no. 293) (1961): 45–57.

Saarinen, Eliel. "Architecture and City Planning." *City Planning* 1 (3) (October 1925): 143–155.

Saarinen, Eliel. "Green-Belts, Traffic Efficiency, and Quietness of Living in Urban Areas." *American City* 58 (April 1943): 57–59.

Sack, Kevin. "New York Told to Repay Westway Fund." *New York Times* (August 11, 1990).

Sale, James, and Eleanor Steinberg. "Effects on Nonrelocated Households of Building a Highway in a Dense Residential Area." *Highway Research Record* 356 (1971): 173.

Samuelson, Robert J. "Cambridge and the Inner Belt Highway: Some Problems are Simply Insoluble." *Harvard Crimson* (June 2, 1967). Available at: http://www.thecrimson.com/article/1967/6/2/cambridge-and-the-inner-belt-highway/.

Schermerhorn, Richard, Jr. "A Practical Program for the Protection and Development of Roadside Beauty." *American City* 42 (March 1930): 140.

Schrag, Zachary M. "The Freeway Fight in Washington, D.C.: The Three Sisters Bridge in Three Administrations." *Journal of Urban History* 30 (5) (July 2004): 648–673.

Schulman, Sy. "Review of *Highway Engineering*, by Laurence I. Hewes and Clarkson H. Oglesby." *Journal of the American Institute of Planners* 22 (2) (Spring 1956): 115–116.

Schuyler, Montgomery, and Liam Dunne. "The Highway's Homeless." *Architectural Forum* 85 (September 1946): 46.

Schwartz, Gary T. "Urban Freeways and the Interstate System." *Southern California Law Review* 49 (March 1976): 173–264.

Sears, Bradford G. "Education and Recruitment of Landscape Architects for Highway Organizations." *Highway Research Record* 23 (1963): 19–21.

Seeley, John R. "New York State Prepares for City Arterial Routes." *American Highways* 23 (4) (October 1944): 5.

Seeley, John R. "New York State's Answer to Urban Traffic Problems." *American City* 63 (July 1948): 72–74.

Seeley, John R. "What Is Planning? Definition and Strategy." *Journal of the American Institute of Planners* 28 (2) (May 1962): 91–97.

Seely, Bruce E. "The Scientific Mystique in Engineering: Highway Research at the Bureau of Public Roads, 1918–1940." *Technology and Culture* 25 (October 1984): 798–831.

Segoe, Ladislas. "Rochester's Traffic Strainer." *American City* 69 (April 1954): 133.

Segoe, Ladislas. "How Urban Expressways Should Be Designed." *American City* 72 (November 1957): 193.

Sells, Charles H. "New York State Prepares for City Arterial Routes." *American Highways* 23 (4) (October 1944): 5.

Sells, Charles H. "New York State's Answer to Urban Traffic Problems." *American City* 63 (July 1948): 72–74.

Sevilla, Charles M. "Asphalt Through the Model Cities: A Study of Highways and the Urban Poor." *Journal of Urban Law* 49 (November 1971): 297–322.

Sewell, Marjorie. "How Blighted Areas in Philadelphia and Boston Might Be Transformed." *American City* 58 (October 1943): 47–49.

Sewell, Marjorie. "Replanning an Obsolete Square Mile." *American City* 58 (December 1943): 46.

Sewell, Marjorie. "Huge Model Visualizes Committee's Plans for 'Toledo Tomorrow.'" *American City* 60 (July 1945): 72–74.

Shapiro, Sidney M. "Parkways in New York Metropolitan Area." *Civil Engineering (New York, N.Y.)* 12 (5) (May 1942): 239–242.

Sheets, Frank T. "The Development of Primary Roads during the Next Quarter Century." *American Highways* 18 (October 1939): 34.

Shurtleff, Arthur A. "Boston Metropolitan Planning." *City Planning* 6 (1) (January 1930): 15–19.

Silen, Arthur R. "Highway Location in California: The Federal Impact." *Hastings Law Journal* 21 (1970): 781–830.

Silver, Christopher. "Neighborhood Planning in Historical Perspective." *Journal of the American Planning Association* 51 (Spring 1985): 161–174.

Silver, Robert H. "Lower Manhattan Expressway." *Architectural Forum* 127 (September 1967): 66–69.

Simmons, Bob. "The Freeway Establishment." *Cry California* 3 (2) (Spring 1968): 31–38.

Siskind, P. "Shades of Black and Green: The Making of Racial and Environmental Liberalism in Nelson Rockefeller's New York." *Journal of Urban History* 34 (2) (January 2008): 243–265.

Skocpol, Theda. "Legacies of New Deal Liberalism." *Dissent* 30 (Winter 1983): 33–44.

Smith, Chloethiel Woodard. "Esthetic Lion-Taming in the City." *Journal of the American Institute of Architects* 38 (November 1962): 36–38.

Smith, Nathan L. "Blighted Areas and Traffic." *Traffic Quarterly* 1 (4) (October 1947): 312–324.

"Speed and Safety at a Bridge Approach." *American City* 42 (February 1930): 161.

Squire, Latham C., and Howard M. Bassett. "A New Type of Thoroughfare: The 'Freeway.'" *American City* 47 (November 1932): 64–66.

Stanberry, V. B. "What Type Regional Planning for the Bay Area." *Journal of the American Institute of Planners* 18 (2) (Spring 1952): 63–67.

"State Won't Abandon I-40 Plans, Shaw Says." *Commercial Appeal*, Memphis, Tenn. (October 4, 1977).

Stein, Clarence S. "The Case for New Towns." *Planners' Journal* 5 (2) (March–June 1939): 39–41. Discussion, 41–44.

Steiner, Richard L. "General Planning, Urban Renewal, and Highways." *Highway Research Board Bulletin* (no. 221) (1959): 37–39.

"Stichman OKs Public Housing for 15th Ward. Plan Lauded as One of Best . . . City Hits Proposals to Shift Site to Suburbs." *Post-Standard*. Syracuse, N.Y. (December 10, 1954).

Stransky, Joseph A. "Superhighway Development in the Milwaukee Metropolitan Area." *American City* 69 (August 1929): 271–273.

Strauss, Peter L. "Revisiting Overton Park: Political and Judicial Controls Over Administrative Actions Affecting the Community." *UCLA Law Review* 39 UCLALR 1251 (1991–1992): 1251, 1252.

Streich, William F. "A Plan for Multiplying the Utility of Business Thoroughfares." *American City* 8 (March 1913): 275–276.

Swan, Herbert S. "The Parkway as a Traffic Artery: Part I." *American City* 45 (October 1931): 84–86.

Swan, Herbert S. "The Parkway as a Traffic Artery: Part II." *American City* 45 (November 1931): 73–76.

"Syracuse Tackles Its Future." *Fortune* (May 1943).

Tallamy, B. D. "The Development of Expressways in New York State." *Traffic Quarterly* 7 (3) (July 1953): 291–302.

Taylor, Brian. "When Finance Leads Planning: Urban Planning, Highway Planning, and Metropolitan Freeways in California." *Journal of Planning Education and Research* 20 (2) (Winter 2000): 196–214.

Taylor, Brian D. "Public Perceptions, Fiscal Realities, and Freeway Planning: The California Case." *Journal of the American Planning Association* 61 (1) (Winter 1995): 43–56.

Taylor, Eugene S. "A Comprehensive System of Elevated Superhighways." *City Planning* 7 (2) (April 1931): 118–120.

Taylor, Harry A. "Depress Those Urban Expressways if at All Possible." *American City* 73 (May 1958): 194.

"Team Concepts for Urban Highways and Urban Design." *Highway Research Record* 220 (1968).

"The Congress Street Superhighway." *American City* 67 (September 1952): 145–146.

"The National Highway Program—A Challenge to Cities." *American City* 71 (August 1956): 11.

"The New Highways: Challenge to the Metropolitan Region." *Urban Land Institute Technical Bulletin* (no. 31) (November 1957).

Thiel, Floyd I. "Social Effects of Modern Highway Transportation." *Highway Research Board Bulletin* 327 (1962): 1–20.

Tilton, L. "Deming. "Post-War Development Plan for San Francisco Waterfront." *Architect and Engineer* 155 (Dec. 1943): 12–23.

Torkelson, M. W. "A 'Practical' Planner Questions a 'Dreamer.'" *American City* 58 (May 1943): 77.

"Townless Highways." *American City* 42 (May 1930): 94–96.

"Traffic Congestion: S.F. Bayshore to Be a Freeway." *Architect and Engineer* 143 (October 1940): 43–45.

"Traffic Jams Business Out." *Architectural Forum* 72 (January 1940): 64–65.

"Transportation and the City." *Architectural Forum* 119 (October 1963): 61–94.

Tsaguris, John S. "Urban Expressways: The Highway Engineer and City Planner." *American Society of Civil Engineers: Journal of the City Planning Division* 85 (no. CP1) (June 1959): 7–13.

Tuemmler, Fred W. "Urban Expressways: Work of Highway and Planning Agencies." *American Society of Civil Engineers: Journal of the City Planning Division* 85 (no. CP1) (June 1959): 15–20.

Tuemmler, Fred W. "Land Use and Expressways." *American Society of Civil Engineers: Journal of the City Planning Division* 87 (no. CP1) (September 1961): 29–39.

Tugwell, Rexford G., and Edward C. Banfield. "The Planning Function Reappraised." *Journal of the American Institute of Planners* 17 (1) (Winter 1951): 46–49.

Tunnard, Christopher. "Cities by Design." *Journal of the American Institute of Planners* 17 (3) (Summer 1951): 142–150.

Tunnard, Christopher. "The City and Its Interpreters." *Journal of the American Institute of Planners* 27 (4) (November 1961): 346–350.

Turner, Daniel L. "The Detroit Super-Highway Project." *American City* 32 (April 1925): 373–376.

Turner, Frances C. "The Case for Highway Planning." *Transportation Law Journal* 4 (2) (July 1972): 167–175.

"Two Notable Examples of Street Widening in New York City." *American City* 36 (March 1927): 340–343.

Tyrrell, Henry G. "The Esthetic Treatment of City Bridges." *American City* 9 (November 1913): 404–411.

Upham, Charles M. "The Last Two Decades in Highway Design, Construction and Maintenance." *American City* 43 (September 1930): 90–92.

Upham, Charles M. "German Highway Design." *Proceedings of the Highway Research Board* (1938): 181–185.

"Urban Design." *Progressive Architecture* 37 (August 1956): 97–112.

"Urban Expressway Needs a Cover." *American City* 82 (July 1967): 50.

"Urbane Freeway." *Architectural Forum* 129 (September 1968): 68–73.

"Urban Renewal Battle: Mead Fought Harriman for City Slum Program." *Post-Standard*. Syracuse, N.Y. (February 6, 1956).

Van Ginkel, Blanche Lemco. "The Form of the Core." *Journal of the American Institute of Planners* 27 (1) (February 1961): 56–69.

Van Schaick, B. L. "The Grand Central Parkway Approach to New York City's Triborough Bridge." *American City* 49 (August 1934): 43.

Van Storch, Earl. "Housing Development and Express Highways." *Highway Research Board Bulletin*, no. 10 (1947): 31–36.

Van Tassel, Roger. "Economic Aspects of Expressway Construction." *Journal of the American Institute of Planners* 20 (2) (Spring 1954): 83–86.

Veiller, Lawrence. "Protecting Residential Districts." *American City* 10 (June 1914): 525–529.

Verman, Marvin. "A Proposal to Use Existing Federal Mechanisms to Make This Expressway a Seam in the City's Fabric." *Architectural Forum* 135 (October 1971): 44–45.

Von Storch, Earl. "Housing Development and Express Highways." *Highway Research Board Bulletin* (no. 10) (1947): 31–36.

Voorhees, Alan M., ed. The Professional Responsibility of City Planners and Traffic Engineers in Urban Transportation: Joint Policy Statement of the American Institute of Planners and the Institute of Traffic Engineers. *Journal of the American Institute of Planners* 27 (1) 1961.

Voorhees, Alan M., ed. Land Use and Traffic Models: A Progress Report [special issue]. *Journal of the American Institute of Planners* 25 (May 1959): 57–104.

Voorhees, Alan M., ed. "The Nature and Uses of Models in City Planning." *Journal of the American Institute of Planners* 25 (2) (May 1959): 57–60.

Voorhees, Alan M., Charles F. Barnes, Jr., and Francis E. Coleman. "Traffic Patterns and Land-Use Alternatives." *Highway Research Board Bulletin* (no. 347) (1962): 1–9.

Wachs, Martin. "Basic Approaches to the Measurement of Community Values." *Highway Research Record* 305 (1970): 88–98.

Wachs, Martin. "Autos, Transit, and the Sprawl of Los Angeles: The 1920s." *Journal of the American Planning Association* 50 (Summer 1984): 297–310.

Wachs, Martin, and Joseph L. Schofer. "Abstract Values and Concrete Highways." *Traffic Quarterly* 23 (1) (January 1969): 133–156.

Walker, Robert A. "The Implementation of Planning Measures." *Journal of the American Institute of Planners* 16 (3) (Summer 1950): 122–130.

Warburton, Ralph. "What Urban Design Means." *American City* 84 (May 1969): 11–12.

"We Are Through with Overton Park Officials Say, Ending Decades of Delay." *Commercial Appeal*. Memphis, Tenn. (October 4, 1977).

Webb, Sam, and Sylvia Webb. "Oh, What a Lovely Plan." *Architectural Design* 39 (May 1969): 234–235.

Webber, Melvin M. "The Engineer's Responsibility for the Form of Cities." *Traffic Engineering* 30 (1) (October 1959): 11–15.

Weinberg, Robert C. "Review of *The Heart of the City*, edited by J. Tyrwhitt, J. L. Sert, and E. N. Rogers." *Journal of the American Institute of Planners* 19 (no. 1) (Winter 1953): 45–49..

Weinberg, Robert C. "Urban Design and the Community." *Journal of the American Institute of Planners* 26 (2) (May 1960): 133–134.

Weiss, Carol H. "Knowledge Creep and Decision Accretion." *Knowledge: Creation, Diffusion, Utilization* 1 (3) (March 1980): 381–404.

Wetmore, Louis B. "Visual Approach to Highway Planning and Design." *Highway Research Board Bulletin*, no. 190 (1958): 29–40.

Whalen, Richard J. "The American Highway: Do We Know Where We're Going?" *Saturday Evening Post* 14 (December 1968): 22.

White, James T. "More Cars Wanted in Fort Wayne's Business District." *American City* 62 (November 1947): 127.

Whitten, Robert. "The Economic Utilization of Land in City Building." *American City* 30 (May 1924): 527–530.

Whitten, Robert. "The Expressway in the Region." *City Planning* 8 (1) (January 1932): 23–27.

"Will 1932 Witness the Beginning of a New Epoch in Highway Design and Construction?" *American City* 46 (January 1932): 104–105.

Williams, Leslie. "Planning Public Transportation on Urban Expressways." *Proceedings of the Highway Research Board* (1945): 363–375.

Williams, Leslie. "What Can Be Done About Traffic Congestion: Part I, The Problem We Face." *Civil Engineering (New York, N.Y.)* 16 (April 1946): 149–151.

Winter, Arch R. "Four Architectural Factors." *Journal of the American Institute of Architects* 38 (November 1962): 29–31.

Wood, Edith Elmer. "Slums and the City Plan." *American City* 41 (August 1929): 93–97.

Wood, Edward W., Jr., Sidney N. Brower, and Margaret W. Latimer. "Planners' People." *Journal of the American Institute of Planners* 32 (4) (July 1966): 228–234.

Wurster, Catherine Bauer. "Architecture and the Cityscape: Notes on the Primitive State of Urban Design in America." *Journal of the American Institute of Architects* 35 (3) (March 1961): 36–39.

Yardley, William. "Seattle Ponders (Some More) the Wisdom of Replacing a Road." *New York Times* (April 10, 2011): 17.

Zapatka, Christian. "The American Parkways: Origins and Evolution of the Park-Road." *Lotus International* (no. 56) (1987): 96–128.

Interview Transcripts

American Association of State Highway Transportation Officials, Interstate Highway Research Project. Transcripts of Interviews with Participants in the Planning and Construction of the Interstate Highway System. Washington, D.C.: Public Works Historical Society.

Leiserson, Alan. Legal Services Director, Tennesee Department of Environment and Conservation. Telephone interview, June 23, 2010.

U.S. Government Materials

U.S. Executive Departments and Commissions

U.S. Bureau of Public Roads. *General Location of National System of Interstate Highways*. Washington, D.C.: USGPO, 1955.

U.S. Bureau of Public Roads. *Highways and Economic and Social Changes*. Washington, D.C.: USGPO, 1964.

U.S. Bureau of Public Roads, Office of Right-of-Way and Location, Environmental Development Division. *Highway Joint Development and Multiple Use*. Washington, D.C.: USGPO, 1970.

U.S. Bureau of Public Roads, Office of Right-of-Way and Location, Environmental Development Division. *Literature References to Highways and Their Environmental Considerations*. July 1969.

U.S. Department of Commerce. *Freeways to Urban Development*. Washington, D.C.: USGPO, 1966.

U.S. Department of Commerce, Bureau of Public Roads, *General Location of National System of Interstate Highways*, 1955.

U.S. Department of Housing and Urban Development. *Joint Project Concept: Integrated Transportation Corridors*. Prepared by Barton-Aschman Associates. January, 1968.

U.S. Department of Transportation, Office of the Secretary. *Urban System Study.* Washington, D.C.: USGPO, 1977.

U.S. Department of Transportation, Federal Highway Administration. *The Freeway in the City: Principles of Planning and Design.* Prepared by the Urban Advisors to the Federal Highway Administrator. Washington, D.C.: USGPO, 1968.

U.S. Federal Works Administration. *Final Report of the WPA, 1933–1939.* Washington, D.C.: USGPO, 1939.

U.S. National Resources Committee. Supplementary Report of the Urbanism Committee to the National Resources Committee. Vol. 2, Urban Planning and Land Policies. Washington, D.C.: USGPO, 1939.

U.S. National Resources Planning Board. *Our Cities: Their Role in the National Economy.* Washington, D.C.: USGPO, 1937.

U.S. President's Advisory Committee on a National Highway Program. *A Ten-Year National Highway Program.* Washington, D.C.: USGPO, January 1955.

Congressional Materials: Documents, Reports
U.S. Congress, House, Committee on Public Works. *Federal-Aid Highway Act of 1968.* Report prepared by U.S. Committee on Public Works. 90th Congress, 2nd Session. 1968. H. Doc. 1584.

U.S. Congress, House, Committee on Roads. *Toll Roads and Free Roads.* Report prepared by U.S. Bureau of Public Roads. 76th Congress, 1st Session, 1939. H. Doc. 272.

U.S. Congress, House, Committee on Roads. *Interregional Highways.* Report prepared by U.S. Interregional Highway Committee. 78th Congress, 2nd Session, 1944. H. Doc. 379.

U.S. Congress, House, Committee to the Committee of the Whole House on the State of the Union. *Department of Transportation Act.* Report prepared by U.S. Committee on Government Operations. 89th Congress, 2nd Session. 1966. H. Doc. 1701.

U.S. Congress, Senate, Committee on Commerce. *National Transportation Policy.* Report prepared by the Special Study Group on Transportation Policies in the United States. 89th Congress, 1st Session. 1961. S. Doc. 445.

U.S. Congress, Senate, Committee on Public Works. *Federal-Aid Highway Act of 1968.* Report prepared by U.S. Committee on Public Works. 90th Congress, 2nd Session. 1968. S. Doc. 1340.

Congressional Materials: Hearings
U.S. Congress, House, Hearing before the Committee on Science and Astronautic, and Senate, Hearing before the Committee on Interior and Insular Affairs. 90th Congress, 2nd Session. *Joint House-Senate Colloquium to Discuss a National Policy for the Environment.* July 17, 1968.

U.S. Congress, House, Committee on Public Works, Subcommittee on Roads. *National Highway Study.* Hearings. Part 1. 83rd Congress, 1st Session. April-May 1953.

U.S. Congress, House, Committee on Public Works, Subcommittee on Roads. *National Highway Study.* Hearings. Part 2. 83rd Congress, 1st Session. June-July 1953.

U.S. Congress, House, Committee on Public Works, Subcommittee on Roads. *National Highway Program: Federal Aid Highway Act of 1956.* Hearings on H.R. 8836, 84th Congress, 2nd Session. February-March 1956.

U.S. Congress, House, Committee on Public Works, Subcommittee on Roads. 90th Congress, 1st Session. *Major Highway Problems in D.C.* December 5 and 6, 1967.

U.S. Congress, House, Committee on Public Works, Subcommittee on Roads. 90th Congress, 2nd Session on H.R. 837. *Completion of George Washington Memorial Parkway.* March 20, 1968.

U.S. Congress, House, Committee on Public Works, Subcommittee on Roads, 90th Congress, 2nd Session on H.R. 16000. *The Interstate System in the District of Columbia.* April 2, 3, and 4, 1968.

U.S. Congress, House, Committee on Public Works, Subcommittee on Roads. 90th Congress, 2nd Session on H.R. 17134 and related bills. *To Authorize Appropriations for the Fiscal Years 1970 and 1971 for the Construction of Certain Highways in Accordance with Title 23 of the United States Code and for Other Purposes.* February 20, and 21, May 23 and 28, and June 4, 5, 11, and 12, 1968.

U.S. Congress, House, Roads Committee. *Federal-Aid for Post-War Highway Construction.* Hearings on H.R. 2426. 2 vols. 78th Congress, 2nd session. 1944.

U.S. Congress, House, Subcommittee of the Committee on Government Operations, 89th Congress, 2nd Session on H.R. 13200, *A Bill to Establish a Department of Transportation, and for Other Purposes.* April 6, 7, 25 and 26, 1966.

U.S. Congress, House, Subcommittee of the Committee on Government Operations, 89th Congress, 2nd Session on H.R. 13200, *A Bill to Establish a Department of Transportation, and for Other Purposes.* May 2, 3, 17, 18, 19, 24 and June 21, 1966.

U.S. Congress, Senate, Committee on Government Operations. 89th Congress, 2nd Session on S. 3010, Part 1. *A Bill to Establish a Department of Transportation, and for Other Purposes.* March 29 and 30, 1966.

U.S. Congress, Senate, Committee on Government Operations. 89th Congress, 2nd Session on S. 3010, Part 2. *A Bill to Establish a Department of Transportation, and for Other Purposes.* May 3, 4, and 5, 1966.

U.S. Congress, Senate, Committee on Government Operations. 89th Congress, 2nd Session on S. 3010, Part 3. *A Bill to Establish a Department of Transportation, and for Other Purposes.* May 18 and 19, 1966.

U.S. Congress, Senate, Committee on Government Operations. 89th Congress, 2nd Session on S. 3010, Part 4. *A Bill to Establish a Department of Transportation, and for Other Purposes.* June 28 and 29, 1966.

U.S. Congress, Senate, Committee on Interior and Insular Affairs. 86th Congress, 2nd Session on S. 2549. *Proposed Resources and Conservation Act of 1960.* January 25, 26, 28, and 29, 1960.

U.S. Congress, Senate, Committee on Public Works. *National Highway Program.* Hearings on S. 1048, S. 1072, S. 1160, and S. 1573. 84th Congress, 1st Session. February-April 1955.

U.S. Congress, Senate, Committee on Public Works, Subcommittee on Roads. 90th Congress, 2nd Session. *Status of the Inspection, Maintenance, and Design of Bridges in the United States.* March 18, 19, and 20, 1968.

U.S. Congress, Senate, Committee on Public Works, Subcommittee on Roads. 90th Congress, 1st and 2nd Sessions, Part 1. *Urban Highway Planning, Location and Design.* November 14, 15, 16, 28, 29 and 30, 1967.

U.S. Congress, Senate, Committee on Public Works, Subcommittee on Roads. 90th Congress, 1st and 2nd Sessions, Part 2. *Urban Highway Planning, Location and Design.* May 1, 6, 7, 8, 27 and 28, 1968.

U.S. Congress, Senate, Committee on Public Works, Subcommittee on Roads. 90th Congress, 2nd Session on S. 2888, S. 3381, and S. 3418. *Federal-Aid Highway Act of 1968.* June 4, 5, 10, and 11, 1968.

U.S. Congress, Senate, Subcommittee on Transportation of the Committee on Environment and Public Works. *Proposed Highway Construction through Overton Park, Memphis, Tennessee.* 95th Congress, 2nd Session. 19 April 1978.

Government and Quasi-governmental Reports Consulted and Cited

Bon Air Environmental Impact Statement (Memphis, Tennesee: City of Memphis, 1972): 1–8 SU.

Clark, Harry J. The Papers of Harry J. Clark. OHA 6725.

Detroit Rapid Transit Commission. *Proposed Super-Highway Plan for Greater Detroit.* Detroit: Detroit Rapid Transit Commission, 1924.

Limber, Ralph C. *Economic Characteristics of the Syracuse Area.* Syracuse-Onondaga Post War Planning Council, Syracuse, New York. 1943.

Mead, Donald H. Blueprint for Progress: The 1956 Program Message to the Common Council. Syracuse, New York. 1956

Memphis, City of. Memphis Park Commission, Public Construction Office. "Overton Park: The Evolution of a Park Space." Prepared for Ritchie Smith Associates, Overton Park Master Plan. John Linn Hopkins (September 1, 1987): 35.

Metropolitan Development Association of Syracuse and Onondaga County. *20/20 Plus.* Syracuse, New York.

Onondaga County Department of Planning, *Transportation in the Onondaga-Syracuse Metropolitan Area.* Catalogued as Blair & Stein in Loeb Design Library, Harvard University VF NAC 2800g 26 NY-Ono.

Onondaga County Department of Research and Development. *Onondaga County and Planning* Syracuse, New York. 1957.

Onondaga Park and Regional Planning Board. *Proposed Parkway around Onondaga Lake.* November 1928.

Post-War Planning Council. *A Program for Progress.* Syracuse, New York. 1946.

Snyder, Roger W. D.A.T.A.* Data Aggregated to Assist: A listing of all publications since 1959 which contains statistics or other information on the Syracuse-Onondaga Metropolitan Area and may be useful in local decision-making. November, 1967.

State of California, Department of Public Works, Division of Highways. Statistical supplement portion of the annual report to the Governor of California by the Director of Public Works, 1966.

State of New York, Department of Public Works. Report State of Arterial Routes in the Syracuse Urban Area. 1947.

Syracuse, New York, City of. *A Community Renewal Program. Preliminary.* September 16, 1963.

Syracuse, New York, City of. *A Community Renewal Program. Summary.* 2003-197 Box 5, Onondaga Historical Association.

Syracuse, New York, City of. An Exciting Redevelopment Opportunity. nd.

Syracuse, New York, City of. Application to the Department of Housing and Urban Development for a Grant to Plan a Comprehensive Model Cities Program. April 12, 1968.

Syracuse, New York, City of. *A Summary of Land Uses.* Circa 1936.

Syracuse, New York, City of. Central Syracuse: A General Neighborhood Renewal Plan. Part 1 Recommended Renewal Action. October 1964.

Syracuse, New York, City of. Central Syracuse: A General Neighborhood Renewal Plan. Part 2 Development Policies and Objectives. July 1965.

Syracuse, New York, City of. Urban Renewal Plan, Survey Area Number 2. 1954.

Syracuse, New York, City of. Advisory Commission on City Planning. *Citizen Commission 1963.*

Syracuse, New York, City of. Bureau of Municipal Research. *Inside Syracuse: Report for Centennial Year 1948.*

Syracuse, New York, City of. City Planning Commission. *Annual Report of the City Planning Commission 1946.*

Syracuse, New York, City of. City Planning Commission. *Annual Report of the City Planning Commission 1948.*

Syracuse, New York, City of. City Planning Commission. *Annual Report of the City Planning Commission, 1949.*

Syracuse, New York, City of. City Planning Commission. *Annual Report of the City Planning Commission, 1950.*

Syracuse, New York, City of. City Planning Commission. *Annual Report of the City Planning Commission, 1952.*

Syracuse, New York, City of. City Planning Commission. *Annual Report of the City Planning Commission, 1953.*

Syracuse, New York, City of. City Planning Commission. *Annual Report of the City Planning Commission, 1955.*

Syracuse, New York, City of. City Planning Commission. *Annual Report of the City Planning Commission, 1967.*

Syracuse, New York, City of. City Planning Commission. *Highlights of 1957.*

Syracuse, New York, City of. City Planning Commission. *Redevelopment Plan: Survey Area Number 1.* 1954.

Syracuse, New York, City of. City Planning Commission. Report of the New York State Department of Public Works—Report on Arterial Routes in the Syracuse Urban Area. 1948.

Syracuse, New York, City of. City Planning Commission. Some Data for Preparation of the Administrative Organization for Urban Renewal. January 23, 1956.

Syracuse, New York, City of. City Planning Department. *A Study of Planning Unit 25.* nd.

Syracuse, New York, City of. Commissioner of Planning. *Planning Central Area, Syracuse 1958.*

Syracuse, New York, City of. Syracuse Urban Renewal Agency. *Preliminary Urban Renewal Plan, Downtown One.* January 1964.

Syracuse Governmental Research Bureau, Inc. "Population Growth in Onondaga County." *For the Record.* October 1 1960.

Syracuse Housing Authority: Its Program and Project. Syracuse, New York. 1939.

Syracuse-Onondaga County Planning Agency. *Clearance, Redevelopment, Urban Renewal.* Archives 45. Nd.

Syracuse-Onondaga County Post-War Planning Council. Postwar Perspective, A Report to the People of the City of Syracuse and the County of Onondaga, 1944 [Draft, Sergei Grimm].

Syracuse-Onondaga County Post-War Planning Council. Postwar Perspective, A Report to the People of the City of Syracuse and the County of Onondaga, 1944.

Syracuse-Onondaga Post-War Planning Council. *Economics.* Syracuse, New York. 1945.

Syracuse-Onondaga Post-War Planning Council. The Report of the Syracuse-Onondaga Post-War Planning Council to the Citizens of the City of Syracuse and Onondaga County. Submitted by William Z.P. Tolley, December 15, 1945.

U.S. Department of Transportation, Federal Highway Administration, Highway History, http://www.fhwa.dot.gov/highwayhistory/data/page01.cfm.

Washington State Department of Transportation. "6 Case Studies in Urban Freeway Removal." *Seattle Urban Mobility Plan (2008).* Available at: http://www.seattle.gov/transportation/docs/ump/06%20SEATTLE%20Case%20studies%20in%20urban%20freeway%20removal.pdf.

Internet Articles

Charlier, Tom. "Justices' 1971 Ruling Protects Parkland from Interstate Intrusion." June 29, 2006. Available at: http://www.harrisshelton.com/articles/article_CA_overtoncourtcase062906.pdf.

Citizens to Preserve Overton Park, Inc., et al., Plaintiff-appellant, v. Claude S. Brinegar, Secretary, United States Department of Transportation, Defendant-appellant, and Charles W. Speight, Commissioner, Tennessee Department of Highways, Defendant-appellee, United States Court of Appeals, Sixth Circuit. 494 F.2d 1212, pages 7–8. Available at: http://cases.justia.com/us-court-of-appeals/ F2/494/1212/112646/.

Clifford, Frank. "Century Freeway Housing Funds Clear Hurdle." *Los Angeles Times*, June 7, 1990. Available at: http://articles.latimes.com/keyword/century -freeway.

Congress for the New Urbanism (CNU). "Freeways Without Futures 2008." Available at: http://www.cnu.orghighways/freewayswithoutfutures.

Congress for the New Urbanism (CNU)."Highway To Boulevard Concept Comes of Age With Today's Joint HUD-DOT Announcement. Shift in Federal Emphasis Supports Efforts to Replace Elevated Highways with Walkable Surface Street." Available at: http://www.cnu.org/node/3744.

Ellis, Virginia. "State Speeds Up Funding of Southland Road Work Prop. 111: Transportation Commission allocates money to be raised by higher gasoline taxes for the Century Freeway and other projects." *Los Angeles Times*, June 14, 1990. Available at: http://articles.latimes.com/keyword/century-freeway.

Faris, Gerald. "1 Century Freeway Housing Project to Be Built, but 2nd Falls Through." *Los Angeles Times*, April 27, 1986. Available at: http://articles.latimes .com/keyword/century-freeway.

Gill, James. "Reviving a New Orleans Neighborhood's Heart." *Times-Picayune*, August 1, 2010. Available at: http://www.nola.com/opinions/index.ssf/2010/08/ reviving_a_new_orleans_neighbo.html.

Hebert, Ray. "Century Freeway—When It's Born, an Era Will Die." *Los Angeles Times*, June 22, 1986. Available at: http://articles.latimes.com/keyword/century -freeway.

Huxtable, Ada Louise. "Ugly Cities and How they Grow." *New York Times*, March 15, 1964. Available at: http://select.nytimes.com/gst/abstract.html?res=F 70612F8395415738DDDAC0994DB405B848AF1D3&scp=1&sq=Ugly+cities+ and+How+They+Grow&st=p.

"I-695 I-95 Inner Belt Expressway Unbuilt." Available at: http://www.boston roads.com/roads/inner-belt/.

Jackson, Ron. "Que Reunion Recalls the 15th Ward. What Urban Renewal Didn't Destroy." *Syracuse City Eagle* 4, Issue 36, September 6 to 12, 2007. From the "Our Stories" collection, Syracuse University Digital Library. Original article owned by: Williams, Margaret. Available at: http://digilib.syr.educdm4_bhpp /item_viewer.php?CISOROOT=/bhpp&CISOPTR=183&DMSCA.

Kimmelman, Michael. "In Madrid's Heart, Park Blooms Where a Freeway Once Blighted." *New York Times*, December 26, 2011. Available at http://www.nytimes .com/2011/12/27/arts/design/in-madrid-even-maybe-the-bronx-parks-replace -freeways.html?_r=1.

Kowsky, Kim. "Poor Win Housing Fight. Hawthorne: Complex Eyed for Military Use Belongs to Poor and Century Freeway Refugees, Judge Rules. *Los Angeles*

Times, September 1, 1991. Available at: http://articles.latimes.com/keyword/century-freeway.

Kutner, Jeremy. "Downtown Need a Makeover? More Cities Are Razing Urban Highways." March 2, 2011. Available at: http://www.csmonitor.com/USA/2011/0302/Downtown-need-a-makeover-More-cities-are-razing-urban-highways/%28page%29/2?source=patrick.net#mainColumn.

Levey, Bob and Jane Freundel Levey. "END OF THE ROADS; In the Interstate Era, Congress ruled Washington like a fiefdom. Then a fight over some freeways inspired a biracial, neighborhood-level movement to fight the federal power." *The Washington Post* (November 26, 2000) Final Edition, Magazine Section, W10. Available at: http://www.washingtonpost.com/wp-srv/metro/endofroads.pdf.

Massachusetts Department of Transportation, Division of Highways. "The Central Artery/Tunnel Project—The Big Dig." Available at: http://www.massdot.state.ma.us/Highway/bigdig/bigdigmain.aspx.

Merina, Victor. "Century Freeway Tour Pleases Deukmejian." *Los Angeles Times*, January 24, 1985. Available at: http://articles.latimes.com/keyword/century-freeway.

Mitchell, John L. "Freeway Feud." *Los Angeles Times*, March 23, 1997. Available at: http://articles.latimes.com/print/1997-03-23/local/me-41257_1_century-freeway.

Nasser, Haya El. "Urban parks take over downtown freeways." *USA TODAY*. Available at: http://www.usatoday.com/news/nation/2010-05-05-urban-parks_N.htm.

Oliver, Marilyn Tower. "Optimism Amid Diversity, Adversity. Lynwood: A Lot of Friendly People Live in This Multicultural Community, Which Looks Forward to the 1993 Completion of the Century Freeway." *Los Angeles Times*, March 3, 1991. Available at: http://articles.latimes.com/keyword/century-freeway.

Onondaga Citizens League. "Rethinking I-81." 2009. Available at: http://onondagacitizensleague.org/pdfs/OCLRethinkingI81_9print.pdf.

Samuelson, Robert J. "Cambridge and the Inner Belt Highway: Some Problems are Simply Insoluble." *Harvard Crimson*, June 2, 1967. Available at: http://www.thecrimson.com/article/1967/6/2/cambridge-and-the-inner-belt-highway/.

Siegel, Charles. "Removing Urban Freeways." March 19, 2007. Available at: http://www.planetizen.com/node/23300.

"State Approves Funds to Complete Century Freeway." *Los Angeles Times*, July 7, 1985. Available at: http://articles.latimes.com/keyword/century-freeway.

Striner, Richard, Ph.D. "The Committee of 100 on the Federal City Its History and Its Service to the Nation's Capital." Available at: http://www.committeeof100.net/Who-We-Are/history.html.

Taylor, Ronald B. "Soaring Interchange on Century Freeway to Be One of a Kind." *Los Angeles Times*, December 10, 1989. Available at: http://articles.latimes.com/keyword/century-freeway.

The Committee of 100 on the Federal City. "Mission." Available at: http://www
.committeeof100.net.

The Preservation Institute. "Removing Freeways—Restoring Cities. Freeway Removal Plans and Proposals" Available at: http://www.preservenet.com/freeways/
FreewaysPlansProposals.html.

Trombley, William. "New Housing Plan Urged for Century Freeway Route." *Los
Angeles Times*, July 25, 1988. Available at: http://articles.latimes.com/keyword/
century-freeway.

Trombley, William, and Ray Herbert. "Bold Housing Program Develops Big Problems: Plan Plagued by Shoddy Construction, Cost Overruns, High Vacancy Rates,
Opposition." *Los Angeles Times*, December 28, 1987. Available at: http://articles
.latimes.com/print/1987-12-28/news/mn-21363_1_high-cost.

Weingroff, Richard F. "Federal-Aid Highway Act of 1956: Creating the Interstate
System." *Public Roads* 60, no. 1 (Summer 1966) (Web page updated April 8, 2011).
Available at: http://www.fhwa.dot.gov/publications/publicroads/96summer/p96
su10.cfm.

Zamichow, Nora. "After Decades of Debate, Century Freeway to Open. Transit:
$2.2-billion Project Has Torn Apart Lives and Communities but Also Brought Job
Training and Housing." *Los Angeles Times*, October 10, 1993. Available at: http://
articles.latimes.com/keyword/century-freeway.

Miscellany

Balakrishnan, Ashwin. "Replacing Sheridan can be good for all." Letter to the editor of the *Hunts Point Express* representing the position of the Southern Bronx
River Watershed Alliance, May 4, 2011. Available at: http://www.southbronxvi
sion.org/.

Century Freeway Corridor Cities Caucus, Presentation to the Honorable Drew
Lewis, Secretary of Transportation, May 4, 1981. On file with author.

Crawford, Holly. "Road: Century Project." Exhibited at the South Bay Museum
of Art, the Museum of Art in Downey, the City of Benecia Art Gallery, and the
California Department of Housing and Community Development, Inglewood Office, December 7, 1991 to January 11, 1992. Available at: http://www.art-poetry
.info/id16.html.

FHWA Route Log and Finder List. http://www.fhwa.dot.gov/reports/routefinder/
index.htm.

"Modern Motor Arteries." Proceedings of the Twenty-Second National Conference on City Planning Held in Denver, Colorado, 23–26 June 1930. Philadelphia:
William Fell, 1930: 61–67.

Nashville I-40 Steering Committee v. Ellington, 387 F. 2d 179 (6th Cir. 1967).

Park East Redevelopment Plan rendering courtesy of Graef, Anhalt, Schloemer &
Associates, Inc. Milwaukee, WI (2003).

Syracuse University. "City Earmarks $170,000 Fund For 15th Ward Slum Cleaning. Mayor at Controls As Crane Wrecks First Area Shack." *The Films of the SU Public Memory Project, Memories of Syracuse's 15th Ward.* Available through: kphillip@syr.edu.

"Urban Highway Planning and Its Relation to General Urban Development." Urban Highway Planning Seminar. Berkeley, California, April 1960.

Wilbur Smith Associates. "Company History." Available at: http://www.wilbursmith.com/history.htm.

Index

Urban and Industrial Environments

Series editor: Robert Gottlieb, Henry R. Luce Professor of Urban and Environmental Policy, Occidental College

Kerry H. Whiteside, *Precautionary Politics: Principle and Practice in Confronting Environmental Risk*

Ronald Sandler and Phaedra C. Pezzullo, eds., *Environmental Justice and Environmentalism: The Social Justice Challenge to the Environmental Movement*

Julie Sze, *Noxious New York: The Racial Politics of Urban Health and Environmental Justice*

Robert D. Bullard, ed., *Growing Smarter: Achieving Livable Communities, Environmental Justice, and Regional Equity*

Ann Rappaport and Sarah Hammond Creighton, *Degrees That Matter: Climate Change and the University*

Michael Egan, *Barry Commoner and the Science of Survival: The Remaking of American Environmentalism*

David J. Hess, *Alternative Pathways in Science and Industry: Activism, Innovation, and the Environment in an Era of Globalization*

Peter F. Cannavò, *The Working Landscape: Founding, Preservation, and the Politics of Place*

Paul Stanton Kibel, ed., *Rivertown: Rethinking Urban Rivers* Kevin P. Gallagher and Lyuba Zarsky, *The Enclave Economy: Foreign Investment and Sustainable Development in Mexico's Silicon Valley* David N. Pellow, *Resisting Global Toxics: Transnational Movements for Environmental Justice*

Robert Gottlieb, *Reinventing Los Angeles: Nature and Community in the Global City*

David V. Carruthers, ed., *Environmental Justice in Latin America: Problems, Promise, and Practice*

Tom Angotti, *New York for Sale: Community Planning Confronts Global Real Estate*

Paloma Pavel, ed., *Breakthrough Communities: Sustainability and Justice in the Next American Metropolis*

Anastasia Loukaitou-Sideris and Renia Ehrenfeucht, *Sidewalks: Conflict and Negotiation over Public Space*

David J. Hess, *Localist Movements in a Global Economy: Sustainability, Justice, and Urban Development in the United States*

Julian Agyeman and Yelena Ogneva-Himmelberger, eds., *Environmental Justice and Sustainability in the Former Soviet Union*

Jason Corburn, *Toward the Healthy City: People, Places, and the Politics of Urban Planning*

JoAnn Carmin and Julian Agyeman, eds., *Environmental Inequalities Beyond Borders: Local Perspectives on Global Injustices*

Louise Mozingo, *Pastoral Capitalism: A History of Suburban Corporate Landscapes*

Gwen Ottinger and Benjamin Cohen, eds., *Technoscience and Environmental Justice: Expert Cultures in a Grassroots Movement*

Samantha MacBride, *Recycling Reconsidered: The Present Failure and Future Promise of Environmental Action in the United States*

Andrew Karvonen, *Politics of Urban Runoff: Nature, Technology, and the Sustainable City*

Daniel Schneider, *Hybrid Nature: Sewage Treatment and the Contradictions of the Industrial Ecosystem*

Catherine Tumber, *Small, Gritty, and Green: The Promise of America's Smaller Industrial Cities in a Low-Carbon World*

Sam Bass Warner and Andrew H. Whittemore, *American Urban Form: A Representative History*

John Pucher and Ralph Buehler, eds., *City Cycling*

Stephanie Foote and Elizabeth Mazzolini, eds., *Histories of the Dustheap: Waste, Material Cultures, Social Justice*

David J. Hess, *Good Green Jobs in a Global Economy: Making and Keeping New Industries in the United States*

Joseph F. C. DiMento and Cliff Ellis, *Changing Lanes: Visions and Histories of Urban Freeways*